THE CAMBRIDGE COMPANION
TO *NINETEEN EIGHTY-FOUR*

George Orwell's *Nineteen Eighty-Four* (1949) remains a book of the moment. This *Companion* builds on successive waves of generational inheritance and debate in the novel's reception by asking new questions about how and why *Nineteen Eighty-Four* was written, what it means, and why it matters. Chapters on a selection of the novel's interpretative contexts, the literary histories from which it is inseparable, the urgent questions it raises, and the impact it has had on other kinds of media, ranging from radio to video games, open up the conversation in an expansive way. Established concerns (e.g. Orwell's attitude to the working class and his anxieties about the socio-political compartmentalization of the post-war world) are presented alongside newer ones (e.g. his views on evil and the influence of *Nineteen Eighty-Four* on comics). Individual essays help us see in new ways how Orwell's most famous work continues to be a novel for our times.

Nathan Waddell is a Senior Lecturer at the University of Birmingham. He is the author of *Moonlighting: Beethoven and Literary Modernism* (2019), *Modernist Nowheres: Politics and Utopia in Early Modernist Writing, 1900–1920* (2012), and *Modern John Buchan: A Critical Introduction* (2009). He has also co-edited volumes of essays on the work of Wyndham Lewis.

T0384472

THE CAMBRIDGE
COMPANION TO
NINETEEN EIGHTY-FOUR

EDITED BY
NATHAN WADDELL
University of Birmingham

CAMBRIDGE
UNIVERSITY PRESS

CAMBRIDGE
UNIVERSITY PRESS

University Printing House, Cambridge CB2 8BS, United Kingdom

One Liberty Plaza, 20th Floor, New York, NY 10006, USA

477 Williamstown Road, Port Melbourne, VIC 3207, Australia

314–321, 3rd Floor, Plot 3, Splendor Forum, Jasola District Centre,
New Delhi – 110025, India

79 Anson Road, #06–04/06, Singapore 079906

Cambridge University Press is part of the University of Cambridge.

It furthers the University's mission by disseminating knowledge in the pursuit of
education, learning, and research at the highest international levels of excellence.

www.cambridge.org
Information on this title: www.cambridge.org/9781108841092
DOI: 10.1017/9781108887090

First published 2020

A catalogue record for this publication is available from the British Library.

ISBN 978-1-108-84109-2 Hardback
ISBN 978-1-108-81471-3 Paperback

CONTENTS

Contents

FIGURES

CONTRIBUTORS

PETER BRIAN BARRY is the Finkbeiner Endowed Professor of Ethics and Professor of Philosophy at Saginaw Valley State University. He is the author of *Evil and Moral Psychology* (Routledge, 2013) and *The Fiction of Evil* (Routledge, 2016). He is working on a book on the ethical philosophy of George Orwell.

DANIEL BUCKINGHAM is a doctoral candidate at the University of Birmingham. His research interests include satire, literary celebrity, and the twentieth-century middlebrow.

SARAH COLE is the Parr Professor of English and Comparative Literature and Dean of Humanities at Columbia University. She is the author of three books: *Inventing Tomorrow: H. G. Wells and the Twentieth Century* (Columbia University Press, 2019), *At the Violet Hour: Modernism and Violence in England and Ireland* (Oxford University Press, 2012), and *Modernism, Male Friendship, and the First World War* (Cambridge University Press, 2003). She is the recipient of a Guggenheim Fellowship.

DILETTA DE CRISTOFARO is a Wellcome Trust funded research fellow at Northumbria University and a specialist in writings responding to twenty-first-century anxieties and crises. She has published widely on the contemporary apocalyptic imagination, including her first monograph, *The Contemporary Post-Apocalyptic Novel: Critical Temporalities and the End Times* (Bloomsbury, 2019).

DAVID DWAN is an Associate Professor in English at the University of Oxford and a Tutorial Fellow in English at Hertford College. He is the author of *The Great Community: Culture and Nationalism in Ireland* (Field Day/Notre Dame, 2008) and *Liberty, Equality and Humbug: Orwell's Political Ideals* (Oxford University Press, 2018).

JONATHAN GREENBERG is Department Chair and Professor of English at Montclair State University. He has written three books: *Modernism, Satire, and the Novel* (Cambridge University Press, 2011), *The Cambridge Introduction to Satire* (Cambridge University Press, 2019), and, with Mo Rocca, *Mobituaries: Great Lives Worth Reliving* (Simon & Schuster, 2019).

ISABELLE LICARI-GUILLAUME is a Lecturer at Université Côte d'Azur, Nice, France. She defended her PhD in Anglophone Studies in 2017. Her research focuses on comic book history and culture, with a special interest in DC's Vertigo imprint and its connection to British scriptwriters. She is also a translator.

JANICE HO is an Associate Professor of English at the University of Colorado, Boulder. She is the author of *Nation and Citizenship in the Twentieth-Century British Novel* (Cambridge University Press, 2015) and has published essays in the fields of modernism, contemporary literature, and world Anglophone literature.

HOLLIE JOHNSON is a teaching affiliate at the University of Nottingham, where she teaches on feminist thinkers and philosophy. She completed her PhD thesis at Nottingham in 2018. Drawing from an interdisciplinary background, her research takes an ecocritical approach to dystopian fiction to explore the role of environmental concerns within the thematic and formal development of the genre.

DOUGLAS KERR was a Professor of English and Dean of the Arts Faculty at Hong Kong University, and has written books on Wilfred Owen, Arthur Conan Doyle, and colonial literature. He is the author of *George Orwell* (for Northcote House's Writers and their Work series) and of some dozen scholarly articles on Orwell.

LISA MULLEN is a Teaching Associate in Modern and Contemporary Literature at Cambridge University, and was previously Junior Research Fellow at Worcester College, Oxford. Her first book, *Mid-Century Gothic: The Uncanny Objects of Modernity in British Literature and Culture after the Second World War*, was published by Manchester University Press in 2019; her next will be *Orwell Unwell: Pathology and the Medical Imaginary in Orwell's Fiction and Journalism*.

SORAYA MURRAY is a visual studies scholar with interests in cultural theory, contemporary art, film, and games. An Associate Professor in the Film and Digital Media Department at the University of California, Santa Cruz, Murray is the author of *On Video Games: The Visual Politics of Race, Gender, and Space* (I. B. Tauris, 2018).

NATASHA PERIYAN is the author of *The Politics of 1930s British Literature: Education, Gender, Class* (Bloomsbury, 2018) and articles and chapters that examine modernism's relationship to education. She was an AHRC Research Associate at the University of Kent on 'Literary Culture, Meritocracy and the Assessment of Intelligence in Britain and America, 1880–1920'.

ADAM ROBERTS is a Professor of Nineteenth-Century Literature and Culture at Royal Holloway, University of London, and Fellow of the Royal Society of Literature. He is the author of twenty-one works of fiction, all but one of them science fiction. He is currently working on a novel that is, at least in part, a sequel to *Nineteen Eighty-Four*.

ELINOR TAYLOR is a Lecturer in English at the University of Westminster. She is the author of a monograph, *The Popular Front Novel in Britain, 1934–40* (Brill/Haymarket, 2019), and a member of the executive committee of the Raymond Williams Society.

NATHAN WADDELL is a Senior Lecturer at the University of Birmingham. He is the author of *Moonlighting: Beethoven and Literary Modernism* (2019), *Modernist Nowheres: Politics and Utopia in Early Modernist Writing, 1900–1920* (2012), and *Modern John Buchan: A Critical Introduction* (2009). He has also co-edited volumes of essays on the work of Wyndham Lewis.

JAMIE WOOD is an independent scholar focused on the genealogy of modernist aesthetics between 1900 and 1940.

ACKNOWLEDGEMENTS

As many others before me have said, working on George Orwell necessarily means being indebted to the extraordinary scholarship of Peter Davison, whose textual labours have made available in authoritative form the material on which Orwell studies depends. At Cambridge University Press, my thanks to Ray Ryan for believing in this project and for supportively and enthusiastically seeing it through from proposal stage to publication. Thanks, likewise, to Edgar Mendez for his unflagging help and encouragement, and to the anonymous peer reviewers of the proposal for suggesting valuable ways in which to improve the book. All of the students with whom I've discussed *Nineteen Eighty-Four* over the years have shaped my opinions about it. My gratitude to them for the intelligence with which they've responded to my ways of thinking and reading; this edited volume is meant as a tribute to, and a 'thank you' for, their determining influence. I'm hugely grateful to the contributors for writing such brilliant, thought-provoking chapters and for tolerating my interminable queries during the preparation of the typescript. A glass raised not only to them but also to Andrzej Gąsiorek, Dorian Lynskey, Kara Reilly, David Ryan, Jean Seaton, Lyndsey Stonebridge, D. J. Taylor, Sylvia Topp, Julian Wolfreys, Gobaloussamy Rangaradjou (Senior Copy Editor at Integra), and Jayavel Radhakrishnan (Senior Project Manager at Integra). Daniel Buckingham was good enough not only to compile the 'Chronology' and the 'Further Reading' section but also to proofread the volume in its entirety at the very last minute with typical good humour.

1903	25 June. Eric Arthur Blair is born in Motihari, Bengal, to Richard and Ida Blair.
1932	November. Eric Blair decides to use a pseudonym. 'George Orwell' is born.
1933	9 January. *Down and Out in Paris and London.*
1934	25 October. *Burmese Days.*
1935	11 March. *A Clergyman's Daughter.*
1936	20 April. *Keep the Aspidistra Flying.*
1937	8 March. *The Road to Wigan Pier.*
1938	25 April. *Homage to Catalonia.*
1939	12 June. *Coming Up for Air.*
1943	28 November. Beginning of the Teheran Conference, later credited by Orwell as the conceptual origin of *Nineteen Eighty-Four.*
1944	June. Orwell and his wife, Eileen Blair, adopt a son named Richard Horatio Blair.
1944	September. Orwell visits, for the first time, the Hebridean island of Jura.
1945	29 March. Death of Eileen Blair.
1945	25 June. Secker & Warburg acknowledge Orwell's completion of the first twelve pages of *Nineteen Eighty-Four.*
1945	17 August. *Animal Farm.*
1945	September. Orwell visits Jura again.
1946	May–October. Having taken residence at Barnhill, Jura, Orwell works on *Nineteen Eighty-Four.*
1946	Mid October. Orwell returns to London.
1947	April. Orwell returns to Jura.
1947	May. While sending Fred Warburg his school memoir, 'Such, Such Were the Joys', Orwell reports that he has completed a third of *Nineteen Eighty-Four.*

1947	July. Orwell publishes 'Toward European Unity', in which he explores the possibility of the division of the world into superstates propped up by isolationism and phoney wars.
1947	November. Orwell completes the first draft of *Nineteen Eighty-Four*.
1947	December. Orwell is admitted to Hairmyres Hospital, East Kilbride, Scotland, and diagnosed with tuberculosis.
1948	January–July. Orwell remains at Hairmyres.
1948	November. Having returned to Jura, Orwell completes the final version of *Nineteen Eighty-Four* in a severely weakened state.
1948	4 December. Orwell sends the completed typescript to Warburg.
1949	6 January–3 September. Orwell is admitted to Cotswold Sanatorium in Cranham, Goucestershire, due to worsening tuberculosis.
1949	8 June. *Nineteen Eighty-Four* is published in the United Kingdom, the first edition comprising 26,575 copies.
1949	13 June. *Nineteen Eighty-Four* is published in the United States with a print run of 20,000 copies.
1949	July. *Nineteen Eighty-Four* is selected for the US Book of the Month Club.
1949	27 August. The first radio adaptation of *Nineteen Eighty-Four* is broadcast, starring David Niven as Winston Smith.
1949	3 September. Orwell transfers to University College Hospital on Gower Street in London.
1949	13 October. Orwell marries Sonia Brownell.
1950	21 January. Orwell, aged 46, dies of pulmonary tuberculosis.

ABBREVIATIONS

References to Orwell's main works of fiction and non-fiction are taken from *The Complete Works of George Orwell*, edited by Peter Davison, in the following imprints:

ACD   *A Clergyman's Daughter* (1935; London: Penguin, 1990)

AF   *Animal Farm* (1945), introd. Malcolm Bradbury (London: Penguin, 1989)

BD   *Burmese Days* (1934), introd. Emma Larkin (London: Penguin, 2009)

CUFA   *Coming Up for Air* (1939; London: Penguin, 1990)

DOPL   *Down and Out in Paris and London* (1933), introd. Dervla Murphy (London: Penguin, 1989)

HC   *Homage to Catalonia* (1938; London: Penguin, 2003)

KAF   *Keep the Aspidistra Flying* (1936; London: Penguin, 1989)

NEF   *Nineteen Eighty-Four* (1949), introd. Julian Symons (London: Everyman's Library, 1992)

RWP   *The Road to Wigan Pier* (1937), introd. Richard Hoggart (London: Penguin, 1989)

References to Orwell's essays, letters, and reviews, and so forth are taken from *The Complete Works of George Orwell*, edited by Peter Davison with the assistance of Ian Angus and Sheila Davison, published in London by Secker & Warburg – as follows:

CW, 10   *A Kind of Compulsion, 1903–1936*, rev. ed. (2000)

CW, 11   *Facing Unpleasant Facts, 1937–1939*, rev. ed. (2000)

CW, 12   *A Patriot After All, 1940–1941*, rev. ed. (2002)

CW, 13   *All Propaganda Is Lies, 1941–1942*, rev. ed. (2001)

CW, 14   *Keeping Our Little Corner Clean, 1942–1943*, rev. ed. (2001)

CW, 15   *Two Wasted Years, 1943*, rev. ed. (2001)

CW, 16   *I Have Tried to Tell the Truth, 1943–1944*, rev. ed. (2001)
CW, 17   *I Belong to the Left, 1945*, rev. ed. (2001)
CW, 18   *Smothered under Journalism, 1946*, rev. ed. (2001)
CW, 19   *It Is What I Think, 1947–1948*, rev. ed. (2002)
CW, 20   *Our Job Is to Make Life Worth Living, 1949–1950*, rev. ed. (2002)

Works by others:

Arendt, OT   Hannah Arendt, *The Origins of Totalitarianism* (1951; London: Penguin, 2017)
Atwood, HT   Margaret Atwood, *The Handmaid's Tale* (1985; London: Vintage, 1996)
Burgess, *1985*   Anthony Burgess, *1985* (1978), introd. Andrew Biswell (London: Serpent's Tail, 2013)
Derrida, AF   Jacques Derrida, 'Archive Fever: A Freudian Impression', trans. Eric Prenowitz, *Diacritics*, 25.2 (Summer 1995), pp. 9–63
Doctorow, LB   Cory Doctorow, *Little Brother* (London: Harper Voyager, 2008)

All italicized emphases in quotations are as in the original source unless otherwise stated.

NATHAN WADDELL

Introduction
Orwell's Book

Writing to his publisher, Fredric Warburg (of Secker & Warburg), on 22 October 1948, George Orwell claimed that the manuscript of the book he was working on was not only 'fearfully long' but also 'unbelievably bad' (*CW*, 19, pp. 456, 457). Orwell added that he was 'not pleased with the book' yet 'not absolutely dissatisfied' (*CW*, 19, p. 457) with it either. The book in question was *Nineteen Eighty-Four* (1949). When Warburg wrote his report on the manuscript nearly two months later, he stated:

> This is amongst the most terrifying books I have ever read. The savagery of [Jonathan] Swift has passed to a successor who looks upon life and finds it becoming ever more intolerable. Orwell must acknowledge a debt to Jack London's 'IRON HEEL', but in verisimilitude and horror he surpasses this not inconsiderable author. Orwell has no hope, or at least he allows his reader no hope, no tiny flickering candlelight of hope. Here is a study in pessimism unrelieved, except perhaps by the thought that, if a man can conceive '1984', he can also will to avoid it. (*CW*, 19, p. 479)

Warburg felt that his extensive and almost entirely positive report on *Nineteen Eighty-Four* gave 'little idea of the giant movement of thought' which Orwell had 'set in motion' in this 'great book'. Nevertheless, Warburg was so disturbed by the novel that he prayed to be 'spared from reading another like it for years to come' (*CW*, 19, p. 481). David Farrer, another executive at Secker & Warburg, suggested that in 'emotive power and craftsmanship' *Nineteen Eighty-Four* 'tower[ed] above the average'. Orwell had done 'what [H. G.] Wells never did, created a fantasy world which yet is horribly real so that you *mind* what happens to the characters which inhabit it'. Farrer added: 'if we can't sell fifteen to twenty thousand copies of this book we ought to be shot' (*CW*, 19, p. 482).

The tone of Farrer's remark now seems acutely misjudged – because of its casualness, and because it aligns the likely fate of Winston Smith, Orwell's doomed protagonist, with a set of purely commercial imperatives. But all the same there is an urgency about Farrer's quip that evokes how *Nineteen Eighty-Four* was always likely to resonate with readers in a world exhausted by two world wars and anxious about the different kinds of political consensus likely to emerge in its aftermath. London-based readers would have been very familiar with the book's allusions to air-raids, Tube station shelters, rubble in the streets, and rationing.[1] It is, as Anthony Burgess pointed out, a book of London in 'war-time or just after' (Burgess, *1985*, p. 14). *Nineteen Eighty-Four* spoke in the 1950s to the concerns of those who had seen the defeat of Nazism and feared the politics and ambitions of the Soviet Union. It appealed, and still appeals, to readers deeply critical of what Orwell elsewhere called 'oratorical way[s] of talking' (*DOPL*, p. 108). It resonated with those who were alarmed by the rapidity of technological advance and the ever more rationalized, efficiency-driven characteristics of modern society. It said something meaningful to the persecuted, the forgotten, the hopeful, the obsequious, the afraid. With its suspicious attitude towards dewy-eyed reminiscence and equally scathing account of authoritarian utopianism in all its forms, *Nineteen Eighty-Four* also brilliantly rang true for those sceptics who, like Hannah Arendt, believed that 'all efforts to escape from the grimness of the present into nostalgia for a still intact past, or into the anticipated oblivion of a better future, are vain' (Arendt, *OT*, p. xii). It was and remains a book of the moment.

Seventy years later, much of the appeal of *Nineteen Eighty-Four* lies in the fact that so many of its readers share in Winston's knowledge 'that something is wrong' with the world, as Louis Menand has put it, 'that we are losing control of our lives', and yet fear, too, that 'we are powerless to resist' the nightmarish transitions of a gradually more technocratic humankind.[2] The novel's account of an all-encompassing paranoia, in which not even the person you love is to be trusted fully and finally, seems disconcertingly compatible with the worst techno-political effects of social media, which for many people have become vehicles of alienation and distrust. Orwell's contemptuous depiction of Ingsoc's anti-intellectual politics holds water for those who have lived through the oppressive regimes of the Eastern Bloc, and still engages readers the world over who are faced with a resurgent anti-intellectual populism. It's a book that shows how experts will only be useful to the state until they are deemed unnecessary and undesirable, at which point they will be cast out, or killed. *Nineteen Eighty-Four* warns us, as Christopher Hitchens once wrote, against 'the awful pleasures and temptations of servility'.[3] It is a book about love, and about enjoying love in secret in order, maybe, to survive, but it also ruminates on how hatred is the hidden freight of a love teetering on the brink of sadism.

This *Companion* builds on successive waves of generational inheritance and debate in the novel's reception by asking new questions about how and why *Nineteen Eighty-Four* was written, what it means, and why it matters. Chapter groupings on a selection of the novel's interpretative contexts, the literary histories from which it is inseparable, the urgent questions it raises, and the impact it has had on other kinds of media, ranging from radio to video games, open up the conversation in a purposefully expansive way. Established concerns (e.g. Orwell's attitude to the working class, his anxieties about the political compartmentalization of the post-war world) are presented alongside newer ones (e.g. his views on evil, and the influence of *Nineteen Eighty-Four* on comics). The goal is to stimulate further exchanges about the novel's significance in an age in which authoritarianism finds itself newly empowered. *Nineteen Eighty-Four* is not a book about Donald Trump, or Kim Jong-un, or Jair Bolsonaro, or even Boris Johnson, but it is a book that tells us something about how individuals of their stripe can push through illiberal political change. It tells us something very important about cults of political celebrity, about 'war-fever and leader-worship' (*NEF*, p. 139). Although *Nineteen Eighty-Four* remains Orwell's book, to these extents it is increasingly *ours*.

Part I of this *Companion*, 'Contexts', establishes four frameworks within which Orwell's novel can be understood from a socio-historical perspective. Natasha Periyan's essay on 'Teaching and Learning in and beyond *Nineteen Eighty-Four*' (Chapter 1) looks at how pedagogy functions in the novel, relating this to Orwell's attitudes towards the school system of his day and to connections between the novel's politics and form. Douglas Kerr's 'The Virtual Geographies of *Nineteen Eighty-Four*' (Chapter 2) takes another look at the post-war geopolitical developments that inspired the eternally warring political blocs of Oceania, Eurasia, and Eastasia. Diletta De Cristofaro's 'The Politics of the Archive in *Nineteen Eighty-Four*' (Chapter 3) considers the novel's presentation of memory and the political workings of archival storage and retrieval. And David Dwan's discussion of 'Orwell and Humanism' (Chapter 4) reminds us of just how thoroughly *Nineteen Eighty-Four* is embroiled in debates not only about human rights – a key context for Orwell, given the appearance of *Nineteen Eighty-Four* just six months after the Universal Declaration of Human Rights in December 1948 – but also about the idea of what it means to be human itself. All of these different perspectives on *Nineteen Eighty-Four* indicate that it continues to tell us about how the way we live now is bound up with unresolved issues from over a lifetime ago.

Putting things like this makes it seem like *Nineteen Eighty-Four* can be boiled down to that oft-caricatured, unhelpfully derided thing: the novel with a message – what Orwell called, in his 1929 essay on John Galsworthy, 'the novel which aims to be a picture and a criticism of contemporary life rather than a straightforward story' (*CW*, 10, p. 140). But although we should be wary of seeing *Nineteen Eighty-Four* as only this, as only a novel seeking to tell us something, it isn't necessarily a problem to emphasize its moralistic dimensions. Orwell certainly thought that *Nineteen Eighty-Four* had urgent things to say about rights and wrongs, clarifying in a statement issued in July 1949 that the novel was not intended 'as an attack on socialism, or on the British Labour Party', which Orwell said he supported, but 'as a show-up of the perversions to which a centralized economy is liable', and which had 'already been partly realized in Communism and Fascism' (*CW*, 20, p. 136). He added that the 'scene of the book' was 'laid in Britain in order to emphasize that the English speaking races are not innately better than anyone else', and that totalitarianism, if it went unchallenged, could 'triumph anywhere' (*CW*, 20, p. 136). *Nineteen Eighty-Four* is a kind of petition, a work asking its readers never to become so complacent that they fail to spot an incipient totalitarianism growing all around them (what Amy Siskind refers to as the 'small signs of normalcy on our march into darkness').[4] Hence Warburg's insistence that the moral to be drawn from the 'dangerous situation' explored in *Nineteen Eighty-Four* 'is a simple one: *Don't let it happen. It depends on you*' (*CW*, 20, p. 134).

Generations of readers have read and valued *Nineteen Eighty-Four* in different ways, ranging from the audiences who first encountered it, in Britain and elsewhere, in the midst of the burgeoning Cold War; to those who read Orwell's books covertly in post-war Eastern Europe; to those who appealed to *Nineteen Eighty-Four* in order to comment on political decisions made in the wake of the 9/11 terrorist attacks; to those who first heard of the novel after the politics it satirizes seemingly came to full fruition, in the West, at least, in the administration of the 45th President of the USA, Donald J. Trump.[5] Dorian Lynskey has recently insisted not only that the book is 'far richer and stranger' than most people probably remember, but also that it has been 'claimed by socialists, conservatives, anarchists, liberals, Catholics, and libertarians of every description'.[6] A staple of school and university curricula, the novel confirms for many young readers the sense that something is rotten in the state, that the world can so often be a place of carefully constructed lies in which we're encouraged to accept unquestioningly the stories and statistics required by the *status quo*. And readers already alert to these problems are not inevitably better prepared for the novel's hard-nosed sombreness. Adult readers are just as likely to be disturbed by *Nineteen Eighty-Four* as are its young enthusiasts. But it is the young who will inherit the world left to them by adults who often don't seem to have learned from the kind of cautionary tale *Nineteen Eighty-Four* so brilliantly exemplifies. For Lyndsey Stonebridge, the novel's 'descriptions of suffering are there to remind us that the pain of others is intolerable; and that what might bind us is not political ideology, but the human capacity to respond to that suffering'.[7] We need such a capacity now more than ever. Our world has never before been more like Winston's: a world of 'false rumours' (*NEF*, p. 74), 'continuously rewritten' histories (*NEF*, p. 222), and degradation through persecution, where the art of ruling (and of being ruled) is to play 'tricks with reality' (*NEF*, p. 223). What we do with such knowledge is for us to decide. Yet who this 'us' amounts to is a complex question.

Discussing the audiences of *Nineteen Eighty-Four* in terms of a universal third-person plural can obscure how it has had a wide and unpredictable readership throughout the last seventy years, with many disparate constituencies finding things in Orwell's novel to value and abhor. Those who study *Nineteen Eighty-Four* in a school classroom in 2020 will think and feel very differently about the novel in contrast to those who once read it surreptitiously, and at significant danger to themselves, behind the Iron Curtain. Czesław Miłosz suggested that Orwell fascinated such individuals through 'his insight into details' of life under Soviet rule and 'through his use of Swiftian satire', which 'tresspass[ed] beyond the prescriptions of socialist realism and the demands of the censor'.[8] Similarly, there is a world of difference between those who furtively consumed *Nineteen Eighty-Four* in Eastern Europe during the post-war period and those who in recent years have bought it openly in China, where it has been available in multiple translations.[9] Readers exposed to *Nineteen Eighty-Four* in China's burgeoning economy, and in the wake of that country's turbulent history, will feel very differently about its contents to those who read it for the first time in America in January 2017, following Trump's inauguration, at which point sales of the novel spiked by 9,500 per cent.[10] And yet what unites all of these different readerships, surely, is a sense that *Nineteen Eighty-Four* speaks in an urgently particular way to the fears of those who find themselves at the whims of dictators, or of would-be tyrants. Bonding child readers at school the world over and the man who chose to read *Nineteen Eighty-Four* in public in Thailand in June 2014, in protest against the military groups who ruled the country until 2019, is a commitment to Orwell's visionary nerve in the face of those hoping to destroy civil liberties as a matter of policy.[11]

Nineteen Eighty-Four appeals to readers everywhere because the central dynamic against which it is positioned – what Leszek Kołakowski called 'the sheer drive for power, for total power as an end in itself' – has lost none of its capacity to mutilate the liberal-democratic principles so many communities still treasure.[12] *Nineteen Eighty-Four* is a book of the 1930s and 1940s. It is clothed in the mental, social, and physical fabric of those decades. It is also sufficiently commodious to speak to readers born in the twenty-first century: the spectre of the omni-regulated life it rejects, to use another Kołakowskian phrase, has not yet been vanquished.[13] The novel remains 'relevant' because, at its heart, it is concerned with the underlying, generalizable structures of thought and action which accompany the drive for power for its own sake, and which incrementally bear down on and erode the resistant mind. So although *Nineteen Eighty-Four* is about the historically specific tensions and possibilities of a certain moment in time, it is also a novel about a set of attitudes the world has not yet vanquished. And this gives *Nineteen Eighty-Four* a flavour of the art defined by the American novelist John Gardner as that which 'beats back', or tries to beat back, 'the monsters', and makes the world safe for frivolous pleasures.[14] When Winston yearns to walk with Julia through the streets 'openly and without fear, talking of trivialities' (*NEF*, p. 146), he evokes an investment of the novel as a whole. *Nineteen Eighty-Four* is a big book about holding on to small things.[15]

One reason why *Nineteen Eighty-Four* is so unsettling is because it doesn't quite let us decide whether it's a hopeful or a pessimistic work. Like the 'shadow-world' (*NEF*, p. 44) of uncertainty in which Winston lives and suffers, the novel's meanings are themselves often shadowy and unclear. Winston addresses himself through his surreptitious jottings in his diary to those living in '*a time when thought is free*' (*NEF*, p. 30). With this move, Orwell turned a critical, if displaced, glance at his own time through the temporal deferrals of Winston's ostensibly private scrawling. Yet *Nineteen Eighty-Four* holds many different temporalities in play, both in terms of the story it tells and in terms of the many readerships it has enjoyed across time and space. It's a novel concerned with the oppressive dynamics of a time 'round about' the date of 1984 (*NEF*, p. 9), a date Orwell himself only settled on, as the novel's manuscript indicates, after toying with the nearby options of 1980 and 1982.[16] To that extent, it announces itself, and has very often been celebrated, as a work of H. G. Wells-inspired futurology – as a text whose 'success' rests on how accurately it predicted a future now almost forty years behind us. *Nineteen Eighty-Four* also pits the time of 'round about' 1984 against other moments in its own internal frame of reference: Winston's half-remembered past; the past of the proles he encounters; the unknown future invoked in his diary; the power-for-power's-sake hereafter theorized by O'Brien; and the apparently transformed world of the future announced in the novel's appendix ('The Principles of Newspeak'), a document which has long been interpreted as a confirmation of Ingsoc's inevitable fall from power.

This proliferation of chronologies helps us get a handle on how and why Winston is so uneasy about his lot in life. He is not a man out of time, or 'outside history' (*NEF*, p. 283), so much as he is a man unable to locate himself *in* time. As we learn at the start of the novel, although he believes 'that he had been born in 1944 or 1945', Oceania's administrative disorientations mean that it's hopeless to try 'to pin down any date within a year or two' (*NEF*, p. 9). Winston's traumatic memories of his mother tear at his heart because he remembers her to have 'died loving him, when he was too young and selfish to love her in return' (*NEF*, p. 32). Dreaming of her and his sister 'down in some subterranean place', 'looking up at him through [. . .] darkening water' (*NEF*, p. 31), Winston is unable to get past his guilt because he has 'deliberately pushed [it] out of his consciousness over many years' (*NEF*, pp. 167–8). The end result of these internal pressures is that Winston is trapped not only in the 'brutal relish' (*NEF*, p. 26) of Oceanic tyranny, but also in the torments of remembrance. He feels as though he wanders 'in the forests of the sea bottom, lost in a monstrous world where he himself [is] the monster' (*NEF*, p. 28), an 'under-water world' (*NEF*, p. 252) from which he swims into the bright-lit torments of the Ministry of Love. Like the so-called traitor Rutherford, Winston belongs at least in part to the grotesque. But whereas Rutherford was a 'monstrous man' who seemed, when Winston saw him in the Chestnut Tree Café, 'to be breaking up before one's eyes, like a mountain crumbling' (*NEF*, p. 80), Winston is more like a desiccated husk who is still further reduced to 'a bundle of bones in filthy underclothes sitting weeping in the harsh white light' (*NEF*, p. 312) of a prison cell.

And Winston finds no solace in his relationship with Julia, a woman whose boldness initially fills him 'with black terror' (*NEF*, p. 12) and who, again in terror, he betrays to O'Brien. Winston and Julia's trysts in the room above Mr Charrington's shop revivify them both, but when they meet again, after Winston's torture, very little seems as it was. Mutual betrayal turns them into 'the dead', as they always knew it would. The 'rigidity and awkwardness' (*NEF*, p. 305) of Julia's body makes it feel like a corpse that Winston once dragged out of a bombed building, whereas he himself is gradually reduced into a living bureaucratic death, ahead of his eventual execution, in which he quibbles meaninglessly with fellow Ministry workers before the life is sucked out of them while they sit round tables 'looking at one another with extinct eyes, like ghosts fading at cock-crow' (*NEF*, p. 308). For much of the novel, Winston's paranoia means he can never quite shake the suspicion that Julia is spying on him. This fact may or may not lead us to argue that she is a member of the Thought Police, as Winston suspects she might be. But it certainly reminds us that fear and hostility are deep-rooted aspects of Winston's psyche.

It may be that the only person in the novel Winston ever feels any genuine closeness to is his torturer. At first, and with no small amount of irony, given the way his conversations with Winston go in Part III of the novel, O'Brien has 'the appearance of being a person that you could talk to' (*NEF*, p. 13). O'Brien's gentility and neatness of manner are also reminiscent of Winston's similarly 'neat' (*NEF*, p. 31) father, a connection reinforced by O'Brien's quasi-parental embrace in the Ministry of Love, where Winston clings to him 'like a baby, curiously comforted by the heavy arm round his shoulders' (*NEF*, pp. 262–3). The comfort is short-lived, not only because O'Brien punishes Winston into compliance, but also because, in torturing him, he acts not as a father but as a kind of gruesome mother. Anna Freud's idea of the mother as the child's 'first external legislator' is helpful here, because it enables us to think of O'Brien as a quasi-maternal surrogate for Winston's absent mother, who along with his father was seemingly obliterated in one of the Party's 'first great purges' (*NEF*, p. 31).[17] O'Brien is Winston's second external legislator. He authorizes Winston fully to be the dissenter he himself has always known he would become, before he has his brains blown out. Not for nothing, after all, does O'Brien give 'an impression of confidence and of an understanding tinged by irony' (*NEF*, p. 182). He is Oceania's supreme ironist: the one who knows that Winston, in being legislated to become who he has for so long imagined himself to be, must cease to exist.

These ironical possibilities, in turn, allow us to think slightly differently about what happens to Winston in Room 101. Winston's dreams of meeting his imagined benefactor, O'Brien, in the 'place where there is no darkness' (*NEF*, p. 107) in fact anticipate his slow interrogation in the ironically named Ministry of Love, whose 'lights [will] never be turned out' (*NEF*, p. 241). The structure of the novel leads us to expect that Winston will meet and be saved by O'Brien in some utopian golden land. Instead, he finds himself subjected to the worst excesses of physical and psychological pain by an oppressor whose knowing duplicity is reflected in the 'ironical gleam' (*NEF*, p. 272) of his spectacles. Winston's narrative arc ends with him becoming reduced to a 'fragment of the abolished past, like a fossil bone' (*NEF*, p. 82), something like the photograph of Jones, Aaronson, and Rutherford he once saw in the Ministry of Truth. And at a certain level, in being reduced to a fragment of the past, like the coral enclosed in the 'tiny world' (*NEF*, p. 154) of the glass paperweight he buys in Charrington's shop, he is simply reduced to the actuality of his place in life. For inasmuch as the novel comes to a climax with Winston confronting his worst fear, rats, in Room 101, this very same scene can also be understood as the moment of O'Brien's ultimate legislative act – that is to say, his bringing of Winston face to face not with the rats *per se*, but rather with what the rats represent: namely, his own entrapment in the iron cage of rationalized existence.

All of this was challenging for the first readers of *Nineteen Eighty-Four*, but it was not unanticipated. Many reviews of the novel pointed out the debts Orwell owed to his literary precursors. Warburg, as we have seen, insisted that Orwell had surely been influenced by Jack London's *The Iron Heel* (1908). He also remarked that the narrative arc of *Nineteen Eighty-Four* reminded him of the story of Arthur Koestler's *Darkness at Noon* (1940), and that the intensity of the third part of the novel was reminiscent of the similarly brooding novels of Fyodor Dostoevsky. Harold Nicolson judged it in relation to Huxley's *Brave New World*, while Philip Rahv, reaffirming the link to Koestler, situated *Nineteen Eighty-Four* in the long sweep of utopian writings going back through Huxley, Edward Bellamy, and William Morris to Tommaso Campanella and Thomas More.[18] To these antecedents we can add Yevgeny Zamyatin's *We* (1924), which Orwell himself viewed as a novel that debunks 'the super-rational, hedonistic type of Utopia' more prominently associated with *Brave New World* (indeed, Orwell suggested Huxley must have 'plagiarised from it to some extent'), one that investigates 'the diabolism & the tendency to return to an earlier form of civilization which seem to be part of totalitarianism' (*CW*, 20, p. 72). And then there's H. G. Wells, a writer whose influence on Orwell arguably began when as an adolescent he read *A Modern Utopia* (1905), Wells's influential account of an ideal, strangely familiar world far away from Earth. In a discussion of Orwell's early relations with Jacintha Buddicom, Peter Davison points out that Orwell's youthful plan one day to write a book like *A Modern Utopia* 'might, with only a little romantic exaggeration, be seen as the moment when *Nineteen Eighty-Four* was conceived'.[19]

However we trace the origins of Orwell's novel in literary-historical terms, clearly we can think about the idea of origins itself in relation to *Nineteen Eighty-Four* in different ways and on multiple chronological scales. Part II of this *Companion*, which is devoted to the theme of 'Histories', presents four such options, moving from broad generic inheritance (the satiric tradition); to immediate literary context (how Orwell can be viewed in relation to other writers of his time); to specific connections between individuals (here, Orwell and Wells); to the influence *Nineteen Eighty-Four* has had precisely as a point of origin for other writers (its shaping presence in the history of post-war dystopian fiction). In thinking about how Orwell fits into different kinds of literary-historical sweep, we can go as far back, as Jonathan Greenberg does in his chapter on Orwell and satire (Chapter 5), to Ancient Greek and Biblical precedent, or we can stick more closely, as Lisa Mullen does in her chapter on Orwell's literary context (Chapter 6), to the immediate networks of stimulus and discrepancy that characterize the literary cultures of the inter-war period. Alternatively, we can relate Orwell to a particularly significant precursor, as Sarah Cole does in her chapter on Orwell and Wells (Chapter 7), or we can think about how *Nineteen Eighty-Four* fits into longer trajectories of literary creativity and innovation, a strategy pursued by Hollie Johnson in her chapter on Orwell's literary inheritors (Chapter 8). Whichever course we take – and these are not exhaustive possibilities, by any means – it becomes increasingly possible to see *Nineteen Eighty-Four* as a work shaped by Orwell's long-digested responses, some more palpable than others, to several centuries' worth of political turmoil, futurological guesswork, and literary innovation.

Part III of this *Companion* indicates how *Nineteen Eighty-Four* has an ethical agenda: it shows the damage done to human beings by state systems built on the politics of cruelty and hatred, encouraging readers to resist and overcome them. This agenda looms large in the scene near the start of the novel when Winston writes in his diary about a war film showing a boatload of refugees bombed into oblivion by helicopters. For Janice Ho, in her chapter 'Europe, Refugees, and *Nineteen Eighty-Four*' (Chapter 9), this scene sits at the heart of a broader anxiety running all the way through the novel about the treatment of foreigners by bloodthirsty nationalists. For Elinor Taylor, in her chapter on 'The Problem of Hope: Orwell's Workers' (Chapter 10), the ethical investments of *Nineteen Eighty-Four* are unmissable, except here the focus falls on Orwell's oft-debated investigations of the fates and fortunes of the proles. Intersecting with some of the issues also discussed by David Dwan, my own chapter, 'Oceania's Dirt: Filth, Nausea, and Disgust in Airstrip One' (Chapter 11), shows how ideas in the novel about dirt and cleanliness are connected with broader political concerns about the health of individuals and nations. Peter Brian Barry's chapter, on 'Room 101: Orwell and the Question of Evil' (Chapter 12), takes a philosophical perspective on how torture functions in *Nineteen Eighty-Four* as an index of intolerance. Placelessness, labour conditions, the politics of grime, malevolence: these are some of the emphases in relation to which Orwell's most ethically charged imaginings took shape.

Nineteen Eighty-Four engages with questions that had been on Orwell's mind for decades. Prominent among them is the slipperiness of the division between human and animal existence, a problem Orwell addresses most often through metaphor and simile. In *Animal Farm* (1945) he found a way to deal with this problem in memorably fabular form, even if animal substitutions and comparisons feature so frequently in Orwell's fiction that it can be hard not to view the *oeuvre* in its entirety as a kind of analogical outspilling from the 1945 work, its fairy-tale gambit implying a unifying mode for all the rest. Next to the allegorical emphases of *Animal Farm*, *Nineteen Eighty-Four* seems rather less animalistically coherent. Yet animal comparisons run through the later work, all the same. Winston's neighbour, Parsons, not only sweats so profusely that the sweat seems like an enzymatic secretion, but he also has a 'froglike face' (*NEF*, pp. 58, 245) that becomes sanctimonious when he yields to his designation as a Thought Criminal. Just as the Party imposes on its members the cruel dictum that the proles are 'natural inferiors who must be kept in subjection, like animals' (*NEF*, p. 74), so too is *Nineteen Eighty-Four* itself, at the narrative level, a work thoroughly invested in the representational tactics of animal equivalence.[20] Dwan notes in *Liberty, Equality and Humbug* (2018) that the animal is 'repeatedly invoked' in Orwell's work 'as a sign of the low and the abject'.[21] He notes, too, in his essay in this *Companion*, that the way animal comparisons work in *Nineteen Eighty-Four* makes it difficult to decide whether the humans compared to animals in the novel are compared in this way by Orwell's narrator or if they themselves have *become* animalistic. Whatever the case may be, it's clear that *Nineteen Eighty-Four* is one of the most imaginatively 'beastly' novels Orwell produced.

The idea of the beastly functions in Orwell's thought, as Margaret Drabble has pointed out, as a mark of 'the goodness of beasts', on the one hand, and of 'the beastliness of human nature', on the other.[22] Hence we find running throughout *Nineteen Eighty-Four* a twin emphasis on humans acting, or seeming to act, in other-than-human ways; and on animalistic comparison as a means with which to account metaphorically for human deeds. The proles are the focus for this strategy: they are said to exist in degrading swarms and to shoot into doorways 'like rabbits' (*NEF*, p. 87), and many of them, as if they are beasts of burden, are little more than 'old bent creatures shuffling along on splayed feet' (*NEF*, p. 86). To reiterate Dwan's point, it's not fully clear whether such descriptions mean that the proles *are* animalistic in some sense, or that, in behaving in certain ways, they have surrendered their claim to be viewed as human subjects – or that the novel is asking us implicitly to criticize Winston and others for how they construct the proletarians' lives in these othering vocabularies. Whatever the case may be, those who are most subdued by or compliant with the Oceanic authorities tend – appropriately enough for a novel in which furry little critters play such a celebrated, distressing role – to be rodent- or primate-like. The poet Ampleforth, for example, is 'a mild, ineffectual, dreamy creature', with 'very hairy ears' (*NEF*, p. 44), whereas Syme's 'dark hair and large, protuberant eyes, at once mournful and derisive' (*NEF*, p. 51), make him sound very much like an acquiescent tarsier.

These cases of animalistic resemblance point to a more general correspondence between submissive or downtrodden types and non-human others. In many instances this is expressed through references to insectoid sameness. In the Records Department alone, 'swarms of workers' are 'engaged in an unimaginable multitude of jobs', every thronging group of them merely one 'cell' (*NEF*, p. 45) among many in a hive-like mass. The 'buzz of conversation' (*NEF*, p. 116) against which Winston hopes surreptitiously to speak to Julia only reinforces this sense of the Oceanic workforce as a kind of arthropodic bulk. So deep-rooted is this idea that Winston himself views the ostensibly limited consciousness of the proles, those 'few scattered survivors from the ancient world' (*NEF*, p. 96) before the birth of the Party, as comparable to the restricted vision of 'the ant, which can see small objects but not large ones' (*NEF*, pp. 96–7) – a description which aligns them with the Eurasian army of his imagination, 'swarming across the never-broken frontier and pouring down into the tip of Africa like a column of ants' (*NEF*, p. 303). Yet although at certain moments in the story, for Winston, the proles seem like 'swarming disregarded masses' (*NEF*, p. 72), at others he insists on their nobility and humanity. He is convinced that the proles, in another echo of *Animal Farm* (via the character of Boxer), need 'only to rise up and shake themselves like a horse shaking off flies' (*NEF*, p. 73) in order to secure their freedom, but it's not so obvious how they can do that when, at least as far as Orwell's narrator is concerned, 'larger evils invariably escaped their notice' (*NEF*, p. 75). But then again, maybe that doesn't matter: there is a fragile possibility that the proles will 'stay alive against all the odds, like birds, passing on from body to body the vitality which the Party did not share and could not kill' (*NEF*, p. 229).

All of which makes it twice as puzzling that John Sutherland should write, in *Orwell's Nose* (2016): 'There is not a single animal in *Nineteen Eighty-Four*. Unless, that is, you count the rat.'[23] From Goldstein's sheep-like face; to the way the Parsons children play with each other like tiger cubs (*NEF*, p. 25); to the 'gorilla-faced' (*NEF*, p. 6) guards standing watch outside the Ministry of Love; to the 'aquiline' (*NEF*, p. 69) features of Winston's wife, Katharine; to the old prole 'with white moustaches that bristled forward like those of a prawn' (*NEF*, p. 90); to the 'sordid colonies of wooden dwellings like chicken-houses' (*NEF*, p. 5) which have spring up all over London; to the woman at the Two Minutes Hate whose mouth opens and shuts 'like that of a landed fish' (*NEF*, p. 16); to the pure orthodoxy of the man in the Records Department Canteen speaking 'in unconsciousness, like the quacking of a duck' (*NEF*, p. 57), and much else besides, there is very little in *Nineteen Eighty-Four* that *isn't* animalistic, at least in the sense that it is so painstakingly ballasted with human-animal semblance. And even where the rats are concerned, Orwell ensured that the spaces through which Winston moves all look forward, in different ways, to the iconic scene at the end of *Nineteen Eighty-Four*, when he literally comes face to face with a rodent. The first inkling of this we get in the novel is the fact that, just like the 'little dark doorway like a rat-hole' (*DOPL*, p. 56) Orwell remembered from his time in Paris, in *Nineteen Eighty-Four* the 'battered doorways' in the area north-east of what used to be St Pancras are 'curiously suggestive of rat-holes' (*NEF*, p. 86). The thought becomes real when Julia tells Winston that she saw a rat dart out of the wainscoting in the room above Charrington's shop. Does she tell him this because she actually saw it happen? Or does she tell him this because she's a goading agent of the Thought Police?

Such questions are very difficult to answer with any certainty, not least because the style of *Nineteen Eighty-Four* is not as far from the ambiguities of the modernist literatures from which in many other respects it diverges.[24] It's also tricky to account for the animalistic dimensions of *Nineteen Eighty-Four* unequivocally. One possibility is that Orwell wanted to suggest that the downtrodden become animalistic under the oppressive circumstances of a world so catastrophically askew. It's also likely, though, that at some level he thought that in spite of all that has happened to them, in spite of all the burdens, scarcities, humiliations, and wrongs, the put-upon citizens of Airstrip One cannot finally be defeated. Orwell wrote in *The Lion and the Unicorn* (1941) of how it takes 'some very great disaster, such as prolonged subjugation by a foreign enemy, to destroy a national culture':

> The Stock Exchange will be pulled down, the horse plough will give way to the tractor, the country houses will be turned into children's holiday camps, the Eton and Harrow match will be forgotten, but England will still be England, an everlasting animal stretching into the future and the past, and, like all living things, having the power to change out of recognition and yet remain the same. (*CW*, 12, p. 409)

Airstrip One is Orwell's vision of an England changed out of recognition and yet uncannily the same, his vision of a dystopian world based on an increasingly authoritarian present, an everlasting animal stretched into the future even as it builds upon the anxieties of the past. And insofar as its dependence on animal comparisons further extends Orwell's concerns about the autonomy of the individual, *Nineteen Eighty-Four* simultaneously implies, through the very manner in which it describes human individuals, that if more or less everyone is liable to behave animalistically, then everyone, more or less, is the same. *Nineteen Eighty-Four* thereby testifies to how difficult it is to maintain one's individuality in a society of increasingly monotonous sameness even as it registers the exceptional challenge of keeping a free mind under conditions of unprecedented technological control.

There are two *coups de grâce* at the end of *Nineteen Eighty-Four*. The first is what surely must be Winston's execution. We don't witness it, but he and we know it's coming. The second is what the novel seems to imply about its own operations in the very act of being finished. Douglas Kerr has argued that the novelistic form of *Nineteen Eighty-Four* itself functions as a riposte to the reductive values of the world it chronicles. 'Although it tells a story that imagines the defeat of individual freedom, community, history, and conscience', Kerr writes, 'it does so in a form of writing that continues to enact these very things every time it is read.'[25] *Nineteen Eighty-Four* is, then, its own imaginative answer to the rubbishy fictions produced by the 'novel-writing machines' (*NEF*, p. 11) in the Ministry of Truth. Even so, the novel works hard to demonstrate just how exhaustively, through a wide variety of techniques and postures of domination, individuals can be kept down, dehumanized, and enchained. Martha C. Nussbaum has written that *Nineteen Eighty-Four* is 'not just about lies and totalitarian projects of domination. It is about the end of human beings as we know them, the political overthrow of the human heart.'[26] What human beings have to contend with in *Nineteen Eighty-Four* is nothing less than the gutting of their humanity as such. So many of Oceania's citizens seem lifeless because the lives they live are so listless and empty. They have been deadened not only by the structures of a 'strictly regimented society' (*NEF*, p. 197), but also by the way they have internalized its authoritarian expectations.

Such factors are a consequence of the exhausting dynamics structuring the lives of almost every character and character-type in *Nineteen Eighty-Four*. At thirty-nine years old, Winston is only on the cusp of middle age, but his body is ulcerated and inflamed. April may or may not be the cruellest month, for him, yet the May sunshine makes him feel 'dirty and etiolated' (*NEF*, p. 125). Like Mrs Parsons, Winston is aged before his time, beginning his days with coughing fits and 'deep, unconscious sigh[s]' (*NEF*, p. 40). Mr Charrington leads a 'ghostlike existence' (*NEF*, p. 157), speaking 'in generalities, with so delicate an air as to give the impression that he had become partly invisible' (*NEF*, p. 144) – and appropriately enough, after all, given that he's a snooping spook. The novel implies that Winston is exhausted simply by thinking about Julia, given her punishing range of interests and abilities. And even O'Brien, so secure in his position of privilege and power, has a 'blunt-featured face' (*NEF*, p. 183) that is 'tired', with 'pouches under the eyes' (*NEF*, p. 256) and sagging skin – a deathly visage whose cadaverousness is reinforced by the way he speaks with a '*grave* courtesy' (*NEF*, p. 186, emphasis added).[27]

The sapped anatomy of Oceania – encapsulated in the name of the disgraced Comrade Withers (*NEF*, p. 47) – pulsates and wanes even as O'Brien points out to Winston that the 'weariness of the cell is the vigour of the organism' (*NEF*, p. 302), thereby suggesting that individual frailty means nothing in the context of the strength of the Party overall. Quite whether O'Brien's confidence in this matter is warranted or not is a moot point. Although, given the nature and extent of the Party's ideological, cultural, social, and technological might, O'Brien is basically correct in thinking that it controls life 'at all its levels' (*NEF*, p. 282), the fitness of the society it dominates is hardly self-evident. It's difficult to imagine a society populated by types in the same state of health as the novel's protagonists surviving for any great length of time. But then again, characters like Winston and Parsons belong to a dwindling generation – they are on the way out, to be replaced by individuals 'taken from their mothers at birth, as one takes eggs from a hen' (*NEF*, p. 280), presumably in order to be raised in an atmosphere ideally conducive to spotless, enduring orthodoxy. Biddable creatures of a 'beetle-like type' (*NEF*, p. 63) proliferate in the Oceanic Ministries, having been reduced into unconscious obedience by the stultifying bureaucracies that employ them. Winston imagines that he and Julia are being surveilled by one of these insectoid types, a suspicion reinforced, for the reader at least, by the fact that the clock in Charrington's room ticks with an 'insect voice' (*NEF*, p. 192). Winston is himself constructed in similar terms; he eventually learns that the Thought Police have watched him for seven years 'like a beetle under a magnifying glass' (*NEF*, p. 289). Others, like the 'jerkily' (*NEF*, p. 244) mobile Parsons, are less like insects and more akin to puppets: Winston feels that the fanatic in the Records Department canteen is 'not a real human being but some kind of dummy' (*NEF*, p. 57); his wife, Katharine, stiffens into a 'jointed wooden image' (*NEF*, p. 70) when she endures his love-making; and he himself, presumably along with every other Outer Party member, is turned into a kind of puppet every morning by the jerking routine he is forced to perform at the behest of the 'shrewish voice' (*NEF*, p. 39) in his telescreen. It's little surprise, then, that so many Outer Party members shudder and lurch their way through their marionette-like existences.[28]

This is one aspect of *Nineteen Eighty-Four* that accounts for its attractiveness to video game designers, who, as Soraya Murray demonstrates below in her chapter on this same subject (Chapter 16), have taken full advantage of the Orwellian 'model'. But the legend of *Nineteen Eighty-Four* has also made its way into film and television adaptations and pop song lyrics. When O'Brien makes Winston accept the proposition that two plus two can in fact equal five, he sets the stage for works like Radiohead's song '2+2=5'

(2003) and, on another front, for what is surely the finest moment in Patrick Stewart's career as an actor: the sight of Captain Jean-Luc Picard, in the *Star Trek: The Next Generation* two-part episode 'Chain of Command' (1992), resisting the surreal logic to which poor old Winston succumbs. Picard's dramatic insistence that there are only four lights, when the Cardassian bully Gul Madred wants him to believe that there are in fact five, implicitly rejects not only O'Brien's account of things, but also, perhaps, Orwell's. In Picard's world, resistance is anything but futile. The final part of this *Companion* focuses on these and other processes of cultural inheritance and creative appropriation, with chapters by Daniel Buckingham on *Nineteen Eighty-Four* and its abundance of radio, stage, and screen adaptations (Chapter 13); Jamie Wood on the novel and its shaping influence on an extraordinary assortment of pop and rock songs, and on opera (Chapter 14); and Isabelle Licari-Guillaume on the different vectors through which *Nineteen Eighty-Four* has made itself heard in the world of comic books (Chapter 15), with Murray's chapter rounding off the set. These contributions bring into focus an Orwellian legacy that keeps on growing in always new and unexpected ways.

***

Despite the obvious temptations, there are good reasons to avoid seeing *Nineteen Eighty-Four* as a map or blueprint for our own times, not least because of Orwell's claim that '[a]ll prophecies are wrong' (*CW*, 11, p. 46). Orwell certainly pitched his books with a particular kind of politically alert audience in mind, but he didn't write *Nineteen Eighty-Four* for 'us' in any straightforwardly transhistorical sense of that word. Although the novel is clearly ours in the sense of having become deeply entrenched in late twentieth- and early twenty-first-century culture and commentary, it remains a book addressed to the 1930s and 1940s, and in response to a sense that certain socio-political tendencies of that period might develop, if left unchecked, along catastrophic lines. Yet for all that, and in a different but important way, *Nineteen Eighty-Four* remains ours, even so. We read it, we live with it, we teach with it. We argue about it, and sometimes we dismiss it. Like it or loathe it, the power *Nineteen Eighty-Four* wields seventy years after it was published suggests that we moderns often love it, too, as Adam Roberts challengingly points out in the 'Coda' to this volume. The amount of attention paid to the book, even in (and perhaps especially in) criticizing it, demonstrates its hold on our times. A question to ask, then, is not what Orwell 'got right' by way of prophetic anticipations in *Nineteen Eighty-Four*, but rather: Why do we go to the novel in search of echoes between now and the now-superseded present of its imagined future?

Every generation, every community makes *Nineteen Eighty-Four* into what it wants the novel to be. One explanation for this is because human beings find it reassuring to see modern problems in old stories, to discover ourselves in our past. In this way, we entertain the fantasy of a way out and through the present by means of a return to a time when the future still seemed unwritten. The meanings of *Nineteen Eighty-Four* are in so many ways 'scraped clean and re-inscribed' (*NEF*, p. 42) by those interpreting it in the wake of those who have interpreted it before. The novel's symbol for this reinscriptive process, the palimpsest – a name for a writing surface on which marks can be made and then removed, but which spectrally peek through the ensuing layers of inscription, like a 'sort of transparency' (*NEF*, p. 117) – represents the technological and administrative means with which history in Oceania is written, rewritten, and then rewritten again. Yet this process of 'ghostly re-appearance' (*NEF*, p. 48) also signals the novel's own operations as a cultural-historical object. The meanings this novel seems to contain vary as each generation or community discovers it anew. If *Nineteen Eighty-Four* is in these respects no different from any other literary work, all such texts being subject to the same palimpsestic mechanisms, it stands out to the extent that it is itself concerned, at the level of plot and theme, with how literary production can be influenced by the most diabolical pressures.

Inscriptive activity – writing, engraving, carving – is suspect in Oceania because the possibility that anything recorded in the form of language has in fact been simulated, or is meant to signal the opposite of itself, or is a prelude to death, is so extraordinarily high. Winston puts faith in the value of writing when he chooses to write freely in his diary, but he knows, right away, that the mere act of buying a diary, let alone putting pen to paper in one, will eventually get him killed. The slogans of the Party are so alarming not because their ironic structures entail a troubling kind of meaninglessness, but because they have been contrived to have the appearance of something concrete and true. 'WAR IS PEACE' isn't disconcerting because it suggests that peace might be war, although that possibility disturbs all the same, but rather because 'WAR IS PEACE' can be taken as a right and proper view of the world. As Winston reflects in Charrington's shop: 'One could not learn history from architecture any more than one could learn it from books. Statues, inscriptions, memorial stones, the names of streets – anything that might throw light upon the past had been systematically altered' (*NEF*, p. 102). Given this knowledge, the 'inscription' (*NEF*, p. 191) at the start of Goldstein's book, *The Theory and Practice of Oligarchical Collectivism* – the fact that it is a piece of writing in the first place – should set Winston's alarm bells ringing, but it does not. The mistake costs him dearly.

One reason why Winston is hoodwinked is because he shares Orwell's sense that a handshake matters. When he and Julia leave O'Brien's apartment, O'Brien shakes Winston's hand with such force that he crushes the bones in his palm (*NEF*, p. 186). The crushing is a betrayal, a trouncing of the solidarity of touch. O'Brien should be Winston's friend in this lying world, but he isn't. *Nineteen Eighty-Four* thereby implicitly looks back to a scene in Orwell's *Homage to Catalonia* (1938). Writing about his meeting, in civil-war-torn Barcelona, with a Spanish police officer who had little reason to trust him, Orwell recalls the 'strange and moving thing' of shaking hands with the man in a 'horrible atmosphere of suspicion and hatred, the lies and rumours circulating everywhere' (*HC*, p. 186). The handshake is, for Orwell, a sign of the nobility inherent in the generous spirit, in the person able to look past rumour in affirming the hopeful carriage of decency. In the story of *Nineteen Eighty-Four*, by contrast, a handshake means nothing. Or, rather, a handshake means what all the essays in this *Companion* show: that for Orwell there was a good deal of creative purchase in the dislocations of a world turned upside down and inside out. In *Nineteen Eighty-Four*, as we will see in so many different ways in what follows, Orwell made a virtue of the end of integrity. He turned hopelessness into craft. We should argue over what this means, and over why we still pay attention to a novel written in a time that already feels impossibly distant, yet terrifyingly near.

Notes

1 See Lawrence Phillips, 'Sex, Violence, and Concrete: The Post-War Dystopian Vision of London in *Nineteen Eighty-Four*', *Critical Survey*, 20.1 (2008), pp. 69–79.
2 Louis Menand, '"*1984* at Seventy: Why We Still Read Orwell's Book of Prophecy' (8 June 2019) [www.newyorker.com/news/daily-comment/1984-at-seventy-why-we-still-read-orwells-book-of-prophecy] (accessed 11 November 2019).
3 Christopher Hitchens, *Orwell's Victory* (2002; London: Penguin, 2003), p. 6.
4 Amy Siskind, *The List: A Week-by-Week Reckoning of Trump's First Year* (New York: Bloomsbury, 2018), p. 1.
5 The two best recent accounts of these dynamics of reader response can be found in Dorian Lynskey's *The Ministry of Truth: A Biography of George Orwell's '1984'* (London: Picador, 2019) and D. J. Taylor's *On 'Nineteen Eighty-Four': A Biography* (New York: Abrams Press, 2019).
6 Lynskey, *The Ministry of Truth*, p. xviii.
7 Lyndsey Stonebridge, *Placeless People: Writings, Rights, and Refugees* (Oxford: Oxford University Press, 2018), p. 75.
8 Czesław Miłosz, *The Captive Mind*, trans. Jane Zielonko (London: Penguin, 2001), p. 42.

9 See Michael Rank, 'Orwell in China: Big Brother in Every Bookshop', *The Asia-Pacific Journal*, 11.23:2 (9 June 2013), pp. 1–11.

10 Adam Gopnik, 'Orwell's "1984" and Trump's America', *The New Yorker* (27 January 2017) [www.newyorker.com/news/daily-comment/orwells-1984-and-trumps-america] (accessed 13 November 2019).

11 'Protesting Thai reader of Orwell's *1984* dragged off by police in Bangkok', *South China Morning Post* (23 June 2014) [www.scmp.com/news/asia/article/1538 616/protesting-thai-reader-orwells-1984-dragged-police-bangkok] (accessed 13 November 2019).

12 Leszek Kołakowski, 'Communism as a Cultural Force' (1985), in *Is God Happy?* (London: Penguin, 2012), pp. 25–42, at p. 36.

13 See *Ibid.*, p. 27.

14 John Gardner, *On Moral Fiction* (1978), introd. Lore Segal (New York: Basic Books, 2000), p.6.

15 For more on this side of Orwell's thought, see Annette Federico, 'Making Do: George Orwell's *Coming Up for Air*', *Studies in the Novel*, 37.1 (Spring 2005), pp. 50–63.

16 George Orwell, *Nineteen Eighty-Four: The Facsimile of the Extant Manuscript*, ed. Peter Davison (London: Secker & Warburg, 1984), pp. 22–3.

17 See Adam Phillips, *On Kissing, Tickling, and Being Bored: Psychoanalytic Essays on the Unexamined Life* (1993; London and Boston: Faber and Faber, 1994), p. 111.

18 Jeffrey Meyers (ed.), *George Orwell: The Critical Heritage* (London and New York: Routledge, 1975), pp. 247, 249, 250, 259, and 267–8.

19 Peter Davison, *George Orwell: A Literary Life* (Basingstoke: Palgrave, 1996), pp. 8–9.

20 There is an ironic link here between form and theme, given that, in Goldstein's book, it is said that one of the many self-preserving skills Party members possess is 'the power of not grasping analogies' (*NEF*, p. 220).

21 David Dwan, *Liberty, Equality and Humbug: Orwell's Political Ideals* (Oxford: Oxford University Press, 2018), p. 86.

22 Margaret Drabble, 'Of Beasts and Men: Orwell on Beastliness', in Abbott Gleason, Jack Goldsmith, and Martha C. Nussbaum (eds.), *On 'Nineteen Eighty-Four': Orwell and Our Future* (Princeton and Oxford: Princeton University Press, 2005), pp. 38–48, at p. 43.

23 John Sutherland, *Orwell's Nose: A Pathological Biography* (2016; London: Reaktion, paperback edition 2017), p. 227.

24 For more on these uncertainties, and on the novel's 'constant ambiguity', see Lynskey, *The Ministry of Truth*, p. 177. Important discussions of Orwell's indebtedness to modernist techniques include Claire Hopley's 'Orwell's Language of Waste Land and Trench', *College Literature*, 11.1 (1984), pp. 59–70, and two pieces by Patricia Rae: 'Mr. Charrington's Junk Shop: T. S. Eliot and Modernist Poetics in *Nineteen Eighty-Four*', *Twentieth-Century Literature*, 43.2 (Summer 1997), pp. 196–220, and 'Surveillance and the "Poetics of Silence": Late Modernist Imagism in George Orwell's *Nineteen Eighty-Four*', in Mark Levene (ed.), *Political Fiction* (Ipswich, MA: Salem Press, 2015), pp. 132–52.

25 Douglas Kerr, *George Orwell* (Tavistock: Northcote House, 2003), p. 88.

26 Martha C. Nussbaum, 'The Death of Pity: Orwell and American Political Life', in Gleason, Goldsmith, and Nussbaum (eds.), *On 'Nineteen Eighty-Four'*, pp. 279–99, at p. 282.

27 See also the moment when O'Brien looks down at Winston 'gravely and rather sadly' (*NEF*, p. 256).

28 In this way, *Nineteen Eighty-Four* reinforces the urgency articulated in the closing sentence of *Homage to Catalonia* (1938), which signals Orwell's fear that those 'sleeping the deep, deep sleep of England [...] shall never wake till [they] are jerked out of it by the roar of bombs' (*HC*, p. 196).

PART I

Contexts

I

NATASHA PERIYAN

Teaching and Learning in and beyond *Nineteen Eighty-Four*

In June 1932 George Orwell wrote a letter from The Hawthorns, the private preparatory school at which he taught between 1932 and 1933: 'I have been teaching at the above foul place for nearly two months. I don't find the work uninteresting, but it is very exhausting [...]. I've hardly done a stroke of writing' (*CW*, 10, p. 249). The letter demonstrates Orwell's ambivalence towards teaching: his charges are 'brats' (*CW*, 10, p. 249), the work is 'not uninteresting', and its tiring nature a distraction from writing. In July 1933 he wrote to a friend hoping that 'I'll be able to drop this foul teaching after next year' (*CW*, 10, p. 319). Orwell's antipathy towards teaching closely informed his depiction of Dorothy Hare's experience of teaching in a suburban private school in *A Clergyman's Daughter* (1935). The school's penny-pinching headmistress, Mrs Creevy, declares: 'It's the fees I'm after, not *developing the children's minds*' (*ACD*, p. 235). The novel breaks into an essayistic polemic against such schools which all share 'the same fundamental evil [...]; they have ultimately no purpose except to make money' (*ACD*, p. 239), an attack Orwell later repeated in *The Lion and the Unicorn: Socialism and the English Genius* (1941).

Orwell's critique of education makes it ironic that his work has formed a spinal part of British GCSE and A-Level educational syllabi and American high school curricula. *Nineteen Eighty-Four*'s chilling portrayal of intellectual control has found particular resonance in US high schools following the Trump administration's 'alternative facts', which, for many teachers and students, offer an eerie parallel to Ingsoc's manipulation of reality.[1] In 2017 UK educationalists gathered to reflect upon the urgency of teaching Orwell's work in the era of post-truth, alternative facts, and fake news at the George Orwell Studies conference on 'Teaching Orwell'. Sessions of the conference likened the surveillance culture of English secondary schools to the society depicted in *Nineteen Eighty-Four*.[2] Orwell's work has historically occupied a less central place on university syllabi, aside from courses on dystopian or utopian fiction. Critics argue that

Orwell's perennial status on school curricula has marginalized his work on university courses.[3] His essays, particularly 'Politics and the English Language' (1946), have attracted debate surrounding their utility as a tool for teaching writing skills in US composition classes.[4] Orwell's status as a public intellectual renders him foundational to Western academic culture. His thinking forms a significant touchstone for academics across the humanities and social sciences. This chapter explores themes of teaching and learning in *Nineteen Eighty-Four* to argue that the novel criticizes the meritocratic social order shaped by mainstream educational policy for much of the twentieth century in its depiction of the dystopian effects of a society ordered around intellectual aptitude. In analysing the novel as Winston Smith's *bildungsroman*, I argue that Orwell manipulates literary form to examine the political slogans that shape Oceania. By exploring how Orwell aligns the processes of teaching and torture in the novel as forms of intellectual control, the chapter interprets Orwell's wider cynicism surrounding teaching as an attack upon individual mental freedom and points to the paradoxically anti-pedagogic pedagogic function of the novel.

Nineteen Eighty-Four's vision of intellectual control in a future socialist state under a totalitarian regime represents an evolution of the educational critique in Orwell's previous work. *The Lion and the Unicorn* proposes a programme for educational reform in a socialist state. The essay is informed by inter-war politics surrounding calls for democratic access to education in an era when most children were educated only to elementary level and left school at 14. It anticipates '[r]eform of the educational system along democratic lines' (*CW*, 12, p. 422) and envisages wiping out the elite public schools, available only to the wealthy, as it calls for the 'abolition of all hereditary privilege, especially in education' (*CW*, 12, p. 410). Orwell's vision of a 'democratic' educational system reflects the meritocratic politics on the British Left during this period. Throughout the inter-war years the Labour Party was committed to expanding educational opportunities and to raising the school-leaving age. In the immediate post-Second World War period, Labour MPs were generally committed to a tripartite system of secondary education which separated children into different educational streams: grammar schools for children who were perceived to be academic, alongside technical and secondary modern schools. Orwell's focus on educational provision for the 'gifted' reflects this current of opinion:

> We could start by abolishing the autonomy of the public schools and the older universities and flooding them with State-aided pupils chosen simply on grounds of ability. [...] It is all too obvious that our talk of 'defending

democracy' is nonsense while it is a mere accident of birth that decides whether a gifted child shall or shall not get the education it deserves.   (*CW*, 12, p. 424)

Orwell's vision of 'flooding' the elite, fee-paying public schools with students from non-fee-paying state schools illuminates an inter-war social context in which literary writers were evolving their democratic ideals through a focus on educational opportunity.[5] The focus on education for the 'gifted' reflects the formation of a meritocratic social order where social advancement was, theoretically, based on intelligence rather than on hereditary privilege. This social order was fostered by a commitment to the concept of intelligence and implemented by the competitive examination and the scholarship ladder. Adrian Wooldridge suggests that meritocratic mobility 'offered a means of reconciling elitism with democracy'.[6] By the 1950s, however, the purportedly objective basis of educational selection was disputed by sociologists and educationists. More recent critiques of meritocracy emphasize that the rhetoric of individual meritocratic self-advancement veils structural inequalities.[7]

Nineteen Eighty-Four (1949) and 'Such, Such Were the Joys' (1952) are critical of meritocratic educational ideals. 'Such, Such Were the Joys' draws on Orwell's experiences as a 'scholarship boy' at preparatory school (in his case, St Cyprian's in Eastbourne, which he attended from 1911 to 1916). It argues that 'making a gifted boy's career depend on a competitive examination, taken when he is only twelve or thirteen, is an evil thing at best' (*CW*, 19, p. 361). The essay depicts the psychological ramifications of an education tied to financial concerns. Intelligence is a fiscal commodity that entails an emotional debt. Orwell's intellectual prowess rendered him eligible for 'greatly reduced fees' at his school because he was 'likely to win scholarships' to prestigious public schools and 'thus bring credit on the school' (*CW*, 19, p. 360). The fiscal term 'credit' is significant in the context of the broader economic critique Orwell makes of the 'financial relationship' (*CW*, 19, p. 363) the scholarship boy has with his preparatory school. The essay asks: 'it is wicked, is it not, to hate your benefactors? So I was taught, and so I believed' (*CW*, 19, p. 366). Critics have discussed the historical veracity of Orwell's account of his preparatory school.[8] The fiscal term 'benefactor' evokes Charles Dickens's *bildungsroman*, *Great Expectations* (1861), and suggests the resonances between Orwell's school experiences and Dickens's novel: both he and Dickens's protagonist, Pip, are beneficiaries of funds that afford them an education that advances their social position. Both are also depicted as weighed down by an emotional debt occasioned by an educational system based on financial transactions and class consciousness.

In the socialist state imagined in *Nineteen Eighty-Four*, the fiscal basis of the educational system forms a less conspicuous focus for Orwell's critique. Instead Orwell depicts a society based on intelligence. *The Lion and the Unicorn* envisaged 'a classless educational system' (CW, 12, p. 427) in a socialist state. Oceania, the state run by Ingsoc (English Socialism), remains unequal in more invidious terms based on an intellectual stratification which keeps 'the ablest people at the top' (*NEF*, p. 218). This societal ordering closely echoes the scenario described by Aldous Huxley, Orwell's former teacher at his public school, Eton, in *Brave New World* (1932). Huxley's novel depicts an intelligence-based social hierarchy of Alphas, Betas, Gammas, Deltas, and Epsilon Semi-morons.[9] Orwell's visions of totalitarian systems in both *Animal Farm* (1945) and *Nineteen Eighty-Four* depict a form of intellectual control exerted by more intelligent members of society. In *Animal Farm*, the pigs are 'the cleverest of the animals' (*AF*, p. 10) and they rule over the animals of lesser intelligence, while in *Nineteen Eighty-Four*, Winston's inquisitor, O'Brien, is repeatedly identified as 'intelligent' (*NEF*, pp. 176, 264, 286).

Conversely, the novel presents the proles, who form 85 per cent of the population of Oceania, as having 'no intellect' (*NEF*, p. 219) and as being largely illiterate. Orwell's dystopian conception of the literacy level of the proles echoes D. H. Lawrence's hierarchical programme in 'Psychology and the Unconscious' (1923): '*The great mass of humanity should never learn to read and write – never.* [. . .] The mass of people will never *mentally under-stand*. But they will soon instinctively fall into line.'[10] However, the proles also form a latent revolutionary force, whose potential power could be stimulated through education. Winston finds that 'hope lies in the Proles' and notes that '*[u]ntil they become conscious they will never rebel*' (*NEF*, p. 74). In the torture scenes of Part III of *Nineteen Eighty-Four*, O'Brien discloses that he 'collectively' wrote the book attributed to Goldstein. The book posits a 'programme' for revolution through the 'secret accumulation of knowledge – a gradual spread of enlightenment – ultimately a proletarian rebellion', a phony curriculum O'Brien dismisses as 'nonsense' (*NEF*, p. 274).

Orwell's depiction of a nefarious society run by the intelligent rather than by those born of 'hereditary privilege' (*CW*, 12, p. 410) revises his 1941 model for an English socialist state and positions him in dialogue with socialist thinking of the time. His vision anticipates Michael Young's depiction of a dystopian future in his essayistic novel *On Meritocracy* (1958), wherein advancement based on intelligence is envisaged as the primary social good and replaces all other social ties. Theoretically, Goldstein's book suggests a meritocratic form of social advancement in Ingsoc whereby intelligence is a means of social transformation. It outlines that admission 'to either branch of the Party is by examination' (*NEF*, p. 217). However, this meritocratic order extends only so far. While members of the 'Outer Party' can graduate into the 'Inner Party', 'gifted' proletarians are 'not allowed to graduate into the Party' (*NEF*, p. 218). Instead, they are 'eliminated' (*NEF*, p. 218) because they could incite sedition. The sophistry of the arguments in Goldstein's book reveals a conflicted relationship to heredity that reflects a contradictory line of reasoning. While the book notes that in principle membership of the Inner Party, Outer Party, and the proletariat is 'not hereditary', it also points out that the world of Ingsoc 'is stratified, and very rigidly stratified, on what at first sight appear to be hereditary lines' (*NEF*, p. 217). Social mobility – a feature of meritocratic societies – is negligible: 'There is far less to-and-fro movement between the different groups than happened under capitalism or even in the pre-industrial ages' (*NEF*, pp. 217–18). The Party redefines heredity as an issue not of capital but of intellect. In doing so, Orwell exposes the focus on hereditary privilege in the English socialist movement as myopic. In the early years of Oceania, the opposition from the 'older kind of Socialist' was neutralized: 'trained to fight against something called "class privilege", [they] assumed that what is not hereditary cannot be permanent' (*NEF*, p. 218). In fact, the 'essence of oligarchical rule is not father-to-son inheritance, but the persistence of a certain world-view and a certain way of life' (*NEF*, p. 218).

Intellectual control is at the foundation of Oceania. The Party's 'central tenet' is the 'mutability of the past' (*NEF*, p. 222): '"Who controls the past controls the future: who controls the present controls the past"' (*NEF*, p. 260). Winston's job in the Records Department is central to the process by which the past is distorted and the record of reality changed. Doublethink, the process by which individual memory is altered to accord with the changing record of 'reality' orchestrated by the Party, is defined early on in the novel as the ability 'to hold simultaneously two opinions which cancelled out, knowing them to be contradictory and believing in both of them; to use logic against logic' (*NEF*, p. 37). Paradoxically, the more intelligent members of Oceania have to subject themselves the most to this 'vast system of mental cheating' (*NEF*, p. 224) because their greater understanding of reality necessitates a more pronounced 'unconscious [. . .] act of hypnosis' (*NEF*, p. 38) to ensure adherence to Party orthodoxy: 'the greater the understanding, the greater the delusion: the more intelligent, the less sane' (*NEF*, p. 224).

The slogans repeated throughout the text – 'WAR IS PEACE', 'FREEDOM IS SLAVERY', 'IGNORANCE IS STRENGTH' (*NEF*, p. 18) – form the backbone of the means through which Party ideology is disseminated. *Animal Farm* explores the implementation of political slogans as a form of intellectual control. It associates political slogans with the mindless consumption of information and the intellectual incapacity of the mass of the population. On first establishing their new society after ousting their human owner, the animals develop a 'Re-education Committee' (*AF*, p. 22). The narrative absorbs the propagandistic voice of the new regime by suggesting the 'reading and writing classes [...] were a great success. By the autumn almost every animal on the farm was literate in some degree' (*AF*, p. 23). It quickly becomes apparent in the paragraphs following this declaration of 'success' that the phrase 'in some degree' offers the 'euphemism [...] and sheer cloudy vagueness' (*CW*, 17, p. 428) that 'Politics and the English Language' identifies as such a problematic feature of political language. The novel identifies a hierarchy of intellectual aptitude among the animals that mirrors the ranking of minds supplied by intelligence testing. While the pigs read and write 'perfectly', the dogs read only 'fairly well' (*AF*, p. 23), and many of the animals on the farm can only learn the first letter of the alphabet. In response to this, the intelligent pig, Snowball, summarizes the Seven Commandments as 'a single maxim, namely: "Four legs good, two legs bad"' (*AF*, p. 24). This enables the 'stupider animals such as the sheep, hens and ducks' to grasp the 'essential principle of Animalism' (*AF*, p. 24). At the text's denouement, the pigs ape their former human masters by walking only on their hind legs and 'the sheep burst out' into a 'tremendous bleating' of '"Four legs good, two legs *better*! Four legs good, two legs *better*!"' (*AF*, p. 97) after having been isolated from the rest of the animals while Squealer, the leader of Animal Farm's deputy, was 'teaching them to sing a new song' (*AF*, p. 96). The episode demonstrates the political purposes of slogans as a means of manipulating the mass into advancing a political dogma they do not truly understand.

Nineteen Eighty-Four depicts Winston's intellectual dissent from the mind control exercised by Ingsoc. His intellectual curiosity shapes the novel. Alex Zwerdling argues: 'the characteristic pattern of Orwell's documentary essays and books is the movement from ignorance to enlightenment. [...] He is anxious to identify himself with people who are capable of learning, whose minds are not closed [...] his characteristic story is the record of an education'.[11] Winston's attempts at intellectual enlightenment are structured around the development of a broader understanding of the slogans that underpin Ingsoc. His self-led learning is particularly evident after he encounters two texts in the novel, a children's history book in Part I, Chapter 7, and Goldstein's book in Part II. After reading them, Winston reflects in similar terms on how far the information he is presented with elucidates his understanding of Ingsoc: 'the ultimate motive was mysterious. He took up his pen again and wrote: *I understand HOW: I do not understand WHY*' (*NEF*,

p. 83); and later: 'He had still, he reflected, not learned the ultimate secret. He understood *how*; he did not understand *why*' (*NEF*, p. 226).

The principles behind two of the three Party slogans, 'WAR IS PEACE' and 'IGNORANCE IS STRENGTH', are explored in Goldstein's book with excerpts that are directly presented to the readers of *Nineteen Eighty-Four*. Orwell's skilled manipulation of rhetoric is reflected in the didactic tones of Goldstein's book and in the sophistry with which it explains the thinking behind Ingsoc's Party slogans. In March 1949, shortly after Orwell had completed *Nineteen Eighty-Four*, the novel was under discussion for selection for the Book of the Month Club, founded by Harry Scherman in 1926, which involved the production of a special issue of the text. The selectors advised that the extracts from Goldstein's book should be removed. Orwell's response affirms the significance of the book-within-the-book (i.e. Goldstein's book) for the broader meaning and structure of the novel in which it appears. Orwell noted that the proposed cuts 'would alter the whole colour of the book and leave out a good deal that is essential', adding that they 'would also [...] make the story unintelligible' (*CW*, 20, p. 66). His comments indicate the significance of questions of intelligibility to the text. This reflects on both Winston's enlightenment and the reading experience of the novel. Winston's response to Goldstein's book positions him as exceptional in his capacity to learn. While Julia falls asleep while listening to him read, Winston reflects critically on the book's information:

> [I]t told him nothing that was new, but that was part of the attraction. It said what he would have said, if it had been possible for him to set his scattered thoughts in order. It was the product of a mind similar to his own, but enormously more powerful, more systematic, less fear-ridden. The best books, he perceived, are those that tell you what you know already.
>
> (*NEF*, p. 208)

> Chapter I, like Chapter III, had not actually told him anything that he did not know, it had merely systematised the knowledge that he possessed already.
>
> (*NEF*, p. 226)

The narrative emphatically establishes that Goldstein's book is introducing no new information but instead offers a 'systematized' or 'systematic' encapsulation of Oceania's principles. Goldstein's book also holds a similar function for the reader, rendering intelligible the principles behind Ingsoc's political philosophy that are disseminated elsewhere in the novel on a more ad hoc basis.

Goldstein's book is also deployed to stimulate the reader's curiosity. Orwell interrupts Winston's reading at a tantalizing moment: when Goldstein seems on the verge of revealing 'the ultimate secret' (*NEF*,

p. 226) surrounding why 'human equality [should] be averted' (*NEF*, p. 225). Winston stops reading, leaving the reader only with a provocative, unresolved ellipsis: 'This motive really consists. ...' (*NEF*, p. 226). This is one localized instance of how *Nineteen Eighty-Four* establishes suspense through its narrative strategies. Winston's death is foretold from the beginning of the novel in his intellectual dissent as he starts writing a diary that provides evidence of his thoughtcrime. From these early moments of the text Winston concludes that '[h]e was already dead' (*NEF*, p. 30). Orwell objected to the early jacket copy of *Nineteen Eighty-Four*, which he suggested made the novel sound like 'a thriller mixed up with a love story'.[12] In *Nineteen Eighty-Four*, the 'thriller' element of the novel is aligned closely with processes of learning. Suspense comes in Winston's attempts to understand Ingsoc, rather than through the question of whether he will or will not survive. The narrative strategies of the book stimulate curiosity and a desire to learn more and so align the reader with Winston, who is similarly positioned as keen for enlightenment.

Winston's engagement with a children's history textbook, as he attempts in Part I, Chapter 7, to teach himself about 'what life before the Revolution had really been like' (*NEF*, p. 75), also establishes his intellectual curiosity. Through this book, Winston encounters how far the parameters of social reality are controlled by Party orthodoxy. As a means through which to access information about the past, the textbook is a particular instance of Ingsoc's mind control. The children's history textbook as a source of indoctrination was previously explored in *A Clergyman's Daughter* when Dorothy has to use 'a horrid little book called *The Hundred Page History of Britain*' (*ACD*, p. 211) dating from 1888. The textbook covers 'Boadicea to the first Jubilee' (*ACD*, p. 221), selectively focusing on imperialistic tales of Britain's military victory at Waterloo and its 'beneficent reforms' (*ACD*, p. 211). Dorothy is keen to 'scrap the repulsive *Hundred Page History*' (*ACD*, p. 219), which she thinks is mostly 'lies' (*ACD*, p. 221). Instead she borrows 'history books out of the public library' (*ACD*, p. 219) to use in class. In the editorial process for *A Clergyman's Daughter*, Orwell was asked to adapt this section of the text, but he responded robustly: 'Description of textbooks in use at the school has not been altered, as it is substantially true' (*CW*, 10, p. 362). In *Nineteen Eighty-Four*, the children's textbook is similarly a tool of indoctrination:

> *In the old days* [it ran], *before the glorious Revolution, London was not the beautiful city that we know today. It was a dark, dirty, miserable place [...]. But in among all this terrible poverty there were just a few great big beautiful houses that were lived in by rich men who had as many as thirty servants to*

look after them. These rich men were called capitalists. They were fat, ugly men
with wicked faces, like the one in the picture on the opposite page. You can see
that he is dressed in a long black coat which was called a frock coat, and
a queer, shiny hat shaped like a stovepipe, which was called a top hat. This was
the uniform of the capitalists, and no one else was allowed to wear it. The
capitalists owned everything in the world, and everyone else was their slave.

(NEF, pp. 75–6)

The textbook closely mirrors the declarative statements and instructive tone
of pedagogic writing. The image of the capitalist presented in the textbook
recurs elsewhere in Orwell's writing. In *The Road to Wigan Pier* (1937) it
shapes Orwell's critique of socialism's crude political teaching that falsely
dichotomizes the interests of the working class and the middle class through
clichéd stereotypes: 'In order to symbolise the class war, there has been set up
the more or less mythical figure of [. . .] a "capitalist", a fat, wicked man in
a top hat and fur coat' (*RWP*, p. 210). Instead, Orwell advocates for a more
nuanced class model as he argues that 'all people with small, insecure
incomes are in the same boat [. . .]. I am implying that different classes must
be persuaded to act together' (*RWP*, p. 211). Analysis of *Nineteen Eighty-
Four* in relation to *The Road to Wigan Pier* demonstrates that Orwell's vision
of a totalitarian future has its origins in his critique of 1930s socialism and
positions Ingsoc's portrayal of capitalism as crude stereotyping. Winston
uncertainly wonders if the information presented in the textbook is 'pure
fantasy' (*NEF*, p. 78).

While two of Ingsoc's slogans are examined in the extracts from
Goldstein's book, in Part I, Chapter 7, Winston reflects on intellectual freedom as he mentally revises Ingsoc's slogan 'FREEDOM IS SLAVERY':

He picked up the children's history book and looked at the portrait of Big
Brother which formed its frontispiece. The hypnotic eyes gazed into his own. It
was as though some huge force were [. . .] battering against your brain, frightening you out of your beliefs, persuading you, almost, to deny the evidence of
your senses. In the end the Party would announce that two and two made five,
and you would have to believe it. [. . .] the very existence of external reality, was
tacitly denied by their philosophy. [. . .] For [. . .] how do we know that two and
two make four? Or that the force of gravity works? Or that the past is
unchangeable? If both the past and the external world exist only in the mind,
and if the mind itself is controllable – what then?
[. . .]
The Party told you to reject the evidence of your eyes and ears. [. . .] Truisms
are true, hold on to that! [. . .] With the feeling that he was speaking to O'Brien,
and also that he was setting forth an important axiom, he wrote:

> *Freedom is the freedom to say that two plus two make four. If that is granted,*
> *all else follows.*   (NEF, pp. 83–4)

In *A Clergyman's Daughter*, the textbook's frontispiece is an imperialistic image of 'Boadicea with a Union Jack draped over the front of her chariot' (*ACD*, p. 211). In *Nineteen Eighty-Four*, the frontispiece of Big Brother's image assaults Winston's senses in order to make him forsake the most basic building blocks of learning. Winston's definition '*Freedom is the freedom to say that two plus two make four*' reworks Ingsoc's slogan that 'FREEDOM IS SLAVERY' as he claims for himself individual intellectual autonomy based on a logical assessment of the facts.

In the torture scenes of the novel, in Part III, Chapters 2 to 4, O'Brien attacks the capacity for independent mental reasoning that Winston explores in Part I, Chapter 7. He does this in order to force Winston to fall in line with the 'doublethink' necessitated by the Party. In Part III, O'Brien reveals to Winston not only the 'how' behind Ingsoc's maintenance of power, but also the 'why': 'we are interested solely in power. [...] Power is not a means, it is an end' (*NEF*, pp. 275–6). O'Brien also explains to Winston the principle behind the axiom 'FREEDOM IS SLAVERY' – 'Has it ever occurred to you that it is reversible? Slavery is freedom' (*NEF*, p. 277) – and suggests that through intellectual submission the individual can escape the defeat of death: 'if he can escape from his identity, if he can merge himself in the Party so that he *is* the Party, then he is all-powerful and immortal' (*NEF*, p. 277). This involves, however, acceding to the Party's control over mind and matter. The elements of seemingly incontrovertible knowledge Winston explores in Part I, Chapter 7 (the earth rotates around the sun, the past is alterable, two and two make four) are systematically debunked in the torture scenes as O'Brien reworks each of these different 'truisms' (*NEF*, p. 84) in his interrogation of Winston.

O'Brien, acting as Winston's interrogator, is identified as an intelligent, knowledgeable figure. He is depicted as omniscient: his 'mind *contained* Winston's mind' (*NEF*, p. 268) with the ability to echo and rework Winston's thoughts. In Part I, Chapter 7, Winston reflects on how far notions of sanity are shaped by intellectual consensus: 'Perhaps a lunatic was simply a minority of one' (*NEF*, p. 83), a phrase closely echoed by O'Brien as he asserts Winston's need for re-education: 'You preferred to be a lunatic, a minority of one. [...] Whatever the Party holds to be truth, *is* truth. [...] That is the fact that you have got to re-learn, Winston' (*NEF*, p. 261). This 're-learning' is depicted as a dystopian education in which the catechistic questioning techniques of both torture and pedagogy become closely aligned.

Julian Symons described the torture scenes as embodying a 'schoolboyish sensationalism of approach'.[13] His comments suggest that a puerile sensibility underpins the ghoulish depiction of Winston's torture but also indicate the pedagogic elements in the interaction between O'Brien and Winston. During this scene O'Brien is repeatedly identified as a teacher: 'He had the air of a doctor, a teacher, even a priest, anxious to explain and persuade rather than to punish' (*NEF*, p. 257); 'he had the air of a teacher taking pains with a wayward but promising child' (*NEF*, p. 260); O'Brien 'assumed again his air of a schoolmaster questioning a promising pupil' (*NEF*, p. 279). The association between education and torture echoes 'Such, Such Were the Joys', which opens with a description of a brutal beating at St Cyprian's. The essay also functions as an analysis of totalitarian power in an educational setting.[14] Its refrain, 'the rules were such that it was actually not possible for me to keep them' (*CW*, 19, p. 359), illuminates the principles by which terror is enacted in *Nineteen Eighty-Four*. The repeated associations made between teaching and torture figure the pupil–teacher relationship as one of coercion, bullying, and totalitarian oppression.

In his process of 're-education', Winston is repeatedly tortured as O'Brien attempts to erode Winston's confidence in his own reasoning processes and to indoctrinate him in the Party's illogical reasoning. O'Brien frames Winston's capacity to respond to this teaching in specifically educational terms: 'You are a slow learner, Winston' (*NEF*, p. 263). Winston eventually succumbs to O'Brien's teaching/torture and manages the doublethink necessary to accord with Party thinking. After repeated testing, when O'Brien holds up four fingers, Winston sees five:

> And he did see them, for a fleeting instant, before the scenery of his mind changed. He saw five fingers, and there was no deformity. Then everything was normal again, [...]. But there had been a moment [...] of luminous certainty, when each new suggestion of O'Brien's had [...] become absolute truth, and when two and two could have been three as easily as five, if that were what was needed. (*NEF*, pp. 270–71)

Alone in his cell, Winston works 'at the task of re-educating himself. [...] It was merely a question of learning to think as they thought' (*NEF*, pp. 289–90). The intricacy of acquiring the capacity of doublethink is presented as necessitating mental exertion. It requires an 'athleticism of mind, an ability at one moment to make the most delicate use of logic and at the next to be unconscious of the crudest of logical errors' (*NEF*, pp. 291–2). Winston 'trained himself in not seeing or not understanding the arguments that contradicted' the Party's propositions, such as 'the earth is flat' or 'two and two make five' (*NEF*, p. 291). The description of the acquisition of doublethink ironically credits the process as one of intellectual effort and reward, a measure of 'ability' (*NEF*, p. 291) that is usually associated with the development of exceptional mental capacity: 'Stupidity was as necessary as intelligence, and as difficult to attain' (*NEF*, p. 292).

The attempts at 'enlightenment' that Zwerdling identifies as characteristic of Orwell's narratives are perversely inverted in *Nineteen Eighty-Four*.[15] Winston's attempts to free his mind from the dogma of the Party in Parts I and II of the text are cruelly thwarted in Part III during O'Brien's torture, which is conceived by the narrator as an act of teaching. Interestingly, the final moments of the narrative appear to allude to Thomas Hughes's *Tom Brown's School Days* (1857), a genre-defining public school story for children.[16] Hughes depicts the mischievous Tom's 'conversion' to the path of moral righteousness and includes a portrait of the influential Rugby head-master Dr Thomas Arnold (1795–1842), whose moralistic, hierarchical teaching more broadly influenced Victorian and Edwardian educational ideals. Jenny Holt argues that Hughes's story had an influential role in the formation of civic ideals in the Edwardian era: in 1910 to 1911 the Board of Education recommended the inclusion of the novel in every elementary school library, and special editions of the text adapted for use in schools were produced.[17] Orwell's 1940 review of T. C. Worsley's anti-public school tract *Barbarians and Philistines* notes the influence of Hughes's novel: '[t]he new class who were coming into power naturally wanted a more civilized type of school than the Rugby described by Tom Hughes, and through the efforts of Dr Arnold [...] they got it' (*CW*, 12, p. 261). The moment of Tom Brown's submission to Dr Arnold's pedagogy is described in terms that denote a power struggle between the two: 'the Doctor's victory was complete from that moment over Tom Brown'.[18] Similar language is used to describe Winston's final submission to Big Brother, which is conceived as a 'victory' over Winston's own internal reasoning processes: 'the struggle was finished. He had won the victory over himself. He loved Big Brother' (*NEF*, p. 311). The appropriation of Hughes's text by Orwell subversively reconfigures the model Victorian and Edwardian pupil–teacher relationship as a prototype for totalitarian politics.

A focus on teaching and learning in *Nineteen Eighty-Four* illuminates both the politics and the form of Orwell's text. A contextually alert reading demonstrates that Orwell's depiction of a society organized around intelligence offers a critique of the meritocratic values that were coming to dominate British socialism. The novel's structure can also be elucidated as a pedagogic exploration of the principles behind Ingsoc, as Winston attempts to release himself from the Party's mind control only to become enslaved to its dictates in the dystopian education scenes of Part III, where teaching is associated with intellectual manipulation. Indeed, there are few portraits of good teaching in Orwell's work. Dorothy in *A Clergyman's Daughter* briefly manages a classroom revolution, teaching her pupils without the interference of meddling parents and an exploitative headmistress. A mark of her success comes in fostering independent thought in her pupils: she 'broke them in to the habit of thinking for themselves' (*ACD*, p. 220) and the children 'showed more intelligence when it was a question of *making* something instead of merely learning' (*ACD*, p. 222). Her temporary triumph provides an instructive contrast to the depiction of teaching as a form of totalitarian mind control in *Nineteen Eighty-Four*. Far from the portrait of oppression that shapes the teacher–pupil relationship of O'Brien and Winston, or Orwell's own frustration with the 'foul' (*CW*, 10, p. 319) work of teaching, *A Clergyman's Daughter* briefly offers a lyrical appreciation of the joys of teaching: 'Those are the times that make teaching worth while – the times when the children's enthusiasm leaps up, like an answering flame, to meet your own, and sudden unlooked-for gleams of intelligence reward your earlier drudgery' (*ACD*, p. 225).

Notes

1 See Rebecca Klein, 'High School Students Reading "1984" See a Mirror, Not Science Fiction', *HuffPost*, 2 February 2017 [www.huffingtonpost.co.uk/entry/teens-1984-george-orwell-trump_n_5892445ce4b070cf8b8060a7?guccounter=1] (accessed 9 December 2019); Katherine Schulten, 'Teaching Orwell and "1984" with the *New York Times*', *New York Times*, 9 February 2017 [www.nytimes.com /2017/02/09/learning/lesson-plans/teaching-orwell-and-1984-with-the-new-york-times.html] (accessed 9 December 2019).

2 A special issue of *George Orwell Studies* included an essay on Orwell's educational experiences contextualized against developments in teacher training. See Tim Crook, 'Orwell the Teacher: Such, Such Were the Joys', *George Orwell Studies*, 2.1 (2017), pp. 38–51.

3 See Neil McLaughlin, 'Orwell, the Academy and the Intellectuals', in John Rodden (ed.), *The Cambridge Companion to George Orwell* (Cambridge: Cambridge University Press, 2000), pp. 160–78, at p. 162.

4 Cleo McNelly, 'On Not Teaching Orwell', *College English*, 38.6 (February 1977), pp. 553–66; George Y. Trail, 'Teaching Argument and the Rhetoric of Orwell's "Politics and the English Language"', *College English*, 57.5 (September 1995), pp. 570–83.

5 See Natasha Periyan, *The Politics of 1930s British Literature: Education, Class, Gender* (London: Bloomsbury, 2018).

6 Adrian Wooldridge, *Measuring the Mind: Education and Psychology in England, c. 1860 – c. 1990* (Cambridge: Cambridge University Press, 1994), p. 175.

7 See Jo Littler, *Against Meritocracy: Culture, Power, and Myths of Mobility* (London: Routledge, 2017).

8 See Robert Pearce, 'Truth and Falsehood: George Orwell's Prep School Woes', *The Review of English Studies*, 43.171 (August 1992), pp. 367–86.

9 Huxley taught at Eton between 1917 and 1919. See Nicholas Murray, *Aldous Huxley: An English Intellectual* (London: Little, Brown, 2002), pp. 96–109.

10 D. H. Lawrence, *Fantasia of the Unconscious, Psychoanalysis and the Unconscious* (London: Penguin, 1971), p. 87.

11 Alex Zwerdling, *Orwell and the Left* (New Haven and London: Yale University Press, 1974), pp. 133–4.

12 Bernard Crick, *George Orwell: A Life* (1980; London: Secker & Warburg, 1981), p. 383.

13 Julian Symons, *TLS*, 10 June 1949, in Jeffrey Meyers (ed.), *George Orwell: The Critical Heritage* (London and New York: Routledge, 1975), pp. 251–7, at p. 256.

14 See John R. Reed, *Old School Ties: The Public Schools in British Literature* (New York: Syracuse University Press, 1964), pp. 226–41 for an analysis of the similarities between *Nineteen Eighty-Four* and 'Such, Such Were the Joys'.

15 Zwerdling, *Orwell and the Left*, p. 133.

16 See Isabel Quigly, *The Heirs of Tom Brown* (London: Chatto & Windus, 1982).

17 Jenny Holt, *Public School Literature, Civic Education, and the Politics of Male Adolescence* (Farnham: Ashgate, 2008), p. 3.

18 Thomas Hughes, *Tom Brown's School Days* (Cambridge: Macmillan & Co., 1857), p. 408.

2

DOUGLAS KERR

The Virtual Geographies of *Nineteen Eighty-Four*

Every novel creates its own map, with its places of dwelling and meeting and conflict, its infrastructure of communication, its borderlands, its inaccessible or disputed spaces. *Nineteen Eighty-Four* (1949) has at least two, showing the topography of its personal and its geopolitical life: the relatively restricted landscape through which Winston Smith moves – basically urban, with one excursion to the countryside – and the global context shaped by the brutal political realities of Orwell's imagined future. These geographies are virtual, in the sense that they are fictional, but in other ways too. The geopolitical map of *Nineteen Eighty-Four* is a story inscribed by ideological forces on the physical geography of the planet. The story, and the map, may change from one minute to the next. Only in a very qualified way could we describe it as the real world, even in the restricted terms of the novel. For Winston Smith it is certainly less real, less present to him, than the Golden Country he dreams about (*NEF*, pp. 32–3). This chapter investigates *Nineteen Eighty-Four*'s geography of interiority, social interaction, and private space, expressed for the most part in novelistic discourse, and that of Oceania, Eurasia, and Eastasia, created in journalistic or strategic language.

A Map of the World

Nineteen Eighty-Four has many sources and motives, but Orwell, in a letter to Roger Senhouse written in December 1948, was explicit about its main deliberate intention. 'What it is really meant to do is to discuss the implications of dividing the world up into "Zones of influence" (I thought of it in 1944 as a result of the Teheran Conference), & in addition to indicate by parodying them the intellectual implications of totalitarianism' (*CW*, 19, p. 487). In 1941, after Hitler had invaded Russia and Japan attacked the American navy, an alliance was formed among the Soviet Union, the United

Kingdom, and the United States, which was to go on to victory in 1945. The members of this alliance were far from being natural political allies, and their military goals too did not always coincide. The alliance was lubricated by a series of summit meetings between the national leaders, to smooth over differences, agree on war strategy, and to make plans for a post-war world. One of these was the Teheran conference at the end of November 1943, attended by Winston Churchill, Joseph Stalin, and Franklin D. Roosevelt. They discussed the co-ordination of offensives against German-occupied Europe planned for the following year, and ideas for the post-war government of Poland.[1]

These meetings were presented to the public of the allied nations as examples of strategic co-operation. To a more jaundiced observer – such as Orwell, who in an 'As I Please' column for *Tribune* (26 January 1945) refers to 'the sordid bargain that appears to have been driven at Teheran' (*CW*, 17, p. 30) – they presented a spectacle of three great powers carving up the world to their own advantage, just as, a century and a half before, the great satirist James Gillray had depicted a caricature of the Emperor Napoleon Bonaparte and the British Prime Minister William Pitt greedily slicing into the terrestrial globe (in the form of a plum pudding) with their swords.[2] From these tripartite summit meetings of wartime allies – chiefly Teheran, Yalta, and Potsdam – emerged the post-war spheres of influence and ultimately the geography of what Orwell was to christen the 'cold war'. That phrase occurs for the first time in a short essay for *Tribune*, 'You and the Atom Bomb' (19 October 1945), in which Orwell looks forward to a dangerous future. 'More and more obviously the surface of the earth is being parcelled off into three great empires, each self-contained and cut off from contact with the outer world, and each ruled, under one disguise or another, by a self-elected oligarchy' (*CW*, 17, p. 320).[3] This, he thought, was the shape of things to come in the second half of the twentieth century, as cooked up in those wartime allied summits, with one important exception: he foresaw that a weakened Britain would soon lose its place at the geopolitical table, to be replaced by a new player, 'East Asia, dominated by China' (*CW*, 17, p. 320). There is thus a straight line from the Teheran conference to the geography of *Nineteen Eighty-Four*, with its three superstates of Oceania, Eurasia, and Eastasia.

The invention of the political world map of *Nineteen Eighty-Four* is a remarkable act of creative imagination, but the strategic thinking behind it was not unique to Orwell. Educated people caught up in a world war they are trying to understand are bound to exercise a strategic imagination, to think globally, and wartime journalism provided daily a stream of more or less expert discourse to assist such thinking. What would be the implications of the surrender at Singapore? How effective was the convoy system in protecting transatlantic trade from U-boat attack? Why did the Germans need to take Stalingrad, at any cost? To keep up with the world war, you needed a world map in your head. As a sometime servant of the British Empire in the East, Orwell was already used to strategic thinking: to think imperially was to think globally, as the example of Kipling had shown. And while he worked in the Indian Section of the BBC's Eastern Service from 1941 to 1943, Orwell wrote and produced a series of weekly radio news commentaries (also referred to as 'newsletters'), interpretations of world events unfolding week by week in the most critical months of the war, in which he tried to help his Indian listeners to understand the conflict in global terms.[4] These bulletins of world news show the deployment of the strategic vision which would later produce the world of *Nineteen Eighty-Four*.

Almost before the war was over, the rivalry between the allies had soured into actual enmity, as they scrambled to establish their respective blocs across the globe and to thwart each other's ambitions. As happens in *Nineteen Eighty-Four*, two of the parties lined up against the third. The ideological differences between the Western powers and the Soviet Union were sharp, but their geopolitical ambitions were not so dissimilar, tending to world domination. What struck Orwell was what they had in common, a practice of *Realpolitik* in which principles were quickly sacrificed to interests. Britain, America, and Russia were allies in the First World War, antagonists after the Russian Revolution of 1917 created the communist Soviet Union, uneasy opponents of Nazism in the 1930s, enemies after Stalin signed a non-aggression pact with Hitler in 1939, allies again after the German invasion of the USSR in 1941, and now again the antagonists of the Cold War. In Spain in 1937, Orwell himself had had first-hand experience of the way the Soviet Union, the principal ally of the socialist Republican government in the Spanish Civil War, had organized the discrediting and purging of anarchist and trade-union forces in Barcelona who were, as a matter of fact, fighting on the same side as the communists.

Of course in *Nineteen Eighty-Four* Orwell was not writing about the political realities of 1944, when he conceived the idea of the novel, nor of the post-war years up to 1948 when he completed it. It is a fictional world we find in the book. Still, the basic ingredients were there, in a globe divided up between combative and power-hungry superstates, each eager to gain control of weaker non-aligned countries, each urging its home population to loyalty to a particular ideology ('democracy', 'socialism') and to hatred and fear of its apparent opposite espoused by foreigners, but open to bewildering changes of allegiance dictated by state or imperial self-interest. In this way Orwell sets the stage, unrolls the world map, and then directs his attention to how this state of affairs impacts on, and variously disables and dehumanizes, the lives of the subjects of these states and ideological systems. 'Oceania is not a portrait, or even caricature, of a single state', Ben Clarke has observed. 'It incorporates features of Stalinist Russia, Nazi Germany and indeed post-war Britain, but is also an exploration of the "pure idea" of totalitarianism.'[5]

Just as the London of the novel is recognizably the bomb-damaged, rationed London of the 1940s, so the political map too has its origins in the geography of the post-war settlement and the Cold War. But it is of course a projection from that geography into an imagined future. Britain no longer exists as a state, and barely as a memory. As Airstrip One, it is an outlying province of Oceania, and London is not a capital but a provincial city. Britain's former dominions, in southern Africa and Canada and Australasia, belong to Oceania, as does South America. Continental Europe has been absorbed into Eurasia, an expanded version of the Soviet Union whose power is exercised on the great landmass from Portugal to the Bering Sea. Eastasian territory stretches from the Japanese islands to Persia. That leaves, in the middle of the map (Figure 2.1), a quadrilateral with its corners at Tangier in Morocco, Brazzaville on the Congo River, Darwin in northern Australia, and Hong Kong on the edge of China. This is unaligned territory with shifting borders, constantly fought over by the three super-powers. It roughly corresponds to what would become known as the Third World. The quadrilateral is politically powerless, but with its great populations it is an almost unlimited source of slave labour for the warring powers. The novel offers no access to the consciousness of this area of darkness surrounded by powerful predators. It is a blank space on the map.

The three superstates are so powerful that no two of them can hope to invade and defeat the third; their rivalry is played out in frontier lands and in the territory of the quadrilateral. Oceania, like the others, is in a permanent state of emergency, its population under relentless government surveillance, encouraged by propaganda and rumour to feel embattled, threatened, and hysterically hostile to enemy forces nobody in London has ever seen, except in the occasional parade of dispirited prisoners of war.

Oceania is a fortress of paranoia: inside its borders there is nowhere to hide, outside is a world of unknowable terrors. No one can ever leave it, or have any contact with the foreigners whose terrifying onscreen images they have been conditioned to hate and fear. They live in a state of enforced solipsism, an induced blindness to other people and to elsewhere. Is Oceania allied with Eurasia, and at war with Eastasia? Or is it allied with Eastasia, and at war with Eurasia? From the point of view of Oceania's citizens, it literally makes no difference.[6] Like the populations of the other superstates, they are sequestered within their own territory, and kept in

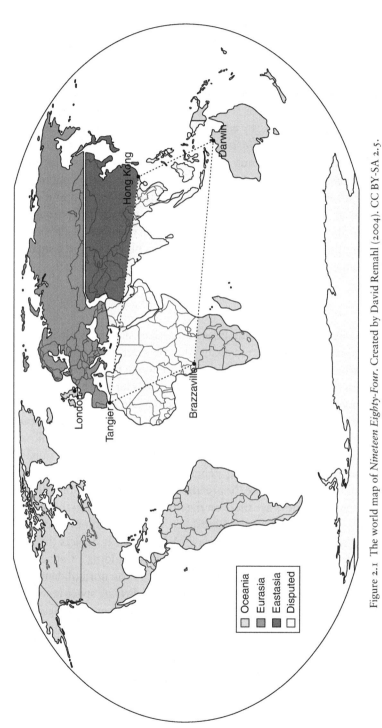

Figure 2.1 The world map of *Nineteen Eighty-Four*. Created by David Remahl (2004). CC BY-SA 2.5.

ignorance and fear of the rest of the world. 'Foreigners, whether from Eurasia or from Eastasia, were a kind of strange animal. One literally never saw them except in the guise of prisoners' (*NEF*, p. 122). There is no empirical geography, just as there is almost no empirical history. All news, being indistinguishable from government propaganda, is fake news or, to put it another way, all news is true, since there is no access to a real world from which a report could be brought back, by which the fake world could be measured.

The great-power politics of *Nineteen Eighty-Four* is a remarkably coherent vision, even if Orwell was not able to integrate it seamlessly into the novelistic discourse of the book. Much of it is consigned to the chapters of Emmanuel Goldstein's book, which Winston Smith reads in chapter nine of Part II. This is an extended passage of expository strategic or journalistic writing which sits rather awkwardly with the literary project of the novel. Meanwhile, another politics, and another history, is played out on a smaller scale in the domain of private space.

Sanctuary Spaces

The first time we see Winston Smith, he is in search of shelter. With 'his chin nuzzled into his breast in an effort to escape the vile wind', he scuttles into the block of flats where he lives, 'though not quickly enough to prevent a swirl of gritty dust from entering along with him' (*NEF*, p. 3). Here we have in trivial form an epitome of a story already told again and again in Orwell's fiction, from *Burmese Days* (1934) to *Animal Farm* (1945), the story of a desperate but unsuccessful effort to escape. Through much of the novel we will see Winston seeking out safe spaces in which to shelter from a hostile outside world, only to find that the spatial geography through which he moves ensures that all his refuges can be, or are already, opened up to surveillance and control. Again, the clues are there on the first page. Tacked to the wall at one end of the hallway of Victory Mansions, there is a coloured poster, a metre wide, 'too large for indoor display' (*NEF*, p. 3). It depicts the face of Big Brother. Victory Mansions is an apartment building, a space for domestic, private life. But something has happened to the normal demarcation between outdoor and indoor, public and private. Private space is subject to intrusion, invasion from outside.[7] The poster, its giant portrait designed for display on the outside of a building, has penetrated indoors, bringing with it a brash public idiom. It is an image that sets up a pattern that will unfold with great consistency through the rest of the novel, and will define its geography, a geography of vulnerable sanctuaries and violated borders.

It is a structure of experience played out again, immediately, when Winston enters his apartment. The panoptical telescreen keeps his private life under constant surveillance, not only subjecting him to unblinking observation, but filling his auditory space too with endless news bulletins (which can be turned down, but never off), or, worse, with shouted commands and humiliations. Not even the bedroom, that inner sanctum of the private life, is insulated from these invasions. And so, prompted by the 'unusual geography' (*NEF*, p. 7) of his living room, Winston seeks refuge in a shallow alcove, outside the range of the telescreen, a sanctuary within the sanctuary, from which to launch his futile rebellion. There he begins to inscribe his freedom in that most private of literary genres, a diary. For this is one of the ironies of life under totalitarian surveillance: while Winston desperately seeks out places where he can be truly alone, he is also made miserable by 'the locked loneliness in which one had to live' (*NEF*, p. 20). Everyone in Airstrip One yearns for human contact, but everyone suspects and fears everyone else; suspicion and fear compound their isolation, like the citizens of T. S. Eliot's *The Waste Land* (1922):

> We think of the key, each in his prison
> Thinking of the key, each confirms a prison[.][8]

Open spaces in this novel are places of discomfort, anxiety, bad weather, and occasional bursts of violence, in the form of a police raid or a rocket bomb. In this hostile environment, Winston Smith lives a quasi-troglodytic existence, huddling in small spaces, seeking out unregarded corners.[9] His workspace cubicle affords him some relief, a place where he can be alone and engaged in work which sometimes offers intellectual satisfaction. But this too is subject to the telescreen, so that he sometimes needs to hide himself in the last refuge, his own body, though even that does not confer invisibility on his inner life. 'To keep your face expressionless was not difficult, and even your breathing could be controlled, with an effort: but you could not control the beating of your heart, and the telescreen was quite delicate enough to pick it up' (*NEF*, p. 82). The instruments of the Thought Police, it seems, can even reach into the most intimate spaces of the body. But Winston keeps trying to burrow down to find an inviolable space. The love nest where his secret assignations with Julia will take place strikes him, when he first enters it, with a sort of nostalgia, an intimation of a kindlier life in the past:

> It seemed to him that he knew exactly what it felt like to sit in a room like this, in an armchair beside an open fire with your feet in the fender and a kettle on the hob: utterly alone, utterly secure, with nobody watching you, no voice pursuing you, no sound except the singing of the kettle and the friendly ticking of the clock. (*NEF*, p. 100)

This cosy domestic fantasy, which Winston recognizes though he has never set foot in it before, is related to the English liberal imaginary, the idea that once all dues have been paid to the public good, there must remain an impregnable space where individuals can do, say, and think what they please.[10]

The map of Oceanic London is punctuated with other potential boltholes. The Party despises the proles, who make up the majority of the population, and does not bother to police them carefully, which is why Winston likes to wander in the snug and squalid prole quarters of the city, where there are few telescreens or police patrols. The pub he visits seems to offer him a chance to reconnect with a past way of life, before the Party rose to power.[11] But his attempt to gain access to that past, questioning an old man about his memories, is hopeless. There is no place for him here.

In public places, the streets or the work canteen in the Records Department or the hall where Party workers gather for the Two Minutes Hate, Winston has to police himself, so as not to betray his true thoughts and feelings. Like John Flory in *Burmese Days*, and like Eric Blair in the Burma Police, he is one of those who are obliged to live their real life in secret.[12] But refuge can be found in unexpected places. Once he is allied to Julia, a more experienced and sophisticated rebel than he is, Winston discovers that a paradoxical privacy is to be found in the densest of crowds. The crush of spectators watching a convoy of prisoners of war cross Victory Square gives the lovers a fleeting chance to make an assignation. Julia, with her history of clandestine affairs, has a strong geographical sense – 'as though she had a map inside her head' (*NEF*, p. 121) – and a knowledge of where to go to escape the gaze of Big Brother, approaching every time by a different route, as she explains to Winston, drawing directions in the dust with a twig (*NEF*, p. 143). The map in Julia's head is a revolutionary geography, a map of freedom.

The places where Winston and Julia do contrive to spend time together – on their first outing into the country, and later in the room above Mr Charrington's shop – are chosen because they seem to be off the map. While the novel's evocations of urban life are meticulous and naturalistic, the description of Winston's arrival in the countryside comes in a quite different style:

> Winston picked his way up the lane through dappled light and shade, stepping out into pools of gold wherever the boughs parted. Under the trees to the left of him the ground was misty with bluebells. The air seemed to kiss one's skin. It was the second of May. From somewhere deeper in the heart of the wood came the droning of ring-doves. (*NEF*, p. 134)

The novel here steps self-consciously into the landscape and language of English pastoral. Orwell was certainly capable of writing about the natural scene in a more realistic way – for example, in his praise of the common toad, a creature which 'unlike the skylark and the primrose, has never had much of a boost from the poets' (*CW*, 18, p. 239) – but here the style draws attention to its own high literariness, with a commonplace trope of English romantic nature writing in every line. In the lovers' country rendezvous, nature itself seems to collaborate with their desires, the bluebells cascading onto the ground to make them a bed, as if of their own accord (*NEF*, p. 125), like flowers in a love poem.[13] This is in line with the novel's deployment of different languages: the idiom of journalism (or what I have called 'strategic writing') for public and political matters, open spaces and events enacted in public, crowds and meetings and propaganda, and political theory, including Goldstein's book – the kind of things you might read about in a newspaper; and the idiom of literature for the sanctuary spaces, for interiority, solitude and uncertainty, physical pleasure, love, memory, secret resistance, and the Golden Country of Winston's dreams.[14]

The room over Mr Charrington's shop is another version of pastoral, lifted out of history, 'a world, a pocket of the past where extinct animals could walk' (*NEF*, p. 173). Like the clearing in the hazel wood (a version of the 'bower of bliss' of pastoral love poetry) where Winston and Julia first come together, their rented room is a place for the enjoyment of illicit pleasures, sex and chocolate, real coffee and sugar, unsupervised leisure. There are aesthetic pleasures too. Winston's reading aloud of Goldstein's book may send Julia to sleep, but there is the quaint picture of old London above the mantelpiece, the haunting nursery rhyme 'Oranges and Lemons', and the song of the washerwoman in the yard below. 'The birds sang, the proles sang, the Party did not sing' (*NEF*, p. 252). Sanctuary spaces offer a weak but authentic aesthetic resistance to both the intrusions of the Thought Police and the grinding march of history. In the story, however, none of these spaces remains inviolable. Winston is not the only one whose path leads to the last false refuge, the Chestnut Tree Café.

> *Under the spreading chestnut tree*
> *I sold you and you sold me[.]*   (*NEF*, p. 80)

Returning to the first of these places of shelter, the shallow alcove in Winston's apartment, apparently invisible to the telescreen, we can see that it shares the qualities of his other refuges. A doubly sequestered space, an alcove within an apartment, it is a place where writing connects with a fast-vanishing past, where Winston composes, not with a mechanical speakwrite such as he uses in the Records Department, but in the 'small [and] childish handwriting' (*NEF*, p. 10) of his unique autograph, with old-fashioned pen-and-ink, on the creamy paper of the diary. The act of writing is eroticized. Having acquired the instruments of writing from a dubious shop and carried them home furtively, Winston crouches in the alcove away from the patriarchal gaze and begins the solitary pleasure of diary writing – 'the beautiful creamy paper deserved to be written on with a real nib' (*NEF*, p. 9).

Writing is a pleasure in itself, an intransitive activity to be enjoyed for its own sake, like the song of the bird in the woods who sang 'to please himself' (*NEF*, p. 230): Winston has not acquired pen and paper in order to write *about* anything.[15] But the act of writing is also the key that unlocks all of his interior world in a flood of words, the secret life of his buried memories as well as his anger and rebellion. Against the domineering ideas, the *Realpolitik* and the brutality of the state, is ranged the private life and its values, a fragile refuge embodied – and this is a discovery of the memories and dreams released by Winston's act of writing – in the recurring figure of his mother and the 'helpless gesture' (*NEF*, p. 172) with which she tries to protect her child. Though defeated, the integrity of his dead mother's feelings give her a kind of nobility in Winston's eyes, because the standards she obeyed were private ones – imagined, inevitably, as a valued space subject to an outside threat. 'Her feelings were her own, and could not be altered from outside. It would not have occurred to her that an action which is ineffectual thereby becomes meaningless' (*NEF*, p. 171). Winston's last sight of his mother, with her arms round her dying daughter (*NEF*, p. 170), recalls the image of the Jewish mother in the lifeboat, clasping her child '*as if she thought her arms could keep the bullets off him*', which Winston remembers seeing in a war film, the first thing it occurs to him to record in his diary (*NEF*, pp. 10–11).[16]

The mother's arms are the most intimate and pitiful of the novel's sanctuary spaces, shrunk to the smallest human dimensions, and too insignificant to show up on any map. The final location where refuge may be sought is in the microgeography of 'the few cubic centimetres inside your own skull' (*NEF*, p. 29), the life of subjectivity and feeling which is surely, Winston believes, beyond the reach of even totalitarian power. When all other aspects of life have been invaded and occupied, abused and enslaved, this space must remain free:

> They could not alter your feelings: for that matter you could not alter them yourself, even if you wanted to. They could lay bare in the utmost detail everything that you had done or said or thought; but the inner heart, whose workings were mysterious even to yourself, remained impregnable.
>
> (*NEF*, p. 174)

Even in the interrogation room in the Ministry of Love, although in the mind he has fully surrendered to his torturers, Winston 'had hoped to keep the inner heart inviolate' (*NEF*, p. 293). We do not need to wait until the final line of the book to understand that, for Winston Smith, this is the last illusion.

Not one of these sanctuary spaces prevails against the pitiless gaze, and disproportionate violence, of the Thought Police and the Party. In the last part of the novel, all enclosed spaces are revealed to be in fact prisons.

The small world maps onto the larger. Doubly sequestered, the predicament of the populations of the earth mirrors that of individuals like Winston Smith, 'the last man in Europe' in the words of an early title for the book that became *Nineteen Eighty-Four*.[17] With remarkable consistency, the macro-landscape of totalitarian geopolitics fits like a glove over the micro-landscape of Winston's London. Both are closed systems. Kept in ignorance and fear by an unapproachable government, the great populations of all three superstates are imprisoned in paranoia, fenced in against the outside world but driven out of the sphere of private life, with no right to be left alone, their strongest desires directed outwards into entirely uncritical patriotism and vicious xeno-phobia expressed in hysterical compulsory public demonstrations of loyalty to their masters and hatred of their enemies, enslaved in a narrative in which foreigners are demonized but friends and family are not to be trusted. The Parsons family, Winston Smith's neighbours, are a microcosm of the global predicament. A minor functionary of paralysing stupidity and imbecile enthu-siasms (*NEF*, p. 24), Parsons has absolutely none of what is called in Newspeak '*ownlife*' (*NEF*, p. 85); he has no free time at all, devoting his after-work hours to endless Party-sponsored activities and causes. He swallows effortlessly all the Party's patriotic propaganda. Yet this blamelessly orthodox citizen is spied on, and eventually betrayed, by his own children, having apparently uttered seditious thoughts in his sleep.

In this world the protective borders of the private life are abolished, while the external frontiers, which ensure there can be no real contact with other people, are impregnably fortified. The ruling powers in each of the three warring states all control and manipulate their citizens in the same way, the endless war (if it exists) and the endless state of emergency justifying the government in demand-ing self-sacrifice from the people and ensuring they are forever vigilant against threats from outside and betrayals from within. Although their official ideol-ogies have different names, they serve the same purpose, the absolute power of government over its subjects. This is the identical state of affairs throughout Oceania, Eurasia, and Eastasia, a totalitarian system so locked down that there seems no possibility of its ever changing or being overthrown. It seems there can be no liberation from within.

For the world and for the individual, it seems an irredeemably bleak picture. The bleakness is qualified, however, in two ways.

Horizons of Freedom

On the smaller scale, we have seen how the things of real value in Winston Smith's world – the tokens of a life of freedom, privacy, pleasure, unselfishness, and inutility, the sharing of thoughts and feelings, the aesthetic and the erotic, a connection to nature and to the past – are sought out and enjoyed in sanctuary spaces, and that these sanctuaries are all in the end (and perhaps already in the beginning) exposed to tyrannical power, and destroyed. But just as we take a step back to understand Winston's predicament in terms of the geopolitical situation, we need to take a further step back to notice the larger framework that encloses both. How after all do we know about Winston Smith, and the threats that surround him? These things are represented in the language of George Orwell's novel. The novel itself is an act of resistance. Novels have always been an assertion of the very things that are valued and threatened in *Nineteen Eighty-Four*. Of all the literary genres, novels specialize in the history of private life – domestic, family, intellectual, emotional, bodily. Telling the story of individuals in a social environment, all novels are about freedom. Further, the novel is produced and enjoyed in private, and offers a unique kind of intersubjectivity, in access to the interiority of other people. The novel is the opposite of tyranny. Even if the story is about imprisonment, the storytelling is a warning and a liberation.

Of course, this is no consolation to the actual inhabitants of the world of *Nineteen Eighty-Four*. There is one more hint, however, that the absolute tyranny of the superstates is not absolutely secure, and this is an insight which, again, is due to Orwell's imperial experience, his strategic thinking, and his global vision. It comes into view if we recall the congruence between the small scale of Winston's city and the large scale of the world map. Those whose lives have placed them within the inexorable lockdown of the Party, like Winston and Julia and almost all the other named characters in the story, can never escape its grip, any more than the populations of the superstates can successfully rebel in current circumstances. Revolution cannot come from within. But there is another group which lies beyond the reach of the Party, and it is this that prompts Winston's tentative belief that '*If there is hope* [...] *it lies in the proles*' (NEF, p. 72).

Perhaps it will lie with the proles to change and liberate Airstrip One. There is an equivalent of this unregarded, despised, but potentially mighty group on the world map, and Orwell, the former colonial policeman who became an impassioned anti-imperialist, knew where they were. Broadcasting on the Eastern Service of the BBC in 1942, in the depths of the Second World War, he asked his listeners in Asia to see 'the whole picture' of world history in their own times as 'the struggle of free peoples who see before them the chance of a fuller and happier existence, against comparatively small cliques who are not interested in the general development of humanity but only in advancing their individual power' (*CW*, 13, p. 324). To put this in terms of the virtual geography of *Nineteen Eighty-Four*: If there is hope, it lies in the quadrilateral.

Notes

1 Teheran failed to produce agreement on Poland. The matter was returned to at a later summit conference on post-war European re-organization and security at Yalta in February 1945, where Poland's fate was settled to Stalin's satisfaction. Later, reviewing Winston Churchill's war memoir *Their Finest Hour*, Orwell hoped that at some time in the future Churchill might disclose 'what really happened at Teheran and Yalta, and whether the policies there adopted were ones that he himself approved of, or whether they were forced upon him by Roosevelt' (*CW*, 20, p. 112).

2 One of the most famous political cartoons of all time, James Gillray's 'The plumb-pudding in danger', was published in 1805 and sold as a popular print.

3 Orwell had decided soon after returning from Spain that Nazism and Stalinism were moving towards a common form of tyranny, which he called 'oligarchical collectivism'. See John Newsinger, *Hope Lies in the Proles: George Orwell and the Left* (London: Pluto Press, 2018), pp. 61–3. It is notable that Orwell foresaw a similar political convergence looming in *all three* great empires which he thought would dominate the post-war world.

4 The commentaries were informative and as truthful as possible in conditions of wartime censorship. But in encouraging a global vision, they were also intended to persuade listeners to see India's fate and interests as bound up with the cause of Britain and her allies. See Douglas Kerr, 'Orwell's BBC Broadcasts: Colonial Discourse and the Rhetoric of Propaganda', *Textual Practice*, 16.3 (Winter 2002), pp. 473–90.

5 Ben Clarke, *Orwell in Context: Communities, Myths, Values* (Basingstoke: Palgrave Macmillan, 2007), p. 155.

6 It is quite possible Julia is correct in her opinion that the war is not actually happening (*NEF*, p. 160).

7 While *Nineteen Eighty-Four* is certainly global in scope, Orwell associated a cherishing of privacy particularly with his own country. In *The Lion and the Unicorn* (1941), he writes appreciatively about 'the *privateness* of English life', while acknowledging that 'this purely private liberty is a lost cause' (*CW*, 12, p. 394).

8 T. S. Eliot, *The Waste Land* (1922), in Christopher Ricks and Jim McCue (eds.), *The Poems of T. S. Eliot – Volume I: Collected and Uncollected Poems* (London: Faber and Faber, 2015), p. 70.

9 It is not irrelevant that most of *Nineteen Eighty-Four* was written in a remote cottage on the island of Jura. For Orwell, uncomfortable isolation was a motive for communication – 'I think from the very start my literary ambitions were mixed up with the feeling of being isolated and undervalued' (*CW*, 18, p. 316) – but also the necessary condition for writing, whether for the book-reviewer in his 'cold but stuffy bed-sitting room' (*CW*, 18, p. 300), or the ailing novelist in his inaccessible Hebridian cottage. For Orwell on Jura, see also the excellent David Dwan, *Liberty, Equality and Humbug: Orwell's Political Ideals* (Oxford: Oxford University Press, 2018), pp. 197–202.

10 Bernard Crick argues that the socialist tradition Orwell inherited maintained that 'there are some areas of life which have to be preserved from politics' ('Orwell and English Socialism', in Peter Buitenhuis and Ira B. Nadel (eds.), *George Orwell: A Reassessment* (Basingstoke: Macmillan, 1988), p. 16).

11 In 'The Moon under Water', an essay of 1946, Orwell described his ideal pub – in every way snug, traditional, and welcoming – only to reveal that it was a fantasy (*CW*, 18, pp. 98–101).

12 See *BD*, p. 70 ('But it is a corrupting thing to live one's real life in secret') and *RWP*, p. 135 ('All over India there are Englishmen who secretly loathe the system of which they are part; and just occasionally, when they are quite certain of being in the right company, their hidden bitterness overflows').

13 Alex Woloch, who writes well about Orwell's style, has little to say about *Nineteen Eighty-Four*, but calls it 'strangely, both naturalistic and futuristic' (*Or Orwell: Writing and Democratic Socialism* (Cambridge: Harvard University Press, 2016), p. 6). He might well have added 'and lyrical'.

14 This pattern is not unique to *Nineteen Eighty-Four*. There are similarities with the struggle between the languages of poetry and commerce (advertising) in *Keep the Aspidistra Flying* (1936), and of course with Orwell's own divided allegiances to political writing and art.

15 Dwan discusses this bird as a symbol of freedom in *Liberty, Equality and Humbug*, p. 46.

16 The possible ethnic identity of the refugee woman – '*might have been a Jewess*' (*NEF*, p. 10) – seems to have been a second thought; the phrase was added in autograph to the typescript of the novel. See *Nineteen Eighty-Four: The Facsimile of the Extant Manuscript*, ed. Peter Davison (London: Secker & Warburg, 1984), pp. 28–9. See also the chapter 'Orwell's Jews' in Lyndsey Stonebridge, *Placeless People: Writing, Rights, and Refugees* (Oxford: Oxford University Press, 2018), pp. 73–95.

17 See Orwell's letter to Fredric Warburg, 22 October 1948 (*CW*, 19, pp. 456–7).

3

DILETTA DE CRISTOFARO

The Politics of the Archive in *Nineteen Eighty-Four*

Four quotations will guide my analysis of the politics of the archive in *Nineteen Eighty-Four* (1949), namely, of how foundational the control of archives, from public historical records to individual recollections such as those preserved in diaries, is to Ingsoc's ideology and totalitarian power and, conversely, to all attempts to counter this ideology and power. First, the claim by philosopher Jacques Derrida that *'There is no political power without control of the archive, if not of memory'* (Derrida, *AF*, p. 11). Second, one of the Party's slogans: 'Who controls the past, [...] controls the future: who controls the present controls the past' (*NEF*, p. 37). Third, the writer Sarah Manguso's meditation on diaries: 'Why do people keep diaries? Prisoners, explorers, regents – of course. But there are so many others, nobly addressing the entire future.'[1] Fourth, Winston's own musings on diary keeping: 'He wondered again for whom he was writing the diary. For the future, for the past' (*NEF*, p. 29). Time is what unifies these quotations and the underlying theme of this chapter. On the one hand, we find power's, and specifically the Party's, hold over the archival traces of the past with the aim of shaping the future. On the other hand, we find the individual's, and specifically Winston's, desire to free the past and the future from power's grip. These two directions structure my chapter's considerations. I begin by analysing images of public archives manipulated by the Party to legitimize itself and to reinforce its totalitarian power, ensuring Ingsoc's continuation into the future. I then turn to images of private archives that seek to fissure the Party's totalitarian control over time in order to recover a sense of individual agency.

Derrida opens his theorization of the notion of the archive by considering the term's etymological meaning. In ancient Greek, '*arkhē*' denotes, first, 'the originary, the first, the principial, the primitive, in short the commencement', and, second, in the related form of '*arkheion*', 'a house, a domicile, an address, the residence of the superior magistrates, the *archons*, those who commanded' (Derrida, *AF*, p. 9). We could say that an archive derives its authority over a specific subject by housing original records and documents about that subject; that is, by revealing something about its origins. Conversely, those who are in power derive their authority by having special access to these documents. 'The archons', Derrida writes, 'are first of all the documents' guardians. They do not only ensure the physical security of what is deposited and of the substrate [namely, the physical place which houses the documents]. They are also accorded the hermeneutic right and competence. They have the power to interpret the archives' (Derrida, *AF*, p. 10). This power to interpret the archive and the records it houses is, in essence, a legal and political power – 'the right to make or to represent the law' (Derrida, *AF*, p. 10) – which leads us back to the first of my opening quotations: '*There is no political power without control of the archive, if not of memory.*' In *Nineteen Eighty-Four*, the control of both the public archive, that is, of what is memorialized and considered historical fact, as well as of the individual's private archive, that is, memory, is a key mechanism through which the Party maintains its dystopian and totalitarian hold. I shall start by considering the Party's control of the public archive before turning to its control of memory.

It is the Ministry of Truth, and specifically its Records Department, that embodies the nexus of political power and the public archive in the world imagined by Orwell. 'The sacred principles of Ingsoc', Winston muses, are 'Newspeak, doublethink, the mutability of the past' (*NEF*, p. 28). The latter principle indicates an extreme version of political power's control of the archive. Indeed, the fact that Winston, the novel's protagonist, works in the Records Department signals how crucial the politics of the archive are to the dystopian society *Nineteen Eighty-Four* depicts. Where Derrida observes that '*[e]ffective democratization can always be measured by this essential criterion: the participation in and the access to the archive, its constitution, and its interpretation*', while '*the breaches of democracy can be measured by* [the presence of] Forbidden Archives' (Derrida, *AF*, p. 11), what is at stake in the Ministry of Truth is not just the power to forbid public access to documents about the past and to posit the Party as the sole interpreter of these documents. Rather, the Party, through the Ministry of Truth, holds the totalitarian power to constantly destroy and fabricate records, and thus the public archive. This is particularly evident in the treatment reserved for any archival trace left by the Party's enemies: '[their] name was removed from the registers, every record of everything [they] had ever done was wiped out, [their] one-time existence was denied and then forgotten. [They] were abolished, annihilated: *vaporized* was the usual word' (*NEF*, p. 21).[2] More broadly, history is to the Party 'a palimpsest, scraped clean and re-inscribed exactly as often as was necessary' (*NEF*, p. 42), and Winston's job for the Ministry of Truth is precisely to do this endless scraping and re-inscribing aimed at protecting the illusion of the Party's infallibility and at propping up its ideologies. Thus, where the etymology of the term signals how foundational original documents are to the archive, the Party's slogan 'who controls the present controls the past' (*NEF*, p. 37) effectively means that in Winston's world there are no longer any original documents about the past at all. The function of the archive has been irremediably perverted to support the Party's totalitarianism.

The palimpsestic nature of history and its continuous rewriting imply that the archival records Winston is tasked with correcting according to the Party's needs have 'no connection with anything in the real world, not even the kind of connection that is contained in a direct lie' (*NEF*, p. 43). This can productively be read through Jean Baudrillard's theory of simulation. Simulation, Baudrillard writes, is no longer 'a referential being or a substance. It is the generation by models of a real without origin or reality.'[3] Simulations are constructions that produce a convincing effect of reality but that do not in fact refer to a world external to themselves. Indeed, they precede and produce what we deem as the real, external world, so much so that simulation 'is no longer a question of imitation, nor duplication, nor even parody [of the real]. It is a question of substituting the signs of the real for the real.'[4] Winston's realization that 'the very existence of external reality [is] tacitly denied by [the Party's] philosophies' (*NEF*, p. 83) is perfectly in line with such a logic of simulation. Ingsoc's 'past' is literally produced by – that is, it does not have an independent existence from – its constantly in-flux simulated archival records. 'Day by day and almost minute by minute the past [is] brought up to date' at the Records Department (*NEF*, p. 42), for the present's control of the past ultimately signifies that the present endlessly recreates the past's simulated public archives to match the Party's most recent conceptions. Consider, for instance, Comrade Ogilvy, a devoted Party member, up to his ultimate sacrifice, and 'a piece of pure fantasy' (*NEF*, p. 49), whose story Winston fabricates to take the place of an article praising Withers, now an '*unperson*' (*NEF*, p. 48). Where Withers, thanks to the vaporization of all his archival traces, 'did not exist: he had never existed' (*NEF*, p. 48), Comrade Ogilvy, 'who had never existed in the present, now existed in the past, [...] and upon the same evidence, as Charlemagne or Julius Caesar' (*NEF*, p. 50), that is, upon the same grounds as archival evidence, albeit entirely simulated. But of course, in the realm of simulation, in which all original documents have been destroyed and records refer to nothing else than to further simulated records, questions about what is true and what is false become moot. As Baudrillard writes, simulation is 'a space whose curvature is no longer that of the real, nor that of truth'.[5] '[T]he systematic erosion of truth [under] the rise of authoritarian politics' is indeed a major concern that Orwell explores in *Nineteen Eighty-Four*, so much so that, for Winston, 'truth remains the ground and even the goal of freedom'.[6] Once again, we can see how *'the question of a politics of the archive [...] determines politics from top to bottom'* (Derrida, *AF*, pp. 10–11). The immense, and constantly fluctuating, simulations that constitute the public archives carefully curated by the Records Department ground the totalitarian attack on the concept of objective truth carried out by the aptly named Ministry of Truth.

The utter lack of original archival documents and the proliferation of ever-changing simulated pasts in Oceania also indicate that Winston's world itself has no entirely knowable origins and is, notwithstanding this proliferation, ahistorical, which is again instrumental in propping up the Party's totalitarian power. A significant part of *Nineteen Eighty-Four*'s plot is occupied by Winston's attempts at recovering a sense of history, both of the pre- and post-Revolutionary periods. For instance, we find Winston trying to remember a time before Ingsoc's perpetual war, questioning an old prole about what life was like before the Revolution, poring over a children's history textbook as well as over the history traced by Goldstein's book, and conversing with Mr Charrington about London's past in his junk shop. Yet these attempts at recovering a sense of history are ultimately impossible in the absence of stable and reliable archival records – and it is significant, in this sense, that both Goldstein's book and Mr Charrington turn out to be simulations fabricated by the Party. As Winston realizes reading the children's history textbook, its words are 'like a single equation with two unknowns' (*NEF*, p. 78). Both the pre- and the post-Revolutionary periods are constituted by endlessly mutable simulations that eliminate the very possibility of putting the two periods into relation, that is, of re-constructing an unequivocal history of the shift from the former to the latter period. Winston's question, 'Was life better before the Revolution than it is now?' (*NEF*, p. 96), cannot but remain unanswered and this is of course to the Party's advantage, as people tolerate Oceania's dystopian living conditions partly because they have 'no standards of comparison' (*NEF*, p. 221) with anything different. As David J. Lorenzo maintains, Ingsoc's treatment of history as infinitely malleable and mutable aims at throwing 'the individual off balance. There is no place to stand in which to make judgements or assert one's individual capacity to make judgements competently. The evidence one would wish to reference will no longer exist in tangible form.'[7] Even Newspeak, Oceania's official new language, is aimed at reinforcing the ahistorical nature of Winston's society. As *Nineteen*

Eighty-Four's appendix, 'The Principles of Newspeak', explains: 'When Oldspeak had been once and for all superseded, the last link with the past would have been severed' (*NEF*, p. 324), for any scattered fragments of past texts would have been made incomprehensible – the appendix, seemingly written from a post-Ingsoc world, reveals that this replacement of language never fully took place. Thus, it is not just political dissidents who are 'lifted clean out of the stream of history' thanks to the erasure of their archival traces (*NEF*, p. 172). It is *Nineteen Eighty-Four*'s entire society that is, in effect, purposefully ahistorical.

Through the Party's constant meddling with archival records, 'The past', Winston reflects, has 'not merely been altered', it has 'actually been destroyed' (*NEF*, p. 38). Erika Gottlieb reads this 'demonization of historical time, the time of man's historical consciousness', as a way to force a 'return to the time of myth, the time of the sacred. [The Party] has to abolish historical time so that it can create a sense of its own timelessness.'[8] As Winston notes, indeed: 'History has stopped. Nothing exists except an endless present in which the Party is always right' (*NEF*, p. 162). Hardly by chance, despite this being a society in which individual time is strictly regulated and filled up with work and leisure activities regimented by the Party – the Physical Jerks, the Two Minutes Hate, Hate Week, and the numerous evenings devoted to various committee activities – so that there is no time left for what Newspeak terms '*ownlife*' (*NEF*, p. 85) and any occupation not aimed at reinforcing faith in the Party, Winston is not sure about what year it is.[9] In an endless present, after all, dates are irrelevant. Winston's first proper act of rebellion is marred by this uncertainty: as he writes down in his diary the date and realizes that he cannot know if it is indeed 1984, he is overcome by a 'sense of complete helplessness' (*NEF*, p. 9), which signifies how deeply the Party's power is intertwined with its control of time. Goldstein's book returns to the significant image of history stopping, arguing that the very purpose of Ingsoc is 'to arrest progress and freeze history at a chosen moment' (*NEF*, p. 212). Winston interrupts his reading of Goldstein's book on another instance of this image: 'what is the motive for this huge, accurately planned effort to freeze history at a particular moment of time?' (*NEF*, pp. 225–6). Winston never resumes his reading of the book, and thus never reads Goldstein's answer, but this question, which Winston has been obsessing over – as he writes in his diary, '*I understand HOW [history is being manipulated]: I do not understand WHY*' (*NEF*, p. 83) – comes up again during his interrogation in the Ministry of Love. Here, O'Brien, one of the authors of Goldstein's book, gives the tautological answer that the 'object of power is power' (*NEF*, p. 276). Arguably, indeed, the Party's control of the archive produces the impression that history has frozen not only in order to make it impossible for the individual to access a past existing independently of – and in contradiction with – the Party's simulations, but also in order to secure the future as mere reproduction of the present, namely, to secure the indefinite continuation of the Party's totalitarian power.

'Who controls the past controls the future', the Party's slogan admonishes us. But, in effect, the Party's control of the past through the control of the public archive is aimed at ensuring that there is no future, strictly speaking, only an endless present. As Gottlieb maintains, 'like most paradoxes in Oceania, the slogan can also be turned backwards, and then you get: "Who controls the future, controls the past." Here Orwell's satire points at the role of prediction in the ideologies embraced by totalitarian systems.'[10] These systems 'predict the end result of the historical process as inevitable', which entails that both past and present are made to conform to this sense of an inevitable and teleological historical development.[11] In *Nineteen Eighty-Four*, the endlessly simulated archival records, through which 'every prediction made by the Party could be shown by documentary evidence to have been correct' (*NEF*, p. 42), arguably seek to fashion Ingsoc's present as the necessary culmination of a long process of historical development and, thus, as something that should, and will, continue in perpetuity unchanged. The '*glorious Revolution*', the children's history textbook explains, has finally righted the capitalists' injustices (*NEF*, pp. 75–6). The telescreens relentlessly regurgitate statistics that prove the Party's successes and its achievement of the predicted utopian – at least according to Ingsoc's ideology – end: 'a world of steel and concrete of monstrous machines and terrifying weapons – a nation of warriors and fanatics, marching forward in perfect unity, all thinking the same thoughts and shouting the same slogans, perpetually working, fighting, triumphing, persecuting' (*NEF*, p. 77). This image of the future – in effect the endless repetition (note the 'perpetually' above) of how the Party's propaganda constructs present conditions – is of course far from the actual reality of 'decaying, dingy cities' and 'underfed people' (*NEF*, p. 77). As O'Brien acknowledges, a more accurate picture of the future under the Party is that of endless dystopian oppression: a 'boot stamping on a human face – for ever' (*NEF*, p. 280).

Ingsoc has thus abolished futurity, which is about possibility and change. Throughout *Nineteen Eighty-Four*, Winston returns to the sense of a future that is fixed, already pre-determined, and thus hardly a future at all, but simply the reproduction of the totalitarian present. He is painfully aware that the 'end [is] contained in the beginning' (*NEF*, p. 166), the beginning being his thoughtcrime of keeping a diary and the end being the 'predestined horror' that will 'happen in the Ministry of Love' (*NEF*, p. 146) – note how Winston's predicted end exposes the dystopian reality of oppression hidden behind the utopian predicted end constructed by the Party's propaganda. At the Ministry of Love, O'Brien echoes Winston's thoughts and reinforces his deterministic conception of time: 'It was all contained in that first act. Nothing has happened that you did not foresee' (*NEF*, p. 286). Even the Brotherhood seemingly abides by a deterministic understanding of the future, at least of the near future. As O'Brien outlines to Winston while pretending to be a member of the Brotherhood: 'You will work for a while, you will be caught, you will confess, and then you will die. Those are the only results that you will ever see. There is no possibility that any perceptible change will happen within our own lifetime' (*NEF*, p. 183). This cancellation of a genuine sense of futurity is aimed at stripping the individual of agency, of the hope and possibility of shaping a different future beyond the Party's grip. Under Ingsoc, what you do or refrain from doing makes 'literally no difference' (*NEF*, p. 172); if anything, as Winston frequently repeats, his rebellion against the Party makes him 'already dead' (*NEF*, pp. 30, 183, 230). Yet, of course, in his acts of resistance, Winston is motivated by the sliver of a sense of possibility, at least for a future beyond his lifetime, and significantly writes his diary for 'the future, for the unborn' (*NEF*, p. 9). This sliver, to which we shall return later on in this chapter, is intertwined with Winston's attempts at recovering his memories, the individual archive that the Party tries to control.

Let us turn, then, to the second half of my opening quotation, '*There is no political power without control of the archive, if not of memory.*' It is 'by means of doublethink', a practice revolving around memory, 'that the Party has been able [. . .] to arrest the course of history' (*NEF*, p. 223) and to erase a genuine sense of futurity, Goldstein's book argues. While the endless alterability of the archive and thus of the past is a central tenet of Ingsoc, the other interrelated tenet is that 'the past, though of its nature alterable, never had been altered. Whatever was true now was true from everlasting to everlasting' (*NEF*, p. 37). Indeed, as Goldstein's book outlines, the Party's 'control of the past depends above all on the training of memory. To make sure that all written records agree with the orthodoxy of the moment is merely a mechanical act. But it is also necessary to *remember* that events happened in the desired manner' (*NEF*, p. 222). This is achieved through doublethink, the power 'to forget whatever it was necessary to forget, then to draw it back into memory again at the moment when it was needed, and then promptly to forget it again' (*NEF*, p. 37). Big Brother's power is totalitarian to the extreme precisely because it does not merely consist in the constant destruction and recreation of the public archive of historical records in the Party's image, but, rather, because it seeks to exercise absolute control over our own private archives and memories. As O'Brien explains to Winston in the Ministry of Love, 'the past exist[s], if at all', in historical records and human memories; 'We, the Party, control all records, and we control all memories. Then we control the past' (*NEF*, p. 260).

Significantly, the key tools of the Party's control over the past are the memory holes, whose name and function bridge the two types of archive. In the memory holes, the employees of the Records Department endlessly destroy the public records that contradict the Party's ideologies, beliefs, and predictions, thus facilitating the effect of reality generated by its simulated archival documents. This practice is so ingrained that the mere sight of a piece of waste paper causes the automatic reflex of disposing of it through the nearest memory hole. Equally, by destroying any traces of the Party's fallibility and manipulations through the memory holes, these employees seek to will upon themselves doublethink and its revisionism of memory's individual archive. This dynamic is perfectly encapsulated by one of the exchanges between Winston and O'Brien at the Ministry of Love. Here, O'Brien produces a photograph that is etched in Winston's memory as the only concrete proof of an act of archival falsification he ever encountered after the falsification was made historical record. When he first happened upon the photograph, Winston immediately destroyed it in a memory hole. Yet his 'defective memory' (*NEF*, p. 258) – defective, of course, according to the standards of the Party – archived it forever. As O'Brien vaporizes the photograph once again in a memory hole at the Ministry of Love, he exhibits the typical 'lunatic dislocation of the mind' (*NEF*, p. 260) at the core of doublethink by triumphally proclaiming: 'It does not exist. It never existed' (*NEF*, p. 259). And to Winston, who protests 'It exists in memory. I remember it. You remember it', O'Brien chillingly retorts 'I do not remember it' (*NEF*, p. 259), a response which epitomizes the revisionist doublethink facilitated by the memory holes. Illustrating the effectiveness of this method of forced collective amnesia, the reason for the nickname 'memory holes' is itself, ironically, unknown (*NEF*, p. 40).

Since memory is so central to the Party's control of the past, it is hardly surprising that Winston's attempts to fissure Ingsoc's totalitarian power over time revolve around memory. The forced collective amnesia he resists is not limited to the memory of historical events, such as who invented airplanes or who Oceania was at war with at any given moment. Rather, the Party's totalitarianism threatens personal memories as well. Winston, for instance, remembers very little about his childhood, and his attempts to recover a sense of history are paralleled by his attempts to recover traces of his personal memories, especially of his family. Significantly, it is when recalling the last time he saw his mother that Winston recuperates a sense of agency, albeit a limited one. Thinking about the final memory of his mother, Winston realizes that the Party has persuaded its subjects that 'mere impulses, mere feelings, [a]re of no account' and that this, in turn, has robbed them 'of all power over the material world' (*NEF*, p. 172), that is, of agency. Yet it 'would not have occurred to her [Winston's mother] that an action that is ineffectual', such as affectionately holding his dying sister in her arms, 'becomes meaningless' (*NEF*, p. 171). As Winston muses, it is in holding true to feelings, the feelings that make us human, that the possibility for agency lies, even under the Party's totalitarian oppression: 'They [the Party] can't get inside you. If you can *feel* that staying human is worth while, even when it can't have any result whatever, you've beaten them' (*NEF*, p. 174). Thus, while the totalitarian present is in effect ahistorical in that access to the past beyond the Party's simulations is impossible, and while Winston has 'no memories of anything greatly different' (*NEF*, p. 62) than his current living conditions, he holds fast to a gut feeling, 'some kind of ancestral memory that things had once been different' (*NEF*, p. 63), as the reason behind the intolerability of present conditions and the need to oppose Ingsoc.[12]

Winston's attempts to recover a sense of the past, in terms of both history and individual memories, are embodied in the private archive represented by his diary. As Theo Finigan argues:

> In opposition to the totalitarian destruction of public history and personal memory, the novel['s] protagonis[t] attempt[s] to institute archives of [his] own. In [his] diar[y] [...] which [he] explicitly imagine[s] as [a] documen[t] for a future history beyond the reach of the regime's control, Winston Smith [...] seek[s] to shore up fragments of the shattered past by attending to those fossilized remains that do persist, sedimented in memory, language, and materiality.[13]

The diary itself is such a fossilized material remain. Its paper is 'of a kind that had not been manufactured for at least forty years' (*NEF*, p. 8), though Winston believes the object is much older. The pen Winston uses to write the diary is also an 'archaic instrument' (*NEF*, p. 8). Together with other objects found at the junk shop, the diary represents a 'little chunk of history that [the Party have] forgotten to alter' (*NEF*, p. 152), namely, these objects represent the resurfacing of the real past, of original documents beyond the Party's endless archival destructions and simulations. Equally, the diary functions as a repository of Winston's scattered memories and, thus, as the sign of the Party's not entirely successful control of the individual archive. This is why the Party cannot but severely punish the act of keeping a diary.

Alongside the inexorable prospect of being caught by the Thought Police for keeping a diary, at the forefront of Winston's concerns about this object is the question of its addressee. Significantly, this is a question that Winston articulates in temporal terms, again indicating how the Party's power depends on its totalitarian control of time and, conversely, how any kind of resistance to the Party needs to work along temporal lines to fissure this control. Immediately after he is overcome by the realization that he does not know if it is indeed 1984, the year he has written down as the date of his first diary entry, Winston wonders: 'For whom [...] was he writing this diary? For the future, for the unborn' (*NEF*, p. 9). To return to the Manguso quotation, through his diary Winston seeks to 'nobly addres[s] the entire future'. The boldness of this aim is soon chipped, however. 'How could you communicate with the future? It was of its nature impossible', Winston muses, for '[e]ither the future would resemble the present', which is what the Party seeks to ensure by freezing history and by erasing a genuine sense of futurity, 'in which case it would not listen to him: or it would be different from it, and his predicament would be meaningless' (*NEF*, p. 9). Thus, the next time Winston returns to the question of his diary's addressee he adds the dimension of the past: 'He wondered again for whom he was writing the diary. For the future, for the past' (*NEF*, p. 29). Naturally, communicating with the past is even more impossible than communicating with the future, but Winston's appeal to the former temporal dimension can be understood by considering the politics of the archive. In this second instance of the addressee question, indeed, Winston approaches the impossibility of communicating with the future from the perspective of the volatility of Oceania's archival records: 'The diary would be reduced to ashes and himself to vapour. [...] How could you make appeal to the future when not a trace of you, not even an anonymous word scribbled on a piece of paper, could physically survive?' (*NEF*, p. 29). In other words, the possibility of Winston's words reaching and shaping a future beyond Ingsoc's grip depends on the recovery of the possibility of stable and reliable archives of the past.

After all, an archive of records is assembled with a future reader in mind, so much so that, as Derrida reminds us, the archive is 'a question of the future, the question of the future itself, the question of a response, of a promise and of a responsibility for tomorrow' (Derrida, *AF*, p. 27). Thus, where the Party's control of the archive seeks to ensure the endless reproduction of the totalitarian present into the future, for this archive simulates the pre-Revolutionary era as a dystopian past and Ingsoc's present as the utopian culmination of history, Winston's hopes for the far future revolve around the resistance forming an alternative archive that will fissure the Party's simulations and its totalitarian erasure of the possibility of a different future. As Winston puts it,

I don't imagine that we can alter anything in our own lifetime. But one can imagine little knots of resistance springing up here and there – small groups of people banding themselves together, and gradually growing, and even *leaving a few records behind*, so that the next generation can carry on where we leave off. (*NEF*, pp. 162–3, emphasis added)

This alternative archive, Winston hopes, will precariously preserve the 'human heritage', those feelings, memories, experiences, and beliefs that indicate how intolerable living conditions are in Oceania and how far Ingsoc is from the necessary utopian culmination of the historical development, thus contributing to shape a far future *'when thought is free, when men are different from one another and do not live alone'*, *'when truth exists and what is done cannot be undone'* (*NEF*, p. 30). In other words, the resistance's alternative archive, which includes Winston's diary, seeks to pry open the closure of the totalitarian archive, which erases any interpretations or views alternative to those in power, creating spaces for the individual's agency to inform a future beyond the Party's endless present.[14]

The volatility and violent erasures characteristic of Oceania's archives entail that Winston's challenge to the totalitarian closure of the Party's endless present – a challenge encapsulated by his diary – is unsuccessful in his lifetime, as he had indeed predicted. Tellingly, the final moments of the novel see Winston completely defeated, rejecting a memory of his mother as a 'false memory' (*NEF*, p. 309). Given the centrality of memory to Winston's rebellion, it is 'the sign of his utter degradation', as Gottlieb argues, 'that in the last scene of the novel he has to give up his right to personal memory, his last chance for keeping a record of the past'.[15] And yet, something of him must have survived the Party's archival revisionisms, for *Nineteen Eighty-Four*'s appendix, which speaks of Ingsoc as a thing of the past, makes a reference to Winston (*NEF*, p. 320). Furthermore, outside of the fictional universe, Winston's story finds its hoped-for future readers in *Nineteen Eighty-Four*'s readership, which includes a series of ensuing authors of dystopian fictions that return to the trope of the diary, or more broadly a recorded testimony, counteracting power's totalitarian control of the archive and history.[16]

Margaret Atwood, for instance, the author of another dystopian classic, *The Handmaid's Tale* (1985), acknowledges that her novel 'takes at least part of its inspiration from George Orwell's *1984* – particularly the epilogue'.[17] Arguably, we can also trace the influence of *Nineteen Eighty-Four* upon Atwood's protagonist, Offred, who, like Winston, finds solace in telling her story, even if she worries it will never find an audience because of the impermanence of archival records under Gilead, the totalitarian regime in which she lives. In attempting to tell and preserve her story, Offred finds a sense of communion with others she lacks under Gilead's oppressive patriarchy: 'if it's a story, even in my head, I must be telling it to someone. You don't tell a story only to yourself. There's always someone else. Even when there is no one' (Atwood, *HT*, p. 49). Just as in *Nineteen Eighty-Four*, the epilogue of *The Handmaid's Tale* reveals that Offred's story, recorded on tapes, has indeed survived Gilead's archival revisionism and reached audiences that inhabit a post-totalitarian and seemingly peaceful future. Similarly, in a society in which the totalitarian state of corpocracy 'outlaws [public access to] *any* historical discourse', the clone Sonmi-451, the protagonist of the fifth narrative of David Mitchell's *Cloud Atlas* (2004), is inspired to rebel against the regime by gaining access to its forbidden archives.[18] These archives significantly include texts by George Orwell, presumably *Nineteen Eighty-Four* itself, and by Aldous Huxley, the author of the canonical dystopia *Brave New World* (1932), thus metafictionally gesturing to one of the aims of the dystopian genre: inspiring its readership to act in order to ward off the societies the genre depicts. Sonmi-451 is executed for her rebellion. Yet her testimony, archived in a technological device called an orison, survives corpocracy and is considered a sacred text in a distant post-apocalyptic future. And in another metafictional gesture, the narrative set in this distant post-apocalyptic future, *Cloud Atlas*'s sixth story, closes on the narrator directly inviting the readers to take heed of Sonmi-451's testimony: 'Sit down a beat or two. Hold out your hands. Look.'[19] Thus, through characters like Offred and Sonmi-451, who carry on Winston's fight against the totalitarian control of the archive, his message endures and his diary finds its future addressees: us.

Notes

1 Sarah Manguso, *Ongoingness: The End of a Diary* (London: Picador, 2018), p. 7.
2 Critics have often pointed out how, in imagining this constant erasure and rewriting of the past, Orwell takes inspiration from actual events: 'He had witnessed the erasure of history in the course of Stalin's purges and in what he took as the rewriting of the narrative of the Spanish Civil War. He saw it again in the British government's manipulation of descriptions of events during World War II' (David J. Lorenzo, *Cities at the End of the World: Using Utopian and Dystopian Stories to Reflect Critically on Our Political Beliefs, Communities, and Ways of Life* (London: Bloomsbury Academic, 2014), p. 160). See also Bernard Crick, '*Nineteen Eighty-Four*: Context and Controversy', in John Rodden (ed.), *The Cambridge Companion to George Orwell* (Cambridge: Cambridge University Press, 2007), pp. 146–59.
3 Jean Baudrillard, *Simulacra and Simulation*, trans. Sheila Faria Glaser (Ann Arbor, MI: University of Michigan Press 1994), p. 1.

4 *Ibid.*, p. 2.

5 *Ibid.*

6 David Dwan, 'Truth and Freedom in Orwell's *Nineteen Eighty-Four*', *Philosophy and Literature*, 34.2 (2010), pp. 381–93, at pp. 382, 381.

7 Lorenzo, *Cities at the End of the World*, p. 161.

8 Erika Gottlieb, 'The Function of Goldstein's Book: Time as Theme and Structure in Dystopian Satire', *Utopian Studies*, 3 (1991), pp. 12–19, at p. 15.

9 On the totalitarian domination of the experience of time in *Nineteen Eighty-Four*, see also Theo Finigan, '"Into the Memory Hole": Totalitarianism and Mal d'Archive in *Nineteen Eighty-Four* and *The Handmaid's Tale*', *Science Fiction Studies*, 38.3 (2011), pp. 435–59.

10 Gottlieb, 'The Function of Goldstein's Book', p. 14.

11 *Ibid.*

12 The image of an ancestral memory recurs when Winston finds himself by chance at the junk shop where he bought the diary. As Mr Charrington shows him the room where he used to live with his now-dead wife, Winston feels 'a sort of nostalgia, a sort of ancestral memory'. This ancestral memory is again closely connected to the gut feeling that, despite the Party's simulations about a dismal pre-Revolutionary past, things were better then. As Winston goes on to articulate his ancestral memory: 'It seemed to him that he knew exactly what it felt like to sit in a room like this, [...] utterly secure, with nobody watching you' (*NEF*, p. 100).

13 Finigan, '"Into the Memory Hole"', p. 435.

14 On the closure of the totalitarian archive, see also Finigan who argues that, by treating the archive 'as though at its "disposal"', totalitarianism effectively 'closes, or disposes of, the archive' ('"Into the Memory Hole"', pp. 448–9).

15 Gottlieb, 'The Function of Goldstein's Book', p. 18.

16 I write more extensively about the trope of the archive in contemporary dystopias in the conclusion to *The Contemporary Post-Apocalyptic Novel: Critical Temporalities and the End Times* (London: Bloomsbury, 2019).

17 Margaret Atwood, '*The Handmaid's Tale* and *Oryx and Crake* "In Context"', *PMLA*, 119.3 (2004), pp. 513–17, at p. 516.

18 David Mitchell, *Cloud Atlas* (London: Sceptre, 2004), p. 243.

19 *Ibid.*, p. 325.

4

DAVID DWAN

Orwell and Humanism

Nineteen Eighty-Four was published on 8 June 1949 – six months after the UN's endorsement of the Universal Declaration of Human Rights at the Palais de Chaillot in Paris. Orwell had been calling for an international charter of this kind for some time. In 1946, for instance, he collaborated with the novelist Arthur Koestler and the philosopher Bertrand Russell on a manifesto for a new organization that would rekindle the language of universal rights. 'The programme of the Rights of Man', the three men argued, 'has to be restated in the light of the experience since the French Revolution'.[1] The UN Declaration provided such a re-statement, building on the same principles of human dignity, individual freedom, and equal right that Orwell, Russell, and Koestler had emphasized two years earlier. Orwell was always more committed to the economic entailments of 'equal right' than the UN was in 1948, though he also believed that an emphasis on economic equality could be overstated to the disastrous exclusion of other values.[2] Nonetheless, the Declaration's emphasis on fundamental freedoms – of speech, conscience, and association – alongside the prescriptions against arbitrary arrest and detention chime with much of what Orwell campaigned for throughout the 1940s.

Nineteen Eighty-Four is a novel that would seem to defend human rights by outlining the moral horror that ensues from their total abrogation. 'No one shall be subjected to torture or to cruel, inhuman or degrading treatment or punishment', the Declaration maintains, but Winston suffers all this at the hands of O'Brien. According to Article 10 of the Declaration: 'Everyone is entitled in full equality to a fair and public hearing by an independent and impartial tribunal.' However, the basic concept of an independent and impartial justice is defunct in *Nineteen Eighty-Four*. Article 12 of the UN Declaration defends the right to privacy, but no such right obtains in Oceania. The very notion of 'thoughtcrime' is a gross contradiction of

Article 18 ('Everyone has the right to freedom of thought').[3] If these violations cause shock or queasiness in a reader, these reactions would seem to perform and entrench a visceral commitment to some fundamental moral norms.

But *Nineteen Eighty-Four* also raises troubling questions about the norms it implicitly sponsors: Why should any rights follow from the mere fact of being human? And how stable is this fact? In her famous reflections on totalitarianism, Hannah Arendt declared that it was a politics committed to the radical reconfiguration of the human mind. 'What totalitarian ideologies [. . .] aim at', according to Arendt, 'is not the transformation of the outside world or the revolutionizing transmutation of society, but the transformation of human nature itself' (Arendt, *OT*, p. 601). Orwell had long been obsessed by this dark power. In 1939, for instance, he suggested that modern dictatorships had shown that 'human nature' is contingent and can be radically repurposed: it is 'just as possible to produce a breed of men who do not wish for liberty', he opined, 'as to produce a breed of hornless cows' (*CW*, 11, p. 317). *Nineteen Eighty-Four* may well feature this new breed of men.

Orwell had often insisted on the need to regard humans as malleable creatures. Like many on the Left, he hoped that the advent of socialism would be accompanied by a psychological revolution – that the acquisitive instincts, for instance, might be 'bred out in a couple of generations' (*CW*, 16, p. 294). Thus, on one point he was adamant: 'human society, and therefore human nature, can change' (*CW*, 14, p. 160). Those who insisted otherwise, stressing the immutability of human nature, simply turned their backs on radical political and social reform. But *The Last Man in Europe* – to adopt the original title of the novel – is clearly concerned about the contingency and finitude of the human. As O'Brien says to Winston: 'You are imagining that there is something called human nature which will be outraged by what we do and will turn against us.' But, as far as O'Brien is concerned, this is a nonsensical hope: 'we create human nature' (*NEF*, p. 282). So, humanity is the product of power, never its moral limit. Here the idea of human rights – viewed as fixed and inalienable properties – would seem to have little traction. If human rights are in trouble here, so too is an ethos that can be loosely called humanism.

Humanism in Context

In 1946 Evelyn Waugh credited Orwell with the invention of 'a new humanism' – the 'humanism of the common man'.[4] Waugh was predictably uneasy about the secular dimensions of this credo, but the qualified welcome he gave to the new humanism may have reflected a common conviction that the old one was in bad shape. Indeed, the prospects and limitations of humanism were hotly contested in the 1940s, as Europeans began to review their moral heritage in the light of another disastrous conflict. Julian Huxley, Gilbert Murray, and Joe Oldham debated its significance in a series of talks for the BBC in 1944.[5] Sartre gave it the thumbs up in France in 1945.[6] In Germany in 1947 Heidegger dismissed humanism as a deeply calloused attitude to the world and gave it the thumbs down.[7]

The vagueness of 'humanism' as a general concept made these debates hard to adjudicate. The term had often simply referred to a system of education in which the Latin classics often took pride of place. The pagan sources of that education partly account for the ways in which humanism would later be associated with a broadly secular outlook. Orwell would speak up for this secularism, but he could also look upon it with mixed feelings: 'when men stop worshipping God, they promptly start worshipping Man, with disastrous results' (CW, 17, p. 227). The potential for man worship arose from the fact that humanism tended to give humans a central role within the universe. As Orwell noted in 1945, the belief that 'man is the measure of all things' – a view once propounded by Protagoras – is a basic axiom of humanism (CW, 17, p. 176).[8] Whatever this might do to God – Orwell seemed to think it dethroned him – it gave humans an exalted position over other animals.[9] Properties like reason and freedom were presented as hallmarks of the human and were judged to set us aside from simpler and baser creatures.[10] In the enlightened humanism of Kant, for instance, it is the freedom to act on the basis of rational principles that gives humans their unique dignity.[11] The UN Declaration draws on this humanist heritage in its defence of the 'inherent dignity', 'reason', and 'conscience' of human beings.

In the debates about humanism in the 1940s, Sartre defended some of its key values – in particular, the principles of freedom and human dignity (though he was arguably setting the bar quite low when he declared that 'man is of greater dignity than a stone or a table').[12] Moreover, respect for these properties in others necessarily entailed that individuals had to evaluate their own responsibilities in universal terms. By casting my own actions through the prism of the universal, 'humanity regulates itself by what I do'.[13] Orwell dismissed Sartre as a windbag and hoped to give him a good kicking in print (CW, 19, p. 457) – while some of Sartre's friends nursed similar views of Orwell (Merleau-Ponty, for instance, had hoped to contribute an article to Horizon rubbishing Orwell's 'so-called humanism').[14] Nonetheless, the affinities between both writers on the question of humanism should not be overlooked. Both were enthusiasts of freedom and were reluctant to impose limits on what it might achieve by signing up to theories of a fixed human nature ('man is free', Sartre insisted, and 'there is no human nature which I can take as foundational').[15] Accompanying this freedom, moreover, was a strenuous sense of moral duty in both writers. 'Our responsibility [...] is much greater than we had supposed', Sartre opined, 'for it concerns mankind as a whole.'[16] This sense of responsibility, moreover, drew both men Leftwards. 'The basis of socialism is humanism', Orwell declared in 1946 (CW, 18, p. 61).

However, the moralistic tenor of Orwell's politics could sound fairly quaint in Marxist ears. Orwell, after all, was an unabashed moralist – a figure who believed in the objective existence, universal scope, and motivational power of 'ordinary human decency' (CW, 18, p. 60). But he was aware that this moral confidence had often been lampooned by Marx. As he put it in 1940: 'Marx exploded a hundred tons of dynamite beneath the moralist position, and we are still living in the echo of that tremendous crash' (CW, 12, p. 31). Marx's attacks on morality are still a matter of dispute. Sometimes it seems that he had simply 'bourgeois morality' in his sights; at other moments, he appeared to take issue with all moral systems.[17] By focussing less on the content of moral propositions than on their practical effect in social life, Marx claimed that morality reflects and sustains asymmetries of power. Moral ideals may pretend to be universal and impartial but they invariably serve sectional interests. The very concept of 'humanity' was, for Marx, one of these suspect abstractions: nursing a purely formal or wishful idea of solidarity, it blinded people to the reality of class conflict and the need for a more radical overhaul of social relationships.[18]

The extent to which Marx remained a humanist – wedded to notions of freedom or human dignity – when critiquing the cant of humanity would be disputed throughout Orwell's lifetime. In 1947, Merleau-Ponty wanted to recall Marxists 'to their humanist inspiration', while also insisting that Marxism was a critique of all existing humanisms.[19] Orwell was certainly receptive to elements of this critique. His hostility to fixed theories of human nature may have been a concession to Marx's brand of historicism (though Marx had never abjured from generalizing about human nature).[20] Orwell frequently disparaged evaluative uses of the word 'human' – presenting them as largely empty forms of appraisal – and ridiculed the shallow benevolence of much humanitarianism.[21] 'A humanitarian is always a hypocrite', he declared in 1942 – a figure whose abstract sympathy for the human race easily co-habited with the structural inequalities it professes to indict (CW, 13, p. 153). However, Orwell was also convinced that 'humanity [...] is not an abstraction' (CW, 12, p. 126), but a serviceable moral ideal.

Orwell would appear to remain committed to this ideal in *Nineteen Eighty-Four*, alongside attendant values such as dignity and freedom. But, as we shall see, these are vulnerable concepts, hard to fathom and easy to abuse (after all, freedom becomes slavery in *Nineteen Eighty-Four*). According to Christopher Norris, the novel simply exposes the fact that 'the individual subject is a fiction' and human dignity a delusion – at least when it is interpreted in individualistic terms. 'What *Nineteen Eighty-Four* thus documents', he concludes, 'is the nihilistic horror unleashed upon itself by an ideology wedded to the values of liberal humanism, but forced to acknowledge their precisely *ideological* character.'[22] Nihilism here may be in the eye of the beholder. The novel certainly puts its own humanism on trial, but this does not mean that the ethos is sent to the dungeons.

On Human Dignity

In a key section of *Nineteen Eighty-Four*, Winston tracks down an old prole and asks him the following question: 'Are you treated more like a human being?' (*NEF*, p. 94). The man struggles to answer the question, but perhaps anyone would. It's not immediately clear what treating like a human being involves outside or within the many different ways in which they are treated. But humans under most forms of humanism were judged worthy of a particular kind of solicitude. This was as a simple function of what they were judged to be: beings endowed with reason and freedom. It was often assumed that these properties were connected: so the ability to act on the basis of rational principles – often in contradistinction to brute appetite – was a hallmark of being free. This freedom was the ground of human dignity in Kant's eyes, and entitled us to equal respect from all. Humans have an 'unconditional, incomparable inner worth', which means that they can never be viewed as a mere means to some other end, but must always be regarded as ends-in-themselves.[23]

It is not exactly clear what treating people as ends-in-themselves really involves. Vague as it may be, it is hard to say that anyone manages to cultivate this kind of respect for all in *Nineteen Eighty-Four*. 'Ownlife' is proscribed and the Party only acknowledges one end-in-itself, namely 'power' (i.e. 'The object of power is power'; *NEF*, p. 276). In the eyes of the Party, 'all was justified by the ultimate purpose', namely, the acquisition and maintenance of power (*NEF*, p. 275). Even Winston and Julia struggle to regard other people – outside of each other – as absolute ends. Signing up to the famous Brotherhood, they blithely assent to the idea of murdering and maiming innocents for the cause. When asked by O'Brien whether they would be prepared to throw sulphuric acid in a child's face if required, they give an unqualified 'yes' (*NEF*, p. 180).

Here Orwell may have been satirizing a certain style of revolutionary commitment. 'The welfare of the revolution – that is the supreme law', Trotsky maintained, and he suggested that any number of practices – from

murder to organized lies – were justified on its behalf.[24] Trotsky had no time
for those who would 'subdue Marxism by means of Kantianism to paralyse
the social revolution by means of "absolute" norms' – or what we might call
human rights.[25] Trotsky continues to be presented as a committed humanist,
but if the universalization of ethics was a key feature of humanism (as some
have maintained), then Trotsky stood askance from this tradition.[26] There
were, Trotsky insisted, 'no eternal moral truths'.[27] He was sometimes prepared to invoke the principle of human dignity: foul language, Trotsky
argued, contravened this principle (Big Brother, incidentally, also disap-
proves of swearing).[28] Yet Trotsky had little regard for those who would
limit the revolution with 'prattle about the "sacredness of human life"'.[29]

Nineteen Eighty-Four takes aim at this ruthless vision, though the novel
has obviously more than Trotsky – or communism – in its sights. The
novel's plot may confirm the thesis that 'the individual is always defeated'
(*NEF*, p. 142), but, focalized as it is through the consciousness of Winston
Smith, the story might seem to defend the 'inner worth' of the individual
person. But what, we might ask, is the root of this dignity in *Nineteen
Eighty-Four*? 'Autonomy', Kant tells us, is 'the ground of the dignity of
human nature and of every rational nature', but very few people would
seem to possess this freedom in *Nineteen Eighty-Four*.[30] Moreover, the
extent to which reason is a constituent of human freedom – as Kant and
other humanists suggest – is difficult to decipher in the novel. Orwell often
maintained that reason could alienate us from our humanity as much as it
could express it – a position that informs his mistrust of intellectuals. All
too often they cut loose from their moral intuitions in the pursuit of some
rational scheme; the average Joe, on the other hand, often finds his
humanity vouchsafed by a benign obtuseness.

This position is partly borne out in *Nineteen Eighty-Four*. O'Brien's
intelligence is repeatedly emphasized, but so too is his moral nihilism. 'The
proles', on the other hand, 'had stayed human', despite – or because of – their
rational deficiencies ('They had held on to the primitive emotions'; *NEF*,
p. 172). Of course, this lack of nous will lead some to deny their humanity. As
Syme maintains: 'The proles are not human beings' (*NEF*, p. 56). Indeed, the
proles are repeatedly lumped together with beasts: they are 'natural inferiors
who must be kept in subjection, like animals' (*NEF*, p. 74). 'Proles and
animals are free' (*NEF*, p. 75), according to the Party, but the novel queries
the integrity of this freedom, since, in a whole range of ways, the proles are
never quite masters of themselves. Winston may feel there is hope in the
proles, but his assessment of their condition is pretty damning: '*Until they
become conscious they will never rebel, and until after they have rebelled
they cannot become conscious*' (*NEF*, p. 74). Given the semantic range of

'consciousness', the rational deficiencies of the proles are potentially extremely high.

The condescension to which the Proles are subject exposes the dangers of making reason a hallmark of the human – clearly it is an assumption that can degrade and exclude – but it is a position to which Winston (and perhaps the novel overall) remains committed. Winston often feels that his compatriots have relinquished their humanity by abandoning their reason. Consider this assessment of one of the zealots of the Party:

> Winston had a curious feeling that this was not a real human being but some kind of dummy. It was not the man's brain that was speaking, it was his larynx. The stuff that was coming out of him consisted of words, but it was not speech in the true sense: it was a noise uttered in unconsciousness, like the quacking of a duck. (*NEF*, p. 57)

Here critical independence is a hallmark of the human, and those who fail to exercise the responsibilities of this freedom are equated with beasts. The zealot quacks like a duck, while the 'imbecile' Parsons swallows the Party's guff 'with the stupidity of an animal' (*NEF*, p. 62). It is difficult to decide whether the narrative denies these people their dignity or whether they have abandoned their claim to it, but it is clear that the animal is a sign of the abject – as it is so often within humanism.

The Abject Animal

In an article on Samuel Butler in 1944, Orwell declared that moderns had come to terms with evolution: 'we do not feel that to be descended from animals is degrading to human dignity' (*CW*, 16, p. 293). Nonetheless, the trace of the animal is something that Orwell often turns from in horror. The basic possession of a body makes this animality difficult to transcend. As Orwell put it in a late essay on Swift: 'The human body is beautiful; it is also repulsive and ridiculous, a fact which can be verified at any swimming pool.' We often shrink from the basic conditions of life: the sexual organs are objects of 'desire and also of loathing', while even eating has a repulsive quality ('all our food springs ultimately from dung and dead bodies'). The average child, in Orwell's eyes, is often overcome by a visceral disgust for material existence: a 'horror of snot and spittle, of the dogs' excrement on the pavement, the dying toad full of maggots, the sweaty smell of grown-ups, the hideousness of old men, with their bald heads and bulbous noses'. Our queasiness about snot, spittle, and excrement may stem from a sense of the body's vulnerability and its susceptibility to disease. Old men may alert us to our own mortality and inevitable decay, which is why we may shrink from them in disgust. Whatever the grounds, we often find the world a loathsome place. Swift's 'endless harping on disease, dirt and deformity' was not mistaken in Orwell's eyes; it was simply one-sided or incomplete (*CW*, 18, p. 430).

The degradation of our animal condition is certainly a feature of *Nineteen Eighty-Four*. On one level, of course, the novel exults in 'the animal instinct': sexual desire, for instance, is a pure kind of life force that may one day destroy the party (*NEF*, p. 132). Yet the human animal is often a repulsive creature in *Nineteen Eighty-Four*. This is partly borne out by the way humans resemble other animals in the novel. So people quack like ducks, breathe like fish, resemble rodents, or move like insects ('It was curious how that beetle-like type proliferated in the Ministries'; *NEF*, p. 63). The novel is alert to the ways in which bodily caricatures operate as propaganda – capitalists were invariably *'fat, ugly men, with wicked faces'* (*NEF*, p. 76) in the eyes of the regime – but the novel itself plays a similar game. 'Nearly everyone was ugly' in Oceania, we are told (*NEF*, p. 63). This may be an aestheticized political or moral judgement of a regime, but everywhere we find signs of the body's squalor. Parsons is memorably obese and has an 'inexhaustible supply of acrid-smelling seat' (*NEF*, p. 156). Winston fixes a blocked pipe in his house and is aghast at what he witnesses ('Winston let out the water and disgustedly removed the clot of human hair that had blocked up the pipe'; *NEF*, p. 24). Winston may learn to love Julia's 'white youthful body' (*NEF*, p. 115), but he has considerably more difficulties accepting his own. His varicose ulcer is an itchy leitmotif of the novel. The ulcer may be another moral symbol – notably, it clears up for a while when he finds love – but it also invites the reader to indulge in the same disgust that he often entertains for himself.

O'Brien will harness this self-disgust, alerting Winston to the sight of his own broken body after weeks of imprisonment and torture. Winston is shocked by what he has become:

> A bowed, grey-coloured, skeleton-like thing was coming towards him. Its actual appearance was frightening, and not merely the fact that he knew it to be himself. He moved closer to the glass. The creature's face seemed to be protruded, because of its bent carriage. A forlorn, jailbird's face with a nobby forehead running back into a bald scalp, a crooked nose and battered-looking cheekbones above which his eyes were fierce and watchful. The cheeks were seamed, the mouth had a drawn-in look. [...] He had gone partially bald. For the first moment he had thought he had gone grey as well, but it was only the scalp that was grey. Except for his hands and a circle of his face, his body was grey all over with ancient, ingrained dirt. Here and there under the dirt there were the red scars of wounds, and near the ankle the varicose ulcer was an

> inflamed mass with flakes of skin peeling off it. But the truly frightening thing
> was the emaciation of his body. [...] At a guess he would have said that it was
> the body of a man of sixty, suffering from some malignant disease.
>
> (*NEF*, p. 284)

Winston struggles to recognize himself in the mirror and to recognize himself as human. He is 'the creature', a 'jailbird', a 'grey-coloured, skeleton-like thing', the hyphenated terms capturing Winston's sense of himself as a strange, hybrid being, once human, but no longer quite so. In O'Brien's estimate, he is simply a 'bag of filth' (*NEF*, p. 285). The dignity of humanity – so lauded by Kant and others – is something that O'Brien sets out to destroy. If Winston remains human, O'Brien invites him to conclude that this humanity is incompatible with any pretensions to dignity: 'Do you see that thing facing you? That is the last man. If you are human, that is humanity' (*NEF*, p. 285).

Encountering his own image in the mirror, Winston experiences 'a feeling of pity for his ruined body' (*NEF*, p. 285). Winston feels compassion for himself, but 'pity' has often been cast as the feeling which unites us best to others. 'Humanity', as a moral disposition, was simply pity extended to 'the species in general'.[31] Moreover, our shared sense of bodily vulnerability is often the source of this compassion.[32] The image of Julia's body, 'helpless in sleep', awakens in Winston 'a pitying, protecting feeling' (*NEF*, p. 132). O'Brien even seems to pity Winston in his abject state and lays 'a hand on his shoulder, almost kindly' (*NEF*, p. 285), but his dominant response is one of disgust – a 'key device of subordination' in Martha Nussbaum's eyes.[33] Disgust erodes equality of respect and concern by emphasizing the base animality of others; it is not, we are told, a very promising basis for political community.[34] Indeed, Orwell suggests that it leads to a 'reactionary' politics (*CW*, 18, p. 428). The problem in *Nineteen Eighty-Four*, however, is that this disgust is ubiquitous. This may reflect the fact that the story is focalized through the sensitive eye of Winston Smith – a figure, as we have seen, whose disgust for himself ultimately outmatches his revulsion for others.

Winston's problems with embodiment partly stem from his commitment to a certain type of freedom or moral autonomy. In other words, he seems to want to live a principled life in which he is a moral legislator for himself, but the body and its needs repeatedly frustrate this endeavour. Winston speaks of the 'treachery of the human body'. 'In moments of crisis', he explains, 'one is never fighting against an external enemy, but always against one's own body.' Principles are forgotten on the battlefield or in the torture chamber, he maintains, because 'the body swells up until it fills the universe' (*NEF*, p. 106). These theories find some vindication in Winston's own experiences of torture and imprisonment. Here Winston is reduced to 'a screaming animal' impervious to his own principles (*NEF*, p. 299). 'The one thing that matters is that we shouldn't betray one another,' he has told Julia, but neither can obey this simple rule (*NEF*, p. 173). The body renders us vulnerable and dependent. In thrall to its dictates, Winston becomes 'as shameless as an animal' (*NEF*, p. 252).

Dignity, according to the UN Declaration, is 'inherent'; it can be violated, but never, it seems, relinquished. But when dignity is felt to derive from autonomy, troublesome questions arise: Is it forfeited when we cease to be autonomous? Perhaps it's the capacity for autonomy rather than its practice that counts here, but by the end of *Nineteen Eighty-Four* Winston seems to lack even the capacity to be a self-legislating being. 'O'Brien had tortured him to the edge of lunacy' and beyond (*NEF*, p. 264). The degree to which he is lost to himself is expressed in rapturous love of Big Brother. Here readers may feel that a simple compassion for a broken, vulnerable animal should override claims about their autonomy or inalienable dignity. The autonomous person, for Kant, was motivated by 'a life independent of animality and even of the whole sensible world', but Orwell implies that we can never be so gloriously insensible.[35] This may suggest that autonomy is a fiction – the real moral of the novel in Norris's eyes – or it may indicate that autonomy requires (perhaps ironically) certain conditions. We can only cut loose from the body when we have satisfied some of its basic needs: in conditions of starvation, intimidation, and torture, we will never succeed in being properly autonomous agents. But more abstract things need to be in place too. *Nineteen Eighty-Four* also implies that it is hard to be free in a world without truth.

The Truth of Humanism

'Only the truth can set us free.' This remark may derive from John's Gospel, but according to Julian Huxley, it is a basic principle of humanism.[36] *Nineteen-Eighty Four* would seem to provide a troubled endorsement of this principle. It is troubled, because it is the tyrant O'Brien who sometimes appears as the novel's greatest enthusiast of truth. The idea of error in the world is something he cannot abide ('It is intolerable to us that an erroneous thought should exist anywhere in the world, however secret and powerless it may be'; *NEF*, p. 267). Moreover, he invites Winston to set himself free from error by submerging himself in the Party – the only reliable foundation for truth in the world in O'Brien's eyes. Room 101 – 'the place where there is no darkness' (*NEF*, p. 256) – is the place where this grim enlightenment is engendered. Here 'all evil and all illusion' are burned out of the individual (*NEF*, p. 267). Winston's final capitulation is a parody of freedom as rational self-mastery: 'He had won the victory over himself. He loved Big Brother' (*NEF*, p. 310).

The basic plot of *Nineteen Eighty-Four*, therefore, is a dark inversion of the humanist mantra that the truth sets you free. The joke, of course, may be on the regime rather than on truth, freedom, or humanism, but O'Brien puts pressure on another contention of humanism, for he, too, seems to believe that man is the measure of all things. Plato had attacked the Protagorean principle for the ways in which it licensed a dangerous relativism: if everything is relative to humanity, then a certain notion of objective truth may never be in reach.[37] For all the evident hubris of the man-as-measure principle, humanism often contained a kind of epistemic humility: it conceded to the impossibility of arriving at a transcendent or god-like view of the universe.[38] 'We can never get outside man', Gilbert Murray reported. 'Beyond man is the unknown, the realm of mystery which cannot be expressed in human language or comprehended by human thought.' The humanist, Murray insisted, 'accepts this fact'.[39] But so, problematically, does O'Brien.

Indeed, the view that we must always see things from a *human* perspective becomes, under O'Brien, a full-blown anti-realism – a denial of a mind-independent reality. According to O'Brien, reality exists 'in the human mind, and nowhere else' (*NEF*, p. 261) – a position that can read like a parody of Murray's humanism or, indeed, of Sartre's.[40] But again the joke may be on O'Brien rather than on humanism. No humanist need consign themselves to the view that there is no external world: we may acknowledge that we will always see things from a human viewpoint, but that viewpoint may require us to regard the world as independent or objective. The laws of gravity may be human inventions – we might even agree with O'Brien that we 'make the laws of Nature' (*NEF*, p. 277) – but most people would be inclined to think that these laws describe something real. We are thus unlikely to share O'Brien's confidence that we can float from the floor like a soap bubble if we wish. Even if everything is a product of mind, as O'Brien suggests, this does not mean we can jettison the mind's inner discipline – rules of logic or rational consistency – in the ways O'Brien thinks he can. Whether the world is entirely mental or not, two plus two can never be five.

But Orwell believed that the world was descending 'into an age in which two and two will make five' (*CW*, 11, p. 311). Since at least the Spanish Civil War – with its orgies of lies and misinformation – Orwell felt that the very concept of objective truth was fast disappearing from the world. Nationalism and the consequent subdivision of world into different units had made relativism a kind of practical fact in Orwell's eyes: every culture was trapped in its own collective solipsism and lacked any external reference point to adjudicate its convictions (in *Nineteen Eighty-Four*, people are similarly subdivided and hermetically sealed). This may lead to relativism in practice, but Orwell was convinced that the Nazis also espoused relativism as a principle: 'Nazi theory indeed specifically denies that such a thing as "the truth" exists. There is, for instance, no such thing as "science". There is only "German science", "Jewish science" etc.' (*CW*, 13, p. 504). In *Nineteen Eighty-Four*, of course, truth is relative to the Party – a position that might appear to parody Bolsheviks as much as Nazis. After all, in the 1920s Trotsky would present the Party as the only reliable criterion of truth in the world.[41] So if humanism suggests that truth is relative to the human race, then this relativism undergoes a terrible contraction in the novel. Here, 'Humanity is the Party' (*NEF*, p. 282) and 'Whatever the Party holds to be truth, *is* truth' (*NEF*, p. 261).

Though truth is bullied and is used to bully in *Nineteen Eighty-Four*, the novel would seem to hold out for some concept of truth, partly by showing the moral disaster that ensues from a neglect of its traditional criteria – universality, consistency, non-coerced consensus, etc. It also seems to endorse the humanist conviction that there is some deep connection between truth and freedom. As Winston declares, '*Freedom is the freedom to say that two plus two make four. If that is granted, all else follows*' (*NEF*, p. 84). It has often been argued that what is at stake here is freedom, not truth: Winston should be free to do his sums; the issue of them being correct does not arise.[42] But Winston seems to pick this particular sum because it serves as a canonical instance of a true statement. Without such basic truths in place, Winton can't make sense of the world, or operate as an agent within it.[43]

'Orwell', we are told, 'represents the confused and self-destructive motives of a liberal humanism finally run aground on its own bankrupt ideology.'[44] It is hard to know whether it's 'liberalism' or 'humanism' that is the real problem here (presumably, it's both), but it's far from clear that either of these credos are exposed as bankrupt in *Nineteen Eighty-Four*. Autonomy and dignity are revealed to be vulnerable ideals and more contingent than we like to think, but that does not mean they should be retired. The novel certainly suggests that humanism often overstates the differences between humans and animals, making us shrink from our own animality, while encouraging us to lord it over other creatures. Moreover, the potential hubris of man-the-measurer is all too evident in figures like O'Brien. Orwell's contemporaries rightly queried the Protagorean principle for the ways in which it sanctions 'man the user and instrumentalizer' – a callous solipsist who acknowledges no value independent of his own will.[45] Orwell, as we have seen, was alert to the dangers of man worship, and he knew that the 'human' could operate as a deeply sectarian principle (for Nazis, for instance, 'only Nordic man is fully human'; *CW*, 12, p. 411). But this doesn't mean that there are not some aspects of the 'human heritage' worth saving (*NEF*, p. 30). For most of *Nineteen Eighty-Four* Winston Smith wants to hang on to ideals of freedom and reason, believing them to be expressive of who we are. This may make him a humanist, but he is unlikely to be the last.

Notes

1 The manifesto is published in David Smith, *George Orwell Illustrated* (London: Haymarket Books, 2018), pp. 230–34.
2 Orwell, Russell, and Koestler worried that economic equality was presented as the only right, 'while *habeas corpus*, freedom of speech and of the press, the right to political opposition and absence of political terrorism were merely phrases designed to side-track the attention of the poor from economic inequality' (Smith, *George Orwell Illustrated*, p. 230).
3 UN, 2015 [www.un.org/en/udhrbook/pdf/udhr_booklet_en_web.pdf] (accessed 19 November 2019).
4 Evelyn Waugh, 'A New Humanism' (*The Tablet*, 6 April 1946), in *Essays, Articles, and Reviews*, ed. Donat Gallagher (London: Methuen, 1983), pp. 304–7, at p. 305.
5 See Julian Huxley, Gilbert Murray, and J. H. Oldham, *Humanism* (London: Watts & Co., 1944).
6 He gave a lecture on humanism in 1945; it was published in 1946. See Jean-Paul Sartre, *Existentialism and Humanism*, trans. Philip Mairet (London: Methuen, 2007).
7 Martin Heidegger, 'Letter on Humanism', in *Basic Writings*, ed. David Farrell Krell, rev. edn (London: Routledge, 1993), pp. 213–66.
8 This is reported by Socrates in *Theaetetus*. See Plato, *Theaetetus*, trans. John McDowell (Oxford: Oxford University Press, 2017), p. 17.
9 Within humanism, Gilbert Murray argued, 'man shows himself higher than the animals, and indeed, with all his horrible imperfections, the highest being yet evolved upon the earth' (Murray, 'Classical Humanism', in *Humanism*, pp. 9–14, at p. 9).
10 Most humanists follow Cicero in believing that 'we all have a share in reason and in the superiority by which we surpass the brute creatures'. See Cicero, *On Duties*, ed. M. T. Griffin and E. M. Atkins (Cambridge: Cambridge University Press, 1991), p. 42.
11 Kant speaks of 'the *dignity* of a rational being, who obeys no law other than that which he himself at the same time gives'. See Immanuel Kant, *Groundwork of the Metaphysics of Morals*, in *The Cambridge Edition of the Works of Immanuel Kant: Practical Philosophy*, ed. and trans. Mary J. Gregor (Cambridge: Cambridge University Press, 1996), p. 84.
12 Sartre, *Existentialism and Humanism*, p. 30.
13 *Ibid.*, p. 35.
14 Hilary Spurling, *The Girl from the Fiction Department: A Portrait of Sonia Orwell* (New York: Counterpoint, 2004), p. 77.
15 Sartre, *Existentialism and Humanism*, p. 46.

16 *Ibid.*, p. 32.
17 In the *German Ideology*, Marx certainly claimed to have 'shattered the basis of all morality'. See Karl Marx and Friedrich Engels, *Collected Works*, 50 vols (London: Lawrence and Wishart, 1975–2000), v, p. 419.
18 As Marx put it, 'all classes melt away before the solemn concept of "humanity"' (Marx and Engels, *Collected Works*, vi, p. 330).
19 Maurice Merleau-Ponty, *Humanism and Terror: The Communist Problem*, trans. John O'Neill (New York and London: Transaction, 2000), p. 179. For Marx's alleged anti-humanism, see Louis Althusser, 'Marxism and Humanism', in *For Marx*, trans. Ben Brewster (London: Verso, 1990), pp. 219–47.
20 On this point, see Norman Geras, *Marx and Human Nature* (London: Verso, 1983).
21 Gordon Comstock ridicules the epithet 'human' in *Keep the Aspidistra Flying* (*KAF*, p. 10); Orwell declares it meaningless in 'Politics and the English Language' (*CW*, 17, p. 425).
22 Christopher Norris, 'Language, Truth, and Ideology: Orwell and the Post-War Left', in Norris (ed.), *Inside the Myth – Orwell: Views from the Left* (London: Lawrence and Wishart, 1984), pp. 242–62, at p. 245.
23 Kant, *Groundwork of the Metaphysics of Morals*, p. 85.
24 Leon Trotsky, 'Moralists and Sycophants against Marxism', *The New International*, 5.8 (August 1939), pp. 229–33, at p. 233.
25 Trotsky, 'Moralists and Sycophants against Marxism', pp. 231–2.
26 On Trotsky's humanism, see Isaac Deutscher, *The Prophet: The Life of Leon Trotsky* (London: Verso, 2015). On the universalization of ethics as humanism, see Huxley, 'Scientific Humanism', in *Humanism*, pp. 3–8, at p. 5.
27 Leon Trotsky, 'Their Morals and Ours', *The New International*, 4.6 (1938), pp. 163–73, at p. 164.
28 Leon Trotsky, 'The Struggle for Cultured Speech', *Pravda* (16 May 1923). Published in Trotsky, *Problems in Everyday Life: And Other Writings* (New York: Pathfinder Press), pp. 65–70, at p. 65. In *Nineteen Eighty-Four*, we learn: 'Party members were supposed not to swear, and Winston himself very seldom did swear, aloud, at any rate' (*NEF*, p. 128).
29 Leon Trotsky, *The Defence of Terrorism: A Reply to Karl Kautsky* (London: Allen and Unwin, 1921), p. 60.
30 Kant, *Groundwork of the Metaphysics of Morals*, p. 85.
31 Jean-Jacques Rousseau, *The Discourses and Other Early Political Writings*, ed. Victor Gourevitch (Cambridge: Cambridge University Press, 1997), p. 153.
32 According to Rousseau, 'it is our common miseries which turn our hearts to humanity'. Jean-Jacques Rousseau, *Émile*, trans. Allan Bloom (London: Penguin, 1991), p. 221.
33 Martha C. Nussbaum, *Political Emotions: Why Love Matters for Justice* (Cambridge: Belknap Press, 2013), p. 182.
34 *Ibid.*, pp. 186, 141.
35 Immanuel Kant, *Critique of Practical Reason*, in *The Cambridge Edition of the Works of Immanuel Kant: Practical Philosophy*, p. 270.
36 Huxley, 'Scientific Humanism', in *Humanism*, p. 5.
37 Plato, *Theaetetus*, pp. 16–18.

38 On this point, see Bernard Williams, 'The Human Prejudice', in *Philosophy as a Humanistic Discipline*, ed. A. W. Moore (Princeton and Oxford: Princeton University Press, 2006), pp. 180–99.

39 Murray, 'Classical Humanism', p. 13.

40 According to Sartre, there is 'no human universe except the human universe, the universe of human subjectivity' (Sartre, *Existentialism and Humanism*, p. 67). This isn't hugely different from O'Brien's claim: 'Outside man there is nothing' (*NEF*, p. 278).

41 As Trotsky declared to the Thirteenth Party Congress: 'The party in the last analysis is always right [...]. One can be right only with the party and through the party, for history has not created any other way of determining what is right.' Quoted in Roy Medvedev, *Let History Judge: The Origins and Consequences of Stalinism* (New York: Columbia University Press, 1989), p. 187.

42 Richard Rorty, 'The Last Intellectual in Europe: Orwell on Cruelty', in *Contingency, Irony and Solidarity* (Cambridge: Cambridge University Press, 1989), pp. 169–88, at p. 176.

43 For a fuller account of this, see David Dwan, *Liberty, Equality and Humbug: Orwell's Political Ideals* (Oxford: Oxford University Press, 2018), pp. 139–68.

44 Norris, 'Language, Truth, and Ideology', p. 245.

45 Hannah Arendt, *The Human Condition*, ed. Margaret Canovan, 2nd edn (Chicago: University of Chicago Press, 1998), p. 158.

PART II

Histories

5

JONATHAN GREENBERG

Nineteen Eighty-Four and the Tradition of Satire

Nineteen Eighty-Four as Satire

Nineteen Eighty-Four (1949) is routinely described as a satire. But why? Satire is usually thought of as a mode of literature or art that uses comic techniques to ridicule and diminish its targets. Yet does any reader find Orwell's chilling vision of the future – a boot stamping on a human face forever (*NEF*, p. 280) – a rollicking good time? The novel's prevailing tone is not even darkly funny in the manner of a writer like Evelyn Waugh, whose bleak judgements are registered with amusement or even delight. If laughter is necessary for satire, *Nineteen Eighty-Four* hardly seems to qualify.

Animal Farm (1945), the novel Orwell completed just before *Nineteen Eighty-Four*, is a different story. It fits comfortably in the category of the beast fable or allegory, an ancient satiric form, and its comic reduction of human actors or social groups to talking barnyard animals has clear precedents in works like Geoffrey Chaucer's 'Nun's Priest's Tale'. In treating a weighty subject like the Russian Revolution through the simple form of a children's 'fairy story', Orwell's fable makes plain its didactic intent, while employing the fantasy, whimsy, and humour normally seen as components of satire. But while *Nineteen Eighty-Four* is pervaded with – even built upon – irony, it contains very little of the wry, playful spirit of *Animal Farm*. True, a reader like Anthony Burgess keenly perceives moments of black comedy in the book. He cites the weary Winston labouring through his morning calisthenics under the dour watch of the telescreen – a surveillance technique, he proposes, that Orwell adapted from Charlie Chaplin's silent comedy *Modern Times* (1936). But it's hard to consent to Burgess's broader judgement that 'Orwell's book is *essentially* a comic book' (Burgess, *1985*, p. 10).[1] It seems far more probable that the word *satire*, having fittingly been applied to *Animal Farm*, was then uncritically transferred to Orwell's follow-up, which shared its anti-communist theme.

Indeed, Orwell's publisher, Fredric Warburg, described *Nineteen Eighty-Four* as '*Animal Farm* writ large' (*CW*, 19, p. 479), and the dust jacket of the first American edition marketed Orwell as 'the author of *Animal Farm*', seeking to capitalize on the earlier book's success.

Yet it is not mere proximity to *Animal Farm* that makes *Nineteen Eighty-Four* a satire. After all, Orwell himself used the term, writing in his statement on the novel: 'I do not believe that the kind of society I describe necessarily will arrive, but I believe (allowing of course for the fact that the book is a satire) that something resembling it could arrive' (*CW*, 20, p. 136). An early reviewer, V. S. Pritchett, agreed, describing the novel as 'a satirical pamphlet'. Yet Pritchett also pointed out that the book lacks the 'irony and unnatural laughter' of satirists like Jonathan Swift and Voltaire. For Orwell, he said, 'hypocrisy is too dreadful for laughter: it feeds his despair'. But if the novel is not funny, then what makes it a satire? Pritchett's answer is a kind of grotesque exaggeration. 'The duty of the satirist', he writes, 'is to go one worse than reality.'[2] Orwell's statement on the novel similarly suggests that his satire consists in his deliberate departure from norms of realism.

If the primary feature of satire in *Nineteen Eighty-Four* is not laughter, then its primary motivation is not amusement. Instead, it is what Pritchett calls 'withering indignation'.[3] With this phrase, Pritchett locates Orwell in the tradition of satire called 'Juvenalian', after the poet-satirist who denounced the decadence of ancient Rome in a series of verses written around the beginning of the second century CE. 'Indignation will drive me to verse', Juvenal declares as he runs through a litany of complaints about a corrupt, unjust, dangerous, filthy metropolis; confronted with such evils, it is, he says, 'difficult *not* to write satire'.[4] A similar outrage often animates Orwell's writing, in *Nineteen Eighty-Four* and elsewhere. As Orwell himself testifies: 'My starting point is always a feeling of partisanship, a sense of injustice. [...] I write [my books] because there is some lie that I want to expose, some fact to which I want to draw attention' (*CW*, 18, p. 319).

Beyond its general tone of indignation, however, *Nineteen Eighty-Four* participates in a more specific satiric tradition, the genre of the literary dystopia.[5] *Dystopia*, from the Greek, means a bad or evil place, the opposite of a *utopia* (which means both 'no place' and a 'good place').[6] Most readers today are familiar with many of its common features: a near-future world of straitened economic or environmental conditions, a repressive government that relies on surveillance and violence, a population cowed into obedience and conformity, and, often, a small resistance whose actions drive the plot. These dystopian conditions, by their very existence in the world of the novel, offer an implicit satiric commentary on present-day circumstances. The dystopia says, in effect, that the conditions it envisions are already discernible in nascent form in reality. For this reason, critical quibbling about whether Orwell's book is best described as a 'warning', a 'prophecy', or a 'satire' is fruitless. It's all of the above.

But although many of the signal features of dystopia exist in *Nineteen Eighty-Four*, Orwell didn't use that term to describe his book. On the contrary, in February 1949 he described it to Julian Symons as 'a Utopia in the form of a novel' (*CW*, 20, p. 35). Of course, the word *dystopia* had not attained the currency in 1949 that it has today. It appears as early as 1747, but isn't used as a literary term until 1952, and doesn't enter the lexicon until the 1960s.[7] Yet even if Orwell had access to the term, his choice of *utopia* remains apt. For as an attentive reading of his novel makes clear, utopia and dystopia are closer in nature than common sense might suppose. A dystopia is often (if not always) a utopia as viewed by those who reject its values, or a utopia gone wrong.

The dystopia, at least in its canonical form, arises from intellectual, social, and technological developments initially thought to be progressive or utopian. As Irving Howe wrote: 'Not progress denied but progress realized is the nightmare haunting the anti-utopian novel.'[8] The dystopia, then, isn't exactly a utopia gone wrong; it's a utopia executed as planned, 'a future [the author] had been trained to desire'.[9] Yet it is simultaneously a future in which the costs of 'progress realized' prove impossible to bear. This reversal, the shift from hope to fear, is precisely the irony that constitutes the dystopia, and the reason that dystopias, though rarely comic, are fundamentally ironic in nature. Dystopia *is* an irony – it is a world that 'means' two opposing things at once. Orwell articulates this insight when he enunciates Oceania's slogans: 'WAR IS PEACE', 'FREEDOM IS SLAVERY', 'IGNORANCE IS STRENGTH' (*NEF*, p. 6).[10] These paradoxes are more than mere political lies; they are doublethink, and as Goldstein's *The Theory and Practice of Oligarchical Collectivism* explains, each contains a truth, albeit a perverse one.

Nineteen Eighty-Four makes explicit the link between dystopia and utopia that Howe observes. Goldstein's book notes that nineteenth-century socialism 'was still deeply infected by the Utopianism of past ages' but that 'from about 1900 onwards the aim of establishing liberty and equality was more and more openly abandoned' (*NEF*, p. 211). O'Brien goes further, boasting that Oceania is 'the exact opposite of the stupid hedonistic Utopias that the old reformers imagined' (*NEF*, p. 279). And in the appendix ('The Principles of Newspeak'), the narrator tells us that with the shift from 'Communist International' to 'Comintern', the Soviets 'narrowed and subtly altered' the meaning of the phrase, jettisoning the high ideals of 'universal human brotherhood' in favour of 'a tightly knit organisation and a well-defined body of doctrine' (*NEF*, p. 321). Whether because of the hypocrisy of its proponents or its own internal contradictions, utopian socialism has become its opposite.

Dystopian Satire: A Brief History

A comprehensive history of utopia and dystopia would begin with ancient myths of societies of peace and abundance such as the Garden of Eden in the Hebrew Bible, or the Golden Age of Saturn described by Hesiod and Ovid; it would surely include Socrates's description of a healthy *polis* in Plato's *Republic*. But the genre of utopia (as well as the word itself) can properly be said to begin in 1516 with Thomas More's *Utopia*, a fictional account of an Atlantic island whose society is free from the evils – greed, inequality, deceit, war – that riddle sixteenth-century Europe. More's book draws upon the ancient genres of the imaginary voyage and the philosophical dialogue – genres often described as *Menippean satire* since they target 'mental attitudes' rather than 'people as such'[11] – but it transforms these influences into a new literary type, combining political philosophy, satire, and prose fiction. Four centuries later, *Nineteen Eighty-Four* offers a similar amalgam, integrating long excerpts from Goldstein's book (which is so boring that Julia falls asleep as Winston reads it to her) and the appendix. These passages read like essays in political history and philosophy of language, yet they are (nominally) written about fictional entities.

More's utopia establishes a standard of perfection by which the reader can measure the fundamental madness of various European institutions, most centrally private property. Yet even More's foundational text hints at dystopian threats embedded in utopian ideals. The communist basis of the imagined society relies on a suppression of the individual self, and while there are no telescreens, we discern the beginnings of a surveillance state. 'Because they live in the full view of all', More writes, the Utopians 'are bound to be working at their usual trades or enjoying their leisure in a respectable way.'[12] Peace and prosperity are achieved through restrictive mechanisms of social control, and the utopian commonwealth only exists because of a founding act of violent conquest. More's imagined world indeed contains the basic paradoxes of Orwell's: violence is peace; freedom is conformity; docility is strength.

Jonathan Swift's *Gulliver's Travels* (1726) similarly presents itself as a true account of the author's journeys to distant lands, sometimes showing social practices that seem far preferable to those of Europe, at other times offering a comic rendition of the absurdities Gulliver has left behind. The talking horses ('Houyhnhnms') whom he encounters on his final voyage are utopian citizens 'wholly governed' by reason, embodying virtues such as strength, modesty, benevolence, cleanliness, and justice.[13] Conversely, the savage primates ('Yahoos') who share the island are dystopian monsters, embodying every imaginable vice: lust, greed, squalor, and selfishness. The perfection of the Houyhnhnms rebukes a debauched European society; the viciousness of the Yahoos reveals grotesque human flaws. Yet the Houyhnhnms themselves come to appear monstrous when they contemplate the extermination of the Yahoo race. Although they ultimately reject mass slaughter, deciding instead on mass castration, Utopia is maintained only through large-scale violence inflicted on the bodies of living beings to regulate their reproduction – an exercise of biopolitical power that foreshadows the importance of the state's control over sexuality in *Nineteen Eighty-Four*. On his return to England, Gulliver finds his wife and children as disgusting as the Yahoos left behind and favours the company of inarticulate horses. Where does this leave us? The rationality of the Houyhnhnms has proven cold and genocidal; the barbaric Yahoos are driven solely by lusts and appetites. Gulliver himself appears mad, yet his indictment of human society retains its satiric power.

Gulliver's Travels still stands at some distance from the literary dystopias of the twentieth century. In between lie not only influential literary and philosophical works, but also real-world historical efforts to put Enlightenment ideals into practice, including the ongoing collective struggles for emancipation on the part of the enslaved, the colonized, workers, women, Jews, and others. During these years, various strains of socialism (including but not limited to Marxism) emerge, and utopia starts to be seen as a socialist concept. The late nineteenth century sees a boom in utopian writing, the most influential texts being Edward Bellamy's *Looking Backward 2000–1887* (1888) and William Morris's *News from Nowhere* (1890). Compared to the works of More and Swift, however, these utopias offer little in the way of satire – neither the slippery ironies that undercut proffered ideals nor the withering indignation that animates the call for change.

Alongside this boom, however, a more satiric counter-tradition of anti-utopia arises. Samuel Butler's *Erewhon* (1872) includes a long passage, 'The Book of the Machines', which questions industrial and technological progress, suggesting that men are becoming slaves to the machines they invented. Jerome K. Jerome's sketch 'The New Utopia' (1891) – known to both H. G. Wells and Yevgeny Zamyatin – offers a gentle comic satire of the socialism of Bellamy and Morris in which the narrator journeys to a twenty-ninth-century society that has eradicated all potential sources of discord, including love, marriage, family, nature, art, and individual difference. In Wells's *The Time Machine* (1895), an inventor, himself a symbol of scientific progress, visits a future that seems to resemble an Edenic socialist utopia but turns out to be a dystopian state of nature in which evolution has split the human race into two species. One has descended from 'the favoured aristocracy', while the other, descended from 'their mechanical servants', now maintain their former masters as 'fatted cattle' to be consumed.[14]

But while these works, which we might call proto-dystopias, are responses, in some measure, to utopian socialism, the rise of dystopian fiction is also driven by the very socio-economic disruptions that motivate the utopian critique in the first place. Its satiric targets include mechanization and industrialization; the standardization and rationalization of production; technocracy, bureaucracy, utilitarianism, and other aspects of modern management; and eugenic thinking and biopolitics. Thus, as the canonical dystopia takes shape in the twentieth century, it must be seen as a reaction to both the modernizing forces of capitalism in the West and to the persistent expectation of a utopian socialist future, for which Wells (sometime dystopian science-fiction author) becomes the leading prophet.[15]

E. M. Forster, for example, described his story 'The Machine Stops' (1909) – another work that features the word *machine* in its title – as 'a reaction to one of the earlier heavens of H. G. Wells',[16] but it equally takes aim at what Tom Moylan calls 'a totalizing administration' of an 'emergent modernity'.[17] Forster's eponymous Machine is a great impersonal network that, while superficially tending to human needs, completely regulates and restrains all aspects of human experience, including love, sex, reproduction, and death. The humans of this future reside in underground hexagonal cells, interacting with other people only through video screens, and with nature not at all; 'it is we that are dying', says the dissident-protagonist, Kuno; 'the only thing that really lives is the Machine'.[18] The Machine has become identical with a Wellsian world state, indeed with modernity itself. In *Nineteen Eighty-Four*, the role of the Machine will go to the Party, a collective entity that similarly survives at the expense of autonomous human beings.

Yevgeny Zamyatin's *We* (1924), written in Lenin's USSR, similarly responds to socialist utopianism. But its attacks on standardization target not only Wells's socialism and Lenin's communism but also the industrial production strategies promulgated by the American engineer Frederick Winslow Taylor, who is described in the novel as 'the most brilliant of the Ancients'. *We* imagines a thoroughly collectivized, urbanized society in which human beings no longer have names but only numbers. Their lives are strictly governed by the state, under the leadership of a great 'Benefactor', supported by Wellsian 'Guardians'. People, or 'ciphers', live in apartments made of glass, subject to constant surveillance. A strict biopolitical regime prevails; the ciphers are permitted only brief periods of privacy for sex, which is regulated by a 'lex sexualis' according to which '[e]ach cipher has the right to any other cipher as sexual product'. Children are raised in factories; to conceive a child without a permit is a crime. A utilitarian ideology subordin-ates individual happiness to the collective good ('forget that you are a gram, and feel as though you are a millionth part of the ton'), reduces personal differences to a minimum ('being original is to violate equality'), and exalts mathematics as the highest ideal ('the multiplication table is wiser, more absolute than the ancient God').[19]

Zamyatin called his book 'a warning against the two-fold danger which threatens humanity: the hypertrophic power of the Machine and the hyper-trophic power of the State'.[20] To articulate this warning, he draws on the writings of Dostoevsky, whose *Notes from the Underground* (1864) lodges a protest against scientism and utilitarianism, which leave no space for human freedom. Dostoevsky's novel *The Brothers Karamazov* (1880), meanwhile, includes a famous parable in which Spain's Grand Inquisitor visits an imprisoned Jesus Christ and propounds the idea that freedom must be abolished for happiness to be achieved. This passage provides a template, both narrative and philosophical, for the climactic confrontation between D-503 and the Benefactor, as well as similar dialogues in Aldous Huxley's *Brave New World* (1932), Arthur Koestler's *Darkness at Noon* (1940), and of course *Nineteen Eighty-Four*. In many other ways, too, *We* directly influences *Nineteen Eighty-Four*. Like Winston, D-503 keeps a secret diary, and rebels sexually as well as intellectually and politically. He joins a resistance but is brought to heel by the state through violent measures. *We* even anticipates Orwell's image of the boot as a symbol of repression; a character tells D-503 that although Adam and Eve, at the behest of the Devil, erroneously chose freedom over happiness, this satanic freedom can be crushed: 'Our boot: on his head – crrunch! And there: paradise is restored.'[21]

Huxley called *Brave New World* a book about 'Wells's Utopia realized, and the absolute horror of it', and it follows *We* in rendering a future where a single technocratic world state promotes uniformity among its citizens.[22] The economy is centrally planned; marriage and family do not exist; the natural world and high culture are scorned. Henry Ford rather than Taylor is the revered figure of efficiency, but the same principles of standardization and mass production have infiltrated society, including the reproduction of the species: babies are produced on assembly lines. It has generally been read as an attack on American-style consumer capitalism rather than Soviet-style totalitarianism; Theodor Adorno called *Brave New World* 'a nightmare of endless doubles like that which the most recent phase of capitalism has spawned into everyday life', finding in it a satire of 'the standardized con-sciousness of millions'.[23] As in *We*, 'everyone belongs to everyone else' sexually, but Huxley envisions a system of excess, not repression, in which sanctioned promiscuity and orgies have the effect of mollifying the populace.

Thus the society lacks the emphasis on surveillance and torture that characterizes Oceania. The government instead controls the population through a combination of genetic engineering, behavioural conditioning, and a hedonist ethos that includes (in addition to the orgies) drugs, sports, and mass entertainment. 'The whole world has turned into a Riviera hotel' (*CW*, 12, p. 211), Orwell commented wryly.

Conventional wisdom holds that *We, Brave New World*, and *Nineteen Eighty-Four* make up a 'canonical dystopian trilogy',[24] but the years leading up to the writing of Orwell's book saw publication of many more now-forgotten titles available to readers. Not all were anti-socialist. An important influence on Orwell was Jack London's *The Iron Heel* (1907), sometimes claimed as the first dystopian novel.[25] It imagines the crushing of the socialist movement in the United States by a reactionary capitalist oligarchy. It is not a portrait of an established dystopian state in the manner of *Brave New World*, but a story about the struggle between socialism and fascism, reminiscent of Wells's futuristic adventure *The Sleeper Awakes*. As a specifically anti-fascist fantasy, it anticipates works from the 1930s such as Sinclair Lewis's *It Can't Happen Here* (1935) and Katharine Burdekin's *Swastika Night* (1937). It is in its formal methods, however, that London's book was most useful to Orwell. Set in the near-future United States, it uses footnotes ostensibly written centuries later to comment on the narrative, and, as in Orwell's book, this framing voice provides a hopeful perspective because it attests to a world in which the totalitarian system has been overcome. Orwell praised the novel, though his compliments are somewhat backhanded: comparing London to H. G. Wells, he said that London, though artless, had the advantage of an unconscious 'Fascist strain' (*CW*, 12, p. 212), a love of power and violence that gave him an intuitive understanding of the ruling class which Wells lacked.

A final influence on *Nineteen Eighty-Four* is Arthur Koestler's *Darkness at Noon*. The book is not set in the future and is not, properly speaking, a dystopia or even a satire but rather a political novel about the Moscow show trials of 1936 to 1938, during which Stalin's political enemies confessed under torture to trumped-up charges. It acquires an allegorical feel because it doesn't identify Stalin specifically, though the Russian names are something of a giveaway. Orwell dubbed this genre 'concentration camp literature': 'the special class of literature that has arisen out of the European political struggle since the rise of Fascism' (*CW*, 16, p. 392) and that analyses 'the special world created by secret police forces, censorship of opinion, torture and frame-up trials' (*CW*, 16, p. 393). Orwell found in Koestler, a Hungarian Jew and disillusioned member of the German Communist Party, a voice of moral integrity who took political writing beyond shallow polemic to approach tragedy. He also admired the keenness with which

Koestler understood the psychic effects of totalitarianism on the individual. In writing *Nineteen Eighty-Four*, Orwell fused elements of *Darkness at Noon* and *The Iron Heel* on to the dystopian template that Zamyatin and Huxley had established.

Orwell's Satiric Technique

As I noted at the start of this chapter, the satire of *Nineteen Eighty-Four* is not generally comic. At certain moments, however, a dark humour surfaces as Orwell's horror and despair give way to a bitter contempt. Such moments occur most frequently when Orwell directs his ire not at the totalitarian state but at less forbidding targets, notably British leftists. Indeed, *Nineteen Eighty-Four*'s mockery of the habits of the socialist intelligentsia is more characteristic of the comedy of manners than the dystopia.[26] Early in the novel, we get a satirical glimpse of the dreary social activities expected of Party members: 'Tonight was one of [Winston's] nights at the Community Centre. He wolfed another tasteless meal in the canteen, hurried off to the Centre, took part in the solemn foolery of a "discussion group", played two games of table tennis, swallowed several glasses of gin and sat for half an hour through a lecture entitled "Ingsoc in relation to chess"' (*NEF*, p. 115). The satire here is more social than political; a phrase like 'solemn foolery' indicates a vantage point outside the ruling ideology from which Orwell can target the posturing of the bourgeois Left. This is the same culture he mocks in 'Inside the Whale' (1940) when he describes the literary climate of England in the 1930s as 'a sort of Boy Scout atmosphere of bare knees and community singing' (*CW*, 12, p. 99).

A darker comic moment occurs in Section Three, when Parsons is brought in for the crime of muttering 'Down with Big Brother!' in his sleep. Winston asks Parsons whether he's guilty:

> 'Of course I'm guilty!' cried Parsons with a servile glance at the telescreen. 'You don't think the Party would arrest an innocent man, do you?' His froglike face grew calmer, and even took on a slightly sanctimonious expression. 'Thoughtcrime is a dreadful thing, old man', he said sententiously.
>
> (*NEF*, p. 245)

But even worse than Parsons's acceptance of his own guilt is his response when Winston asks who turned him in:

> 'It was my little daughter', said Parsons with a sort of doleful pride. 'She listened at the keyhole. Heard what I was saying and nipped off to the patrols the very next day. Pretty smart for a nipper of seven, eh?'   (*NEF*, p. 245)

Breaking up the bleakest section of the novel, this moment reads as a bit of comic relief. We can laugh at the 'servile' party member who takes pride in the daughter who has betrayed him in a way that we cannot laugh at Winston's own misery.

For the most part, however, the novel's satire focuses not on the social or moral failings of individual Party members but on the ideology and practices of the Party itself, which is the object not of scorn but of fear. Consequently, Orwell's prevailing method is not to poke fun, but to outline the conditions of Oceania in 1984 and imply their relevance to England in 1949. The satire registers not in bursts of laughter but in the slow narrative work of world building. Orwell uses various narrative techniques to do this work: Winston's thoughts, perceptions, and memories, conveyed through free indirect discourse; his conversations with Julia; his long interrogation by O'Brien; and the interpolated texts of Goldstein's book and the Newspeak appendix. Sometimes the conditions of the world are explained directly in expository prose, sometimes more indirectly and subtly.

Consider the famous first sentence: 'It was a bright cold day in April, and the clocks were striking thirteen' (*NEF*, p. 3). The disorienting surprise of 'thirteen' subtly signals that we are in an alternative reality, in the way that a science-fiction film might place a second sun in the sky to let us know we're not on Earth. Thirteen is an unlucky number, an odd number, a prime. Perhaps it indicates a shift to military time. More subtly still, a new way of measuring time might also allude to the calendar implemented during the French Revolution, which, in its efforts to reshape human society, dispensed with traditional systems of months, weeks, and hours in favour of a decimal system. From the first sentence, then, Orwell hints at a world in which utopian aspirations have distorted everyday experience.

Over the course of the novel, Orwell fills in the outline of the dystopia, allowing us to see how *Nineteen Eighty-Four* both continues and departs from its precursors. Orwell follows Forster, Zamyatin, and Huxley in satirizing the loss of the individual at the hands of the collective. As O'Brien says to Winston: 'Alone – free – the human being is always defeated. [...] But if he can make complete, utter submission, if he can escape from his identity, if he can merge himself in the Party so that he *is* the Party, then he is all-powerful and immortal' (*NEF*, p. 277). As in the earlier works, prohibitions on political dissent and even on great art and literature produce not only 'complete obedience to the will of the State' but also 'complete uniformity of opinion on all subjects' (*NEF*, p. 214). This control extends into reproduction and sexual life; human beings have become resources serving the collective. The nuclear family is intact, but it has become an instrument of the surveillance state, and O'Brien envisions a future more dire yet, when the final links between parents and children will be cut: 'Children will be taken from their mothers at birth, as one takes eggs from a hen' (*NEF*, p. 280). Sex, already a joyless duty between Winston and Katharine, will become, with the aid of state-sponsored neurology, devoid of physical pleasure.

As Julia explains to Winston, state control over sex is part of a greater ambition to control the entire interior affective life. Julia understands that 'the sex instinct created a world of its own which was outside the Party's control', and which, by creating an interior space of freedom, poses a threat to collectivism. Moreover, unsatisfied sexual feelings can then 'be transformed into war-fever and leader-worship' (*NEF*, p. 139). In this regard, too, *Nineteen Eighty-Four* aligns with previous dystopias in recognizing the role of the state in creating collective rituals that stoke public emotion (e.g. Hate Week) and buttress the cult of personality. But Orwell, more keenly than any of his major precursors, recognizes what he called (in a 1946 review of *We*) 'the irrational side of totalitarianism' (*CW*, 18, p. 15), its harnessing of atavistic, unconscious sexual and aggressive drives. For Orwell, who has absorbed the lessons of Freud, the rational Houyhnhnm always has a violent Yahoo within.

But Orwell departs from his predecessors in important ways. His dystopia envisions not a single Wellsian world state but a fractured Cold War world with three superpowers engaged in a perpetual standoff. Unlike his precursors, he's largely unconcerned with technology as a dystopian force; far more threatening than the telescreens are the low-tech methods of the Thought Police and the use of citizens to monitor each other. Nor is the efficient, utilitarian state, deploying the management techniques of Taylor and Ford, a primary target. After all, '[n]othing is efficient in Oceania except the Thought Police' (*NEF*, p. 206); the shortages of basic goods and the terrible quality of gin affirm that the state has relinquished the aspirations of Forster's or Huxley's dystopias to meet people's material needs. (A version of Huxley's hedonistic dystopia does survive in the world of the Proles, who are not indoctrinated but instead placated with alcohol, pornography, and popular music.) The outdated socialist ideal of equality has been abandoned, revealing the Party's true aim as the consolidation of power. Brutality, which earlier regimes justified as a regrettable means to an end, is now an end in itself. Thus, although Orwell borrows from Dostoevsky (via Zamyatin) when he has Winston assert, *'Freedom is the freedom to say that two plus two make four'* (*NEF*, p. 84), he is actually reversing the terms of Dostoevsky's critique. For Dostoevsky, freedom means the freedom to be eccentrically wrong, freedom from the ruthless rule of mathematics. For Orwell it means the freedom to be mathematically correct, to hold to an objective truth that is beyond the power of the Party to rewrite.[27]

Finally, two developments seem to be special concerns of Orwell. The first is the (mis)use of language for political purposes, a topic also examined in one of Orwell's most-read essays, 'Politics and the English Language' (1946). To be sure, utopia and dystopia have long been concerned with language, its use and misuse, how it shapes and reflects human thought and society. Swift's Houyhnhnms lack a word for lying or falsehood, and when Gulliver describes various outrageous features of English society, his dubious Houyhnhnm master assumes that Gulliver has said 'the thing which is not'. The lack of a word for lying reflects the utter honesty of the equine species. In Gulliver's England, however, lying is a common practice, and when he describes lawyers – a professional class unthinkable in the Houyhnhnms' utopia – he is thrown back upon the most basic language: 'there was a society of men among us, bred up from their youth in the art of proving, by words multiplied for the purpose, that white is black, and black is white, according as they are paid'.[28]

Readers of *Nineteen Eighty-Four* will recall the importance of the Newspeak word *blackwhite*:

> Like so many Newspeak words, this word has two mutually contradictory meanings. Applied to an opponent, it means the habit of impudently claiming that black is white, in contradiction of the plain facts. Applied to a Party member, it means a loyal willingness to say that black is white when Party discipline demands this. (*NEF*, p. 221)

This fear – that language can be manipulated to turn reality upside down, to convince people that black is white – is an ancient one, going back to Plato's attacks on Protagoras and the Sophists. Satirists deploy it across the centuries: Juvenal lashes out at builders who secure contracts 'by swearing black is white', while Jane Austen's villain Lady Susan uses her 'command of Language [...] to make Black appear White'.[29] Nonetheless, Orwell was sensitive to a new kind of mid-century bureaucratic speech, parodied as Newspeak, designed to cover over violence. He feared that the proliferation and acceptance of such language would enfeeble human thought, curtailing dissent and resistance. It is more than historical accident that in 1949, the year of the book's publication, the United States replaced its Department of War with a Department of Defense.[30] And it was almost 1984 when the Reagan administration first tested an inter-continental ballistic missile paradoxically named the 'Peacekeeper'. It is appropriate, then, that Orwell, the diagnostician of political language, himself created words and phrases – *doublethink*, *Thought Police*, *Big Brother* – that have become as essential to our political discourse as Thomas More's coinage *utopia*. That we rely on Orwell's neologisms attests to the relevance of his analysis to our current moment.

Yet the debasement of language is ultimately just a symptom of a greater threat, the power of governments to obliterate history and indeed reality itself. This threat is obvious enough to any reader of *Nineteen Eighty-Four*; because human beings are mortal and memory is fragile – as Winston's conversation with the old man in the pub illustrates – only written history can counter the flood of false information put out by a totalitarian state that fully controls the mass media. Forster hints at distortion of reality by emphasizing the degradation of experience and the stigmatization of new ideas; Zamyatin's hero is forced to undergo a 'fantasiectomy' to remove his imaginative faculties; Huxley's brave new worlders follow Henry Ford in believing that history is bunk. But in Orwell's imagined future, the manipulation of past and present reality reaches extremes his precursors do not imagine. Writing after Hitler and Stalin, he confronts the malleability of the past with a new urgency and indignation. This indignation, directed at ideologues and sadists who obliterate history so that the Party can keep its grip on power, makes it impossible for Orwell not to write satire.

Notes

1 Chaplin is mentioned at p. 12.
2 V. S. Pritchett, 'The Most Honest Writer Alive', *The New Statesman*, 18 June 1949 [reprinted at www.newstatesman.com/books/2009/06/orwell-eighty-thought-party] (accessed 15 October 2019).
3 *Ibid.*
4 Juvenal, *The Sixteen Satires*, trans. Peter Green (London: Penguin, 1998), pp. 5, 4.
5 I will use *anti-utopia* broadly, to describe a work that critiques a utopian project or utopian thinking, reserving *dystopia* for those fictional works that comprehensively imagine an arrangement of society that leads to human misery. More narrowly still, *canonical dystopia* will refer to novels such as Yevgeny Zamyatin's *We* (1924), Aldous Huxley's *Brave New World* (1932), and *Nineteen Eighty-Four*, in which the dystopian society is established and its dystopian nature is the novel's main theme.
6 From Thomas More's first usage, the word has played on both meanings: the Greek *outopia* means 'no place', while *eutopia* means a good or happy place. A utopia is thus an ideal society but also a non-existent one.
7 Gregory Claeys, *Dystopia: A Natural History* (Oxford: Oxford University Press, 2017), p. 274.
8 Irving Howe, 'The Fiction of Anti-Utopia', *The New Republic* (23 April 1962), pp. 13–16, at p. 14.
9 *Ibid.*, p. 13.

10 *Animal Farm*'s signature slogan relies on the same literary device of paradox: 'ALL ANIMALS ARE EQUAL BUT SOME ANIMALS ARE MORE EQUAL THAN OTHERS' (*AF*, p. 97).

11 Northrop Frye, *Anatomy of Criticism: Four Essays* (Princeton, NJ: Princeton University Press, 1957), p. 309.

12 Thomas More, *Utopia* (1516), trans. Robert M. Adams (New York: W. W. Norton, 2010), p. 53.

13 Jonathan Swift, *Gulliver's Travels* (1726), ed. Christopher Fox (Boston: Bedford/ St. Martin's, 1995), p. 242.

14 H. G. Wells, *The Time Machine* (1895), ed. Roger Luckhurst (Oxford: Oxford University Press, 2017), pp. 55, 59.

15 'British intellectuals largely ignored the earlier Wells, to concentrate their fire on the later propagandist of the world-state' (Krishan Kumar, *Utopia and Anti-Utopia in Modern Times* (Oxford: Basil Blackwell, 1987), p. 205).

16 E. M. Forster, *Collected Short Stories* (Harmondsworth: Penguin, 1954), p. 6.

17 Tom Moylan, *Scraps of the Untainted Sky: Science Fiction, Utopia, Dystopia* (Oxford: Westview Press, 2001), p. 111.

18 Forster, 'The Machine Stops' (1909), in *Collected Short Stories*, pp. 109–46, at p. 131.

19 Yevgeny Zamyatin, *We* (1924), trans. Natasha Randall (New York: The Modern Library, 2006), pp. 102, 27, 59.

20 Kumar, *Utopia and Anti-Utopia in Modern Times*, p. 229.

21 Zamyatin, *We*, p. 55.

22 Aldous Huxley to Sydney Schiff (7 May 1931), in *Selected Letters of Aldous Huxley*, ed. James Sexton (Chicago: Ivan R. Dee, 2007), p. 255.

23 Theodor W. Adorno, 'Aldous Huxley and Utopia' (1942), in *Prisms*, trans. Shierry Weber Nicholsen and Samuel Weber (1955; Cambridge, MA: MIT Press, 1967), pp. 95–118, at p. 98.

24 Fredric Jameson, *Archaeologies of the Future: The Desire Called Utopia and Other Science Fictions* (London: Verso, 2007), p. 202.

25 Claeys, *Dystopia*, p. 332.

26 On this distinction, see Jonathan Greenberg, *The Cambridge Introduction to Satire* (Cambridge: Cambridge University Press, 2019).

27 Adrian Wanner, 'The Underground Man as Big Brother: Dostoevsky's and Orwell's Anti-Utopia', *Utopian Studies*, 8.1 (1997), pp. 77–88, at p. 81.

28 Swift, *Gulliver's Travels*, p. 227.

29 Juvenal, *The Sixteen Satires*, p. 15; Jane Austen, *Northanger Abbey, Lady Susan, The Watsons, and Sanditon*, ed. James Kinsley and John Davie, introd. Claudia L. Johnson (Oxford: Oxford University Press, 2003), p. 198.

30 Thomas Pynchon notes the Orwellian nature of the phrase 'Department of Defense' in his 'Introduction' to the 2003 Penguin edition of *Nineteen Eighty-Four* (see George Orwell, *Nineteen Eighty-Four* (1949; London: Penguin, 2003), p. xi).

6

LISA MULLEN

Orwell's Literary Context: Modernism, Language, and Politics

'It is an instructive book; there is a good deal of What Every Young Person Ought to Know – not in 1984, but 1949.'[1] *The Guardian*'s first review was clear in its priorities: Orwell's novel was a source of wisdom and warning, which must be urgently attended; if it happened to be 'brilliantly constructed and told', these qualities were instrumental to the novel's communication of its message. Yet Orwell was a writer to his bones, a connoisseur of language and style who considered the effect of every word and paragraph. Even in his most scrappy hack work – the quickie book reviews, op-eds, and colour pieces which paid the rent for much of his career – his voice is unmistakable. In 'Why I Write', an essay he wrote in 1946 just as he began work on *Nineteen Eighty-Four* (1949), Orwell declared that 'what I have most wanted to do throughout the past ten years is to make political writing into an art' (CW, 18, p. 319). The premise of this chapter is that we should take his stated ambition seriously, and consider the literary merit of the novel on its own terms, as an essential component of its enduring power, and not an incidental corollary of it.

In his recent study of Orwell's non-fiction style, Alex Woloch has laid out the case that Orwell's ideal of a perfect fusion of politics and aesthetics always (and perhaps inevitably) eluded him, so that his 'political desire, precisely as it is unfulfilled, generates a compulsive and sustained attachment to the praxis of writing itself'.[2] What this chapter will consider is how this attachment plays out in Orwell's final novel, and how his conscious intention of yoking art to politics may be contextualized in relation to the literary problems and practices of his precursors and contemporaries. In order to do so, we will look first at his relationship with literary modernism and its legacies, and examine how he understood the 'praxis of writing' to be at work in authors such as James Joyce and Henry Miller; we will then consider *Nineteen Eighty-Four* as a response to earlier dystopian and speculative fiction; and finally, we will assess depictions of writing and the politics of language within the novel itself, and how their treatment might relate to Orwell's sense of his place within twentieth-century literature.

Orwell's most sustained analysis of the literary context in which he was writing is contained in his essay 'Inside the Whale'. This was written in 1940, a key year, as we shall see, in the development of Orwell's attitude to political writing, which he elaborated in a number of important book reviews written in response to the urgency of the Second World War. 'Inside the Whale' was ostensibly an analysis of Henry Miller's 1934 novel *Tropic of Cancer*, but it was really an opportunity for Orwell to discourse on recent developments in literature more generally, and it lays out some principles which have a bearing on the intentions and processes which led him away from the realist style of his earlier novels, and towards the allegorical manner of *Animal Farm* and *Nineteen Eighty-Four*. The responsibility (or otherwise) of a writer to engage with politics is one of the essay's major themes: Orwell notes that Miller, writing as an expat in Paris who is concerned only with the textures and impressions of a particular time and place, excuses himself from any obligation to reflect on the issues of the day. In this, he sees an affinity between Miller and what Orwell calls 'the Joyce-Eliot school' – a group we might now refer to as the high modernists; as Orwell describes it, this style of writing drenches the reader in an exhilarating stream of everyday details, personal impressions, and minutely drawn observations, but elides the larger questions of the public sphere.[3] 'What is noticeable about all these writers', Orwell says, 'is that what "purpose" they have is very much up in the air. There is no attention to the urgent problems of the moment, above all no politics in the narrower sense. Our eyes are directed to Rome, to Byzantium, to Montparnasse, to Mexico, to the Etruscans, to the Subconscious, to the solar plexus – to everywhere except the places where things are actually happening. When one looks back at the 'twenties, nothing is queerer than the way in which every important event in Europe escaped the notice of the English intelligentsia' (*CW*, 12, p. 97).

Thus, his praise of Miller as a writer who delivers above all a sense of somatic satisfaction through the power of his words is hedged within an implied critique of the glibness entailed by this sensuous pact with the reader: *Tropic of Cancer* is the 'book of a man who is happy' (*CW*, 12, p. 90), a man who accepts the *status quo* and is untroubled by political urges. Miller's approach will not pass muster, Orwell implies, in the 1940s:

> To say 'I accept' in an age like our own is to say that you accept concentration-camps, rubber truncheons, Hitler, Stalin, bombs, aeroplanes, tinned food, machine-guns, putsches, purges, slogans, Bedaux belts, gas-masks, submarines, spies, provocateurs, press-censorship, secret prisons, aspirins, Hollywood films and political murders. [...] [I]n general the attitude is 'Let's swallow it whole'. [...] To accept civilisation *as it is* practically means accepting decay.
>
> (*CW*, 12, p. 91)

Orwell was an expert proponent of the withering list, and the eccentricity of this one, which appears to put aspirins and Charlie Chaplin on a par with Hitler and machine guns, should not distract us from the fervour of his main point: to consent to any of it is, according to Orwell, to consent to an entire system of moral bankruptcy and despotism: to swallow is *to be swallowed*. 'Of course', he concedes, 'a novelist is not obliged to write directly about contemporary history, but a novelist who simply disregards the major public events of the moment is generally either a footler or a plain idiot' (*CW*, 12, p. 87).

By the time he was working in earnest on *Nineteen Eighty-Four* six years later, Orwell had turned up the dial on this viewpoint considerably: the appeal of a Miller-esque immersion in the shallow detail and affect of the everyday had not only receded, it had become an attitude to be satirized, and he does so forcefully in his depiction of the easily met emotional needs of the facile citizens of Oceania, who happily consume, with obedient equanimity, all kinds of machine-made popular culture, bouts of vapid flag-waving, and the all-purpose catharsis of the Two Minutes Hate. In contrast, Orwell's novel offers little in the way of conceptual resting places for the brutality-fatigued reader: just as Winston Smith tries in vain to carve out for himself a shallow sanctuary – an alcove in his flat, a clearing in an isolated piece of woodland, a room above a junk shop – from the watchful eye of Big Brother, so the reader ducks hopefully into Winston's dreams, his memories, his revolutionary stirrings, his desires and longings, only to find the Thought Police have not only got there first, but have been there all along.

Nevertheless, in framing his dystopia, Orwell had an agenda which was fundamentally optimistic: his purpose was not simply to reflect past atrocity or predict future iterations of it, but to circumvent its inevitability by projecting an alternative perspective which might be reverse-engineered from the contours of his nightmare. In this, he was engaging consciously with a line of genre writing which had its roots in utopian fictions such as Richard Jefferies's *After London; Or, Wild England* (1885), Edward Bellamy's *Looking Backward: 2000–1887* (1888), and William Morris's *News from Nowhere* (1890). The sense of a lurching dislocation in time and space, which makes the opening of *Nineteen Eighty-Four* so disconcerting, can be traced back to these earlier examples. Morris, like Orwell, had taken the real geography of London as his novel's geographical blueprint; but while Morris imagined an idyllically reforested 'Kensington Gardens' where children would be allowed to run free, and to learn through experiment and play, Orwell's London has grown shabbier and more bomb-blasted than it was even in Orwell's time. While Morris's city park blossoms into a scene of prelapsarian innocence, in *Nineteen Eighty-Four*, St Clement Danes church cycles through a range of heavily mediated half meanings: it exists as an antique etching, a snatch of a nursery rhyme, and a shibboleth of dissident memory. In Morris, the architecture of the British Museum and the Houses of Parliament persists as a shell of form into which new content can be decanted (the museum houses an archive of the revolution; Parliament is put to use as a dung-heap), but Orwell counters this essentially reactionary dependence on cultural familiarity by overlaying London with vast, invented ziggurats of concrete: the ministries which soar over the cityscape, disciplining both the space and the discourse of the city.

A more convincing analogue for Orwell's emphasis on spatial discipline is perhaps found in E. M. Forster's short story 'The Machine Stops' (1909). Here, an underground culture in which individuals are confined within a honeycomb of tunnels signifies the end of autonomous individuality. All the necessities of life, from food and drink to entertainment and social interaction, are supplied by an inhuman entity known as 'The Machine' and delivered via a system of tubes to an irritable and overwhelmed population. These isolated cell-dwellers emerge into the light only occasionally, and experience the surface of the earth only from above, on long-distance journeys by airship. In the story's bitter denouement, the world is pitched into chaos when the Machine malfunctions; the main characters are crushed beneath the airships, which plunge to the ground in the absence of the Machine's disciplinary guidance: the verticality of the utopian perspective, which confers an automatic and unthought quality to cultural interactions and habitual forms of knowledge, ultimately wreaks havoc and devastation.

In the aftermath of the First World War, and with the rise of fascism in the 1920s and 1930s, the utopian genre took a yet darker turn. Although there is no evidence that Orwell read them, two dystopian precursors, written by women, are of particular note: Katharine Burdekin's *Swastika Night* (published under the pseudonym Murray Constantine in 1937) and Storm Jameson's *In the Second Year* (1936).[4] Burdekin's novel is set seven centuries after the victorious ascent of Nazism, and focuses its political lens on the position of women in the new world order. Stripped of their humanity, coerced into shaven-headed herds, and useful only as breeding stock, these women are symbols of the uglification of humanity under fascism: the grim flipside of Nazism's Manichaean mythology, which has evolved by this time into a full-blown religion complete with an origin story about a golden-haired Hitler springing fully formed from the head of a god. For Jameson, too, fascism is a question of misdirected faith or superstition. *In the Second Year* extrapolates from the rise of Hitler in Germany to imagine an English brand of fascism taking hold only a few years into the future, thanks to the opportunism of an ideologue named Frank Hillier, who understands that '[p]eople wanted to believe. More than they wanted anything, they wanted belief. [...] He promised all of them what they wanted, and in their revulsion from despair and the cynicism of despair they never asked themselves if he were more able than others to give it to them.'[5] Hillier's brand of fascism, which pretends to be an answer to cynicism, is itself entirely cynical; it is ambition enabled by bureaucracy and amplified by process: politics at its most mechanical. In a sense, the novel's main purpose is to remonstrate against quietism and the assumption that an unexamined, instinctive liberal-ism suffices as a notional default to which British culture must inevitably revert.

Another writer, Rex Warner, pursued a similar theme in three semi-dystopian novels published between 1937 and 1941: *The Wild Goose Chase* (1937) outlines the overthrow of a tyrannical regime by means of a quasi-Marxist rebellion; *The Professor* (1938) exposes the insufficiency of academic liberalism when confronted with the uncompromising forces of repression; and *The Aerodrome* (1941) pitches the cyborgian logic of air war – with its uncanny fusion of man and machine – against a romantic ideal of rural harmony and cyclical temporality. What Warner, in addition to Burdekin and Jameson, offers is a conceptual structure which contrasts a bad set of fascistic or tyrannical values with a recognizably humane alter-native, instantiated conceptually via political theory, psychologically via personal memory of the before-times, or (in the case of Burdekin) via the textual truth of a dissident book, passed from hand to hand in secret. This binary conceptualization of dystopia was a legacy of Wells and Morris, but it was informed by a political agenda which Orwell would come to consider simplistic. Indeed, *Nineteen Eighty-Four* explicitly denies Winston access to the remedies propounded in these precursor novels: authentic memory is impossible when history itself can be erased and rewritten in an instant, and both Goldstein's book, and the theory it purports to contain, turn out to be the invention of O'Brien and his fellow Inner Party autocrats.

In 1940, the reprinting of Jack London's *The Iron Heel* (1908) prompted Orwell to write a review in *Tribune* (CW, 12, pp. 210–13) which compared this novel to three other dystopian works: Aldous Huxley's *Brave New World* (1932), H. G. Wells's *When the Sleeper Wakes: A Story of the Years to Come* (1899), and the now largely forgotten *The Secret of the League* by Ernest Bramah (1907).[6] Orwell's relationship with Wells's fiction is considered in more detail in Chapter 7 of this volume; it is enough here to mention that, despite the vivid style and emotional impact of Wells's novel, Orwell felt that it lacked something which London's 'hugely inferior' work achieved. '[B]ecause of his own streak of savagery London could grasp something that Wells apparently could not,' Orwell writes, 'and that is that hedonistic societies do not endure' (*CW*, 12, p. 211). Huxley, in Orwell's view, writes a 'parody of the Wellsian Utopia' which exaggerates the 'soft, cynical and faithless' tendencies of a pampered upper caste, and is thus even less adequate to the task of extrapolating future dangers from the desperate present. 'Here the hedonistic principle is pushed to its utmost, the whole world has turned into a Riviera hotel. But though *Brave New World* was a brilliant caricature of the present (the present of 1930), it probably casts no light on the future. No society of that kind would last more than a couple of generations' (*CW*, 12, p. 211).

For Orwell, Jack London's advantage resided in his tendency towards a fascistic mindset – based on his 'love of violence and physical strength, his belief in "natural aristocracy," his animal-worship and exaltation of the primitive' – which enabled him to understand the likely consequence of any move to detach the ruling classes from their accustomed privilege (*CW*, 12, pp. 211–12). Socialist writers, in contrast, are too 'mechanistic' in their understanding of history and their assumption of a Marxist dogma which stipulates that the contradictions of capitalism must eventually lead to its destruction. As far as Orwell is concerned, only one dystopia comes close to anticipating the potential backlash to this idea, because it is written from the point of view, not of populism and demagoguery, but of the self-interested bourgeoisie themselves. He resurrects Bramah's *The Secret of the League* as an example of how a basically 'decent and kindly writer' could nevertheless relish 'the crushing of the proletariat' in a novel about a dissident group of wealthy conspirators who use their purchasing power and economic savvy, via a plot about coal and oil, to overthrow a Labour government (*CW*, 12, p. 213). They are motivated, Orwell stresses, by the sense that their hazily defined but talismanic 'way of life', rather than mere financial advantage, is under threat. Once again, Orwell is making the point that a pragmatic approach to human irrationality, and not a materialist system of historical cause and effect, is the basis of (and by implication the solution to) fascism and totalitarianism.

In an earlier 1940 essay, 'Notes on the Way', Orwell – inspired by Malcolm Muggeridge's 'brilliant and depressing' book *The Thirties* (1940) – had argued that literature was emerging from 'a long period during which nearly every thinking man was in some sense a rebel, and usually a quite irresponsible rebel' (*CW*, 12, p. 124).[7] Citing Gibbon, Voltaire, Rousseau, Shelley, Byron, Dickens, Stendhal, Samuel Butler, Ibsen, Zola, Flaubert, Shaw, and Joyce as all 'in one way or another [...] destroyers, wreckers, saboteurs', he likens this oppositional mindset to a process of sawing away at a branch you are sitting on:

> For two hundred years we had sawed and sawed and sawed [...]. And in the end, much more suddenly than anyone had foreseen, our efforts were rewarded, and down we came. But unfortunately there had been a little mistake. The thing at the bottom was not a bed of roses after all, it was a cesspool full of barbed wire. (*CW*, 12, p. 124)

The essay coalesces into an attack on the idea that realism offers a way out of the horrors of the modern world; men are motivated by 'abstractions' like patriotism, but '[a]ll that this really means is that they are aware of some organism greater than themselves, stretching into the future and the past, within which they feel themselves to be immortal' (*CW*, 12, pp. 125–6). The answer is not more realism, but a better kind of enchantment: 'A very slight increase of consciousness, and their sense of loyalty could be transferred to humanity itself, which is not an abstraction' (*CW*, 12, p. 126). In a curious anticipation of Theodor Adorno and Max Horkheimer's *Dialectic of Enlightenment*, Orwell is calling here for a truly radical solution to the problems of a scientific, post-religious modern era.[8] Huxley's *Brave New World* – again referred to as a 'good caricature of the hedonistic Utopia' – fails to predict the future because it ignores the necessity of 'reinstat[ing] the belief in human brotherhood, without the need for a "next world" to give it meaning' (*CW*, 12, p. 126). He ends the essay by returning to Marx's famous adage about religion and opium, noting that it is often misunderstood as meaning that religion serves no purpose and has no political content. 'What is [Marx] saying except that man does *not* live by bread alone', Orwell asks, 'that hatred is *not* enough, that a world worth living in cannot be founded on "realism" and machine guns?' (*CW*, 12, p. 126).

Orwell's turn away from literary realism in the 1940s was connected to this instinctive suspicion of socialist realism. In 1940, Orwell had not yet read Yevgeny Zamyatin's *We*, first published in English in 1924; indeed he did not read it until 1945, although he had learned of it a year earlier from Gleb Struve's *Twenty-Five Years of Soviet Russian Literature* (see *CW*, 16, p. 99). The stark difference between Orwell's earlier vision of a politically constructive form of speculative literature and the desolate pessimism of *Nineteen Eighty-Four* can arguably be attributed in part to the influence of Zamyatin; like *Nineteen Eighty-Four*, *We* critiques the idea of Soviet socialism, not by pointing out its misunderstanding of human nature, but by positing a nightmare society where human nature is outlawed altogether: the nexus of motivational beliefs, abstract or not, which agitated Orwell so much in 1940 become abruptly irrelevant in a world where privacy and person-hood are forbidden. All the same, certain key differences between *We* and *Nineteen Eighty-Four* demonstrate Orwell's greater philosophical, as well as literary, sophistication. While Orwell describes a grimy metropolis brought to its knees by a looming, top-down surveillance state, Zamyatin's glassy suburbia was premised on ideals of mutual openness and communal scrutiny: 'we live in broad daylight inside these walls that seem to have been fashioned out of bright air, always on view', the narrator of *We* records. 'We have nothing to hide from one another.'[9] In Airstrip One, the idea of a 'glittering antiseptic world of glass and steel and snow-white concrete' is – according to Goldstein's book – already a superannuated dreamscape, a vision of a future which will never come to pass (*NEF*, p. 196). The sheer exhaustion and squalor of Winston Smith's London, with its bombsites and boilersuits, its canteen slop and boiled-cabbage smells, set it apart from its predecessors, and point to a different calibration of Orwell's political and moral aims as a writer.

In order to understand Orwell's position, we must recall the distinction between utopian writers inspired by Morris, who were informed by a Marxian eschatology of capital, and the inter-war dystopian novels by Zamyatin, Huxley, Warner, and Burdekin, which tended to centre collectivism and technophilia as the essential precursors of modern oppression. Orwell was just as interested in how ideological rigidity could suppress or supplant humanity and free will, but technology and mechanization are less politically and morally central to *Nineteen Eighty-Four* than they were either to Zamyatin's novel, or even to Orwell's own earlier accounts of the dangers of modernity and progress, such as the long diatribes against tinned food and the factory mindset in *The Road to Wigan Pier* (1937; see for instance *RWP*, pp. 173–201), or George Bowling's nauseated recoil from 'shininess and streamlining' in *Coming Up for Air* (1939; *CUFA*, p. 22). In *Nineteen Eighty-Four*, the material technology of surveillance ineluctably defines the dominant culture of the Party, but it fails to encompass the disorderly Proles, to give one example, and it serves a political purpose which is itself messy, inarticulate, and fundamentally irrational. In Oceania, oppression does not arise from mechanized thinking which mirrors a sleekly efficient set of social parameters and norms. The real danger lies in the flesh-and-blood operatives who consume the citizens' technologically mediated outputs – members of the Thought Police who are all too human in their lust for power for its own sake. O'Brien – the initially blank apparatchik who morphs slowly from rebel ally, to agent provocateur, and finally to torturer as Winston's downfall achieves terminal momentum – becomes more and more human as his evil expresses itself. For O'Brien, and for Orwell, the idea of power as a motivator is the opposite of mechanistic; as David Dwan has noted in his recent study of Orwell's political philosophy, far from being *about* mathematical logic, the Big Brother doctrine in fact expressly *forbids* any recourse to scientific empiricism, by insisting that two plus two might or might not equal five, according to expediency or mere whim.[10]

The conversations between Winston Smith and O'Brien in the final section of *Nineteen Eighty-Four* resonate more clearly with another book Orwell greatly admired: Arthur Koestler's *Darkness at Noon* (1940). Based on the 1936 to 1938 Moscow show trials, this thinly disguised allegory depicts a society governed by a nonsensical adherence to rigid ideology, and it outlines an argument about propaganda and injustice which exercised Orwell from *Homage to Catalonia* (1938) onwards. Orwell's review of Koestler's novel suggests that its plot about trumped-up charges, torture, confession, and execution merely 'follow[s] the normal course'; its 'whole interest', he states, centres on the 'intellectual struggle' between the man on trial, Rubashov, and his two accusers (*CW*, 12, p. 358). The older of these two, Ivanov, is relatively humane and pragmatic. He argues that Rubashov's guilt or innocence is simply irrelevant; he just ought to confess to murder for the good of the revolutionary project and the stability of society. The younger man, Gletkin, is more sinister. He has grown up under the regime of the party and knows nothing else; he suggests that Rubashov's deviation from official doctrine is *identical* to the crime of murder: he should therefore confess because he *is* guilty, despite the fact that he has empirically committed no crime. 'Gletkin's strength', Orwell writes, 'lies in the complete severance from the past, which leaves him not only without pity but without imagination or inconvenient knowledge' (*CW*, 12, p. 358). There are echoes here, not only of O'Brien's weaponization of bad history and circular logic, but also something of Julia's numbed, second-generation internalization of the prevailing ideology of the Party, which renders her immune to the kind of existential panic which consumes Winston. Orwell notes Koestler's introduction of an even more pragmatic normalization at the end of the novel, in the character of 'a young girl in whose house Rubashov has once lodged' who 'wonder[s] whether to denounce her father to the Secret Police as a way of securing a flat for herself and her future husband' (*CW*, 12, p. 358). The effect of this attrition of decency and morality is to render Rubashov incapable of resistance. When he gives in, Orwell writes, 'it is not because of the torture [...] so much as from complete inner emptiness' (*CW*, 12, pp. 358–9). In the end, he is, like the self-deceiving Winston, effectively complicit in his own downfall: 'Any right to protest against torture, secret prisons, organised lying and so forth he has long since forfeited. He recognises that what is now happening is the consequence of his own acts – even feels a sort of admiration for Gletkin, as the kind of subhuman being probably needed to guide the Revolution through its present stage' (CW, 12, p. 359). In effect, Rubashov loves Big Brother.

The cataclysmic impact of that famous closing line of Nineteen Eighty-Four can partly be attributed to its terseness. The sophistication of Orwell's novel is revealed as much in its narrative restraint as in its imaginative structure. Many of its precursors – Brave New World is a particularly egregious offender – deliver their dystopian freight via heavy slabs of universe-building description; in contrast, the almost complete lack of exposition in Nineteen Eighty-Four (if we discount the paratextual Goldstein's book and the appendix, to which we will shortly return) is remarkable. It is a stylistic choice on Orwell's part, but also a political one; it enables the flawed perspective of the weak protagonist to be both foregrounded and problematized. Throughout the novel we, as readers, have no better grasp of what 'Big Brother' really stands for than Winston does because, like him, we can only grope towards understanding, and towards an idea of ideological resistance which, again like him, we have to invent for ourselves, ad hoc and with very little to go on. Thus we share his predicament both intellectually and viscerally; we are flooded with doubt about our own sanity, just as he is.[11] And whereas authors like Morris and Wells used the dislocation of the time traveller to organize their expositionary and polemical discourse, Winston does not have the luxury of anthropological distance; he lives in a world which is as real to him as it is familiar to the novel's readers, so that his (and our) cognitive disarray is structured by language and disciplined by the aporias of an impoverished vocabulary, rather than by a narrative trick of forced defamiliarization.

The invention of Newspeak as a way of abolishing curiosity and empathy in Oceania marks a stark reversal of the optimism which Orwell had felt about new languages earlier in his lifetime. In 'New Words', an unpublished essay which was probably written in early 1940, Orwell outlines the prospectus for a project to 'discover the now nameless feelings that men have in common. All the powerful motives which will not go into words and which are a cause of constant lying and misunderstanding, could be tracked down, given visible form, agreed upon, and named' (CW, 12, p. 134). Crucially, this would have to be a communal project as Orwell conceives it. 'For one man, or a clique, to try and make up a language, as I believe James Joyce is now doing [in Finnegans Wake], is [...] absurd [...]. What is wanted is several thousands of gifted but normal people who would give themselves to word-invention as seriously as people now give themselves to Shakespearean research. Given these, I believe we could work wonders with language' (*CW*, 12, p. 133). Later in the 1940s, however, he became more interested in simplifying language rather than adding new vocabulary. In his BBC wartime broadcasts to India, Orwell drew on 'Basic English', a system codified in 1930 by the linguist and philosopher Charles Kay Ogden, which stripped out all but 850 essential words from the English vocabulary.

The residue of this experiment with simplicity can be detected most directly in his call for plainness in 'Politics and the English Language' and 'Why I Write' (both 1946). '[O]f late years', Orwell states in 'Why I Write', 'I have tried to write less picturesquely and more exactly' (*CW*, 18, p. 320). Yet somewhere in the course of writing *Nineteen Eighty-Four* over the following two years, Orwell seems to have decided that a demand for clarity might tip into an authoritarian insistence on rectitude of thought. To read these two essays as a manifesto of Orwell's late style is to ignore the extent to which that style was still evolving. Indeed, it is important to realize that the 'manifesto' itself is one of the literary forms of which *Nineteen Eighty-Four* is deeply suspicious; it is in the act of reading one (Goldstein's book) and attempting to write one (his diary) that Winston is at his most vulnerable, both to self-delusion and to detection by the Thought Police.

The failure of such manifestos is made clear in the novel's appendix, 'The Principles of Newspeak', in which a future historian looks back to Winston's time and explains the philosophical and political underpinnings of Oceania's linguistic experiment.[12] The implied reader lives in a post-Big Brother world of renewed intellectual curiosity, who might see the truncation of thought as an oddity rather than a matter of life and death. Orwell considered this appendix and the excerpts from the Goldstein book, despite their peripheral relationship with the main text of *Nineteen Eighty-Four*, to be essential to his novel; he refused to allow the publication of a Book-of-the-Month Club edition with these elements removed.[13] Yet these pseudo-paratexts threaten the formal unity of their host narrative, and Orwell was aware that he was engaged in a careful balancing act. In a letter to Fredric Warburg written in May 1947, Orwell warned his publisher: 'I will tell you now that this is a novel about the future – that is, it is in a sense a fantasy, but in the form of a naturalistic novel. That is what makes it a difficult job – of course as a book of anticipations it would be comparatively simple to write' (*CW*, 19, p. 149).

This putative 'naturalism' of *Nineteen Eighty-Four* (whether realized or not) is distinct from Orwell's idea of 'realism' in that it exists in a dialectical relationship with its fantasy elements; Orwell continued to feel that a text untethered by an empirical relationship with reality would be both aesthetically and politically inadequate. In 'Why I Write', Orwell argues that a mature style must temper artistic ego with a 'historical impulse' and a 'political purpose' fuelled by a desire 'to push the world in a certain direction'. Nor was this kind of praxis optional: it was merely a question of how far an author was conscious of it. As Orwell puts things: 'The opinion that art should have nothing to do with politics is itself a political attitude' (*CW*, 18, p. 318). For Orwell, a 'good' style was essential to truth-telling, or as he expresses it in his famous dictum: 'Good prose is like a window pane' (*CW*, 18, p. 320).

The windowpane through which Winston gazes in the opening chapter of *Nineteen Eighty-Four* does not deliver a simple transfer of information: it both reveals and occludes, despite its apparent transparency. It can be read as one of a series of writerly frames through which Orwell views his text: glassy spaces – the telescreens, the antique framed etching of St Clement Danes church, the talismanic coral paperweight which Winston carries round with him as a material symbol of his secret thought crimes – which are ways of seeing, or being seen, or both; none is apolitical. Orwell knew he was writing his last book, and he knew, as he admitted in 'Why I Write', that it would be a 'failure' in its own aesthetic terms, since 'every book is a failure'. He scatters these framing opportunities through the novel as a way of acknowledging his consciousness of this, just as he seeds the book with paratexts which place *Nineteen Eighty-Four* into a constellation of similarly failed books.

Unlike a 'book of anticipations', Orwell's novel must confront its own limitations. *The Last Man in Europe* – Orwell's original title – was written by a man on his deathbed, and it reverberates with its author's sense that time is running out for writing of all kinds. Thus, we are almost immediately confronted with Winston Smith's failure as a writer, a failure which arises partly from an overemphasis on form, as symbolized by the beautiful diary with its creamy pages, and the illicit fountain pen which promises to write pleasing words via the sympathetic magic of its own archaic functionality. The 'naturalistic novel', too, is a superannuated object in Winston's world, where readers wish only for the machine-tooled prose produced in Julia's Fiction Department, or the stodgy polemic of the phoney book by Goldstein which sends Julia straight to sleep. Winston's diary is indeed a failure of style as much as of politics. It begins as an unfiltered stream of consciousness – '*theyll shoot me i dont care theyll shoot me in the back of the neck i dont care down with big brother*' (*NEF*, p. 21) – and eventually resolves into a tone of self-conscious pomposity: '*To the future or to the past, to a time when thought is free, [...]. From the age of uniformity, from the age of solitude, from the age of Big Brother, from the age of doublethink – greetings!*' (*NEF*, p. 30). These two modes of writing seem to satirize two strands of Orwell's literary predecessors, first puncturing the unpunctuated modernist experiments of Joyce and others, and then lancing the overblown histrionics of the futuristic fiction of the past. By addressing 'the future' or 'the past', the diary evokes an atemporal nowhere – a utopia from Winston's point of view – and marks a divergence both from the simple futurism of the novel's dystopian predecessors, and from the aesthetic newfangledness of modernism.

As we have seen in this chapter, the progress of Orwell's thinking about dystopian fiction closely tracked the evolution of his attitudes towards modernism: he rejected both for their tendency towards abstraction. For Orwell, both style and ideology, pursued for their own sake, could endanger truth; art and politics had to be reclaimed as material actors in the world. Only then could humanity itself be revealed as irreducible and, finally, salvageable.

Notes

1 'Nineteen Eighty-Four by George Orwell: first review – archive, 1949', The Guardian (10 June 1949) [www.theguardian.com/books/1949/jun/10/georgeorwell.classics] (accessed 5 August 2019).

2 Alex Woloch, Or Orwell: Writing and Democratic Socialism (Cambridge, MA: Harvard University Press, 2016), p. 10.

3 For a fascinating discussion of the conflicted relationship between Nineteen Eighty-Four, modernist poetics, and T. S. Eliot, see Patricia Rae, 'Mr. Charrington's Junk Shop: T. S. Eliot and Modernist Poetics in Nineteen Eighty-Four', Twentieth-Century Literature, 43.2 (Summer 1997), pp. 196–220.

4 Nineteen Eighty-Four is unfavourably compared to Swastika Night in Daphne Patai, 'Orwell's Despair, Burdekin's Hope: Gender and Power in Dystopia', Women's Studies International Forum, 7.2 (1984), pp. 85–95. For Jameson's critique of The Road to Wigan Pier (1937), see Storm Jameson, 'Documents', Fact (July 1937), pp. 9–11.

5 Storm Jameson, In the Second Year (1936), ed. Stan Smith (Nottingham: Trent Editions, 2004), p. 185.

6 For further discussion of Orwell's relationship with Wells and Huxley, see Gregory Claeys, 'The Origins of Dystopia: Wells, Huxley, and Orwell', in Claeys (ed.), The Cambridge Companion to Utopian Literature (Cambridge: Cambridge University Press, 2010), pp. 107–31. For an examination of Warner's utopian politics, see Glyn Salton-Cox, 'Syncretic Utopia, Transnational Provincialism: Rex Warner's The Wild Goose Chase', in Alice Reeve-Tucker and Nathan Waddell (eds.), Utopianism, Modernism, and Literature in the Twentieth Century (Basingstoke: Palgrave Macmillan, 2013), pp. 111–29.

7 Muggeridge's book argued that the totalitarian politics on both the Right and the Left arose from a love of pure power for its own sake. See William Steinhoff, George Orwell and the Origins of 1984 (Ann Arbor: University of Michigan Press, 1975), p. 205.

8 Theodor W. Adorno and Max Horkheimer, *Dialectic of Enlightenment*, trans. John Cumming (London: Verso, 1997). See, for instance, pp. 30–31 for their discussion of the political necessity of reasserting the radical potential of enchantment. For a discussion of Orwell's attitude towards religion at this time, see Michael G. Brennan, *George Orwell and Religion* (London: Bloomsbury, 2017), pp. 76–90.

9 Yevgeny Zamyatin, *We (1924)*, trans. Clarence Brown (New York: Penguin, 1993), p. 19.

10 See David Dwan, *Liberty, Equality & Humbug: Orwell's Political Ideals* (Oxford: Oxford University Press, 2018), pp. 166–7.

11 For more on the politics of sanity and insanity in the novel, see Lisa Mullen, '"The Few Cubic Centimetres inside Your Skull": A Neurological Reading of George Orwell's *Nineteen Eighty-Four*', *Medical Humanities*, 45 (2018), pp. 258–66.

12 For more on this sense of slippery temporality, see for instance Thomas Pynchon's 'Foreword', in George Orwell, *Nineteen Eighty-Four* (1949; London: Penguin, 2003).

13 See Michael Shelden, *Orwell: The Authorised Biography* (London: Heinemann, 1991), p. 430.

7

SARAH COLE

Wells, Orwell, and the Dictator

Here is the first thing to say: Big Brother is not a dictator. Big Brother is not actually a person at all. Or rather, as we know from O'Brien, he is a person only in the terms made possible by doublethink: he does exist and he doesn't, he is a real person and he isn't, he will live forever and therefore he cannot be any living person. At the same time, the concept of Big Brother perseveres as the ultimate emblem of the dictator in the twentieth century, and his resemblance in the novel to Joseph Stalin seems to confirm the analogy. In today's surveillance state, the relevance not only of the telescreen but of the figure allegedly doing the watching bursts back into pressing contemporaneity.

But Orwell's configuration of the dictator is, in many ways, of its time. The evolution of the dictator from Napoleon in *Animal Farm* to Big Brother in *Nineteen Eighty-Four* illuminates Orwell's developing understanding of how power can be exerted in the modern totalitarian state. Moreover, it represents an engagement with other contemporary theories of modern state power, emanating not only from the totalitarian regimes themselves but from England, and especially from Orwell's greatest influence, the writer against whom Orwell most directly set his own work, H. G. Wells. Wells was a major figure in Orwell's conception of his own writerly praxis, and to consider them together, in the context of dictatorship and the state, is to re-enliven the historical period from the late 1920s through to the publication of *Nineteen Eighty-Four* in 1949. Questions of how history and the future would be forged, and how the individual might be imagined to effect change in the modern world – these were urgent provocations not only for political theorists, but for novelists. *Nineteen Eighty-Four*, with its excruciating and extensive documentation of the destruction of the individual, ultimately finds no space for the great man at the top either. It is the functionary – the torturer, the brilliant man whose face is on no posters or telescreens – that actually epitomizes power in its human form. There may be no dictator in

Nineteen Eighty-Four, but there is someone who knows how to make and use one: O'Brien. In this sense, Orwell and Wells converge: both can see how the individual matters, and equally where he will be eclipsed, in the long futures they imagined. Ultimately, both are taking stock of the future itself, asking whether the very possibility of imagining a better future – or any future – can have a place in the twentieth century.

To begin at the beginning of this story: there was no more potent influence on Orwell as a writer than Wells, by his own admission. We find Wells sprinkled throughout his writings, credited as a key figure in his intellectual and political formation, his work and ideas engaged directly in various contexts (*The Road to Wigan Pier*, 1937; *Coming Up for Air*, 1939; 'Wells, Hitler, and the World State', 1941).[1] It was in many ways a personal influence, with Wells commanding the field of leftist political writing, as well as providing some of the fictions that stayed with Orwell as a boy and young man. And yet, as intimate as this influence was, Orwell sees the significance of Wells largely in generational terms. In 'Wells, Hitler, and the World State' he sums it up bluntly:

> Thinking people who were born about the beginning of this century are in some sense Wells's own creation. How much influence any mere writer has, and especially a 'popular' writer whose work takes effect quickly, is questionable, but I doubt whether anyone who was writing books between 1900 and 1920, at any rate in the English language, influenced the young so much. The minds of all of us, and therefore the physical world, would be perceptibly different if Wells had never existed. (*CW*, 12, p. 539)

It is a startling statement to read today, given the literary-historical amnesia about Wells's influence and visibility in the early decades of the twentieth century. But for readers of Orwell, the sense of patrimony is clear (he jokes just before this passage about literary patricide), and represents an essential feature in Orwell's writerly formation. Dorian Lynksey has noted, in a recent volume on the sources and afterlife of *Nineteen Eighty-Four*, that 'H. G. Wells loomed over Orwell's childhood like a planet – awe-inspiring, oppressive, impossible to ignore – and Orwell never got over it', and there is ample evidence throughout Orwell's writing that when he thought about his own evolution as a political writer, Wells stood near the crucible.[2]

The key question, however, is not whether Wells mattered to his successor, but how; what was the nature and meaning of that connection? One could draw a variety of lines between them. Most generally, Orwell might be seen as occupying a new voice for the left, in that sense following Wells, or, as is typical of generational lineage, superseding him. His 'Wells, Hitler, and the World State' essay is largely a critique of Wells for having become, in essence, outmoded – for relying on the intellectual formations of the Victorians to understand (or rather misunderstand) the threat posed by Hitler. Elsewhere he argues that Wells gets it wrong with machines, with people's motivations, with socialism. In *Coming Up for Air*, his protagonist George Bowling flirts with Wellsian forecast on several occasions, though each time rejecting it as so much fantasy. The novel ends this way, with the penultimate chapter swelling into a Wellsian spirit ('It was as though the power of prophecy had been given me. It seemed that I could see the whole of England'; *CUFA*, p. 238), only to be instantly deflated ('Illusion! Baloney!'; *CUFA*, p. 239). What matters is now.

Orwell's structure of presenting himself as the natural successor to Wells, a model of lineage and generational change, is familiar – the young left, the old left – and yet, for these two iconoclasts, also a bit ill-fitting. Orwell and Wells were both highly unorthodox in their socialism and their political convictions more broadly. Wells for decades bucked the trends and refuted the doxa of all the left groups with which he intersected, whether Fabians, communists, or the Labour Party, while Orwell's experience in Spain inaugurated a wrath against Soviet communism that continued until his death and animated his great political novels. In that sense, Orwell and Wells together represent a kind of moving, shifting sphere of leftist literary expression that confutes the norms of strict political affiliation. It irked some of Wells's peers on the left, for instance, that he was chummy with Henry Ford, and others that he felt comfortable scolding Stalin for his failure to think internationally (this in a 1934 interview published in the *New Statesman*). Placing Wells in clear political camps has never been productive. Equally, Orwell disappointed many in his socialist circles when *The Road to Wigan Pier* (1937) came out, and failed to sustain a fully socialist message. Victor Gollancz (his publisher, of the Left Book Club), upset about *Wigan Pier*, subsequently dropped *Homage to Catalonia* (1938), which, when it appeared, displayed even more questionable orthodoxy. *Homage to Catalonia* sold only 800 copies in its first run.[3] At the same time, as Alex Woloch notes, Orwell himself claimed that 'every word' of his writing fell into the service of democratic socialism.[4]

Notwithstanding these suggestive overlaps and continuities between them, the drama of Orwell reacting to and against Wells is vivid, and was fully internalized by Orwell as part of his writerly persona. The optimist versus the pessimist: here is the difference. Can we in fact say that Orwell's pessimism proved the critical feature of his modernity? That in seeing darkly through the ruses of ideology, the mistaken progressivism of his predecessors, the traps of language itself, he offered an outlook that would help to define a generation – his own? Such seems incontrovertible, but what is less recognized is how fully Wells inhabited this space as its other and counterpoint.

For Orwell and many others of these years, Wells was above all else the optimist, the utopian. Almost by the time Orwell was born, Wells had achieved world fame as a writer of utopia, and, moreover, as the person willing to declare that such futures were possible – even, he wanted to insist, inevitable. Wells wrote several overt and full-fledged utopian fictions (*A Modern Utopia*, 1905; *Men Like Gods*, 1923; *The Dream*, 1924), and even more frequently, constructed elaborate works full of war and extreme destruction, that would open out, in their concluding stages, to brilliant utopian futures (*In the Days of the Comet*, 1906; *The World Set Free*, 1914; *The Shape of Things to Come*, 1934; *Things to Come* (film), 1936). Even his world history *The Outline of History* (1920) operates in this way. After 1,000 pages of global history, beginning with the birth of the planet, and running along through pre-history, ancient history, and up through the modern world, the final two chapters elaborate, first, the insane slaughter of the First World War and its aftermath in the Versailles negotiations (which Wells, like his friend John Maynard Keynes, foresaw as a disaster), followed by a final chapter not of *history* but of forecast, where Wells's narrative dilates to imagine a united, peaceful, and thriving world community. Here is the conclusion to *The Outline* (a world bestseller):

> History is and must always be no more than an account of beginnings. We can venture to prophesy that the next chapters to be written will tell, though perhaps with long interludes of setback and disaster, of the final achievement of world-wide political and social unity. But when that is attained, it will mean no resting stage, nor even a breathing stage, before the development of a new struggle and of new and vaster efforts. Men will unify only to intensify the search for knowledge and power, and live as ever for new occasions. Animal and vegetable life, the obscure processes of psychology, the intimate processes of matter and the interior of our earth, will yield their secrets and endow their conqueror. Life begins perpetually. Gathered together at last under the leadership of man, the student-teacher of the universe, unified, disciplined, armed with the secret powers of the atom and with knowledge as yet beyond dreaming, Life, for ever dying to be born afresh, for ever young and eager, will presently stand upon this earth as upon a footstool, and stretch out its realm amidst the stars.[5]

It was this aspect of Wells's writing above all others to which Orwell reacted, seeing the utopian as the signature of Wells's enormous *oeuvre*, and ultimately crafting his own voice as the antithesis to such futural exuberance. Of course, some skewing was required, and Orwell tends to overstate the utopian strain in Wells and also massively to exaggerate Wells's attachment to mechanization. Yet this perhaps is inevitable, as Orwell took it upon himself to be, in effect, an anti-Wells (perhaps an or-Wells). It is a rich relationship of distance but also shared preoccupation. Noting Wells's faith in the 'sanity' of people as a foundation for his utopian vision, for instance, Orwell writes that Wells 'was, and still is, quite incapable of under-standing that nationalism, religious bigotry and feudal loyalty are far more powerful forces than what he himself would describe as sanity. Creatures out of the Dark Ages have come marching into the present, and if they are ghosts they are at any rate ghosts which need a strong magic to lay them. [...] Wells is too sane to understand the modern world' (*CW*, 12, p. 540).

That saner minds will prevail was in fact an article of faith for Wells. He believed fervently that people ultimately will do what's best for them, as here, in one of many such articulations in his work:

> I am bound to believe [...] that this world community will be growing in knowledge, power, beauty, interest, steadily and delightfully. They will be capable of knowledge I cannot even dream about; they will gain powers over space, time, existence, such as we cannot conceive. [...] Like a great door beginning to open. Sanity coming, sanity growing [...] such a great life ahead as will make the whole course of history up to the present day seem like a crazy, incredible nightmare before the dawn.[6]

This idea that collective sanity and reason would generate a beautiful future represented, in Orwell's view, an unforgivable failure to understand both humanity, with its love of tribes, loyalties, and romanticized violence, and power, which would always be ruthless in exploiting the weakness of its subjects and in accruing more and more dominance to itself. In *Nineteen Eighty-Four*, sanity indeed is an essential term, the sign of mental self-control (and therefore crimethink), against which the party avowedly sets itself. It is precisely by accepting *in*sanity – taking it as sanity, or rejecting the very possibility that sanity exists – that Winston crosses to the final stage in the Ministry of Love, nearing his defeat. 'It is not easy to become sane' (*NEF*, p. 263), says O'Brien, as he slowly twists Winston into accepting that two plus two may well equal five.

Wells's faith in the ultimate sanity of people, who will, he was certain, be ready to exchange their personal loyalties in the name of a united and well-governed world polity, one that would usher in untold benefits for mankind, makes other appearances in *Nineteen Eighty-Four* as well. Here, for instance, is part of the history lesson in Emmanuel Goldstein's (aka O'Brien's) book: 'In the early twentieth century', the book states, 'the vision of a future society unbelievably rich, leisured, orderly and efficient – a glittering antiseptic world of glass and steel and snow-white concrete

[Orwell's rendition of a Wellsian utopia] – was part of the consciousness of nearly every literate person' (*NEF*, p. 196). What naiveté! Everything in *Nineteen Eighty-Four* mitigates against such a view, and O'Brien is particularly at pains to remind Winston to give up any hope for change in the future. The Party's dominance is not only absolute in the extent of its present power, controlling every aspect of life and thought, but also in the temporal dimension, controlling both past and future. 'There is no way in which the Party can be overthrown', says O'Brien: 'The rule of the Party is for ever' (*NEF*, p. 274).

In some sense, then, Wells operates in Orwell's thought and writing as a straightforward foil and generational predecessor. And yet, of course, the connection is more complicated, in part because Wells himself cannot be reduced to a simple figure for optimism, in part because both writers were deeply engaged with issues around history, the state, and the individual in ways that carry complex meanings and belie an easy opposition of optimist to pessimist. Rather than merely supersede Wells, Orwell pursues an urgent moral agenda in which Wells's questions are re-asked, his worlds re-written. As Mark Hillegas puts it: 'To an extraordinary degree the great anti-utopias [such as those by Orwell] are both continuations of the imagination of H. G. Wells and reactions against that imagination.'[7] We will thus learn more about Orwell's major political fictions if we see them not as simple rejections of Wells, but for their deep engagement with the topics Wells had also pursued over several decades. These include, of greatest exigency, the question of power and the state: can we count on people to build a political system that will operate fundamentally in the interest of themselves and their descendants, or is the trend of mid-century totalitarianism the beginning of the end of human freedom?

Human freedom: this is where *Nineteen Eighty-Four* stakes its ground. Freedom, the sovereignty of the individual, the ability even, as Winston thinks, to control one's own thoughts: 'nothing was your own', he ponders early on, 'except the few cubic centimetres inside your skull' (*NEF*, p. 29). And in more romantic terms: 'They could lay bare in the utmost detail everything that you had done or said or thought; but the inner heart, whose workings were mysterious even to yourself, remained impregnable' (*NEF*, p. 174). Though the shortcomings of such faith will become violently apparent over the course of Winston's torture and reconstruction, Winston still clings – almost to the last moment – to the principle that freedom might be imagined to exist, if only for a few seconds of recantation before death. 'To die hating them, that was freedom' (*NEF*, p. 294), he imagines, just before O'Brien sends him to Room 101. We will not know if, in the end, Winston gets those final seconds of hate before his death; a tragic aporia for us as readers. In 1949, when the novel was published, the total loss of human freedom seemed plausible, given the annihilations of the previous decade, and Orwell wondered, throughout the 1940s, about the survivability of the individual at all. In a radio broadcast on literature and totalitarianism, aired in 1941, he reluctantly declared that 'we live in an age in which the autonomous individual is ceasing to exist' (CW, 12, p. 502), and that totalitarianism, which he foresees as moving to encompass the world, 'has abolished freedom of thought to an extent unheard of in any previous age' (CW, 12, p. 503).

In imagining the end of the individual, Orwell engaged with some of the large questions of his contemporaries, who could recognize, simultaneously, a glorious submission of the self to the greater good, and the obliteration of freedom and the triumph of power. These contrasting possibilities occupied thinkers and politicians across the board. All of the major nineteenth-century European political movements, from liberalism to anarchism, socialism to communism, along with their twentieth-century followers in Soviet communism and fascism, can be seen to define themselves according to these questions of how the individual fits into a collective, and writers from the first half of the twentieth century were deeply engaged with these conundrums. Think of T. S. Eliot envisioning 'the mind of Europe', D. H. Lawrence inventing strange new religions to allow his stultified Western characters to shed their modern individualism and subsume themselves, or Virginia Woolf testing out models of shared subjectivity.

Wells drew out this drama over the course of five decades of writing. His utopian vision, always Orwell's focus, relied on the idea that the individual was not, finally, the most meaningful unit. What would it mean to imagine the individual subservient to a greater good, without either glorifying that larger power or relinquishing the Enlightenment values that remained at the basis of Western culture and, in many ways, of Wells's own work (where individual fulfilment and freedom are dominant)? These were Wells's questions, and he answered them through a range of scenarios and works, but always, in Orwell's estimation, with an eye toward the ideal. Take, for instance, *Things to Come* (1936), a film detailing world destruction and rebirth, where the great advances of the future are figured through characters who act out essential human types, and where, moreover, self-sacrifice looms as a primary driver of progress. Wells's utopias are always, in some essential way, collective. Their ultimate object is the species (as Wells thought it) – also called humanity – even as they are run through the stories and language of individuals, and take shape around the unification of all the world's people. As he wrote in his 1934 *Experiment in Autobiography* (another bestseller):

So long as one lives as an individual, vanities, lassitudes, lapses and inconsistencies will hover about and creep back into the picture, but I find nevertheless that this faith and service of constructive world revolution does hold together my mind and will in a prevailing unity, that it makes life continually worth living, transcends and minimizes all momentary and incidental frustrations and takes the sting out of the thought of death. The stream of life out of which we rise and to which we return has been restored to dominance in my consciousness, and though the part I play is, I believe, essential, it is significant only through the whole.[8]

Orwell of course recognized the collective passion of Wells's goals for the future, and set his own vision on the dark and unredeemable realities, as he saw it, of such tendencies.

Yet for both Wells and Orwell, this was no simple balance; the individual finds her way into and out of history in strange spurts and bouts, and this uncertainty about the status and meaning of an individual life in the political currents of time persists for those at the top of the hierarchy as much as for those at the bottom. When it came to dictators, and other 'great men', Wells took essentially a pragmatist view of the situation, willing to grant them a role in some contexts, and wave them away in others. Thus he allows his everyman protagonist Bert Smallways in *The War in the Air* (1908) to have outside importance in the world narrative Wells is telling in that novel, while attempting, in his historical writings such as *The Outline of History*, to see the major figures as embodiments of trends rather than shapers of human life. Wells's overall theory of history stressed forces rather than individuals, and placed events in long spans of time, therefore minimizing the significance of any individual historical actor. Proffering such a view widely, he was naturally confronted with this question – it was unavoidable – about someone such as Napoleon. Here is what he had to say (from a lecture, later published as a short book, both entitled *The Discovery of the Future*): 'these great men of ours are not more than images and symbols and instruments taken, as it were, haphazard by the incessant and consistent forces behind them; they are the pen-nibs Fate has used for her writing'.[9] In *The Outline of History*, Wells cannot help but become absorbed in various historical personalities, and the effort, then, is to find a logic to account for them without suspending the view that, ultimately, they cede to larger collectives. The individual may instead constellate the energy of a particular historical moment; or his importance, over longer spans of time, may diminish in estimation. In the case of Pericles, to take just one example, Wells presents the Athenian leader not as a cultural hero (or failure) but instead as an especially brilliant embodiment of the currents that moved fifth-century Athens. 'The reader', he cautions, 'must bear in mind that illuminating remark of Winckler's, which says that this renascent Athens bore for a time the face of Pericles. [...] Athens wore his face for a time as one wears a mask, and then became restless and desired to put him aside.'[10] At the same time, *The Outline*, over its thousand pages, naturally comes to dwell on a variety of figures, most notably Napoleon, to whom Wells devotes a rare whole chapter. Interestingly, one of Orwell's complaints about *The Outline* was precisely this emphasis on Napoleon. Orwell saw in Wells's disdain for Napoleon a fundamental indication of Wells's own limitations, that he, 'like Dickens, belongs to the non-military middle class' (*CW*, 12, p. 538), and therefore cannot understand the appeal of militaristic symbolism.

It is striking, given Orwell's impatience with Wells's choice to take Napoleon as the model for what has gone wrong in world history, that he selects this very name for his own prototypical dictator in *Animal Farm* (1945). What does one make of this dramatic instance of self-misrecognition? One possibility is that, in the seven years that elapsed between his 'Hitler' essay and *Animal Farm*, Orwell came to recognize that these nineteenth-century military would-be emperors do share some key traits with their twentieth-century dictator followers. It is also possible to read the animals in *Animal Farm*, with their allegorical names, as in some ways *consciously* acting out the part indicated by those names (akin, then, to the way Stephen Dedalus grows into his name through introspection and self-awareness) as distinct from simply embodying those characteristics unbeknownst to them (in the classic allegorical style). Mostly, though, what the Napoleon/Napoleon contradiction shows is that in fact both Wells and Orwell find themselves drawn to the charismatic figure of an earlier epoch, one whom both see as entirely willing to sacrifice the good of the community – for Wells, the potential world community; for Orwell, the farm – for their own gratification. That Orwell's modern dictator has brilliantly discovered a system for extracting ever more labour and passivity from his subjects suggests, too, that what is exceptionally modern here also has roots in earlier models of power and domination. What the nineteenth-century emperor gained through military victories the contemporary authoritarian slowly constructs through subtle psychic manipulation, along with the methods of terror.

Do personalities matter in *Animal Farm*? Are these animals (Napoleon, Squealer, Benjamin, Snowball, etc.) individuals, or purely allegorical expressions, playing out the political and economic forces the novel dramatizes through its technique of parody and allegory? Clearly, it is both. Napoleon's devious strategies, his effective use of terror, his understanding of how to manipulate time: each of these suggest a mind at work, and a specific disposition. And we do see him at times thinking on his feet (or hooves), as in the scene after the windmill has been destroyed by a storm. Surveying the damage, he immediately devises a scapegoating strategy that effectively deflects the animals' potential demoralization into hatred and outrage. 'Napoleon paced to and fro in silence, occasionally snuffing at the ground. His tail had grown rigid and twitched sharply from side to side, a sign in him of intense mental activity. Suddenly he halted as though his mind were made up' (*AF*, p. 52), after which he pronounces Snowball the villain in this calamity (as in all others on the farm). In *Animal Farm*, then, Orwell maintains the vestige, at least, of individual agency and consequence. Especially since 'Animal Farm' remains anomalous in its neighbourhood and does not in fact set off an animal revolution, the novel never indicates that its turn of events is inevitable, and of course the reversion at the ending suggests that the experiment of the farm was a temporary blip in an otherwise solid capitalist, human-dominated world. Perhaps that is why Napoleon has his name, to signal that these older models of power still have credence, even if, in this case, Napoleon the pig's methods cut straight to the core of modern terror, taking full advantage of its political and economic malleability and utility.

Both Orwell and Wells continued to worry and wonder over this essential question about authoritarianism in the modern state, whether it follows from the personality and power of a given leader, or whether it is a matter purely of forces in the world, social, political, and economic. For good (Wells) or evil (Orwell) the key outcome was the amalgamating of people into ever-larger groups, seen variously as the consolidation of power in the interest of power itself, in the case of *Nineteen Eighty-Four*, or the benign governance by a technocratic elite, in the name of world peace, in Wells's utopias (such as *A Modern Utopia*, 1905; *The World Set Free*, 1914; *The Shape of Things to Come*, 1934; and *Things to Come*, 1936). By the 1930s, there was nothing notional about these possibilities, and with the rise of Hitler, Franco, and Mussolini, both authors turned their attention to the question of historical actors. For Wells, who had declared the 'great man' school to be misguided, the 1930s demanded some rethinking. His most elaborate attempt to get to the bottom of the person/force problem came in his 1939 novel *The Holy Terror*, which details the rise of a home-grown English dictator by the name of Rud Whitlow, suggestive of English fascists like Oswald Mosley, as well as Hitler (his given name is actually Rudolf). Rud's political movement serendipitously spreads into world leadership, following on a series of wars and global catastrophes; and it seems as if his personal cult functions in the aid of an ultimately peaceful world commonwealth. Along the way, however, the dictator himself is born (Rud becoming increasingly paranoid, anti-Semitic, and repressive as his power grows). He will ultimately have to be assassinated for the movement to shed its authoritarianism and give way to the genuine world state, Wells's goal. The individual, then, is a transitional actor, who galvanizes and articulates world forces and directions, eventually to be nullified once the revolution has succeeded.

Nineteen Eighty-Four, by contrast with *The Holy Terror* and others of Wells's futural fictions (such as *In the Days of the Comet*, *The Shape of Things to Come*, and *Things to Come*, the film), gives very little by way of history; we know almost nothing of how the world arrived where it is when we meet Winston Smith on the dreary, bleak day that opens the novel. Goldstein's book offers a fascinating gloss on the state of power, but not on its genesis (and anyway, can we trust it?), and of course it is the Party's job to destroy the past. In that sense, we readers resemble the novel's own characters, where ambiguous and fading memories provide the only connection with a lost world. As the residents of Oceania move forward, these last relics will gradually disappear, and the triumph over the past will be complete. The Party, however, is not entirely ready to dispense with the individual; at least one must remain, Big Brother. Big Brother's history and characteristics are ever-changing and malleable, in keeping with the principle of doublethink, but his presence as a human face and concept is consistent and omnipresent. It would seem, then, a pure irony; only by elevating one fictional person can the personhood of all others be destroyed. Big Brother is nothing like Rud Whitlow, in other words. It is not that some individuals with charismatic personalities are needed to push the revolution that will then eradicate individual leadership, but that the collective group constructs such a fake person in the interest of vesting power in itself only. And yet, what about the inner party? What about O'Brien?

From his first appearance in *Nineteen Eighty-Four*, O'Brien holds a unique place. Winston sees him as somehow connected with himself, recognizing semi-consciously as a facet of his own life the same role of double O'Brien plays for us as readers. What transpires, as we know, is that Winston was right (though not in the way he thought): the personal tie does exist, O'Brien and he are destined to interact intimately and consequentially ('in the place where there is no darkness'; *NEF*, p. 256). As this doubling of inside intuition and literary figuration about O'Brien suggests, he seems to have a special spot in the novel's apparatus, straddling the line between functioning as a character, and hence capable of subjectivity and individuality (and for Winston, to be almost a friend, in a perverse way), and embodying the logic and power of the party, like Big Brother. O'Brien himself stresses the functionary side of his existence. Fond of language in the 'Winston, you know this and you have always known this' variety, he stresses the inevitability of all that happens to Winston, his own role being something of a facilitator rather than the person scripting and managing the events. His ability to read Winston's mind, which seems to Winston a marker of his superiority as an intellect, instead is treated as a sign of the Party's prior knowledge of all its subjects.

But the novel cannot do without O'Brien. Big Brother may be the figure that is remembered from *Nineteen Eighty-Four*, the emblem of surveillance and the totalitarian state in the modern world, but within the text he is a fixed entity, a template onto which Winston's (and all other citizens') affect must be grafted. The drama of Winston's torture and reconstruction wends entirely around O'Brien, not only his power but his personality. It is his sessions with Winston that the text documents (whereas a great deal of physical assault and deprivation is left unnarrated), and these provide Winston with the aspects of his ordeal that constitute his re-education, a kind of sadistic anti-therapy. All this attention for one person! It is a question Winston himself asks, and O'Brien's response provides an interesting take on the question of the individual. In contrast to all past dictatorships and regimes of terror, the Party eliminates the very being of its critics: 'You must stop imagining that posterity will vindicate you', he tells Winston. 'Posterity will never hear of you. You will be lifted clean out from the stream of history' (*NEF*, p. 266). But of course what matters is not only that the Party lavishes all of this time and effort to eradicate the mind and being of Winston, but also that it spares this much of O'Brien's effort for the cause (the project of Winston having been ongoing for years before the novel began). In a sense, O'Brien's ingenuity and understanding of character stands behind the full narrative; he has been pulling the strings all along, even before he openly recruits Winston and Julia. And I think we can say, too, that Room 101 itself relies on the continued existence of individual personalities, indeed on the deep and intimate nature of the psyche. It seems to go without saying that O'Brien is the master of Room 101, its engineer.

There is no one like O'Brien in the writing of H. G. Wells. Wells's villains are more likely to fall into the category of deluded idealists or else fabulous monsters. Furthermore, Wells is less motivated to craft individuals who stand astride the events and complexities of his fiction than to find pro- and antagonists who exemplify a problem, or force, or dilemma, and ramify according to the logic and consequences of these issues. O'Brien is, in that sense, a deeply un-Wellsian figure (whereas Winston comports beautifully with a full cast of everymen across Wells's texts, from Kipps (*Kipps*, 1905), to Mr. Polly (*The History of Mr. Polly*, 1910), to Bert Smallways (*The War in the Air*), and on from there). Wells sought to write for and of the planet, to marshal history into a story of the future, and to find collectivity at both the political and writerly levels. Orwell also honed in on the forms and forces of history and politics, but never lost the attraction to indelible individuals, in this case, one whose own powers epitomize the intelligence of his novelistic worlds. O'Brien is a character deeply rooted in the tradition of the English novel, with its core commitment to character; more, he is a world destroyer, whose deep understanding of the nature of psychology and the state allows him to eradicate one in the name of the other. *Nineteen Eighty-Four* thrives, too, on working through doubles, and where would Winston be without O'Brien? Big Brother hovers over the entire social sphere, but O'Brien belongs to Winston, and, we might say, to us. Dictatorship, it seems, begins at home.

But what about the future? For all the differences and connections between Wells and Orwell, the final question for both of them – a profound one for them and, indeed, for their twenty-first-century readers, faced with global climate change – is whether and how the future can be imagined. Wells was his generation's most exuberant and famous futurist, often looking ahead not only by decades or centuries, but into the millions of years as well, as in his first novel, *The Time Machine* (1895), which offered forecasts that ranged from 802,701 to 30 million years into the future. Orwell set his futurist work just thirty-five years forward in time. But *Nineteen Eighty-Four*, whose date, coincidentally, is now thirty-five years behind us, makes a wager that is, in some way, in line with the society it documents: it blocks out any alternate future. 'If you want a picture of the future', says O'Brien, in one of literature's most chilling statements, 'imagine a boot stamping on a human face – for ever' (*NEF*, p. 280). What constitutes forever? Is there a knowledge base that would allow one to conclude that any given future *might* be plausible? Wells believed in the ultimate dynamism of the future, as of the past; change, evolution and movement are its hallmarks. And yet, the future becomes all the more discernible for those very principles. It is because we all subscribe to the laws of science that our own future can, like that of planets, be predicted. 'I am venturing to suggest to you', he commented in 1902, 'that along certain lines and with certain qualifications and limitations a working knowledge of things in the future is a possible and practicable thing.'[1] It is perhaps this sense of certainty about the future – we can know it, we must seek to envision it – that most fully connects these writers. The year 1984 is quickly receding, but have we followed its author, and his favorite foil, in seeking to know, and perhaps even to direct, what comes next?

Notes

1 For discussion of Wells's influence on Orwell, see John S. Partington, 'The Pen as Sword: George Orwell, H. G. Wells, and Journalistic Parricide', *Journal of Contemporary History*, 39.1 (January 2004), pp. 45–56; and Dorian Lynskey, *The Ministry of Truth: A Biography of George Orwell's 1984* (New York: Doubleday, 2019). For discussion of *Coming Up for Air* and Wells, see

Howard Fink, '*Coming Up for Air*: Orwell's Ambiguous Satire on the Wellsian Utopia', *Studies in the Literary Imagination*, 6.2 (Fall 1973), pp. 51–60.

2 Lynskey, *The Ministry of Truth*, p. 60.

3 For discussion of these issues, see Peter Davison, *George Orwell: A Literary Life* (London: St. Martin's Press, 1996), pp. 79–87; Michael Shelden, *Orwell: The Authorized Biography* (London: Heinemann, 1991), pp. 263–85; and Bernard Crick, *George Orwell: A Life* (London: Secker and Warburg, 1981), pp. 207–36. I wish to thank Ameya Tripathi for bringing these dynamics to my attention.

4 Alex Woloch, *Or Orwell: Writing and Democratic Socialism* (Cambridge, MA: Harvard University Press, 2016).

5 H. G. Wells, *The Outline of History: Being a Plain History of Life and Mankind*, 2 vols (London: George Newnes Ltd, 1920), ii, p. 758.

6 H. G. Wells, *Star Begotten: A Biological Fantasia* (New York: Viking, 1937), p. 199.

7 Mark R. Hillegas, *The Future as Nightmare: H. G. Wells and the Anti-Utopians* (New York: Oxford University Press, 1967), p. 5.

8 H. G. Wells, *Experiment in Autobiography: Discoveries and Conclusions of a Very Ordinary Brain (Since 1866)*, 2 vols (1934; London and Boston: Faber and Faber, 1984), pp. 824–5.

9 H. G. Wells, *The Discovery of the Future* (1902), in Harry W. Laidler (ed.), *Social Anticipations* (New York: Vanguard Press, 1927), pp. 61–85, at p. 77.

10 Wells, *The Outline of History*, i, pp. 211–12.

11 Wells, *Social Anticipations*, p. 69.

8

HOLLIE JOHNSON

Orwell's Literary Inheritors, 1950–2000 and Beyond

Evaluating George Orwell's lasting reputation, John Rodden asserts that '[e]xcept possibly for [D. H.] Lawrence, it is likely that Orwell has exerted deeper influence on young Anglo-American writers than any other English writer of the last half-century'.[1] In particular, among Orwell's fiction, *Nineteen Eighty-Four* (1949) has proved itself an enduring work of literature that is read worldwide and has been translated into over sixty different languages. Not only was the novel successful when it was first published, but it achieved new bursts of popularity in the 'countdown' to 1984; in 2002–2003 in anticipation of the centenary of Orwell's birth; and in 2017 when it rose to the top of the Amazon bestseller list following the inauguration of Donald Trump as US president.[2] Along with the equally popular *Animal Farm* (1945), *Nineteen Eighty-Four* was adopted into the British and American school and university curricula soon after its publication and continues to be taught today. Indeed, Rodden notes that a major element of 'Orwell's appeal for new generations of readers may lie in the widespread, pleasurable association of his name with our earliest reading experiences [...]. Probably no other modern English-language writer's work has been so woven into the texture of the popular imagination.'[3] The evidence of this legacy is clear to see. A quick internet search reveals numerous articles and commentaries from the 1990s to the present that suggest Orwell's dystopian vision remains at the forefront of the public imagination: from a *Telegraph* article titled 'Are we still living in 1984?', to a BBC Culture piece on 'Why Orwell's 1984 could be about now', and finally to a CNN column stating 'We're living "1984" today'.[4] Despite the fact that *Nineteen Eighty-Four* was written as a satire responding to the specific historical context of the 1930s and 1940s, Orwell's novel clearly remains relevant to the political dynamics of the late twentieth and early twenty-first centuries.

As the title of Haruki Murakami's *1Q84* (2009) and the name of Ursula K. Le Guin's protagonist 'George Orr' in *The Lathe of Heaven* (1971) suggest, the last half-century of literary fiction includes different kinds of reverential, literary nods to Orwell. *Nineteen Eighty-Four* has been a significant and lasting influence upon the literary imagination of the post-war world, establishing the forms and preoccupations of what would become an increasingly popular genre of speculative fiction. Although examples of 'proto-dystopia' have been identified in the nineteenth and very early twentieth centuries, it was *Nineteen Eighty-Four*, alongside other works such as Aldous Huxley's *Brave New World* (1932) and Ray Bradbury's *Fahrenheit 451* (1953), that cemented and popularized the form as a recognizable genre.[5] In fact, the prominence of Orwell's novel means that any author now proposing to write a dystopian vision of the future inevitably writes in the shadow of *Nineteen Eighty-Four*. This chapter considers the creative legacy of Orwell's novel and the authors who have appropriated and adapted its formal structures and themes in order to address the anxieties of their own times. As the perceived threats of nuclear war and a communist takeover of the West have faded, new crises have arisen to fuel the literary imagination, including the fear of international terrorism, growing anxiety around climate change, and the invasive presence of social media. Although the language and ideas of *Nineteen Eighty-Four* still find purchase in addressing these fears, later authors have also identified conflicts and omissions in Orwell's vision and have challenged these shortcomings in their own texts. By examining how post-Orwellian authors have been influenced by *Nineteen Eighty-Four* this chapter addresses Orwell's legacy and the continued role played by the creative imagination in confronting fears of an oppressive future.

One of the first and best-known responses to *Nineteen Eighty-Four* is Anthony Burgess's *1985* (1978). Burgess was greatly influenced by Orwell, and many elements of *Nineteen Eighty-Four* appear in Burgess's own fiction, including the use of war and violence as a method of social control in *The Wanting Seed* (1962) and the question of individual freedom versus social good, as represented through Alex's brainwashing, in *A Clockwork Orange* (1962). However, *1985* is an explicit attempt to write back to Orwell. While its title announces the status of *1985* as a sort of sequel to Orwell's work, Burgess also deliberately distances his novel from its predecessor.

1985 is divided into two halves. The first is a series of critical essays or interviews reflecting on Orwell's novel. The discussion they generate represents an appreciation of Orwell's literary achievement and a critique of its apparent failures, contextualizing *Nineteen Eighteen-Four* in relation to its historical and literary roots and exploring how Orwell's vision has misjudged the future. In particular, Burgess takes issue with Orwell's representation of an omnipotent state and his depiction of the supposedly powerless proles. In the final critical essay which closes the first half of *1985*, Burgess writes: 'Orwell has, in *Nineteen Eighty-Four*, opened a gap that cannot exist, and in that gap he has built his improbable tyranny. [...] We are so fascinated by it that we will not use the dissolving power of disbelief and send it silently crashing. 1984 is not going to be like that at all' (Burgess, *1985*, p. 89).

The second half of the book is Burgess's attempt to 'contrive an alternative picture – using [Orwell's] own fictional technique' (Burgess, *1985*, p. 9). Burgess's critical vision of the future presents a society ruled by the trade unions, overwhelmed by the wealth of Islamic oil, and saturated with crude and violent popular entertainment. Unlike *Nineteen Eighty-Four*, the state in *1985* is powerless in the face of ceaseless demands from Union leaders, who call mutual strikes in order to hold the country to ransom. The result is widespread social chaos, which Burgess suggests leaves the country open to a foreign takeover.

Although the content of *1985* varies greatly from *Nineteen Eighty-Four*, it shares several preoccupations with its predecessor. Burgess may transfer power from the state to the people, but the dangerous abuse of power by the collective to subjugate the individual remains. The novels share a vision of the last man, alone in his capacity for logic and isolated from society. Winston and Bev, Burgess's protagonist, struggle to find pleasure in their day-to-day existences, and both figures engage in a futile resistance against the *status quo*. In both cases, the government dismisses their arguments as the product of insanity. 'You are mentally deranged', O'Brien tells Winston: 'you are clinging to your disease under the impression that it is a virtue' (*NEF*, p. 258). Similarly, in response to Bev's protests, Dr Schimmel tells him: 'That's undemocratic. Insanity is defined as a rejection of the majority ethos' (Burgess, *1985*, p. 195). This depiction of the alienated protagonist has become a convention of the dystopian narrative, which explicitly addresses the psychological and material disconnection between individuals and their societies.

Burgess takes issue with the validity of Orwell's vision of the future, suggesting that *Nineteen Eighty-Four* '*is no more than a comic transcription of the London of the end of the Second World War*' (Burgess, *1985*, p. 11) and that it presents 'the unrealizable ideal of totalitarianism which mere human systems unhandily imitate' (Burgess, *1985*, p. 40). Yet *1985* is equally no more than a comic transcription of the 1970s. In his review of Burgess's novel, Martin Amis levelled this exact criticism, describing *1985* as a 'stoked-up 1976'.[6] It is not the predictive accuracy of Orwell's vision alone that has made it so influential, but its use of an imagined future as a method to confront what Orwell viewed as the corrupting influence of power and the dangers of a perverted socialism. This is the precise value of dystopian narratives, which 'by focusing their critiques of society on spatially or temporally distant settings, [...] provide fresh perspectives on problematic social and political practices that might otherwise be taken for granted or considered natural or inevitable'.[7] Although they have an extrapolative function, the criticisms offered by dystopian texts are primarily levelled at the present in which they are written. As Paolo Bacigalupi, author of *Ship Breaker* (2010) and *The Windup Girl* (2009), writes: 'something like George Orwell's *1984* is not the template we want to live into. But it gives us a language and a set of metaphors to talk about the hazards of our new social world. [...] If you don't have the language to identify it, you can't get a grip on it'.[8] *Nineteen Eighty-Four* gave people a language for labelling and calling out perceived examples of political state oppression. It is a language that continues to be spoken today.

Despite Burgess's insistence that Orwell got it wrong when it came to the shape of the future, many elements of *Nineteen Eighty-Four*'s totalitarian society have reappeared in later fiction. In Jeanette Winterson's *The Stone Gods* (2007), the world is likewise divided into three superstates which, although peaceful in theory, constantly compete against each other and plot to gain dominance. The Western state, named the 'Central Power', exercises the same strict controls as the Party of Oceania: identity is documented, behaviour is strictly monitored, and '[t]he official line is that the Resistance has been smashed. There is no Resistance to the Central Power.'[9] In particular, the use of violence as a method of maintaining social order ('WAR IS PEACE') has been a recurring feature of dystopian fiction, where the threat of war or terrorism is used to justify the strict controls implemented by the state. The state remains the central power in Suzanne Collins's *The Hunger Games* (2008), in which the populations of the various outlying districts of Panem face surveillance and military supervision from the Capitol, the political centre. Here, mandatory conflict and enforced scarcity misdirect the energies of the population under the excuse that they serve the greater good of the state. Yet in an alternative development, the worlds imagined in many recent dystopian texts have dismissed the all-powerful state to focus instead on the power of international conglomerates who act in a state-like capacity. In the place of seemingly absent or ineffectual government, these dystopias are instead dominated by powerful corporations with names such as 'HelthWyzer' (Margaret Atwood's *Oryx and Crake*, 2003), 'AgriGen' (Bacigalupi's *The Windup Girl*), and 'MORE' (Winterson's *The Stone Gods*). Bearing similarities to the hyper-consumerist populace of the

World State in Huxley's *Brave New World*, citizens in these societies have relative freedom and access to a wide range of technological innovations and hedonistic pastimes, even as they are strictly controlled by the companies that provide these same opportunities.

These two types of dystopian society are not entirely separate, however. Atwood suggests that the

> twentieth century could be seen as a race between two versions of man-made Hell – the jackbooted state totalitarianism of Orwell's *Nineteen Eighty-Four* and the hedonistic ersatz paradise of *Brave New World* [. . .].
>
> But with the notorious 9/11 World Trade Center and Pentagon attacks in 2001, all that changed. Now it appears we face the prospect of two contradictory dystopias at once – open markets, closed minds – because state surveillance is back again with a vengeance.[10]

In the neoliberal dystopias portrayed in Atwood's *Oryx and Crake* and Winterson's *The Stone Gods*, the dominating presence of surveillance and company 'security' forces carry clear echoes of *Nineteen Eighty-Four*'s totalitarian state. The renewal of state oppression in response to external violence is the topic of Cory Doctorow's *Little Brother* (2008), a title chosen in obvious homage to Orwell. The main character, Marcus Yallow, using the alias w1n5ton, is a teenage hacker who is mistakenly arrested and subjected to torture until he admits to a crime he didn't commit. The novel contains various elements that owe much to Orwell's precursor text, including the surveillance culture, the use of show trials, and anonymous denunciation. While Orwell's novel played on the threat of despotism and the dangers of a centralized economy, Doctorow looks at how the threat of international terrorism produces a police state. Like Orwell, Doctorow does not locate his dystopia abroad, but uses his narrative to suggest how the United States of America could be susceptible to the dangers of fascism.

Comparing Doctorow to Orwell, Susan L. Stewart argues that *Little Brother* is 'a novel that speaks to fascism, is a dystopia becoming', in comparison to the already-established 'full-blown fascist government' in *Nineteen Eighty-Four*.[11] In particular, it explores the roots of the Party's slogan 'Slavery is Freedom', which captures the conflict between the promise of security through oppression and the dangers of anarchy in freedom. When Marcus is detained as a possible terrorist suspect, he protests his arrest, stating: 'You're talking about defending my freedom by tearing up the Bill of Rights' (Doctorow, *LB*, p. 47). In the aftermath of a deadly terrorist attack, the 'Patriot Act II' (a reference to the 2001 Patriot Act passed by George W. Bush's administration) allows the government to install cameras in schools and to monitor credit card transactions and metro pass activity with the excuse that it shouldn't matter '[i]f you don't have anything to hide' (Doctorow, *LB*, p. 115). As Aunt Lydia in Atwood's *The Handmaid's Tale* (1985) explains: 'There is more than one kind of freedom, [...]. Freedom to and freedom from. In the days of anarchy, it was freedom to. Now you are being given freedom from' (Atwood, *HT*, p. 34). Yet Marcus maintains that '[t]here's something really liberating about having some corner of your life that's yours, that no one gets to see except you. [...] It's about your life belonging to you' (Doctorow, *LB*, p. 49). Like Winston, Marcus identifies privacy as a cornerstone of individual identity and autonomy. People around him insist that such security measures help them feel safer, but Marcus continues to believe that cameras and tracking can't stop terrorists, and that they only succeed in enforcing a culture of fear.

Because it is set before a typical dystopian society has been fully established, *Little Brother* is more optimistic than *Nineteen Eighty-Four* in its depiction of resistance. For example, the book's front cover bears the tagline 'Big Brother is watching you. Who is watching back?' Marcus repeatedly quotes the Declaration of Independence, which states the responsibility the Government owes to the consent of the people and the resulting legal right of the people to protest against those measures they deem unfit (Doctorow, *LB*, p. 172). And while Winston is largely alone, Marcus recruits his friends on a hidden internet to fight back. *Little Brother* is thus representative of a recent and more openly utopian wave of young adult dystopian fiction, which in the shadow of *Nineteen Eighty-Four* responds to Orwell as a more hopeful vision of what the public, and what young people in particular, can do to fight back against state oppression enforced in the name of security and order.[12]

Significantly, the slogan 'BIG BROTHER IS WATCHING YOU' (*NEF*, p. 3) is perhaps the most enduring legacy of *Nineteen Eighty-Four*, a novel that has become synonymous with surveillance culture. There are few dystopian novels that don't include some form of surveillance or tracking, whether it's through a security force like 'the Eyes' in *The Handmaid's Tale*, ubiquitous identity tracking and cameras like those found in *The Stone Gods*, or the tracing of internet search history and messages that takes place in *Little Brother*. For Peter Boxall, *Nineteen Eighty-Four* is 'a vision of a mechanised, posthuman state, a state in which the forms of interiority and autonomy that are the foundations of human being have been banished'. This loss of privacy prevents the individual's sense of private ownership over their own body.[13] Surveillance is thus a major factor in the conflict between the collective state and the individual that defines the dystopian narrative, not only preventing rebellion but also undermining the protagonist's sense of self.

However, while surveillance in *Nineteen Eighty-Four* and novels like *Little Brother* is used aggressively by the state as a form of socio-political control, other dystopian novels have explored how constant transparency can become its own form of dystopian structure. Ben Elton's *Blind Faith* (1993) imagines a society where a culture of compulsory sharing leads to the characterization of privacy not only as abnormal, but also as perverse and socially dangerous. Meanwhile, in *The Circle* (2013) Dave Eggers goes one step further to imagine surveillance as something voluntarily embraced by, rather than autocratically imposed on, society. As Eggers explains: 'in *Nineteen Eighty-Four* you have submission to a totalitarian regime that you cannot resist or they will torture or kill you. I wanted *The Circle* to be pointedly such that everyone is participating, doing it willingly.'[14] Consequently, instead of a fascist autocracy, Eggers presents a neoliberal meritocracy where power lies in the hands of a technology giant that monopolizes the market. Rather than being a tool of the state, the surveillance structure is reversed as citizens not only watch each other but are also given access to the inner workings of their legislators and government when politicians are forced to 'go transparent'. As in *Little Brother*, this elimination of the private is perpetuated through the argument that one would only resist if you have something to hide. Consequently, rather than a single figure, the whole of society becomes a judgemental Big Brother.

The technology of the Circle connects everyone to each other at all times. 'SeeChange', the distribution of cameras worldwide, offers the opportunity for humanity to see and know everything, leading to the company motto that 'ALL THAT HAPPENS MUST BE KNOWN', a striking inversion of the Party's claim that 'IGNORANCE IS STRENGTH'. Eggers deliberately echoes Orwell's doublethink slogans with his own, having the Circle encourage conformity through the declarations that 'PRIVACY IS THEFT' and 'SECRETS ARE LIES'. This parallelism, which Eggers writes 'was very much on purpose', emphasizes the inversion, acknowledging the literary debt owed to *Nineteen Eighty-Four* while simultaneously affirming that the twenty-first century faces a very different kind of threat to the one portrayed by Orwell.[15]

The Circle aims to reduce crime by increasing accountability, which indeed it does, but it also eliminates the possibility of privacy. Although the transparency of this shared network is meant to build a sense of collective community, it instead further isolates the individual because everyone is held to impossibly high standards of achievement, moral virtue, and distinctiveness, while waiting to confer judgement on, and fearing judgement from, the group. The constant pressure of this system erodes established bases of identity and relationships to others, preventing any meaningful solidarity and thus resistance to the real powers that be, much as it does in *Nineteen*

Eighty-Four. Boxall argues that the varicose ulcer that Winston suffers from throughout the narrative is a symptom of Winston's estrangement from his self as his body becomes 'numb material upon which the state exercises its bio-power'. He comments that 'this irritant is the mark of a wide gulf between public body and private mind, a kind of radical disassociation that signifies the disintegration of the human compound'.[16] When Winston begins his narrative of resistance, his ulcer begins to heal as he starts to reformulate his notion of identity apart from the Party, reclaiming ownership over his sense of self.

Similarly, in *The Circle*, Mae exhibits symptoms of this estrangement from the self. As she becomes fully immersed in the society of the Circle, she begins to

> [feel] this, this black rip, this loud tear, within her, a few times a week. It didn't usually last long, but when she closed her eyes she saw a tiny tear in what seemed to be black cloth, and through this tiny tear she heard the screams of millions of invisible souls. It was a very strange thing[.][17]

This tear and screaming appear at moments in the text when Mae is badgered by online messages and demands to engage with the social network, suggesting a slow effacement of her identity. In a stark contrast to *Nineteen Eighty-Four*, Mae complies with this effacement and actively embraces her personal transparency even as it destroys her friends and family. This depiction of the complicit protagonist has become a theme in more recent dystopian fiction where, whether due to ignorance or investment in relative privilege, characters like Jimmy, in Atwood's *Oryx and Crake*, and Saul, in Maggie Gee's *The Ice People* (1998), participate in their own oppression.

However, it is not only Orwell's critique of political autocracy and surveillance that has influenced the writers who have followed him. *Nineteen Eighty-Four* is also a warning against the abuse of language that supports this autocracy. Writing that 'if thought corrupts language, language can also corrupt thought' (*CW*, 17, p. 428), Orwell was highly attuned to the power that language exerts, and although many mid-century reviews focused on the novel as a work of political critique, subsequent critics have emphasised the importance of the novel's stylistic creativity and narrative imagination.[18] 'If *Nineteen Eighty-Four* is concerned with the understanding of power, it is also concerned with the fate of narrative under such conditions', writes Steven Connor. '*Nineteen Eighty-Four* does have a marked and sustained preoccupation with the question of writing and of narrative writing in particular.'[19] This preoccupation with language is evident in Orwell's depiction of Newspeak, the official language in the society of Airstrip One, which is designed to control communication and suppress creativity by dramatically reducing the range of linguistic expression. For example, by reducing the number of verbs available for everyday communication, Newspeak restricts the capacity to imagine possible actions. Language is removed from the material reality it attempts to represent and meaning is manipulated to support the doublethink ('WAR IS PEACE') that marks the corrosive politics of Big Brother's totalitarian government.

Suitably, it is the defiant action of writing in a private journal that first marks Winston's resistance to the control of the Party, while his attempts to retrieve old memories challenge the Party's totalizing narrative of the past. These acts assert Winston's independence and his ownership of the space inside his head by reclaiming language as his own and thus by establishing values and explanations outside the orthodoxy of Big Brother. This preoccupation with the value of creative narrative has persisted in dystopian writing to become a staple feature of the genre. The act of recording private thoughts plays a key role in the counternarrative of Fowke, the protagonist in David Ely's *A Journal of the Flood Year* (1992), whose ignored reports on the failing structure of 'the Wall' become a protest against his repressive and technocratic society. In other novels, such as Kazuo Ishiguro's *Never Let Me Go* (2005), storytelling and narrative are essential to the protagonist's attempts at identity formation and resistance. Protagonists do not always keep a physical journal, but the narrative is often given in first-person voice or focalized from a first-person perspective in order to frame the story as a private and subjective account. As a result, the dystopian protagonist is, like Winston, framed as an isolated individual, alienated from society, perhaps the last citizen capable of resisting the totalizing structure of a dystopian society.

Considering this focus on narrative, it is apt that one of Margaret Atwood's primary reactions to reading *Nineteen Eighty-Four* was to share Winston's 'desire to write his forbidden thoughts down in a deliciously tempting secret blank book'.[20] Atwood has acknowledged how reading Orwell in her youth was a significant influence on her own work as an author, particularly for *The Handmaid's Tale*. Her novel depicts a society where, in the face of mass infertility, unmarried or divorced women have been enslaved as 'Handmaids' and assigned to upper-class families to act as surrogates for supposedly infertile wives, actions justified through the manipulation of language found in biblical texts. The influence of *Nineteen Eighty-Four* upon *The Handmaid's Tale* is evident in the novels' shared anxieties about totalitarian oppression, police surveillance, and the ritualization of hate and violence (compare, for example, the Two Minutes Hate with the 'Particicution'; Atwood, *HT*, p. 290), and through the preoccupation with the nature of language and the erasure of alternative narratives. The politics of Gilead are based on a selective interpretation of biblical scripture, modified to serve the government's purpose. Despite the fact that Offred recognizes the omissions and changes to the scriptures, just as Winston recognizes the changes in Party politics and history, in the absence of physical proof she is unable to check them for accuracy. Reading and writing are similarly restricted, while televised news is nothing but propaganda. Even the Handmaids' verbal exchanges are restricted by the imposition of standardized exchanges: responding to Ofglen's greeting of 'Blessed be the fruit', Offred replies 'May the Lord open' – 'the accepted response' to 'the accepted greeting' (Atwood, *HT*, p. 29). Like Orwell's Newspeak, language in Gilead is restricted in order to curb any potential for individual creativity, and thus for individual and collective resistance.

Against this restriction of thought and language, Offred and Winston attempt to challenge the ruling order through the act of writing. Winston himself is a writer, employed by the Party to rewrite and 'correct' historical records so they support the current politics of the Party: '"Who controls the past," ran the Party slogan, "controls the future: who controls the present controls the past"' (*NEF*, p. 37). Challenging this fabrication of events, Winston's counter-narrative against Big Brother starts when he first begins to record his own version of events, writing '*To the future or to the past, to a time when thought is free, when men are different from one another and do not live alone – to a time when truth exists and what is done cannot be undone*' (*NEF*, p. 30). Winston's act of narrative creation is thus a hopeful one: not only does he keep a record of his own thoughts, but he asserts the existence of a like-minded person to read them. Similarly, Offred narrates her own version of events in *The Handmaid's Tale*, which is later revealed to be a reconstruction of a recording captured on cassette tapes. Earl Ingersoll argues that Winston and Offred are associated through the privacy and 'illusory refuges' of their rooms, noting that it 'is in her reading of Orwell's focus upon Winston as a writer in his room that Atwood's narrative encourages us to see Offred as a "writer" of a kind, or at least as the generator of a "text," in her room'.[21] Like Winston, Offred's act of 'writing' insists on the existence of someone to read her narrative: 'But if it's a story, even in my head, I must be telling it to someone. You don't tell a story only to yourself. There's always someone else. Even when there is no one' (Atwood, *HT*, p. 49).

Within their acts of reportage, Winston and Offred also reach back for memories of a time before Oceania and before Gilead. Such memories allow the protagonist to imagine possibilities outside of the autocracy that traps them and thus to assemble the basis for future resistance. Winston insists that memories allow him to prove facts contrary to the Party's narrative: 'It does exist! It exists in memory. I remember it' (*NEF*, p. 259). Meanwhile, memories of his mother offer a link 'to a time when there was still privacy, love and friendship' (*NEF*, p. 32), challenging the nature of society Winston lives in now. Although O'Brien will later dismiss the legitimacy or value of Winston's memories, attesting to the totality of Big Brother's control, their presence at the beginning of the novel gives value to the past as a space of possible resistance and alterity.

However, Winston's recourse to memory is not unproblematic. The association between the incomplete memories of his childhood with dreams of a pastoral and idyllic 'Golden Country' betrays a nostalgia that limits the critical parameters of Winston's memory. In contrast, Rafaella Baccolini underlines how in *The Handmaid's Tale* Offred's memories are already coloured with the misogynistic beginnings of Gilead and consequently offer no space for nostalgic retreat. Instead, memory becomes a subversive space that allows Offred to position herself as protagonist in her own story and to challenge the hegemonic narrative of Gilead. Baccolini argues that '[b]ecause language defines reality and gives power, it is precisely the combination of language with memory and imagination that provides Atwood's character a source of freedom. By narrating the past to herself, but also by creating and imagining different versions of the past.'[22] This ability to imagine alternatives to the present allows characters to challenge the singular and static narratives of dystopian societies. As a result, even though protagonists like Offred and Winston apparently fail in their attempt at resistance, the fact that they are able to imagine an alternative to their dystopian reality is an important expression of hope within the novels in which they feature. Furthermore, this ability invites readers to do the same by encouraging them to question the inevitability of the dystopian society they are presented with and to act, in the present, to prevent such dystopian worlds coming to pass.

While Winston reaches for an objective, external truth that lies outside the Party's totalizing control ('*the freedom to say that two plus two make four*'; *NEF*, p. 84), Atwood's Offred instead finds reassurance in the possibility that objective truth is simply not possible and that an individual's perspective can only be one among many competing *versions* of the truth. Speaking in an interview, Atwood stresses the importance of multiple versions of a story, arguing that '[t]he truth is composite and that's a cheering thought. It mitigates tendencies toward autocracy.'[23] In other words, while Winston tries to challenge one 'truth' with another, Offred dismantles the idea of a singular truth altogether. She continually emphasizes the constructed nature of her narrative as 'a reconstruction' (Atwood, *HT*, p. 144), stating: 'I made that up. It didn't happen that way. Here is what happened' (Atwood,

HT, p. 273). The addition of the 'Historical Notes' postscript at the end of the book further complicates the text by presenting Offred's narrative as a scholarly reconstruction of Offred's already reconstructed story, emphasizing how all narratives are subject to distortion as Offred's tale is once again reclaimed by the agents of yet another kind of patriarchy.

The constructed nature of narrative is the ultimate danger in *Nineteen Eighty-Four*. This much is evident in the way that the novel relies, for the most part, on a realist mode of storytelling. Commenting on the realist mode of Orwell's 1930s novels, Michael Levenson argues that for Orwell, realism was 'the only acceptable aesthetic in an epoch of self-delusion'.[24] Characterizing his text as 'a naturalistic novel', Orwell aims to ground the depiction of his speculative future by providing a level of authenticity and solidity through the narrative style, even as this is balanced by Winston's limited point of view. In contrast, the postmodernist shift in fiction means that many later dystopian texts emphasize the constructed nature of narrative and the existence of multiple perspectives on reality. This multiplicity is reflected in Atwood's use of language. While Orwell argued that '[g]ood prose is like a window pane' (*CW*, 18, p. 320), Offred resists Gilead's textual reductionism by revelling in the semantic possibilities of words such as 'chair' or 'lie' (Atwood, *HT*, pp. 120, 47). Listing their various and unconnected meanings, Offred emphasizes the potential of words to mean different things while also recognizing the way in which (mis)interpretation is inherent to the nature of language. The constructed nature of narrative is also present in dystopian texts like Gee's *The Ice People*, where a layered understanding of the narrative requires the reader's recognition that Saul is an unreliable narrator and that his account cannot be taken at face value. Meanwhile, in Chang-rae Lee's *On Such a Full Sea* (2014), the protagonist never gives an account of events; instead, her story is forged from the multiple perspectives of others.

This shift in narrative style is reflected in the legacy of *Nineteen Eighty-Four*'s appendix. The central purpose of the 'Newspeak' appendix is to provide a commentary on the mechanics of social control through an analysis of the restriction of language, attesting to the specifically political and social purpose of Orwell's dystopian novel. The fact that Atwood deliberately includes a similar post-script in *The Handmaid's Tale* demonstrates the usefulness of this textual feature, which uses a scholarly perspective to dissect and analyse the characteristics of Gilead. This strategy has become a generic convention in its own right. Yet while Orwell used his appendix to add a greater layer of detail to his portrayal of Big Brother's dystopian government, other authors have generally followed Atwood in presenting appendices as retrospective appraisals which complicate the narratives they supplement by foregrounding questions of reconstruction and interpretation. For example, in George Turner's *The Sea and Summer* (1987), the main narrative is presented as a reconstruction by a professor of history, while the narrative in Naomi Alderman's *The Power* (2016) is framed by a discussion between author and editor that presents the text as a historical fiction, complete with historical records and artefacts. Like Orwell, these authors use this scholarly perspective to provide a commentary on the mechanics of the dystopian societies they represent, but they also highlight the constructed nature of history as they do so.

For Atwood, the 'Principles of Newspeak', 'written in the past tense', is a hopeful narrative gesture because it 'can only mean that the regime has fallen, and that language and individuality have survived', despite the Party's efforts to control them.[25] In the 'Historical Notes' that close *The Handmaid's Tale*, Atwood repeats this strategy to assert the downfall of Gilead, even as the scholarly framing of the 'Notes' implies a patriarchal reclamation of Offred's narrative. However, the fact that Atwood locates the post-script in her narrative's future is, according to Loraine Saunders, a misinterpretation of Orwell's text. Analysing the syntax of the appendix, Saunders argues that 'it becomes clear that it could only have been written by someone situated firmly in 1948'.[26] Written from the narrative present, Saunders argues, the appendix cannot provide the hopeful post-script that Atwood argues for. Yet Atwood's apparent misinterpretation of tense has created its own accidental legacy: these retrospective post-scripts not only offer a critical analysis of their dystopian societies, but also suggest an additional warning. Professor Pieixoto's attempt to interpret Offred's narrative repeats the offences of Gileadean society by silencing Offred through his pursuit of a singular, 'objective' version of historical truth. Similarly, the conversation between writer and editor in Alderman's *The Power* repeats the sexist attitudes in the narrative it supplements. In such narratives, the post-script serves as a warning about a failure to learn lessons from dystopian pasts.

In his comparison of Orwell's *Nineteen Eighty-Four* and Robert Harris's *Fatherland* (1992), Juan Francisco Elices notes that our responses to 'Orwell's narratives can be substantially enriched if we examine his legacy on other contemporary novelists that draw on the same strategies to build up their dystopias'.[27] The debates around Orwell's post-script demonstrate how the reading of each new text that has drawn upon and responded to *Nineteen Eighty-Four* also rewrites how we read the original, inviting us back to reconsider the way it has been read and interpreted by generations of readers. Today, *Nineteen Eighty-Four* is a key presence in the popular imagination and continues to be widely read in its own right. But it has also produced a literary legacy through the numerous authors who have been able to draw upon its ideas and structures in order to create their own, increasingly unsettling dystopian visions of futures whose implications we are only just beginning to grasp.

Notes

1 John Rodden, *George Orwell: The Politics of Literary Reputation* (1989; London: Routledge, 2017), p. 19.
2 'During 1983 and 1984, what the mass media called "Orwellmania" spurred *Nineteen Eighty-Four* alone to sales of almost 4 million copies' (John Rodden and John Rossi, *The Cambridge Introduction to George Orwell* (Cambridge: Cambridge University Press, 2012), p. 103). Sales spiked following a comment made by Kellyanne Conway, an adviser to Donald Trump, in which she used the term 'alternative facts' to defend a dubious and unproven claim regarding the president's inauguration. The resulting controversy also gave rise to the phrase 'fake news'.
3 Rodden, *The Politics of Literary Reputation*, p. 16.
4 'Are we still living in 1984?', *The Telegraph* (4 June 1999) [www.telegraph.co.uk/culture/4717571/Are-we-still-living-in-1984.html] (accessed 15 October 2019); Jean Seaton, 'Why Orwell's 1984 could be about now', *BBC Culture* (7 May 2018) [www.bbc.com/culture/story/20180507-why-orwells-1984-could-be-about-now] (accessed 15 October 2019); Lewis Beale, 'We're living "1984" today', *CNN* (3 August 2013) [https://edition.cnn.com/2013/08/03/opinion/beale-1984-now/index.html] (accessed 15 October 2019).
5 Tom Moylan suggests Jack London's *The Iron Heel* (1908) and E. M. Forster's 'The Machine Stops' (1909) as examples of 'proto-dystopia', but credits Gorman Beauchamp with the term. See Raffaella Baccolini and Tom Moylan (eds.), *Dark Horizons: Science Fiction and the Dystopian Imagination* (London: Routledge, 2003).
6 Martin Amis, 'A Stoked-up 1976', *The New York Times* (19 November 1978), pp. 3, 60, 62.
7 M. Keith Booker, *The Dystopian Impulse in Modern Literature* (Westport, CT: Greenwood Press, 1994), p. 19.
8 Interview with C. S. Peterson, 'Paolo Bacigalupi: Chilling Worlds of Warning', *Fiction Unbound* (22 April 2016) [www.fictionunbound.com/blog/paolo-bacigalupi-interview] (accessed 15 October 2019).
9 Jeanette Winterson, *The Stone Gods* (2007; London: Penguin, 2008), p. 31.
10 Margaret Atwood, *In Other Worlds: SF and the Human Imagination* (London: Virago, 2012), p. 148.
11 Susan L. Stewart, '1983: Cory Doctorow's *Little Brother*', in M. Keith Booker (ed.), *Critical Insights: Dystopia* (Ipswich, MA: Salem Press, 2013), pp. 241–56, at p. 243.
12 Tom Moylan, *Scraps of the Untainted Sky: Science Fiction, Utopia, Dystopia* (Oxford: Westview Press, 2001), p. 188.

13 Peter Boxall, 'Science, Technology, and the Posthuman', in David James (ed.), *The Cambridge Companion to British Fiction since 1945* (Cambridge: Cambridge University Press, 2015), pp. 127–42, at p. 132.

14 Sean Bex and Stef Craps, 'An Interview with Dave Eggers and Mimi Lok', *Contemporary Literature*, 56.4 (2015), pp. 545–67, at p. 556.

15 *Ibid.*, p. 556.

16 Boxall, 'Science, Technology, and the Posthuman', p. 131.

17 Dave Eggers, *The Circle* (London: Hamish Hamilton, 2013), p. 196.

18 The quotation comes from Orwell's essay 'Politics and the English Language' (1946).

19 Steven Connor, *The English Novel in History, 1950–1995* (London: Routledge, 1996), p. 206.

20 Atwood, *In Other Worlds*, p. 143.

21 Earl Ingersoll, 'Margaret Atwood's *The Handmaid's Tale*: Echoes of Orwell', *Journal of the Fantastic in the Arts*, 5.4 (1992), pp. 64–72, at p. 65.

22 Rafaella Baccolini, 'Journeying through the Dystopian Genre: Memory and Imagination in Burdekin, Orwell, Atwood, and Piercy', in Raffaella Baccolini, Vita Fortunati, and Nadia Minerva (eds.), *Viaggi in utopia* (Ravenna: Longo, 1996), pp. 343–57, p. 353.

23 Interview with Jan Garden Castro (20 April 1983), in *Margaret Atwood: Vision and Forms*, ed. Kathryn Van Spanckeren and Jan Garden Castro (Carbondale: Southern Illinois University Press, 1988), p. 232.

24 Michael Levenson, 'The Fictional Realist: Novels of the 1930s', in John Rodden (ed.), *The Cambridge Companion to George Orwell* (Cambridge: Cambridge University Press, 2007), pp. 59–75, at p. 60.

25 Atwood, *In Other Worlds*, pp. 145–6.

26 Loraine Saunders, *The Unsung Artistry of George Orwell: The Novels from 'Burmese Days' to 'Nineteen Eighty-Four'* (Aldershot: Ashgate, 2008), pp. 144–5.

27 Juan Francisco Elices, 'The Satiric and Dystopic Legacy of George Orwell in Robert Harris's *Fatherland*', in Alberto Lázaro (ed.), *The Road from George Orwell: His Achievement and Legacy* (Bern: Peter Lang, 2001), pp. 199–224, at p. 222.

PART III

Questions

9

JANICE HO

Europe, Refugees, and *Nineteen Eighty-Four*

'Why "1984" Is a 2017 Must-Read' was the 26 January 2017 headline of a *New York Times* article by its then chief book reviewer, Michiko Kakutani. One of the reasons Kakutani proffers for *Nineteen Eighty-Four*'s timeliness lies in its portrayal of a 'world of endless war, where fear and hate are drummed up against foreigners, and movies show boatloads of refugees dying at sea'.[1] Kakutani was writing not long after what has often been described as the worst refugee crisis since the Second World War, when more than one million migrants sought asylum in Europe in 2015, with more than 3,500 dying in the attempt. Arriving mainly through boat crossings through the Mediterranean Sea, many of these asylum seekers were fleeing war-torn countries and repressive regimes, among them the Syrian civil war that began in 2011; Taliban insurgents in Afghanistan; the militant group Daesh's incursions in Iraq; and forced conscriptions by the state in Eritrea.[2] How might *Nineteen Eighty-Four*, a novel published more than half a century earlier in 1949, help us to reflect on one of the most distinctive socio-political issues of our time: the causes of statelessness and the plight of refugees?

Nineteen Eighty-Four makes only a single reference to refugees, but it occurs at the novel's beginning and sets up its key concerns. The protagonist Winston Smith sits in front of a blank diary he has purchased to record his thoughts. This is an act of defiance – a 'thoughtcrime' – against the totalitarian regime of Oceania that seeks to control how its citizens think, feel, and act at every moment. Paralysed by the 'blankness of the page', Winston begins to write in panic, only semi-conscious of his words. His first entry, and the novel's first scene of transgression, reads thus:

> *April 4th, 1984. Last night to the flicks. All war films. One very good one of a ship full of refugees being bombed somewhere in the Mediterranean.*

Audience much amused by shots of a great huge fat man trying to swim away with a helicopter after him. first you saw him wallowing along in the water like a porpoise, then you saw him through the helicopters gunsights, then he was full of holes and the sea round him turned pink and he sank as suddenly as though the holes had let in the water, audience shouting with laughter when he sank. then you saw a lifeboat full of children with a helicopter hovering over it. there was a middleaged woman might have been a jewess sitting up in the bow with a little boy about three years old in her arms. little boy screaming with fright and hiding his head between her breasts as if he was trying to burrow right into her and the woman putting her arms around him and comforting him although she was blue with fright herself, all the time covering him up as much as possible as if she thought her arms could keep the bullets off him. then the helicopter planted a 20 kilo bomb in among them terrific flash and the boat went all to matchwood then there was a wonderful shot of a child's arm going up up up right up into the air a helicopter with a camera in its nose must have followed it up and there was a lot of applause from the party seats but a woman down in the prole part of the house suddenly started kicking up a fuss and shouting they didn't oughter of showed it not in front of kids they didnt it aint right not in front of kids it aint until the police turned her turned her out i dont suppose anything happened to her nobody cares what the proles say typical prole reaction they never –   (NEF, pp. 10–11)

Why is this scene the first thing that comes to Winston's mind? The passage opens up two inter-related questions that this chapter takes up in turn: first, what are the political conditions that have enabled this mass slaughter of refugees? Second, how should we explain the audience's differing reactions to this carnage? This chapter will show how, in *Nineteen Eighty-Four*, the totalitarian state employs a regime of racist nationalism and economic scarcity to scapegoat foreigners as threats. The killing of the refugees – with the significant implication that they are Jewish – reflects political systems responsible for cultivating hostility towards outsiders, feelings that continue to reverberate in today's geopolitical landscape. Second, insofar as the passage stages different responses to the war film – most of the audience delights in the violence while the 'prole' (proletarian) is aghast at it – *Nineteen Eighty-Four* suggests that ethical responses to the spectacle of refugee suffering are neither innate nor pre-given. Instead, human sensibility – one's capacity to be indifferent, callous, or empathetic – is shaped by the political systems one inhabits.

Threats to the Nation

Orwell's lifespan from 1903 to 1950 coincided with the emergence of a new figure in world history: the refugee. In *The Origins of Totalitarianism*, published two years after *Nineteen Eighty-Four*, the political theorist

Hannah Arendt, who herself had been a refugee, described statelessness as 'the newest mass phenomenon in contemporary history' and stateless persons as 'the most symptomatic group in contemporary politics' (Arendt, *OT*, p. 362). The scale of global displacement in the early twentieth century was unprecedented, caused by, among other things, the collapse of the multinational Russian, Austro-Hungarian, and Ottoman empires into ethnically homogenous nation-states in the wake of the First World War (1914–18); the Spanish Civil War (1936–39), which forced nearly half a million Spaniards to flee the Franco regime; and the persecution and genocide of Jews in Nazi Germany and other Eastern European states, which led to deportations and a mass exodus of Jewish refugees. By 1926, there were an estimated 10 million refugees in Europe, a figure that grew to 60 million after the Second World War (1939–45).[3] Beyond numerical scale, what was also unprecedented, argued Arendt, was not so much 'the loss of a home [by the refugees] but the impossibility of finding a new one' (Arendt, *OT*, p. 384). Mass expulsions and forced migrations were not historically new but, for the first time, refugees had nowhere to go, caught in limbo between sovereign nation-states that did not want them.

Although the refugee crisis in the first half of the twentieth century unfolded over different geographies and affected multiple nationalities, it became largely identified with Jewish emigration in the decades leading up to Orwell's composition of *Nineteen Eighty-Four*. In Winston's diary entry, '*a middleaged woman [who] might have been a jewess*' is in the refugee boat. The Jewish presence in a crossed-out line in the novel's manuscript is more emphatic: the boat is described as being 'full of Jews', and Orwell had originally written the figure of the '*great huge fat man trying to swim away*' as that of 'an old fat Jew'.[4] In her reading of the novel, Lyndsey Stonebridge points out that there would have been a plethora of midcentury images of Jewish refugees on boats for Orwell to draw on: both during and after the war, many Jews undertook clandestine sea voyages to reach Palestine where Zionists were attempting to establish a national home, but Britain had imposed strict restrictions on immigration and sought to intercept these boats, either turning these refugees back or interning them.[5] Orwell's thinking about refugees, Stonebridge argues, was primarily shaped by his witnessing of the historical experience of Jews, in particular, the anti-Semitism that constructed them as threats and sought their expulsion from the nation-state, not just in totalitarian regimes like Hitler's Germany, but also in liberal democracies like Britain.

In a 1945 essay ('Anti-Semitism in Britain'), Orwell writes: 'anti-Semitism is part of the larger problem of nationalism, which has not yet been seriously examined, [...] the Jew is evidently a scapegoat, though *for what* he is a scapegoat we do not yet know' (CW, 17, p. 69). If Orwell thought the 'problem of nationalism' was under-examined, Hannah Arendt would soon provide a comprehensive analysis of how nationalism transformed the nation-state from an 'instrument of law' into an 'instrument of the nation' from the late nineteenth century onwards. The founding of the nation-state in the American and French Revolutions of 1776 and 1789 established the liberal principle of equal citizenship before the law: in the eyes of the state, all citizens are theoretically equal, even if they may not be so in fact. But the subsequent rise of ethno-cultural and racial definitions of the nation-state during Orwell's lifetime meant that citizenship was no longer seen as an abstract legal category open to all regardless of one's identity, but was instead determined by one's racial, ethnic, or cultural origins. In this view, 'only nationals could be citizens, only people of the same national origin could enjoy the full protection of legal institutions, [while] persons of different nationality needed some law of exception' (Arendt, OT, p. 359). Minorities, even those with legal citizenship, began to be seen as outsiders and threats – as 'scapegoat[s]', in Orwell's term – to nations increasingly bound by racial and ethnic ties. Arendt attributes the tide of refugees in the early twentieth century to forces of nationalism that sought to enforce the principle of ethno-racial homogeneity, effecting the mass relocation of minorities who were subsequently welcomed nowhere.

Racial nationalisms resulted in tighter external borders to shut out foreigners and in internal paranoia about who was part of the nation. Orwell took note of this new political cartography: reflecting in his 'As I Please' column for 12 May 1944 that 'there was almost no restriction on travel' in the nineteenth century, he contrasted this with the present day of his writing when 'all along the [national] frontiers were barbed wire, machine-guns and prowling sentries, frequently wearing gasmasks'. Migration had 'practically dried up', since all countries including the United States, Britain, and the USSR were restricting immigration, sealing the fate of persecuted Jews. 'Europe's Jews had to stay and be slaughtered because there was nowhere for them to go' (CW, 16, p. 183), Orwell wrote with characteristic bluntness. For those who escaped as refugees, virulent anti-Semitism greeted them. Orwell frequently attributed this xenophobia to prevailing fears that Jews were threats to national culture: 'anti-Semitism is rationalized by saying that the Jew is a person who spreads disaffection and weakens national morale' (CW, 17, p. 69). Elsewhere, in 'Notes on Nationalism' (1945), he suggested that conservatives are more prone to anti-Semitism because they suspect Jews of 'diluting the national culture' (CW, 17, p. 152). Nor was Orwell immune from such assumptions, writing in his wartime diary on 25 October 1940 that he believed 'any Jew, i.e. European Jew, would prefer Hitler's kind of social system to ours, if it were not that he happens to persecute them. Ditto with almost any Central European, e.g. the refugees. They make use of England as a sanctuary, but they cannot help feeling the profoundest contempt for it.'[6] His insinuation about the immigrants' lack of loyalty to Britain is reflective of the widespread sentiment that Jews could not really belong to the nation-state, given their ethnic and cultural differences.[7] Orwell could not overcome his anti-Semitism – for him, such feelings were a 'neurosis' that could not be rationally argued against – but he was at least self-conscious about its consequences. Suspicions that Jewish refugees were secret German spies led to the internment of many of them in 1940 in a camp on the Isle of Man, and to the deportation of others to Australia that same year. Orwell later regarded this as an example of 'British atrocities'.[8] He also recognized that anti-Semitism in its 'milder' form – as expressions of dislike or distrust – could be 'just as cruel in an indirect way, because it causes people to avert their eyes from the whole refugee problem and remain uninterested in the fate of the surviving Jews of Europe' (*CW*, 15, p. 111). Anti-Semitism hence not only led to nation-states closing off their borders, but also cultivated general indifference amongst the populace towards the predicament of Jewish refugees.

The world of *Nineteen Eighty-Four* is predicated on what Stonebridge has called 'the psychopathologies of nationalism' that are saturated with the hatred of racialized foreigners.[9] Winston's semi-conscious recollection of the refugee boat reminds him of the incident that triggered his original impulse to begin his diary: the ritual of the Two Minutes Hate when the denizens of Oceania stir themselves into a frenzy of 'fear and anger' (*NEF*, p. 15) against projected images of 'the face of Emmanuel Goldstein, the Enemy of the People' (*NEF*, p. 13). Goldstein is an allusion to Leon Trotsky (and Big Brother to Joseph Stalin), to be sure, but what is important is Winston's acute registration of Goldstein's racial features: 'It was a lean Jewish face, with a great fuzzy aureole of white hair and a small goatee beard – a clever face, and yet somehow inherently despicable, with a kind of senile silliness in the long thin nose' (*NEF*, p. 14). The Jewish Goldstein functions as the scapegoat upon which all the threats to Oceania are concentrated and displaced. But this fear of foreign others extends beyond Goldstein. In *The Theory and Practice of Oligarchical Collectivism* – the proscribed book ostensibly written by Goldstein but which will turn out to have been composed by O'Brien and others as a decoy to entrap Winston – the totalitarian government of Oceania is described as a system where there is no 'racial discrimination', since 'Jews, Negroes, [and] South Americans of pure Indian blood are to be found in the highest ranks of the Party' (*NEF*, p. 217). This statement, however, is belied by the deep awareness of racial difference that shapes the perception of Oceania's enemies (alternately the superstates of Eurasia and Eastasia). Big Brother is seen as a 'fearless protector' (*NEF*, p. 17) and as the 'rock' against which 'the hordes of Asia dashed themselves in vain' (*NEF*, p. 310). Prisoners paraded through the streets are marked by their 'yellow' and 'sad Mongolian faces' (*NEF*, p. 121). During Hate Week, a popular poster depicts 'the monstrous figure of a Eurasian soldier, [. . .] with [an] expressionless Mongolian face and enormous boots, a sub-machine-gun pointed from his hip' (*NEF*, p. 156). The novel heightens the same paranoia around foreigners that Orwell would have witnessed during the Second World War: children follow a man wearing 'a funny kind of shoes', suspect him of being a foreigner, and report him as an 'enemy agent' (*NEF*, p. 60); an 'old couple' who are 'suspected of being of foreign extraction' have their house set on fire and perish by suffocating (*NEF*, p. 156); and the population's mobility is heavily restricted with 'patrols hanging about the railway stations', asking to examine passports and papers (*NEF*, p. 123). Oceania enforces the same homogeneity that racial nationalisms desire to achieve. Nowhere is this clearer than in the explanation given in Goldstein's book as to why Oceania will never conquer its enemies in spite of its constant wars against Eurasia and Eastasia. All the superstates, the book declares, adhere to the principle of 'cultural integrity', so '[i]f Oceania were to conquer the areas that used once to be known as France and Germany, it would be necessary either to exterminate the inhabitants [. . .] or to assimilate a population of about a hundred million people' (*NEF*, p. 204). Since neither option is practicable, the superstates refrain from infringing on each other's core territories. Culture is not the same as race, to be sure, yet the discourse of a nation's 'cultural integrity' was historically laden with racial overtones. The extreme alternatives presented here – either the extermination or the assimilation of outsiders – echo the exact fate that Arendt sees confronting minority populations in the era of ethno-nationalisms: 'minorities within nation-states must sooner or later be either assimilated or liquidated' (Arendt, *OT*, p. 357) if the principle of ethno-cultural 'integrity' is taken to its logical conclusion. The latter fate is starkly illuminated in *Nineteen Eighty-Four*'s scene of refugees being killed.

The war film, then, implicitly points to the xenophobic nationalism undergirding Oceania's totalitarianism. *Nineteen Eighty-Four* and Orwell's other writings also gesture at a second factor behind the antipathy towards refugees at this time. In 1946, Orwell observes that 'hundreds of thousands of homeless Jews are now trying desperately to get to Palestine', and asks: 'How about inviting, say, 100,000 Jewish refugees to settle in this country? [. . .] Why not solve their problem by offering them British citizenship?' The question, however, is rhetorical – and Orwell knows this because he knows that most British people do not support 'foreign immigration', partly from 'simple xenophobia, partly from fear of undercutting wages, but above all from the out-of-date notion that Britain is overpopulated and that more population means more unemployment'. Orwell points to economic anxieties that can manifest in xenophobic ways, since one common refrain against refugees is that 'They're only after our [British] jobs' (*CW*, 18, p. 482). Furthermore, working-class and trade union opposition, he notes, in part prevented a larger intake of German Jewish refugees before the war. In 1947, he saw the same rhetoric deployed against post-war Polish immigrants (many of them refugees), who were likewise accused of taking jobs from the local population and he deemed such anti-Polish sentiments 'the contemporary equivalent of anti-semitism' (*CW*, 19, p. 24). Orwell acknowledges that structures of racism cannot be explained in purely economic terms by 'unemployment, business jealousy, etc.' (*CW*, 16, p. 92). But it is nonetheless the case that the Great Depression and wartime rationing contributed to a climate of economic insecurity that exacerbated hostility towards immigrants who were perceived to be competitors for limited national resources. According to the historian Michael R. Marrus, 'economic depression conditioned attitudes towards immigration', and 'refugees ran into a wall of restrictions hastily erected in Western European countries in the early 1930s'.[10]

In *Nineteen Eighty-Four*, the same atmosphere of economic austerity – what Sheldon Wolin has called an 'anti-economy'[11] – is artificially engineered by the totalitarian state, which delimits any increase in 'the wealth of the world' (*NEF*, p. 196) and restricts living standards to brutal conditions because, 'if leisure and security were enjoyed by all alike, the great mass of human beings who are normally stupefied by poverty would become literate and would learn to think for themselves' (*NEF*, p. 198). This economic scarcity provokes viciousness towards others – even towards family members, instantiated in Winston's treatment of his mother and sister. As a perpetually hungry young boy, Winston would 'shout and storm' over not having enough food, stealing his mother's and sister's portions, even though he 'knew that he was starving the other two, [. . .]. The clamorous hunger in his belly seemed to justify him' (*NEF*, p. 169). The deprivation of 'leisure and security' and the ravages of poverty make the world seem like a zero-sum game in which people are pitted against each other in a constant battle for survival. This dog-eat-dog world is symbolized in the repeated image of the sinking ship. The image is first evoked by the refugee who '*sank as suddenly as though the holes had let in the water*' (*NEF*, p. 10), but Winston also dreams of his mother and sister in 'the saloon of a sinking ship' (*NEF*, p. 31), much like the refugees; Winston 'was out in the light and air while they were being sucked down to death, and they were down there *because* he was up here' (*NEF*, p. 32, original emphasis). In the merciless logic of a world with insufficient resources, Winston's survival depends on his mother and sister's deaths; he lives *because* they die. By the same logic, refugees are perceived as rivals for scanty resources who need to be blocked or eliminated for national citizens to thrive.

Given *Nineteen Eighty-Four*'s exploration of the forces of racial nationalism and economic austerity that underlie the spectacle of refugees dying at sea, it is unsurprising that Michiko Kakutani saw the novel as immediately relevant to contemporary times. After all, the historical circumstances attending the 2015 European refugee situation paralleled those of the early twentieth century in key ways. In place of the figure of the Jewish saboteur or the Mongolian soldier with his machine gun, it was the figure of the Islamic terrorist that haunted national paranoia about refugees fleeing from predominantly Muslim countries like Syria, Afghanistan, and Iraq. Likewise, decades of economic austerity imposed by European regimes of neoliberalism, coupled with the global financial crash of 2008, fostered widespread concerns that refugees would become financial burdens on the nation. Many states sought to demarcate between ostensibly illegitimate 'economic migrants' – those in search of better prospects – and legitimate refugees, those fleeing political persecution. A report conducted by the Pew Research Center in 2016 was headlined 'Europeans Fear Wave of Refugees Will Mean More Terrorism, Fewer Jobs'.[12] Orwell would have found these fears all too familiar. Not only does *Nineteen Eighty-Four* depict socio-political realities that continue to inform the refugee crises of our time; the text also raises the ethical question of how we respond to such crises and whether we can do so with compassion instead of fear.

Human Suffering, Pity, and Pitilessness

The hostility towards refugees in 2015 was not entirely uniform. One explosive image that emerged in the media coverage at that time was the photograph of the lifeless body of Aylan Kurdi, a three-year-old Syrian boy, lying face down on a beach in Bodrum, Turkey, drowned from the attempt at crossing the Mediterranean Sea.[13] This image was widely regarded as a turning point, prompting global outrage about the humanitarian crisis and a surge of pity for its victims. The British prime minister, David Cameron, declared himself 'deeply moved'; Nicola Sturgeon, the first minister of Scotland, insisted that refugees 'are the responsibility of all of us'; while the French prime minister, Manuel Valls, called for a 'Europe-wide mobilization' to address the crisis.[14] Donations to organizations to aid Syrian refugees increased dramatically, and petitions calling for governments to take in more asylum-seekers were circulated. The image of the boy's tragic end called forth an outpouring of global compassion. How reliable and efficacious are such responses to the spectacle of refugee suffering? Do images of bodily vulnerability invariably evoke sympathy on the part of witnesses?

Winston's diary entry stages these questions. The allusion to the '*middle-aged woman [who] might have been a jewess*' (*NEF*, p. 10) gestures to the racial and economic histories driving the phenomenon of statelessness, but the bulk of Winston's observations focuses on the audience's response to the film's violence. Far from expressing horror at the slaughter or pity towards the refugees' plight, the audience's enjoyment of the spectacle is clear; they are '*much amused*' and '*shouting with laughter*' at the carnage (*NEF*, p. 10). In an influential reading, the philosopher Martha Nussbaum argues that *Nineteen Eighty-Four* depicts 'the political overthrow of the human heart'. Emotions such as pity, sympathy, and compassion that Nussbaum sees as fundamental to human morality are destroyed by a political regime that seeks to remake 'human nature' altogether.[15] Indeed, Oceania is a place where denizens thrill to witness brutalities such as executions. One of Winston's colleagues, Syme, remarks how much he enjoys watching prisoners 'kicking' when they are hanged, with 'the tongue sticking right out, and blue – a quite bright blue. That's the detail that appeals to me' (*NEF*, p. 52). Winston demonstrates the same aestheticized appreciation for violence when he recalls the '*wonderful shot of a child's arm going up up up right up into the air*' (*NEF*, p. 10). The image of the arm recurs when, after a bombing, Winston sees 'a human hand severed at the wrist', and kicks 'the thing into the gutter' (*NEF*, pp. 87–8). This indifference to violations of the body – the severed hand is a mere object, a crafted filmic 'shot' or a 'thing' to be kicked – speaks of 'the death of pity' that Nussbaum sees characterizing this world and its inhabitants. Given this, the audience's joy at the killing of the refugees is unsurprising.

But Winston's diary entry also depicts an alternative to such pitilessness. In response to a '*little boy screaming with fright and hiding his head between her breasts*', the Jewish woman tries to protect him by '*putting her arms round him and comforting him although she was blue with fright herself*'. And the prole expresses outrage, '*kicking up a fuss and shouting they didnt oughter of showed it not in front of the kids*' – which Winston condescendingly dismisses as a '*typical prole reaction*' (*NEF*, pp. 10–11). The woman's gesture of protection of the boy, which is verbally echoed in the prole's desire to shield children from such images, is subsequently repeated in a dream-cum-memory that Winston has of his mother and sister: 'The dream had also been comprehended by – indeed, in some sense it had consisted in – a gesture of the arm made by his mother, and made again thirty years later by the Jewish woman he had seen on the news film, trying to shelter the small boy from the bullets, before the helicopters blew them both to pieces' (*NEF*, p. 167). The same gesture has occurred in Winston's past when 'his mother drew her arm round the child [his sister] and pressed its face against her breast' (*NEF*, p. 170) after Winston forcibly takes his sister's chocolate. In both cases, the protective gesture reveals an instinctive physical reaction to another's vulnerability. Winston realizes that these actions are 'ineffectual': the refugee's embrace cannot shield the child from bullets, just as his mother's embrace cannot produce more food for his sister. But these feelings, he maintains, have intrinsic value, and the horror of Oceania's totalitarian government, '[t]he terrible thing that the Party had done', was 'to persuade you that mere impulses, mere feelings, were of no account' (*NEF*, p. 172). Winston's kicking of 'the severed hand [. . .] into the gutter as though it had been a cabbage-stalk' (*NEF*, p. 172) is the logical consequence of a regime that seeks deliberately to eradicate 'mere feelings' and to cultivate callousness in its denizens. But whereas Party members like Winston are desensitized to cruelties, he recognizes that the proles, left to their own devices by the state, are not. 'The proles', he thinks, 'had stayed human. They had not become hardened inside. They had held on to the primitive emotions which he himself had to re-learn by conscious effort' (*NEF*, p. 172). These emotions are displayed in the prole woman's disgust at the violence against the refugees in contrast to the '*applause from the party seats*' (*NEF*, p. 11). Hence Winston's conclusion: '*If there is hope*, wrote Winston [in his diary], *it lies in the proles*' (*NEF*, p. 72).

In describing compassion for victims and horror at cruelty as 'primitive emotions', Winston suggests, like Nussbaum, that these are innate reactions that have been repressed through a political regime that has perverted 'the human heart'. Left to our natural impulses, human beings, like the proles who have 'stayed human', would respond to suffering with kindness, in much the same way a vast wave of pity for refugees emerged in the wake of the image of Aylan Kurdi's dead body in 2015. And on several occasions, *Nineteen Eighty-Four* does suggest that witnessing another person's vulnerability automatically elicits a sympathetic response in the spectator. Consider the moment when Julia trips, falls, and injures herself in front of Winston. At this point, he believes her to be a member of the Thought Police who will turn him in and who is therefore his nemesis. Yet '[a] curious emotion stirred in Winston's heart. In front of him was an enemy who was trying to kill him: in front of him, also, was a human creature, in pain and perhaps with a broken bone. Already he had *instinctively* started forward to help her. In the moment when he had seen her fall on the bandaged arm, it had been as though he *felt the pain in his own body*' (*NEF*, p. 111, emphasis added). Despite his violent animosity towards Julia – he has fantasized about murdering her in the previous chapter – when confronted with her fall, Winston's reaction is 'instinctive' in his desire to help and he feels her pain as if it were inflicted on his own body. This episode instantiates what the eighteenth-century moral philosopher Adam Smith described as our natural 'moral sentiments' at work, that is, our capacity to enter into the experience of others whose sorrow we witness and to empathize with their pain. 'Pity and compassion', Smith writes, are the 'emotion[s] we feel for the misery of others, when we are made to see it'. Thus, '[w]hen we see a stroke aimed and just ready to fall upon the leg or arm of another person, we naturally shrink and draw back our own leg or our own arm; and when it does fall, we feel it in some measure, and are hurt by it as well as the sufferer; we enter as it were into his body'.[16] Bodily instinct functions as the basis for ethics, facilitating a visceral identification with those experiencing states of injury. Such emotions do political work by generating solidarities and 'fellow feeling', argues Nussbaum, fuelled by the recognition of common vulnerabilities between people.[17] When 'the Party [tells] you to reject the evidence of your eyes and ears' (*NEF*, p. 84), then, it is not merely an attempt to go against the empirical truth of sensory perception; it is an attempt to deform instinctual human morality.

But embodied instinct proves a rather unreliable locus of ethics, functioning alternately as an instrument of sympathy, exemplified in the episode above, and as an instrument of self-preservation, a doubling most visible in the novel's climax when Winston is physically and psychologically tortured. In Room 101, O'Brien threatens to unleash his greatest fear on him – rats – and Winston becomes a mindless 'screaming animal', feeling that '[t]here was one and only one way to save himself. He must interpose another human being, the *body* of another human being, between himself and the rats' (*NEF*, p. 299, original emphasis). Seeking to sacrifice another 'body' to whom 'he could transfer his punishment', Winston screams in betrayal of his love, 'Do it to Julia! Do it to Julia! Not me!' (*NEF*, p. 300). The emphasis is again on the sensations of the body, but instead of it being the wellspring of natural compassion for another, the body is now the source of an instinctive selfishness that seeks to displace pain onto somebody else. This moment is foreshadowed in Winston's earlier reflections:

> It struck him that in moments of crisis one is never fighting against an external enemy but always *against one's own body*. [...] On the battlefield, in the torture chamber, on a sinking ship, the issues that you are fighting for are always forgotten, because the body swells up until it fills the universe, and even when you are not paralysed by fright or screaming with pain, life is a moment-to-moment struggle against hunger or cold or sleeplessness[.]
>
> (*NEF*, p. 106, emphasis added)

This passage links the 'torture chamber' – Room 101 – to the 'sinking ship' of the refugees, pointing to the instinct of self-preservation that may lead all ethical concerns, all 'the issues that you are fighting for', to be forgotten and abandoned. Winston will sacrifice Julia – make her a scapegoat – believing it will preserve his life and sanity, just as national citizens will sacrifice foreign refugees, believing it to be in their own interests. In *Nineteen Eighty-Four*, then, embodied instinct points in two radically different directions, capable of generating an ethical impulse for pity on the one hand, and a ruthless impulse to violence on the other. This ambivalence also characterizes the gesture of protection made by the woman refugee and Winston's mother. As we saw earlier, that gesture – in which a child is pressed 'against [the] breast' of a protecting figure – seems to Winston to encapsulate the quintessence of all that is benevolent about humanity, to be the expression of primitive emotions that seek to shelter those who are most vulnerable. But Orwell transforms this image into something far more sinister by the novel's end, when Winston is finally broken and praises the regime: 'O stubborn, self-willed exile from the loving breast! [. . .] He loved Big Brother' (*NEF*, p. 311). Instead of the human breast symbolizing the capacity of human kindness, it becomes an image of human subservience to totalitarianism, with Winston occupying the place of the child seeking the protection of Big Brother's 'loving breast'.

Figures of ethical humanism – the instinctive body, the protective gesture – in *Nineteen Eighty-Four* are thus highly unstable, morphing just as quickly into figures of unethical inhumanism. What this suggests is that, contrary to Nussbaum's argument, 'the human heart' may not be naturally predisposed to pity, emotions she sees artificially suppressed by totalitarianism. Instead, the reality of human nature may be closer to what O'Brien tells Winston: 'You are imagining that there is something called human nature which will be outraged by what we do and will turn against us. But we create human nature. Men are infinitely malleable' (*NEF*, p. 282). This malleability is what the philosopher Richard Rorty emphasizes in his reading of *Nineteen Eighty-Four*. Like Nussbaum, Rorty sees the novel depicting 'a world in which human solidarity [is] – deliberately, through careful planning – made impossible'. Unlike Nussbaum, he suggests that 'there is nothing deep inside each of us, no common human nature, no built-in human solidarity, to use as a moral reference point'.[18] For Rorty, whether or not one feels pity or pitilessness towards people who suffer – such as Jewish refugees fleeing death camps – ultimately depends on one's socialization and therefore on historical contingency; human solidarities are not pre-given, but forged. Insofar as symbols of human beneficence in *Nineteen Eighty-Four* are slippery, morphing easily into symbols of human cruelty, the novel reinforces

O'Brien's and Rorty's anti-essentialist view of human nature as 'infinitely malleable'. Orwell was clearly aware of the capriciousness of human sensibilities, writing: 'What is most striking of all is the way sympathy can be turned on and off like a tap according to political expediency.'[19] Far from being intrinsic to human nature, the capacity for pity and pitilessness is contingent on one's ideological worldview.

If this is the case, the surest way to ensure that citizens respond compassionately to humanitarian crises such as the ongoing displacement of refugees is to foster political systems that will in turn foster such ethical responses. Orwell recognized that private conscience and public institutions were fundamentally inseparable. As he insisted in 1944: 'The fallacy is to believe that under a dictatorial government you can be free *inside*. [...] The secret freedom which you can supposedly enjoy under a despotic Government is nonsense, because your thoughts are never entirely your own' (*CW*, 16, p. 172). Citizens in an unfree political system are more likely to be unfree in thought. By the same token, citizens in a nation-state hostile to refugees are more likely to be indifferent to their plight. The capacity for ethical or unethical action is not immutable in human beings, but is inextricable from the political worlds we inhabit and that we reciprocally both shape and are shaped by. *Nineteen Eighty-Four* depicts a totalitarian world, one in which the historical regimes of racial nationalism and economic austerity were not only responsible for originating the myriad refugee crises of Orwell's time, but also for encouraging the indifferent and cruel responses of many nation-states and their citizens who turned a blind eye to such suffering. In its imaginative rendering of such a world, *Nineteen Eighty-Four* presciently anticipates the future – that is to say, our present.

Notes

1 Michiko Kakutani, 'Why "1984" Is a 2017 Must-Read', *The New York Times* (26 January 2017) [www.nytimes.com/2017/01/26/books/why-1984-is-a-2017-must-read.html] (accessed 30 October 2019).

2 It is important to note that the refugee situation became visible to the media and politicians as a 'crisis' only once it reached the shores of Europe and the West, as it did in 2015. But in fact, the displacement of people from these countries had and has been ongoing, with the majority of these refugees taken in by countries of the global south, rather than the wealthier north.

3 For helpful histories of refugees, see Michael R. Marrus, *The Unwanted: European Refugees in the Twentieth Century* (New York: Oxford University Press, 1985) and Peter Gatrell, *The Making of the Modern Refugee* (Oxford: Oxford University Press, 2015).

4 George Orwell, *Nineteen Eighty-Four: The Facsimile of the Extant Manuscript*, ed. Peter Davison (London: Secker & Warburg, 1984), pp. 28–9.

5 Lyndsey Stonebridge, *Placeless People: Writing, Rights, and Refugees* (Oxford: Oxford University Press, 2018), pp. 76–7. I am greatly indebted to Stonebridge's reading of Orwell and this chapter follows her line of argument regarding anti-Semitism and racial nationalism. But I also draw attention to conditions of economic austerity that exacerbate hostility towards foreigners who are seen as economic threats.

6 George Orwell, *Diaries*, ed. Peter Davison (London: Penguin, 2009), pp. 285–6.

7 For additional scholarship on Orwell's anti-Semitism, see Melvyn New, 'Orwell and Antisemitism: Toward *1984*', *Modern Fiction Studies*, 21.1 (Spring 1975), pp. 81–105; David Walton, 'George Orwell and Anti-Semitism', *Patterns of Prejudice*, 16.1 (1982), pp. 19–34; and John Newsinger, 'Orwell, Anti-Semitism, and the Holocaust', in John Rodden (ed.), *The Cambridge Companion to George Orwell* (Cambridge: Cambridge University Press, 2007), pp. 112–25.

8 Orwell, *Diaries*, p. 346.

9 Stonebridge, *Placeless People*, p. 80.

10 Marrus, *The Unwanted*, p. 136.

11 Sheldon Wolin, 'Counter-Enlightenment: Orwell's *Nineteen Eighty-Four*', in Robert Mulvihill (ed.), *Reflections on America, 1984: An Orwell Symposium* (Athens: University of Georgia Press, 1986), pp. 98–113, at p. 102.

12 Richard Wilkes, Bruce Stokes, and Katie Simmons, 'Europeans Fear Wave of Refugees Will Mean More Terrorism, Fewer Jobs', Pew Research Center (11 July 2016) [www.pewresearch.org/global/2016/07/11/europeans-fear-wave-of-refugees-will-mean-more-terrorism-fewer-jobs/] (accessed 30 October 2019).

13 The photograph was taken by a Turkish journalist, Nilüfer Demir, and circulated widely across social media and newspapers from 2 September 2015 onwards. The boy's real name is Aylan Shenu, but this chapter uses the name given by the Turkish authorities and subsequently used by the media. For a detailed account of the reception and impact of the photo, see Farida Vis and Olga Goriunova (eds.), *The Iconic Image on Social Media: A Rapid Research Response to the Death of Aylan Kurdi* (Visual Social Media Lab, December 2015). The report is accessible at https://research.gold.ac.uk/14624/1/KURDI%20REPORT.pdf (accessed 30 October 2019).

14 Quotations are taken from Ishaan Tharoor, 'Death of Drowned Syrian Toddler Aylan Kurdi Jolts World Leaders', *The Washington Post* (3 September 2015) [www .washingtonpost.com/news/worldviews/wp/2015/09/03/image-of-drowned-syrian-toddler-aylan-kurdi-jolts-world-leaders/?utm_term=.3c2de5bb719c] (accessed 30 October 2019).

15 Martha C. Nussbaum, 'The Death of Pity: Orwell and American Political Life', in Abbott Gleason, Jack Goldsmith, and Martha C. Nussbaum (eds.), *On 'Nineteen Eighty-Four': Orwell and Our Future* (Princeton and Oxford: Princeton University Press, 2005), pp. 279–99, at p. 282.

16 Adam Smith, *The Theory of Moral Sentiments* (1759), ed. Knud Haakonssen (Cambridge: Cambridge University Press, 2002), pp. 11–12.

17 Nussbaum, 'The Death of Pity', p. 282.

18 Richard Rorty, *Contingency, Irony, Solidarity* (Cambridge: Cambridge University Press, 1989), pp. 189, 177.

19 Orwell, *Diaries*, p. 336.

10

ELINOR TAYLOR

The Problem of Hope
Orwell's Workers

'*If there is hope,* [...] *it lies in the proles*' (*NEF*, p. 72). Thus writes Winston
Smith in his secret diary, in one of the most famous formulations from
Nineteen Eighty-Four (1949). This chapter takes a historical and historicist
view of this remark, situating Winston's and the novel's account of the Oceanic
proletariat in relation to Orwell's understanding of the economico-political
predicament of the working class in the 1930s and 1940s. The chapter considers the highly contentious bind into which *Nineteen Eighty-Four* puts the so-
called 'proles', a group it constructs from a largely exterior point of view:
caught between Winston's belief in that group's inevitable, albeit temporally
distant, victory, and O'Brien's insistence that the alleged 'animalism' of the
proletariat will prevent it from gaining any kind of purchase on the future.
I begin by outlining how Orwell's thinking on the relationship between socialism and the working class developed through the 1930s and 1940s, from *The
Road to Wigan Pier* (1937) to the welfare state. I then discuss the moral and
reproductive functions ascribed to the proles in the novel in light of Orwell's
political commitments, before addressing the question of whether the novel
despairs of class politics, as thinkers such as Raymond Williams have argued.

Orwell and the Working Class

To locate 'hope' in the 'proletariat' is to evoke a Marxist account of history in
which the working class is the class destined to overthrow capitalism and
liberate all humanity. In the *Communist Manifesto*, published in 1848, the
proletariat are defined by Karl Marx and Friedrich Engels as

> a class of labourers, who live only so long as they find work, and who find work
> only so long as their labour increases capital. These labourers, who must sell
> themselves piecemeal, are a commodity, like every other article of commerce,
> and are consequently exposed to all the vicissitudes of competition, to all the
> fluctuations of the market.[1]

They are industrial capitalism's creatures, and by consequence also its 'grave-diggers'; Marx and Engels foresaw an inexorably increasing antagonism between the wage labourers and the owners of the means of production that would give rise to revolution abolishing exploitation. In this sense the proletariat is a 'universal' class that cannot 'emancipate itself from the class which exploits and oppresses it (the bourgeoisie), without at the same time forever freeing the whole of society from exploitation, oppression, [and] class struggle', as Engels argued.[2] During the revolutionary decades of the early twentieth century, fierce debate turned on the questions of the agency of the working class to make such a revolution itself, the role of historical conditions in making revolution possible or inevitable, and the role of intellectuals and political parties in relation to working-class movements; but hope in the proletariat, for revolutionaries, was hope for humanity. There are also the longer traditions, well developed in Britain and closely entwined with the history of trade unionism, of utopian and reformist socialism, which aimed to improve conditions through legislative rather than revolutionary means; there, the working class might be aligned with 'hope' in a more pragmatic, less theoretical way, as a function of its strength as the productive class. It produced value and maintained strength in numbers such that it could withdraw its labour as leverage for better conditions and certain other political demands. By the 1930s, the Labour movement was in crisis as a result of the failure of the 1926 General Strike and the Depression, which caused the collapse of the second Labour government and seemingly irremediable mass unemployment. The collapse of revolutionary movements and the destruction of organized labour under fascism in Europe made the possibility of socialism in the West increasingly distant, even as many British writers and intellectuals aligned themselves with the political Left against fascism.

Orwell's lifelong commitment to socialism is not seriously in doubt, but he was hostile to approaches he thought overly theoretical or abstract. He particularly disputed the 'orthodox' Marxist emphasis on the economic at the expense of the cultural aspects of life. His thinking on class after the mid-1930s placed increasing emphasis on the cultural dimension of working-class life, even to the point of essentializing working-class people as somehow naturally and inherently different from others, and this is vital for understanding the construction of the proles in *Nineteen Eighty-Four*. In *Down and Out in Paris and London* (1933), he was keen to assert, against his own class-conditioned preconceptions, that there was nothing fundamentally different between people of different classes: 'The mass of the rich and the poor are differentiated by their incomes and nothing else, and the average millionaire is only the average dishwasher dressed in a new suit'

(*DOPL*, p. 127). While in some ways Orwell remained faithful to this as a basic truth, the cultural distinctions of class nonetheless came to be increasingly important to him, and shaped his final novel. This shift begins to emerge in *The Road to Wigan Pier*, commissioned by the Left-wing publisher Victor Gollancz and researched in the early months of 1936 in the depressed areas of industrial England beset by mass unemployment. The first half of the book presents Orwell's account of his experiences in those areas. The second consists of a discussion of the prospects for socialism and a critique of socialist intellectuals whom Orwell considered out of touch with the realities of working-class life, committed to a joyless, puritanical vision of life that would never inspire support, and credulous towards to the Stalinized Soviet Union. As in *Down and Out*, Orwell insists there is no natural difference between working-class people and everyone else; they are not more inured to squalor, deprivation, and injustice, nor more passive and acquiescent. Observing a woman unblocking a drain, he asserts: 'She knew well enough what was happening to her – understood as well as I did how dreadful a destiny it was to be kneeling there in the bitter cold, on the slimy stones of a slum backyard, poking a stick up a foul drainpipe' (*RWP*, p. 15). Even though he claimed that working-class people had grown 'servile' since the Depression had begun (*RWP*, p. 118), that passivity was not an expression of an inherent tendency to submission but rather the outcome of constant bullying and intrusive subjection to anonymous bureaucracy that middle-class people cannot imagine. Working-class cultural pursuits such as gambling, drinking, and the cinema are not symptoms of inherent intellectual inferiority, but the 'cheap palliatives' (*RWP*, p. 83) necessary to make such a life bearable.

The second part of *Wigan Pier* announces a theme that would become a defining feature of Orwell's non-fiction: an attack on socialism as a 'theory' abstracted from experience. Capital-S-Socialists are condemned for their desire to make the world resemble a theory, a desire emanating from a 'hypertrophied sense of order' (*RWP*, p. 166) that aims at a tidy rather than a just world and which assumes poverty can only be remedied with top-down intervention, an assumption that leads to a tolerance of dictatorship. Orwell never believed that socialism as an abstract theory of economic equality would win popular consent; by emphasising the economic at the expense of the cultural and social dimensions of life, socialists had in fact hastened the advance of fascism: 'With their eyes glued to economic facts, they have proceeded on the assumption that man has no soul, and explicitly or implicitly they have set up the goal of a materialistic Utopia' (*RWP*, p. 199). Orwell's research had taught him that his conclusion in *Down and Out* that class differences were nothing other than functions of the economic was insufficient; he now saw that culture and economics were woven together to produce a 'shadowy caste-system' (*RWP*, p. 114). Social change could not come purely through economic intervention.

Writing *Wigan Pier* had therefore convinced Orwell that the English working class were not inherently passive and tolerant of subjection, but nor were they inherently revolutionary, as the theorists of socialism supposed. His experiences in the Spanish Civil War furthermore convinced him that they were not inherently internationalist, either, since, as he put it in *The Lion and the Unicorn* (1941), '[f]or two and a half years they watched their comrades in Spain slowly strangled, and never aided them by even a single strike' (*CW*, 12, p. 398). He came to the view that all-out class war in Britain was rendered impossible by cultural factors, primarily patriotism and cultural overlaps between classes. But if this forestalled revolution, Orwell began to conceive of certain features of working-class culture as strengths both in the struggle against fascism and on the road to socialism. After the outbreak of the Second World War, we find an extension of working-class culture into an imagined national-popular ('common') culture, based in tradition, that stood against what he saw as the political culture of the internationalized and authoritarian elite (usually socialists, in Orwell's eyes). This much is clear in his 1940 essay on Charles Dickens, which is worth quoting at some length.

> No grown-up person can read Dickens without feeling his limitations, and yet there does remain his native generosity of mind, which acts as a kind of anchor and nearly always keeps him where he belongs. It is probably the central secret of his popularity. A good-tempered antinomianism rather of Dickens's type is one of the marks of Western popular culture. One sees it in folk-stories and comic songs, in dream-figures like Mickey Mouse and Popeye the Sailor (both of them variants of Jack the Giant-killer), in the history of working-class Socialism, in the popular protests (always ineffective but not always a sham) against imperialism, in the impulse that makes a jury award excessive damages when a rich man's car runs over a poor man; it is the feeling that one is always on the side of the underdog, on the side of the weak against the strong. In one sense it is a feeling that is fifty years out of date. The common man is still living in the mental world of Dickens, but nearly every modern intellectual has gone over to some or other form of totalitarianism. From the Marxist or Fascist point of view, nearly all that Dickens stands for can be written off as 'bourgeois morality'. But in moral outlook no one could be more 'bourgeois' than the English working classes. The ordinary people in the Western countries have never entered, mentally, into the world of 'realism' and power-politics. They may do so before long, in which case Dickens will be as out of date as the cab-horse. But in his own age and ours he has been popular chiefly because he was able to express in a comic, simplified and therefore memorable form the native

decency of the common man. And it is important that from this point of view people of very different types can be described as 'common'. In a country like England, in spite of its class-structure, there does exist a certain cultural unity. All through the Christian ages, and especially since the French Revolution, the Western world has been haunted by the idea of freedom and equality; it is only an *idea*, but it has penetrated to all ranks of society.   (*CW*, 12, p. 55)

This passage sums up Orwell's view, by this point, of a 'common' culture, associated with but not exclusively belonging to the working class, that is infused with moral principles of fairness and resistance to tyranny, and an immanent desire for 'freedom and equality'. The principles of socialism were thus already embedded in English popular culture. (Orwell's examples include American cartoons, but he traces their origins to the English fairy tale.) But notable too is the implied opposition between this cultural forma-tion and 'power politics'. As we shall see, in *Nineteen Eighty-Four* the moral authority of the proles is a function of their absolute exclusion from the politics of the state. At this point, however, Orwell did not see popular culture and its values as necessarily separated from formal politics. In the early phase of the war, Orwell argued in *The Lion and the Unicorn* against the Labour Party's 'timid reformism' (*CW*, 12, p. 420) and for turning the war into a 'revolutionary war' (*CW*, 12, p. 426) for socialist transformation. While he offers a six-point programme for that transformation, he also stresses that the impetus for it must come from 'the people', through their own decision about what they are fighting for, rather than through the direction of any intellectual or institution that claims to speak in their name. The people are thus configured as the moral driving force for social-ism, that drive emerging organically from their own, 'native' traditions and practices. A radical socialism 'from below', as imagined there, would not be susceptible to the authoritarianism of Soviet-style communism, but would be rooted in the communality of 'the pub, the football match, the back garden, the fireside and the "nice cup of tea"' (*CW*, 12, p. 394). In *The English People*, too, written during the war but published in 1947, Orwell affirms the legalism and moral integrity of the 'English people' who have not succumbed to the 'modern cult of power-worship' (*CW*, 16, p. 205) or the hypocrisy and puritanism of the intellectuals. But by this point Orwell accepted that 'the proletariat of Hammersmith will not arise and massacre the *bourgeoisie* of Kensington: they are not different enough' (*CW*, 16, p. 210). Socialism, if it came, would have to come through constitutional means.

The test of those means, and of Orwell's faith in the English public's socialist instincts and values, came with the foundation of the post-war welfare state. The Beveridge Report of 1942 set out the foundations for the welfare state, and its proposals to remedy the 'five giant evils' of want, ignorance, squalor, idleness, and disease through a programme of comprehensive national insurance, alongside those for the nationalization of essential industries, gained popular and political support through the war years. The 1945 general election returned a Labour government with an unprecedented mandate for wide-ranging social and economic reforms. Orwell's attitudes to these developments were complex, however. He moved closer to the Labour Party, which he had previously dismissed as overly timid, through the course of the war and supported the party at the general election.[3] But he had doubts about how far-reaching the reforms would really be, and was also suspicious of the cross-party consensus that formed around them, seeing this as presaging a closing down of political possibility. 'Thirty years ago', he noted in *The English People*, 'any Conservative would have denounced [the Beveridge proposals] as State charity, while most Socialists would have rejected it as a capitalist bribe. In 1944 the only discussion that arose was as to whether it would be adopted in whole or in part' (CW, 16, p. 210). He was disappointed by the limits of the reforms as well as by the electorate's willingness to accept this 'capitalist bribe'. The new system of national insurance removed many of the cruelties that had blighted the lives of the unemployed in *Wigan Pier*, such as the hated Means Test, but war rationing and austerity continued, and working-class wages were restrained to pay for the reforms. In *The Lion and the Unicorn*, he had warned against economic reform without social reform: nationalization and a planned economy would not deliver equality without commensurate democratization in civil society. The Attlee government fell short on both counts: although it nationalized essential industries, its reforms left the economic underpinnings of the class system intact, while offering social reforms that would reconcile working-class people to that system. This was not to be the political realization of the latent socialism of English popular culture, and this disappointment resonates in the seemingly unbreachable divide between the proles and the Party in *Nineteen Eighty-Four*.

By 1947, indeed, socialism had become something like an article of faith, something both necessary and, it increasingly seemed, impossible. The 'socialist today', Orwell wrote in 'Toward European Unity' (1947), published in *Partisan Review*, 'is in the position of a doctor treating an all but hopeless case. As a doctor, it is his duty to keep the patient alive, and therefore to assume that the patient has at least a chance of recovery. As a scientist, it is his duty to face the facts, and therefore to admit that the patient will probably die' (CW, 19, p. 163). In the same essay, he countenanced an atomic world order in which the worst scenario would be the division of the world among two or three vast super-states, unable to conquer one another and unable to be overthrown by any internal rebellion. In all probability their structure would be hierarchic, with a semidivine caste at the top and outright slavery at the bottom, and the crushing out of liberty would exceed anything that the world has yet seen. Within each state the necessary psychological atmosphere would be kept up by complete severance from the outer world, and by a continuous phony war against rival states. Civilizations of this type might remain static for thousands of years.

(CW, 19, p. 163)

History did not quite turn out like this, but Orwell's two predicaments here – his feeling that socialism was receding into an irrational hope, and his fear of a new world order in which *any* political action was effectively impossible – constitute the nexus of class politics in *Nineteen Eighty-Four*.

Proletarian Morality

Nineteen Eighty-Four expresses Orwell's abiding but increasingly diminished faith in a socialist revolution from below, his insistence on the value of what he considered the moral values of 'native' English culture, as well as his fears of the paralysing effects of economic collectivization without democratization. Winston's famous assertion that '*If there is hope* [...] *it lies in the proles*', and his testaments of faith in the absence of providential signs, echo Orwell's metaphor of the doctor ministering to the gravely ill. The novel maintains that the proles are the location of morality and futurity, but it does so in a way that also means they can never be expected to act politically. It is significant that the first episode Winston recounts in his forbidden diary without really knowing why is an incidence of moral rebellion by a prole woman:

> then there was a wonderful shot of a child's arm going up up up right up into the air a helicopter with a camera in its nose must have followed it up and there was a lot of applause from the party seats but a woman down in the prole part of the house suddenly started kicking up a fuss and shouting they didnt oughter of showed it not in front of kids they didnt it aint right not in front of kids it aint until the police turned her turned her out i dont suppose anything happened to her nobody cares what the proles say typical prole reaction they never –
>
> (NEF, pp. 10–11)

While the prole woman's rebellion might appear instinctive and purely emotional, it comes with a moral charge – '*it aint right*' – and is furthermore a '*typical*' reaction, suggesting that moral outbursts of this kind are common, and while nothing may have happened to the woman as a consequence,

Winston perhaps unconsciously converts this moral rebellion into an intellectual one in the form of his diary. But another connection is unconsciously made too: while engaged in this forbidden act of writing, 'a totally different memory had clarified itself in his mind, to the point where he almost felt equal to writing it down' (*NEF*, p. 11): his first, ambiguous encounter with Julia and O'Brien in the Ministry of Truth during the Two Minutes Hate. The linking of these memories – one an act of moral rebellion, the other a sense of political possibility – indicates the connection underlying Winston's later statement that '*If there is hope* [...] *it lies in the proles.*' The unconscious element here also complicates the assumption that Winston is the conscious intellectual and the proles are the unconscious bearers of possibilities they cannot themselves understand. But although this possibility is suggested at the outset, Winston himself only realizes it too late. His first declaration that hope lies in the proles is primarily a logical deduction: it is the proles' sheer numerical strength, together with their exclusion from the Party, that means hope 'must' lie therein, and though each subsequent re-articulation of this hope indicates a revision of his thought, the moral and the political remain in a mutually destructive antagonism.

In a certain way, *Nineteen Eighty-Four* is a vision of Orwell's worst fears about socialism without democratization; a nightmare of what might happen to the abject populace of *Wigan Pier* if the state imposed on them a set of basic provisions and occasional social mobility in exchange for a fundamental powerlessness and political disqualification. The proles are 'turned loose', allowed to live

> a style of life that appeared to be natural to them, a sort of ancestral pattern. They were born, they grew up in the gutters, they went to work at twelve, they passed through a brief blossoming-period of beauty and sexual desire, they married at twenty, they were middle-aged at thirty, they died, for the most part, at sixty. Heavy physical work, the care of home and children, petty quarrels with neighbours, films, football, beer and, above all, gambling, filled up the horizon of their minds. To keep them in control was not difficult. [...] In all questions of morals they were allowed to follow their ancestral code. The sexual puritanism of the Party was not imposed upon them. Promiscuity went unpunished, divorce was permitted. For that matter, even religious worship would have been permitted if the proles had shown any sign of needing or wanting it. They were beneath suspicion. (*NEF*, pp. 74–5)

Yet their 'ancestral' connection to the past and the moral autonomy granted to them by their exclusion from the Party is a key source of the 'hope' Winston sees in them. Winston seems to grasp this when he rearticulates his hope in the register of faith, rather than logic: 'But if there was hope, it lay in the proles. You had to cling on to that. When you put it in words it sounded reasonable: it was when you looked at the human beings passing you on the pavement that it became an act of faith' (*NEF*, p. 89). Perhaps unconsciously seeking to test this faith, Winston turns social investigator and tries to find out from an old prole in a pub whether life really was freer before the Ingsoc revolution. The answers he gains, however, disappoint him because they are in the form of fragmented, particular memories, not general judgements. He concludes that 'all the relevant facts were outside the range of their vision' (*NEF*, p. 96), but this reveals the failure on Winston's part to recognize the political content of those fragments. The 'million useless things' despairingly itemized by Winston – 'a quarrel with a workmate, a hunt for a lost bicycle pump, the expression on a long-dead sister's face, the swirls of dust on a windy morning seventy years ago' (*NEF*, p. 96) – would seem highly relevant, concrete particulars that might substantiate his declaration of 'faith', but he cannot read them as such. This would seem to satirize not the proles themselves but rather the growing rift Orwell saw in the 1940s between political activity and everyday working-class life. The values of the latter, which he had hoped might inform an English socialist revolution, could only survive in an autonomous but fundamentally depoliticized space.

This position – implied, but not fully articulated in Orwell's essays – is even clearer in Winston's next affirmation of hope in the proles. Once the Party caught you, he thinks,

> [y]ou were lifted clean out of the stream of history. And yet to the people of only two generations ago, this would not have seemed all-important, because they were not attempting to alter history. They were governed by private loyalties which they did not question. What mattered were individual relationships, and a completely helpless gesture, an embrace, a tear, a word spoken to a dying man, could have value in itself. The proles, it suddenly occurred to him, had remained in this condition. They were not loyal to a party or a country or an idea, they were loyal to one another. For the first time in his life he did not despise the proles or think of them merely as an inert force which would one day spring to life and regenerate the world. The proles had stayed human. (*NEF*, p. 172)

On the one hand, this suggests that Winston has revised his assessments of the old man's anecdotes and recognized their moral import. It echoes Orwell's respect for the instinctive morality and mutual solidarity he considered characteristic of working-class culture, and which he considered signs of a socialist impulse. But on the other hand, the price paid for the survival of those values that enable the proles to 'stay human' is a complete deprivation of political agency: they survive because they are not put in the service of any attempt to 'alter history', and any attempt on their part to act politically will destroy that way of life and their humanity.

Embodying the Future

The proles are therefore a living connection to a past felt to be implicitly freer and more humane, but they are also placed in a bind where the very survival of the traces of that past depends on their total political disempowerment. They can be a moral force, as the woman in Winston's first diary entry is, but not a political one. There is another element to this bind, however, whereby the proles embody human survival *because* they are excluded from politics, and that is their status as reproducers of human life. This is evident in Winston's final meditation on the proles just before his arrest. Looking at a proletarian woman in the street, he and Julia agree that she is 'beautiful', and Winston thinks:

> The woman down there had no mind, she had only strong arms, a warm heart and a fertile belly. He wondered how many children she had given birth to. It might easily be fifteen. She had had her momentary flowering, a year, perhaps, of wildrose beauty and then she had suddenly swollen like a fertilised fruit and grown hard and red and coarse, and then her life had been laundering, scrubbing, darning, cooking, sweeping, polishing, mending, scrubbing, laundering, first for children, then for grandchildren, over thirty unbroken years. At the end of it she was still singing. The mystical reverence that he felt for her was somehow mixed up with the aspect of the pale, cloudless sky, stretching away behind the chimney-pots into interminable distances. It was curious to think that the sky was the same for everybody, in Eurasia or Eastasia as well as here. And the people under the sky were also very much the same – everywhere, all over the world, hundreds of thousands of millions of people just like this, people ignorant of one another's existence, held apart by walls of hatred and lies, and yet almost exactly the same – people who had never learned to think but who were storing up in their hearts and bellies and muscles the power that would one day overturn the world. If there was hope, it lay in the proles!
>
> (*NEF*, pp. 228–9)

Where Winston had earlier identified hope in the survival of older forms of (moral) sociability within the proles' culture, here it is specifically identified with the proletarian body, and particularly the female body, as it is out of 'those mighty loins a race of conscious beings must one day come' (*NEF*, p. 230). What prevents the proles from simply being relics of a distant, diminishing past is their reproductive capacity, and thus the proles' relationship with the future is deeply entangled with the novel's treatment of sexuality. What Winston realizes here is that the 'ugliness' of the woman's body is a mark of 'humanity', insofar as it marks her participation in the heterosexual, reproductive family. Proletarian life consists and is reproduced in the 'natural' social form of the family, which is contrasted with the 'political' family as dictated by the Party, in which marriages are regulated and children betray their parents. Unsurprisingly, perhaps, Julia and Winston's sexual relationship is marked by fantasies of proletarianization, as Julia obtains the perfume and make-up only used by the proles, and they dream that they could 'learn to speak with proletarian accents, get jobs in a factory and live out their lives undetected' (*NEF*, p. 159). If their sexual relationship can only be a 'perverse' one, the working-class woman represents the normative integration of sexuality in the 'natural' form of the family. Discussing this association of class and reproduction, Glyn Salton-Cox argues that the novel expresses Orwell's 'reproductive anxieties', as expressed in his journalism through his preoccupation with the national birth rate, as well as a fundamentally heteronormative view of sexuality that associated any attempt to think politically about sex with perversion. Winston's eventual capitulation consists not only of the betrayal of his lover but also the cancellation of heterosexual desire in general by his 'love' for Big Brother, so that the novel ends in 'a vision of anti-Communist, homophobic, incestuous despair'.[4] Julia and Winston's attempt to rebel politically through the emulation of proletarian sexuality can only end in brutal dehumanization: they cannot 'stay human' and attempt to 'alter history'.

Defeat and Despair?

Orwell's proles, then, are a moral force in the novel and the key to the survival of humanity, but both these aspects are constructed in a way that excludes in advance any possibility of political agency. They defy the Party in moral and sexual autonomy, but they do so unthinkingly, 'naturally', in ways that cannot alter history. The novel has been read as a testament of double despair: in the possibility that a top-down revolution can avoid becoming totalitarian, and in the capacity of ordinary people to exercise political agency for themselves. The socialist critic Raymond Williams made this case influentially at several points in his career. In 1958, he argued that the novel articulates the impasse Orwell reached at the end of his life, whereby he remained committed to socialism but no longer saw any hope for its realization. As Williams writes: 'He was a believer in equality, and a critic of class, who founded his later work on a deep assumption of inherent inequality, inescapable class difference.'[5] For Williams, this paradox was based on a false and despairing extrapolation from the failures of Orwell's own moment to a vision of a world that offered no possibility of *any* success, a world where all political actions against injustice are not only predestined to fail but also to be erased from the historical record altogether. This generalization effectively repressed historical realities: ordinary people, as Orwell knew, *had* risen against tyranny, at Kronstadt, in Barcelona, and in Warsaw, for instance; and likewise he knew that not everyone breaks down, not everyone betrays one another.[6] He depicts the colonized populations of the novel's disputed territories as just as passive as the proles, yet he knew that anti-colonial movements were gathering force in his own time (it never occurs to Winston that the future might lie with *them*, of course). Yet he 'projects an enormous apathy on all the oppressed'.[7] He saw only a world of heroic but doomed individual actions, against a background of implacable power structures and pacified working classes, because 'that is how he really saw present society'.[8] Williams's charge that Orwell excludes what he knew to be true about the possibilities of revolt is difficult to refute, though one might suggest this is one strand of the novel's anxiety about the loss of historical memory. The reduction of the proles to mindless, breeding bodies is also difficult to deny, even if Winston acknowledges their humanity (and in that lies the novel's bleakly reduced account of what it means to be human). It is worth pointing out that there are signs in the book that contradict O'Brien's claim that the proles will never rebel: one is the moral rebellion of the proletarian woman that Winston records in his first entry; another is the acknowledgement that the proles do sometimes become 'discontented'; and finally, the sheer amount of labour that goes into the production of 'prolefeed' seems disproportionate to the threat they pose if O'Brien is right. But what O'Brien means is that they will never politically rebel, will never turn isolated outrages into attempts to 'alter history' by radically changing their conditions, and, indeed, any attempt to do so would break the pact under which they have been allowed to 'stay human'.

Orwell's underlying problem, for Williams, was that his suspicion of the totalitarian and reductive tendencies of theory in general and Marxist theory in particular meant he could not develop a 'critical analysis of structures' with regard to the ways that cultural forms relate to social and economic ones.[9] This led him to generalize from the particular failures he saw in the relationship between culture and politics in the 1940s to *Nineteen Eighty-Four*'s fantasy of the absolute separation of culture (the proles' sexual and moral autonomy) and politics (the world of the Party). Orwell, for Williams, saw culture largely in terms of tastes, accents, and consumer preferences that were mostly reproduced through upbringing in families, without an account of their economic determinations. Indeed, Williams argued, Orwell saw English society as a 'family with the wrong members in control' (*CW*, 12, p. 401), but this metaphor revealed his inability to think of society as an economic and political system since he could not explain *why* the wrong members were in control. It was accidental, as family relations are. Nor could he explain the underlying reasons why the working class accepted the offer of the Attlee government rather than demanding a fuller socialist transformation. If history has proved Orwell's diagnosis of popular pacification wrong in any number of ways – from the revolts against Soviet power in Europe and the anti-colonial liberation struggles of the twentieth century to the Arab Spring and beyond – within Western nation-states, it is the case that class struggle at the national level was subdued by post-war prosperity, welfarism, and the stimulation of consumption by the expansion of credit. The subsequent decomposition of the working class in the epochal restructuring of the 1970s and 1980s means our world, at the level of class composition, whatever dystopian elements we see in it, is not Orwell's. From the point of view of the twenty-first century, though, the accuracy of the novel's predictions are less salient than the political assumptions that led Orwell to locate futurity in a group whose humanity depends on their dehumanization.

Notes

1 Karl Marx and Frederick Engels, *Manifesto of the Communist Party* (trans. Samuel Moore, 1848), section 1 [www.marxists.org/archive/marx/works/1848/commu nist-manifesto/] (accessed 16 October 2019).
2 Frederick Engels, 'Preface to the 1883 German Edition', *Manifesto of the Communist Party* (trans. Samuel Moore) [www.marxists.org/archive/marx/ works/1848/communist-manifesto/index.htm] (accessed 16 October 2019).
3 For an extensive study of Orwell's political positions, see John Newsinger, *Hope Lies in the Proles: George Orwell and the Left* (London: Pluto Press, 2018). An overview can be found in Ian Williams, 'Orwell and the British Left', in John Rodden (ed.), *The Cambridge Companion to George Orwell* (Cambridge: Cambridge University Press, 2007), pp. 100–11.
4 Glyn Salton-Cox, *Queer Communism and the Ministry of Love: Sexual Revolution in British Writing of the 1930s* (Edinburgh: Edinburgh University Press, 2018), p. 173.
5 Raymond Williams, *Culture and Society* (1958; London: Hogarth Press, 1987), p. 286.
6 Raymond Williams, *Orwell* (London: Fontana, 1971), pp. 78–9.
7 Williams, *Orwell*, p. 78.
8 Williams, *Culture and Society*, p. 293.
9 Williams, *Orwell*, p. 23.

NATHAN WADDELL

Oceania's Dirt
Filth, Nausea, and Disgust in Airstrip One

Orwell's friend and literary executor, Richard Rees, described the author of *Nineteen Eighty-Four* (1949) as 'one of the most squeamish and easily disgusted of men. He went through life wincing at its small sordid horrors.'[1] Orwell's most famous character, Winston Smith, likewise 'winces' at many 'sordid horrors', small and large. His story, putting it mildly, is a tale of hardship from start to finish. Old before his time, paranoid, haunted by repressed memories, unable to love without first feeling homicidal, alienated from his wife and their joyless marriage, increasingly alcoholic, and struck by the idea that he might be a lunatic, Winston seems defeated well before he is turned into the 'bowed, grey-coloured, skeleton-like thing' (*NEF*, p. 284) he sees reflected back at him in the Ministry of Love's three-sided mirror. The paranoia is justified: *they really are out to get him*, and he knows it right from the moment he decides to write in his diary. His 'end', as he comes to appreciate all too viscerally, is contained 'in [his] beginning' (*NEF*, p. 166). But his other traits appear to be a consequence of how Oceania forces its citizens to live in perpetual 'fear and hatred' (*NEF*, p. 133). The Two Minutes Hate, with its rage-filled gestures and vocalizations, is the most obvious outlet for these feelings, which materialize in a general edginess, a tension liable at any moment 'to translate itself into some visible symptom' (*NEF*, p. 67) of rebellious thought. In Winston's case, they emerge in his impulse to smash in Julia's skull with a cobblestone; in his sudden habit of becoming 'violently angry' (*NEF*, p. 145); in his urges to bang his head against walls or to kick over tables (*NEF*, p. 67); and possibly in his urges to shout 'filthy words at the top of his voice' (*NEF*, pp. 66–7). Existence in Oceania involves many torments, but it seems that Winston is at the centre of them all.

By the end of the novel, Winston has experienced a terrible change in circumstances: he moves from being someone who likens a bowl of stew to a pool of vomit, to being someone whose degradations include being beaten so violently that he gets covered in his own puke. When Winston meets Syme in the canteen in the Ministry of Truth, they are served the 'regulation lunch' (*NEF*, p. 52), the main part of which is a bilious casserole in which both figures trace patterns with their spoons. For Winston, the pattern might be rendered as the course his life will subsequently take from herdish subjugation to the more concrete thrashings of bruised muscles and pounded bones. Along the way he meets a woman, who is possibly his mother, in a crowded, 'evil-smelling' (*NEF*, p. 238) prison. Part of the 'constant come-and-go of prisoners of every description' (*NEF*, p. 239) in its cells, her first actions are to sit upright, curse at the guards, belch, and vomit over the floor, before breathing bile and alcohol into Winston's face. Presumably the woman's exhalation is nothing like the 'wave of synthetic violets' (*NEF*, p. 149) that emanates from Julia's body, though it is probably reminiscent of the 'hideous cheesy smell of sour beer' (*NEF*, p. 91) that hits him in the face when he enters a public house in one of the proletarian neighbourhoods. Much later, after Winston has been tortured into submission by O'Brien, we learn that during his abuse he has been 'kicked and flogged and insulted', that he has 'screamed with pain', and that he has 'rolled on the floor in [his] own blood and vomit' (*NEF*, p. 286). Immersed in his own filth, and treated as roughly as one might handle an ordinary sack of potatoes (*NEF*, p. 253), Winston disgusts and is disgusting. Caught in revolt, he has travelled from a condition of being revolted by the world to being one of the world's revulsions. He has been made pure and clean, but only insofar as he has been soiled, dirtied, and fouled.

There is a link, amid all of this, to Orwell's earlier novel *Keep the Aspidistra Flying* (1936). At one point, the novel's protagonist, Gordon Comstock, wakes up in a prison cell after a night of debauchery. Upon waking, he is overcome by 'a frightful spasm of nausea'; promptly vomits 'three or four times' into a nearby toilet; and is then painfully overcome by the glare of the cell's white porcelain walls. The light streaming through the cell's little barred window is particularly severe: 'He could scarcely stand on his feet, his head throbbed as though it were going to burst, and the light seemed like some scalding white liquid pouring into his brain through the sockets of his eyes' (*KAF*, p. 198). Aside from the nature of the light source, Gordon could be in the 'high-ceilinged windowless cell with walls of glittering white porcelain' (*NEF*, p. 237) where Winston finds himself after he is moved out of the prison lock-up. But the key detail, in *Keep the Aspidistra Flying*, is the squeamishness induced by a certain kind of contrast: between Comstock's aching head and the ache-engendering daylight, which forces him to turn 'his face to the wall' and to 'pull the blanket over his head' to shut it out (*KAF*, p. 199). Squeamishness, for Comstock, is the medium of captivity. For Winston, by contrast, it might be the vehicle of integrity.

Queasy comportments of one kind or another appear throughout Orwell's work, but they have an important function in *Nineteen Eighty-Four* in particular. And as Beci Carver has demonstrated, squeamishness unexpectedly has a political role to play in this text. As she puts it, referring to Winston's image of swimming in gin – 'his life, his death and his resurrection' (*NEF*, p. 307) – 'the idea of immersing oneself in a hated substance consistently describes the reflex of recoil in the novel'. For Carver, squeamishness in *Nineteen Eighty-Four* is 'a mode of recoil that may not be dictated', and thus it 'describes the only possible site of resistance' Winston can, as it were, enjoy.[2] The Party can control what he thinks, but it can't control what he shrinks from, or at what he shudders and winces. Such feelings are his and his alone. Yet they're also related to an essential biliousness that structures the extent of Winston's very capacity for revulsion. His disgorgings are simply a more precise version of what Jean-Paul Sartre called the 'dull and inescapable nausea' that perpetually reveals the body to human consciousness, and which lies beneath 'all concrete and empirical nauseas' (such as those instigated by spoiled meat, fresh blood, and excrement).[3] They are a gastrointestinal focusing of the protest that is always in Winston's stomach, of the lifelong feeling that he has been cheated out of something he 'had a right to' (*NEF*, p. 62). Queasiness, for Winston, is a kind of freedom – a mark of how, despite being thoroughly brutalized, he remains human in abject squalor. Sickness, as Winston experiences it, is liberty.

My goal in this chapter is to show how the representations of things like mess and dirt and feelings like nausea, disgust, and squeamishness are bound up, in *Nineteen Eighty-Four*, in revealing ways with its depictions of the differences between totalitarian rulers and the subjects they rule. Although we can understand Winston's squeamishness, as Carver does, in terms of how it operates as an 'imaginative act' that 'may not be micro-managed in the way that his pain is', thereby focusing on how it 'slackens' the relationship between 'oppressor and oppressed', we can also think about how Winston's queasy experiences belong to an alternative (albeit related) group of narrative emphases, one that, in a different way, evokes the tensions and paradoxes upon which authority in Oceania is based.[4] Moving in sequence through considerations of how Orwell gives filth, nausea, and disgust interesting things to do in *Nineteen Eighty-Four*, I trace a pattern of symbolic relations which culminates in the differences between the apparent cleanliness of Oceania's political systems and the nigh-on inescapable muck of its citizens, and of the spaces they inhabit. It doesn't matter that there are differences between what Oceania's rulers, the Inner Party, say and what they do, because these discrepancies generate the power used to keep the Outer Party and the proles in line. Orwell wrote in an article on 'Censorship in England' (1928) that the source of a 'prudery which would suppress Chaucer and Shakespeare as well as James Joyce, but for the snobbish regard for an established reputation', is 'that strange English puritanism, which has no objection to dirt, but which fears sexuality and detests beauty' (*CW*, 10, p. 118). The puritanism of Ingsoc accepts the reality of dirt, seeks to annihilate the sex instinct, and is temperamentally opposed to the aesthetic. In tracing that puritanism, Orwell made a narrative virtue of squalor.

The Politics of Disorder

One of the first things we learn about Airstrip One is how unkempt it is. When Winston slips through the glass doors of Victory Mansions, he isn't quick enough, in closing them, 'to prevent a swirl of gritty dust from entering along with him' (*NEF*, p. 3). The dust is a sign, already, of a future society increasingly given over to the powdery constitution of the reality it dominates, yet doesn't quite want to control completely. The dust is power: the power to ignore mess, of the kind that leaves its trace in the wrinkled faces of its citizens, that represents an enveloping, all-encompassing authority. In Oceania, dust covers and constitutes who and what is controlled: faces, streets, rooms, gadgets, cigarettes, picture-frames – in other words, everything. Opposed to the utopian visions of the late nineteenth and early twentieth centuries, Oceania's scrappiness is the proof of its ordering, regulating command. In Orwell's future, dust isn't dusted away because dust itself is a silent remainder and reminder of the powerful.

The dustiness of Airstrip One implicitly reiterates the entropic certainties of life as Winston experiences it. He and everyone else in Oceania are as sure to become 'handfuls of dust and splinters of bone' (*NEF*, p. 184) as the 'mammoths and mastodons and enormous reptiles' (*NEF*, p. 278) were destined to harden into fossils. Yet dust also evokes the spectre of authority. In the cold-looking streets outside Winston's apartment block, 'little eddies of wind' turn 'dust and torn paper into spirals' (*NEF*, p. 4), while the windows of the 'dingy little pub' in which he meets the old prole seem frosted over but are in fact 'merely coated with dust' (*NEF*, p. 90). Winston's world is a dusty, dirty, grubby place of fastidiously calibrated disorder. His workplace, the Ministry of Truth, towers 'vast and white above the grimy landscape' of a London filled with 'rotting nineteenth-century houses, their sides shored up with baulks of timber, their windows patched with cardboard and their roofs with corrugated iron, their crazy garden walls sagging in all directions' (*NEF*, p. 5). The vitiating qualities of these 'sordid colonies'

(*NEF*, p. 5) of dwelling places are obvious enough, but there is meaning to their muddle, too: their very tangledness, seemingly so random and haphazard, can be understood as yet another sign of the Party's grip on its population. Just as the 'labyrinthine corridors of [the] Ministries' (*NEF*, p. 64) reflect the mystifying strategies of the officials who govern them, so too do the confusions of streets and thoroughfares – an update of the 'planless chaos' (*RWP*, p. 46) Orwell saw in the industrial north of England – reflect the priorities of the overlords who have elected to leave them just the way they are. This is messy space left as mess by design. In Oceania, mess is control.

Dirt, and its avoidance, can be thought about in similar terms. Mess serves the Party's needs, and so does grime and filth. Despite the fact that London is very obviously one of the 'decaying, dingy cities' that runs counter to the Oceanic ideal of a 'huge, terrible and glittering' world (*NEF*, p. 85), a state-sanctioned children's textbook confidently proclaims that before the rule of the Party, London was 'a dark, dirty, miserable place' in contrast to 'the beautiful city' (*NEF*, p. 75) it has supposedly become. Here, the 'labyrinthine' (*NEF*, p. 37) operations of doublethink make dirt clean, make the memory of dirt itself something to be polished up and smoothed away. The dirt perceived by the senses must be denied by a society and an ideology tending in principle towards the sparklingly hygienic. The novel's famous image of a boot stamping on a human face forever expresses this code more straightforwardly: that which doesn't conform to Party ideology must not only be trampled down like so much dirt underfoot, but also be hermetically sealed off from the entity doing the trampling, as a leather boot keeps the body uncontaminated by mud and mulch. It's a small move from ideas of this sort to the worst kind of xenophobic violence – that which sees other bodies as dirt, and seeks to purify them. Hence the fact that (to reiterate a point made in Janice Ho's chapter; Chapter 9, this volume) although it's claimed in *The Theory and Practice of Oligarchical Collectivism* that there is no racial discrimination in Oceanic ideology (*NEF*, p. 217), in practice Oceanic society is built on hatred of the racial other – an attitude enshrined in its rancid animosity to the Jewishness of Emmanuel Goldstein and to the weaponized difference of the so-called Eastasian and Eurasian 'hordes'.

The critique of xenophobia, centralized power, and propaganda offered in *Nineteen Eighty-Four* can be traced back to Orwell's account of his political 'enlightenment' in *Homage to Catalonia* (1938). 'There is much of Orwell's Spanish experience in *Nineteen Eighty-Four*', writes Douglas Kerr.[5] But another crucial link between these texts – between *Nineteen Eighty-Four* and the rest of his major writings, in fact – is their shared preoccupation with the blemishing stains and smears of an astonishing compendium of filth,

among them the greasy effusions of unwashed bodies, the slovenly disorder-
ings of men living at close quarters, and the oleaginous surfaces of constantly
handled cooking utensils. The gloopiness of battlefield- and trench-
saturating mud, that terrible, life-threatening medium which is so common
a feature of early twentieth-century war memoirs, doesn't appear in Airstrip
One, but in many other details *Nineteen Eighty-Four* reiterates the experience of mess and dirt established in Orwell's chronicle of his time fighting in
Spain. The filthiness of Airstrip One, that is to say, wasn't spun out of thin
air. Orwell emphasized it on account of motivations which had taken him to
the 'cold, filthy kitchen[s]' (*DOPL*, p. 113) of Paris and the greasy work-
houses of London; to the dusty, sweaty climes of Burma; to the grime and
strife of northern England's industrial communities, as told in *The Road to
Wigan Pier* (1937); and into Spanish trenches filled with 'mud, lice, hunger,
and cold' (*HC*, p. 18). This matters because it means that Oceania's polluted
grubbiness has more than one narratological function: it signifies a means
with which Orwell subjects Ingsoc, whose rhetoric of cleanness falls rather
short of its reality in mess and muck, to critique; and it reflects a wider
concern with the physicality of modern life as Orwell had experienced it in
the 1930s and 1940s, and which in his view characterized not only a nation,
but also possibly a world.[6]

Grease, Sweat, Orifices

In Oceania, filth mediates and extends the power of the state. Winston thinks
about this most visibly in the canteen sequence, during which he reflects
'resentfully on the physical texture of life' (*NEF*, p. 62). Everything around
him – from the disgusting food, to the grimy walls, to the battered tables, to
the greasy benches, to the grime-laden crevices between bricks and mortar, to
the 'sourish, composite smell of bad gin and bad coffee and metallic stew'
(*NEF*, p. 62) – reveals that there is very little in the Ministry of Truth, in
Oceania, even, that doesn't seem encrusted with muck of one kind or
another. The nib of the pen he buys from Charrington's shop is greasy, the
metal tray he picks up in the canteen is greasy, the hair of the so-called traitor
Rutherford is greasy; seemingly everything and everyone in Airstrip One is
oily, filthy, dirty, and unctuous. The swing doors of the proletarian pub are
covered in grime, as is most of the bread that people eat. Everyone needs
a bath. Despite the gleaming whiteness of her naked body, even Julia is
occasionally made 'oily' (*NEF*, p. 11) by the machines she operates in the
Fiction Department. When Winston is finally allowed to wash himself, in the
midst of his ideological purification, the joy of cleanliness doesn't last long.
The temporary purity of his body doesn't match up with the deeper impurity

of his mind, which must be made clean. The dirtiness of this world exists in necessary contrast to the 'cleaning' actions of the figures who bear down on those who seek to escape it.

Poor old Parsons, then. A sweaty man from a sweaty home, whose plug-holes tend to block up with stomach-churning clots of hair, his fate is to be turned in to the authorities not because he is unconsciously disloyal (although he is certainly that), but because, in being so clammy and foul, *he has to be cleaned*. The logic of the Oceanic system demands it. Julia Kristeva's view of sweat is that it is part of the economy of bodily substances which do not signify death, but, rather, that which is ignored by human subjects in order to maintain the performance of being alive. 'A wound with blood and pus, or the sickly, acrid smell of sweat, of decay, does not *signify* death', Kristeva writes. 'No, as in true theatre, without makeup or masks, refuse and corpses *show me* what I permanently thrust aside in order to live.'[7] For Kristeva, the experience of abjection marks out the limits and nature of the self. For Parsons, and for those who have to get a whiff of him, the smell of his sweat and the stench of his 'abominable' (*NEF*, p. 246) defecations in the Ministry of Love attest to 'the strenuousness of his life' (*NEF*, p. 24). They remind Winston in particular not only of what he himself puts aside in order to live, but also of what he constantly comes up against in the act of living: the 'discomfort and dirt and scarcity, the interminable winters, the stickiness of one's socks, the lifts that never worked, the cold water, the gritty soap, the cigarettes that came to pieces, [and] the food with its strange evil tastes' (*NEF*, p. 63). In Oceania, life is one long stream of grime and disquiet.

Winston's rubbishing begins in earnest when he is caught by the authorities, but his dirtiness is evident from the outset – not only in his dusty overalls but also in the way he writes a 'stream of rubbish' (*NEF*, p. 11) in his diary. He *is* rubbish, in a sense, a 'stain' (*NEF*, p. 267), as O'Brien calls him, who must be cleaned up and wiped out.[8] Warping the imagery of Christian salvation, O'Brien notes that all traitors against the Party are 'washed clean' (*NEF*, p. 268) before their executions. A ghastly priest of power, O'Brien's job is to sterilize the traitor's body and soul; to distil him into a disinfected essence; to 'turn [him] into gas and pour [him] into the stratosphere' (*NEF*, p. 266). Winston's visions and associations of being immersed in deep, dark water – from his sense that he is a kind of underwater sea monster; to the way a thought rises in his mind 'like a lump of submerged wreckage breaking the surface of water' (*NEF*, p. 291) – evoke a cleansing he never experiences. He comes up from deep water *into* deep water. And he doesn't swim: he sinks. Hence the account of the moment after he betrays Julia to O'Brien: 'He was still strapped in the chair, but he had fallen through the floor, through the walls of the building, through the earth, through the oceans' (*NEF*, p. 300). An ink stain on a finger or a make-up mark on a face can be rubbed off without much pain, but Winston's soggy purification takes a great deal more effort.

The irony here, as Winston understands it – as the reader understands it, too – is that this 'cleansing' process is in fact a sullying, soiling disgrace. The curing of Winston is in the Party's eyes an ablution, of sorts, but to him it is much more like a dirtying calamity. Interrogated and beaten down to the point of becoming corpse-like in the incongruously named Ministry of Love, where he is all but emptied of his humanity and smeared with dirt, beneath which lie the 'red scars of wounds', he ends up looking twenty years older than he actually is, with a body seemingly 'suffering from some malignant disease' (*NEF*, p. 284). His respite from these miseries is short-lived, but so are his insights into the ideological convolutions which accompany them. Shortly before he is taken to Room 101, and before the possibility of keeping his 'inner heart inviolate' (*NEF*, p. 293) is taken away from him, Winston toys with the odds of holding on to his dissent, even in a barely discernible, unconscious form. He believes that the truest kind of freedom would be to unleash his withdrawn rage at the last possible moment in order to 'die hating *them*' (*NEF*, p. 294, my emphasis) – that is, to die hating the Oceanic authorities having only moments before existed in a guise of complete subordination to them, and in that way deny them the victory of having killed a man absolutely converted to their cause. Yet this process would, even so, entail a kind of tarnishing self-abnegation. 'From now onwards', he perceives, 'he must not only think right; he must feel right, dream right.' And the cost to himself will be considerable. It will be, he thinks, 'a question of degrading himself, mutilating himself', of plunging 'into the filthiest of filth' (*NEF*, p. 294). What Winston doesn't bargain for is that the authorities have an ace up their sleeve – or, to use the novel's idiom – a checkmating move: the rats.

Winston's encounter with the worst thing in the world, in Room 101, amounts to the worst kind of abjection. Taken 'as deep down as it [is] possible to go' (*NEF*, p. 296) in the Ministry of Love, into the hydrodynamical basement of his mind, Winston is confronted with the creature which makes him go 'quite pale' (*NEF*, p. 151) in the room he rents with Julia above Charrington's shop. It is 'unendurable' then, and it is 'unendurable' in the Ministry of Love, but on quite another scale of distress. As the cage with the rats inside is brought closer to Winston's face he smells not only their stench, but also his own sick-making fear: 'Suddenly the foul musty odour of the brutes struck his nostrils. There was a violent convulsion of nausea inside him, and he almost lost consciousness. Everything had gone black' (*NEF*, p. 299). This is worse than the 'tremor' (*NEF*, p. 9) which goes through

Winston's bowels just before he writes for the first time in his diary; worse than the 'inward shudder' (*NEF*, p. 81) he remembers feeling at the sight of Jones, Aaronson, and Rutherford in the Chestnut Tree Café. No, this is *terrible*. So terrible, in fact, that faced with the violent reality of the rats his bowels seem to 'turn to water' (*NEF*, p. 297). It is a moment of drowning give and take that can only be survived through disloyalty. The abject, for Kristeva, 'simultaneously beseeches and pulverizes the subject', at the same time entreating the self into full being and pushing it into darkness.[9] For Winston, to quote words from earlier in the novel, the abject idea of submitting to the rats is a moment of crisis in which his body 'swells up' and 'fills the universe' (*NEF*, p. 106), grounding and ungrounding him in the same stroke. He survives by interposing another body, Julia's, between himself and the rats. In this way his soul is made as 'white as snow' (*NEF*, p. 311) through the insensitivities of abject panic.

According to Patrick Reilly, in this moment Winston savours 'the full shame of his selfhood and acknowledges the humiliating truth': 'the bag of filth' that is his body 'is the most precious thing in the universe, and he will discard any love, grovel to any abomination, if only the panel restraining the rats stays closed'. The episode is one of 'shameful self-recognition' in which 'Winston is helpless before the demands of self-transcendence', which cannot be met.[10] In this extraordinary predicament Winston confronts and fails to overcome his imperfections, thereby implicating Orwell's readers, with all their comparable frailties, in the very same quandary. The scenario is ethical (should Winston betray Julia? can he do anything *but* betray Julia?), yet it's also material. In confronting a debased version of himself, Winston also confronts the defining material characteristic of Oceanic London: its squalor. He doesn't just come face to face with a pair of rats, although that's bad enough. He faces two 'enormous' (*NEF*, p. 298) rats, one of which is dirt, waste, and disease incarnate – 'an old scaly grandfather of the sewers' (*NEF*, p. 299). O'Brien explains Winston's probable response to the situation as an entirely predictable auto-protective instinct. Using yet another fluidic comparison, he notes: 'If you have come up from deep water it is not cowardly to fill your lungs with air' (*NEF*, p. 297). Winston's fate is to remain in the deep water into which he has been cast. Having risen from rock bottom, having filled his lungs, he falls into the 'enormous depths' (*NEF*, p. 300) of obedience.

Compliance is the lasting focus for Winston's shame and disgust. To be enveloped by irresistible, inevitable darkness, to give in to the authorities he has spent a lifetime resisting, is to be fully and finally undone – to be made 'blind, helpless, [and] mindless' (*NEF*, p. 299). And in a certain sense, Winston has been here before. Aside from his encounter with the rats, one of Winston's most traumatic experiences in *Nineteen Eighty-Four* is what he makes of his meeting with the prostitute. At least insofar as it takes shape in Winston's mind, the entire affair is a matter of dirt, and of being dirtied. Attracted to the woman's thickly painted face, he is nevertheless disgusted by the stuffy odours of her basement kitchen; unsettled by the way she reminds him of his wife, Katharine; repulsed by her manner of drawing up her skirt; alarmed at her age; and unsettled by the way her make-up looks 'as though it might crack like a cardboard mask' (*NEF*, p. 72). The cardboard is an important detail, simultaneously aligning the woman with the decay implied by the cardboard-patched windows on so many Oceanic dwellings and, far more tellingly, with his vexing memory of the smell of the 'damp cardboard' (*NEF*, p. 309) that packages the game of Snakes and Ladders his mother bought him when he was a child. But an even more important detail is the mask-like quality of the prostitute's make-up. Fractured and split, the make-up on her face is, as far as Winston is concerned, the sign of something terrible.[11] What lies beneath, in this case, is the woman's aged skin. And beneath *that* lies the toothless, 'cavernous blackness' (*NEF*, p. 72) of her mouth. Disgusted by these 'dreadful detail[s]' (*NEF*, p. 72), the gerontophobic Winston goes ahead and uses her all the same.

The disgust here is real. As John Sutherland has pointed out, old people 'cut a very poor figure in Orwell's fiction'.[12] But it is *Winston's* disgust, even so, a claim reinforced not only by the way the sequence hews closely to his viewpoint, but also by the way it defers to his thoughts about the prostitute as he writes them down in his diary. Winston finds the old woman's cavernous mouth repulsive, and remembers it likewise on a later occasion (*NEF*, p. 149), because to a certain extent he is unnerved by the idea of oral cavities in general. He's troubled by the prostitute herself, but he's also made uneasy by the sight of the 'little sandy-haired woman' screaming at Goldstein with a mouth 'opening and shutting like that of a landed fish' (*NEF*, p. 16) during the Two Minutes Hate; by the 'large, mobile mouth' (*NEF*, p. 57) of the apparatchik in the canteen; by a stormtrooper's 'slit' (*NEF*, p. 232) of a mouth; and by the pneumatic 'orifices' (*NEF*, p. 40) – a tube for written messages, a tube for newspapers, and a memory hole – in his cubicle in the Ministry of Truth. Winston's disgust originates in a fear of being consumed by some exterior agency (most obviously and terribly by the rats, who are the last and most terrible instrument of an all-consuming tyranny), and is intensified by his knowledge that he is unable to resist his desire for the prostitute. In her kitchen and in Room 101 alike, disgust is the source for and mechanism of compliance. And it is bound up, from bottom to top, with the politicized idiom of cleanliness.

Cleanliness and Hypocrisy

One of the more revealing contrasts urged in the prostitute sequence is the juxtaposition of the dirt and odours in the old woman's room and the literal and symbolic chastity of the women of the Party. Unlike the prostitute, who lives amid the 'smell of bugs and cheap scent' (*NEF*, p. 70), these women have had natural sex-feeling 'driven out of them' by 'careful early conditioning' and, in still another fluidic emphasis, 'by games and cold water' (*NEF*, p. 71). Julia is the exception to this rule. Winston hates her at first due to 'the atmosphere of hockey-fields and cold baths and community hikes and general clean-mindedness' (*NEF*, p. 12) she exudes. Angered by the thought that he will never 'go to bed with her', he fantasizes in the worst possible terms about beating and raping her (*NEF*, p. 17). When Julia does in fact consent to sleep with him, Winston discovers that she is sexually promiscuous and corrupt, and that she enjoys her abasements (*NEF*, pp. 131–2). Or, rather, she *tells* him that she is and enjoys these things, and he is ready – because he *needs* to be ready – to believe her. Julia's promiscuity and rebelliousness alert Winston to the 'wild hope' (*NEF*, p. 131) that all in Oceania is not what it seems. Just as the prostitute's make-up hints at some ghastly secret beneath its crumbling façade, there is the possibility that the Party itself is, in contradiction to the righteous certainties of its propaganda, 'rotten under the surface, its cult of strenuousness and self-denial simply a sham concealing iniquity' (*NEF*, p. 131). The way forward, for Winston, is to find some way further 'to rot, to weaken, to undermine' (*NEF*, p. 132) the whole rancid edifice.

Intimacy seemingly provides the revolutionary answer to Winston's yearning. But in a certain sense the Party is already undermined, or at the very least mired in hypocrisy, by the continuities it perpetuates between itself and the historical utopian projects from which it supposedly differs. Again, a vocabulary of dirt is what structures this dimension of *Nineteen Eighty-Four*. Winston learns from Goldstein's book that the 'bare, hungry, dilapidated' world of the year 1984 starkly contrasts with 'the vision of a future society unbelievably rich, leisured, orderly and efficient – a glittering antiseptic world of glass and steel and snow-white concrete – [that] was part of the consciousness of nearly every literate person' (*NEF*, p. 196) in the early twentieth century. O'Brien rejects the terms of such a vision when he distinguishes between the Oceanic 'world of fear and treachery and torment' and 'the stupid hedonistic Utopias that the old reformers imagined' (*NEF*, p. 279). Putting his faith in pain, O'Brien argues that all pleasures, except 'an endless pressing, pressing, pressing upon the nerve of power' (*NEF*, p. 281), will be destroyed. A world of dirt and dirtying triumph will replace worlds of sparkling cleanliness and truth. And O'Brien's urgent investment in such an outcome would be credible were it not for the fact that the physical and ideological evidence stands against him. Airstrip One is dirty, no doubt about that, but Oceania – as an entity, as the manifestation of an ideology – has a curious attachment to the pristine.

Indeed, for a society built on hatred and decay, there is a lot in Oceania that glistens and glows. Think, for example, of the physicality of the Ministry of Truth. Said to be 'startlingly different from any other object' in London's skyline, it is 'an enormous pyramidal structure of glittering white concrete, soaring up, terrace after terrace, three hundred metres into the air' (*NEF*, pp. 5–6). Or consider the glittering porcelain prison cells in the Ministry of Love, or the black-uniformed officer whose outfit seems 'to glitter all over with polished leather, and whose pale, straight-featured face', in an inversion of the prostitute's rickety veneer, is 'like a wax mask' (*NEF*, p. 241). Think of the 'exquisitely clean' (*NEF*, p. 175) entryway into O'Brien's luxurious apartment, in which he enjoys wine that gleams 'like a ruby' (*NEF*, p. 178). Think of the way his spectacles shine, simultaneously alluring and fear-inducing. Think of how the principles of Ingsoc declare one thing and its ideologues do another. The obvious explanation is that Oceanic society is built on the terms of an ideology which thrives on its contradictions – no great surprise there. But the point is that, in contradicting itself, it is positioned as a tyranny whose indulgences raise the possibility of its undoing. O'Brien uses rhetoric to differentiate Oceania from the utopias of the past, but his fondness for rich, dark-blue carpets suggests that he is not a million miles away from the decadent wastrels he holds in such contempt. Oceania is pure only insofar as its purity relies on self-contradiction; it remains clean by indulging in dirt.

Coursing through *Nineteen Eighty-Four*, in other words, is a pattern of relations to do with the political work of filth and the ideological consequences of its avoidance (or apparent avoidance). Orwell stated in a letter to Brenda Salkeld that it is 'a great mistake to be too afraid of dirt' (*CW*, 10, p. 206), and despite Winston's various entanglements in different categories and kinds of filth, grime, and abjection, the dirt-laden imaginary of *Nineteen Eighty-Four* itself shows how being *unafraid*, in this context, could have its rewards. In part, the novel continues Orwell's interest in what in *A Clergyman's Daughter* (1935) he called the hypocrisies of 'pseudo-religion[s] of "progress" with visions of glittering Utopias and ant-heaps of steel and concrete' (*ACD*, p. 293). But *Nineteen Eighty-Four* is also a document that charts how dirt can structure a world, in which it can be the cause of fearful disgust and arrogant hauteur. And in that sense, the novel bears out Raymond William's claim that Orwell was 'a humane man who communicated an extreme of inhuman terror; a man committed to decency who actualized a distinctive squalor'.[13] This actualizing of squalor enabled Orwell to create a perennially applicable literary dystopia. It also helped him think through the complexities and inconsistencies of a politics built on the logics of filth.

Notes

1 Richard Rees, *George Orwell: Fugitive from the Camp of Victory* (London: Secker & Warburg, 1961), p. 33.
2 Beci Carver, 'Orwell's Squeamishness', in Richard Lance Keeble (ed.), *Orwell Today* (Bury St Edmunds: Abramis, 2012), pp. 62–76, 73, 74.
3 Jean-Paul Sartre, *Being and Nothingness: An Essay on Phenomenological Ontology*, trans. Hazel E. Barnes (London and New York: Routledge, 2003), p. 362.
4 Carver, 'Orwell's Squeamishness', p. 74.
5 Douglas Kerr, *George Orwell* (Tavistock: Northcote House, 2003), p. 76.
6 I am thinking here of Orwell's claim in *The Road to Wigan Pier* that in England's 'industrial areas one always feels that the smoke and filth must go on forever and that no part of the earth's surface can escape them' (*RWP*, p. 15).
7 Julia Kristeva, *Powers of Horror: An Essay on Abjection*, trans. Leon S. Roudiez (New York: Columbia University Press, 1982), p. 3.
8 In this respect, O'Brien holds to a version of the prejudice that makes Ellis, in *Burmese Days* (1934), hate 'Orientals' with 'a bitter, restless loathing as of something evil or unclean' (*BD*, p. 21).
9 Kristeva, *Powers of Horror*, p. 5.
10 Patrick Reilly, *'Nineteen Eighty-Four': Past, Present, and Future* (Boston: Twayne Publishers, 1989), p. 119.
11 Compare the prostitute's make-up with the way Ma Hla May, in *Burmese Days*, coats 'her face so thick with powder that it was like a clown's mask' (*BD*, p. 158), or with the young women, in *A Clergyman's Daughter* (1935), whose tired eyes contrast with their pink make-up in a way that suggests 'a girl's mask with an old woman's face behind it' (*ACD*, p. 143).
12 John Sutherland, *Orwell's Nose: A Pathological Biography* (London: Reaktion, 2016), p. 228.
13 Raymond Williams, *Culture and Society, 1780–1950* (London: Chatto & Windus, 1960), p. 286.

12

PETER BRIAN BARRY

Room 101
Orwell and the Question of Evil

The word 'evil' appears nine times in the text of *Nineteen Eighty-Four* (1949), but it is capitalized only once – that is, only once does Orwell write 'Evil' rather than 'evil'. That singular occasion occurs in the novel's final pages:

> He examined the chess problem and set out the pieces. It was a tricky ending, involving a couple of knights. 'White to play and mate in two moves.' Winston looked up at the portrait of Big Brother. White always mates, he thought with a sort of cloudy mysticism. Always, without exception, it is so arranged. In no chess problem since the beginning of the world has black ever won. Did it not symbolize the eternal, unvarying triumph of Good over Evil? The huge face gazed back at him, full of calm power. White always mates.   (*NEF*, p. 302)[1]

The duality in this passage is suggestive. It evokes a Manichaean world view of the sort that tempted a young Saint Augustine on which the universe is composed of 'principles' of Good and Evil, symbolized by lightness and darkness, that are always in conflict. No surprise, then, that when Winston is startled from his chess problem by a war bulletin announcing a breakthrough in Oceania's war against Eurasia, he imagines a 'white arrow tearing across the tail of the black' (*NEF*, p. 310) – the forces of Oceania represented by white, those of Eurasia by black. With victory over evil secure, Winston imagines himself back in the Ministry of Love, his soul as 'white as snow' (*NEF*, p. 311), walking down a white tiled corridor on his way to be shot in the head.

Winston's Manichaean sympathy only emerges after he is broken by O'Brien, who chides his forays into abstract philosophy: 'metaphysics is not your strong point' (*NEF*, p. 279), Winston is told. But talk of evil does not require cloudy mysticism. After all, it is an author as tough-minded as Orwell who authored *Nineteen Eighty-Four*, a novel in which evil is pervasive. And while Orwell called for purging various swindles and perversions from the English language, and especially from political discourse, 'evil', the word, was not among them.

While Orwell explicitly distanced himself from philosophical theorizing, he does implicitly take some sides in philosophical debates about evil. In particular, Orwell curiously straddles a philosophical divide between *evil-realism* and *evil-scepticism*, and *Nineteen Eighty-Four* provides evidence of his sympathies with each. On the one hand, the narrative of *Nineteen Eighty-Four* is pretty clearly driven by agents and events that are reasonably regarded as evil; I suspect, at any rate, that the typical reader will agree that the Party is a force for evil, that totalitarian regimes are evil, that O'Brien is an agent of evil, that what happens in Room 101 is evil, and so forth. Yet *Nineteen Eighty-Four* suggests some reasons for abandoning talk of evil altogether. *Nineteen Eighty-Four* poses many questions about evil, not the least of which is whether we ought to be talking about it at all. In what follows, my goal is to illuminate Orwell's thinking about evil and to situate Orwell in a current and live philosophical debate about evil and evil people.

Evil-Realism and Evil-Scepticism

It will be helpful to define some terms already in use. I have suggested that Orwell expresses sympathy with two rival theses: evil-realism and evil-scepticism. Consider the following characterization of evil-scepticism and its advocates:

> Evil-sceptics maintain that, although there might be many evil characters and evil deeds in fiction, there is much less evil in the real world than is commonly thought. Some evil-sceptics go so far as to claim that no actual people or actions are evil. Other evil-sceptics allow that there are some evil agents and evil actions but remain sceptical of the revival of evil. According to evil-sceptics, many so-called evil actions are wrong, but not evil, and many so-called evil agents are bad, but not evil.[2]

So described, evil-sceptics advocate specific theses that vary along at least two dimensions. First, evil-sceptics vary with respect to the *object* of their scepticism. Most of us are sceptics about the evil substance postulated by Manichaeans. Other evil-sceptics are sceptical about the existence of evil people, about the existence of evil actions, and perhaps both. However, and this is the second dimension, evil-sceptics also vary with respect to the *scope* of their scepticism. With respect to evil people, some evil-sceptics allow that evil people exist, albeit a vanishingly small number of them. Others allow that there might be evil people in the non-actual, merely possible worlds of fiction, but none in the actual world in which we reside. Some evil-sceptics insist that evil people are *impossible* – that there are no evil people in any possible world. Evil-realists too vary with respect to the object and scope of their realism, but to distinguish their position from that of evil-sceptics, evil-realists must allow that there are more than a vanishingly small number of evil people, evil actions, evil events, or whatever. A conception of evil personhood that renders the evil person a bare logical possibility is oddly regarded as a realist conception even if it does not quite rule them out.

Note that the debate between evil-realists and evil-sceptics is only interesting when 'evil', the term, is understood in a specific sense. The primary definition offered by the *Oxford English Dictionary* states that evil is the 'antithesis of good in all its principal senses', the most comprehensive adjectival expression of disapproval in English. This is the *ordinary sense* according to which 'evil' is synonymous with 'bad', nothing more.[3] Just about everyone is an evil-realist given the ordinary sense, since just about everyone thinks that there are bad people who do bad things. Things are more complicated when 'evil' is understood in its extreme sense, according to which 'evil' is a superlative and functions as the strongest term for expressing moral condemnation in the English language.[4] So understood, evil actions are not just bad; they are 'the worst wrongs people do'.[5] Evil people are not just bad persons; they are the morally worst sort of person. And so forth.

Typically, when 'evil' is used in *Nineteen Eighty-Four*, it is used in the ordinary sense. For example, Winston laments the 'strange evil tastes' (*NEF*, p. 63) of the Party's food, he describes his detention cell as an 'evil-smelling place' (*NEF*, p. 238), and he complains that his mouth has become 'sticky and evil-tasting' (*NEF*, p. 250). Surely these tastes and smells and sensations are bad, but hardly among the worst sort of mental states we can experience, as Winston soon learns. In other works, Orwell condemns more strongly and appears to be using the extreme sense: when he enumerates the worst evils of poverty (e.g. *DOPL*, pp. 193–4) and unemployment (e.g. *RWP*, pp. 69–83) he is not merely recording their unfortunate consequences, and when he denounces imperialism as evil (e.g. in 'Shooting an Elephant' (1936); *CW*, 10, p. 501) he is not simply recording his disapproval.

Orwell's willingness to plainly reference social and political evils puts him at odds with a fairly popular thesis that evil is unintelligible, occult, or otherwise incomprehensible. We are told variously that 'it is ultimately not possible to understand evil',[6] that 'evil in the end is always the inexplicable',[7] that evil is properly equated with something 'unspeakable',[8] and that we are 'at a loss to define what we mean'[9] when we talk about evil. Why accept the view that evil is incomprehensible? When an argument is actually produced, it usually begins with premises linking talk of evil with an archaic world view saturated with antediluvian religious or philosophical concepts. Thus, we are told that 'we have a sense of evil but no longer the religious or philosophical language to talk intelligently' about it,[10] that moral philosophers have avoided talking about it since 'evil is so intimately tied to religious discourse',[11] and that talk of evil 'has an inherently antiquated ring about it'.[12] If comprehending evil requires antiquated religious or philosophical concepts that we no longer understand, then an inability to comprehend evil follows straightforwardly.

Nineteen Eighty-Four should seem like a tonic to this sort of argument. Insofar as evil seems manifest in it and insofar as legions of Orwell's readers *seem* to understand what they are reading, we seem full well to be able to conceive evil events and persons. And, supposing the truth of a popular philosophical thesis that what is conceivable is therefore possible, those evil events and persons are themselves possible, a result that is at odds with any strong version of evil-scepticism. Orwell himself seemed to think that the events that make up *Nineteen Eighty-Four* are genuinely possible and not mere fantasy – that 'something like NINETEEN EIGHTY-FOUR *could* happen' (*CW*, 20, p. 134). Crick too describes *Nineteen Eighty-Four* as 'a warning that "something like this could happen even here [i.e. in England]"'.[13] All of this suggests that Orwell is squarely in the camp of the evil-realist.

The evil-sceptic might complain that things are moving too quickly. Are the events of *Nineteen Eighty-Four* really conceivable and therefore possible? Focus on Room 101 for the moment. If Orwell only means that he cannot rule out the future existence of Room 101 a priori – that is, prior to any experience of it – then Room 101 is merely *negatively* conceivable. But negative conceivability is a less reliable guide to possibility than *positive* conceivability, which requires a bit more: at its upper limit, positively conceiving of Room 101 requires forming a conception of Room 101 where all of the relevant details are filled in without contradiction.[14] Things may come in degrees, but positive conceivability requires, at least, giving some account of the events in question that is consistent with the laws of nature as we understand them and with the fundamental facts of the actual world. And, the evil-sceptic might complain, once we are clear about what positive conceivability requires, Room 101 is hardly positively conceivable.

To see why the evil-sceptic might wonder whether we can really positively conceive of Room 101, consider what we know about it. It is but one room inside the Ministry of Love, 'the really frightening one' (*NEF*, p. 6), and while Winston suggests that 'one did not know what happened inside the Ministry of Love' (*NEF*, p. 174), other characters understand what awaits in Room 101 to varying degrees: Ampleforth, the 'hairy-eared poet' (*NEF*, p. 119), is 'vaguely perturbed, but uncomprehending' when he is ordered to go there

184

(*NEF*, p. 244), while the skull-faced man with whom Winston shares a prison cell begs for death in lieu of being sent to it (*NEF*, p. 248). Winston is eventually told that Room 101 contains 'the worst thing in the world' (*NEF*, p. 296) – not just one bad thing among many but something rightly regarded as evil in the extreme sense. The definite description 'the worst thing in the world' is context-sensitive: just as the referent of 'the tallest man in the room' is partly a function of the person in it, the referent of 'the worst thing in the world' varies according to the denizen of Room 101. Sometimes Room 101 contains painful and gruesome death, sometimes 'some quite trivial thing, not even fatal' (*NEF*, p. 296), depending on the psychological economy of its victim.

A fair-minded reader might wonder how all of this is supposed to work. The rat mask seems like a simple enough contraption, but what if I am most afraid of dragons or vampires? Then what? Terrifyingly convincing simulations? Computer-generated imagery? Drugs paired with post-hypnotic suggestion? And how exactly does one's greatest fear come to be known? Winston suggests that O'Brien could not possibly know his greatest fear, and not without cause. Inside the rented room where Winston and Julia are unknowingly surveilled, he confesses his fear of rats, but he doesn't say *that* much; he exclaims 'Of all horrors in the world – a rat!', and after Julia recounts some horror stories from London, Winston shuts his eyes and implores her '*Don't go on*' and turns pale (*NEF*, p. 151). That's about it. Generally, within Room 101 O'Brien is portrayed as an omniscient telepath: he cautions Winston that 'I am always able to detect a lie' (*NEF*, p. 295), and he consistently anticipates and responds to Winston's unspoken thoughts with devastating effect. If Room 101 requires literal mind-reading, then its conceivability is very much in doubt.

That said, I am inclined to think that Room 101 is positively conceivable, complicating details notwithstanding. O'Brien's skill as an interrogator is impressive, but not unexpected given what we know about Oceania. If the ruling caste of a totalitarian state has to seem infallible, as Orwell himself thinks, it should not be a surprise if O'Brien is highly skilled in manipulation, rhetoric, and cross-examination. Further, while scientific research in Oceania has largely been suspended, there remain 'two great problems which the Party is concerned to solve', one of which is to discern what people are thinking. There remains a kind of scientist, a 'mixture of psychologist and inquisitor' (*NEF*, p. 201), presumably skilled in interpreting facial expressions, gestures, vocal tones, and various autonomic responses. Given these resources, paired with the many and sundry details undoubtedly collected from continual surveillance, perhaps it isn't *that* surprising that O'Brien seems beyond error and that he can anticipate what his subjects are thinking.

A related problem with supposing that Room 101 is positively conceivable is that it seems to promise the impossible. Winston is well on his way to believing the fantastic and the ridiculous just before he is taken to Room 101: he entertains the propositions that the laws of nature are nonsense, that O'Brien can float in the air like a soap bubble, that the past is alterable, that he never saw the exculpatory photo of Jones and Aaronson and Rutherford, and so forth. But getting people to say that they believe fair nonsense is one thing; getting them to *actually* believe it is quite another. Winston says that he can accept anything, that '[a]nything could be true' (*NEF*, p. 291), but his crimestop training is necessary to keep his doubts at bay and he acknowledges that it is not easy to avoid considering contrary arguments. It is only after his time in Room 101 that he affirms that two plus two equals five without hesitation or qualm, a result that suggests that Room 101 does not simply get persons to act and talk like they believe that anything could be true, but ensures that they *really do believe*, and in the absence of sceptical residue. Room 101 thus functions as totalitarianism's apotheosis, as Orwell understands it: whatever else totalitarianism demands, it 'probably demands a disbelief in the very existence of objective truth' (*CW*, 17, p. 374).

But what if objective truth is not abandoned so easily? The promised abandonment of objective truth leaves an opening for Socratic paradoxes. (Is the proposition *There is no objective truth* itself objectively true?) Other paradoxes emerge pretty quickly too if truth is identified with what the Party says is true. (Let *P* stand for *Truth is whatever the Party says is true*. What if the Party says that *P* is false?) But whether we can really conceive of how someone might come to believe that anything – literally *anything* – is possible is a matter of philosophical dispute. In *Dialogues Concerning Natural Religion*, David Hume insists: 'Nothing, that is distinctly conceivable, implies a contradiction.'[15] Since the impossible does imply a contradiction, the impossible cannot be conceived. But if there are limits to what can be believed and if Room 101 is supposed to be the sort of place where subjects are made to believe the impossible, then Room 101 is itself impossible, a result that undermines the supposed conceivability of *Nineteen Eighty-Four*.

Alice, who thinks that the impossible cannot be believed, has her philosophical defenders. So does the Queen of Hearts: Hegel thought it mere prejudice to suppose that contradictions cannot be thought. Note too that at least many of the things Winston believes at the end of *Nineteen Eighty-Four* are not strictly speaking impossible; some of them should be familiar to philosophy students. Winston questions how we could prove that there are objects that exist in space and time absent my awareness of them: 'But how could there be such a world? What knowledge have we of anything, save through our own minds?' (*NEF*, p. 291). Kant more or less wondered the same. Winston's suggestion that '[a]ll happenings are in the mind' (*NEF*, p. 291) is an expression of the idealism that George Berkeley thought was needed to escape radical scepticism. If Room 101 does not result in subjects who believe literally anything but only those who are conditioned to assent immediately to whatever the Party says, then Room 101 is no philosopher's thought experiment. We know all too well that conditioning can undermine the epistemic tethers that normally bind rational agents.

I am thus of the opinion that the evils in *Nineteen Eighty-Four*, including those in Room 101, can be positively conceived of and thus are possible, a result that suggests that Orwell is some stripe of evil-realist. But Orwell is not clearly an evil-realist across the board. *Nineteen Eighty-Four* includes a powerful argument for at least one version of evil-scepticism.

Orwell's Scepticism about Evil People

In *Homage to Catalonia* (1938), Orwell explains: 'I have the most evil memories of Spain, but I have very few bad memories of Spaniards' (*HC*, p. 178). I cannot offer a full survey of Orwell's use of 'evil', but there is some reason to suspect that Orwell is prone to using the extreme sense to describe some*thing* as evil, not some*one*. Another example, from his essay 'No, Not One' (1941), is pertinent here:

> [T]he choice before human beings is not, as a rule, between good and evil, but between two evils. You can let the Nazis rule the world; that is evil; or you can overthrow them by war, which is also evil. There is no other choice before you, and whichever you choose you will not come out with clean hands.
>
> (*CW*, 13, p. 43)

War is evil and so is letting Nazis rule the world, but Nazis themselves are not described as such. Even Hitler is only slightly bruised by Orwell's reflection, in his 1940 review of *Mein Kampf*, that 'I would certainly kill [Hitler] if I could get within reach of him, but that I could feel no personal animosity' (*CW*, 12, p. 117).[16] Orwell's hesitancy to describe people as evil demands justification, one hinted at within the pages of *Nineteen Eighty-Four*.

Some evil-sceptics about evil personhood are sceptical that anyone could have the sort of psychological profile needed to be an evil person. For example, Phillip Cole is convinced that someone must be *monstrous* to be evil, that evil people are 'not [...] genuine human beings' but 'monsters in human shape, human/inhumans, or inhuman/humans' who 'constitute a distinct class, different from the rest of humanity, with a different *nature*'.[17] Of course, there are no literal monsters in human shape, so if we can only make sense of evil people by mythologizing them in ways that invariably fail to describe reality, we are better off simply abandoning the concept of the evil person altogether, as Cole suggests.

Deliberately or not, Orwell has arguably mythologized the evil person in *Nineteen Eighty-Four*. Consider what we are told about O'Brien. At the conclusion of a long passage from Goldstein's treatise, Winston reflects that he does not understand what led to the rise of the Party, 'the never-questioned instinct that first led to the seizure of power'. Winston 'understood *how*; he did not understand *why*' (*NEF*, p. 226). When O'Brien directs Winston to explain, he can only muster the meek reply that the Party rules for the good of those unfit to govern themselves, the sort of explanation that the Grand Inquisitor offers to the silenced Christ in Dostoevsky's *The Brothers Karamazov*.[18] O'Brien tortures Winston for his 'stupid' answer and reveals the hidden secret:

> Now I will tell you the answer to my question. It is this. The Party seeks power entirely for its own sake. We are not interested in the good of others; we are interested solely in power. Not wealth or luxury or long life or happiness: only power, pure power. What pure power means you will understand presently. (*NEF*, p. 275)

O'Brien is clear that power is 'not a means, it is an end' (*NEF*, p. 276). What O'Brien and the Party want and want intrinsically is power over human beings, 'above all, over the mind' (*NEF*, p. 277).

Some commentators hold that Orwell does a 'credible job' in explaining the personalities of totalitarian leaders.[19] But some of Orwell's closest readers doubt that Orwell should be taken literally on this point.[20] Surely some putative evil persons have an inordinate thirst for power, but the proposed psychological profile of O'Brien and Inner Party members is pretty crude moral psychology, and explaining the psychological economy of every putative evil person solely in terms of a fetish for power-for-its-own-sake weirdly aggrandizes their motives. Generally, we ought to be wary of inferring psychological explanations from literary turns, since appealing storylines can seduce us into thinking that people frequently act in ways they rarely do and for reasons that seldom apply.[21] If one suspects that the actual aims and purposes of putative evil people are more complicated than those proffered by O'Brien, then there is good reason to suppose that the evil person is mythologized in *Nineteen Eighty-Four*.

Some philosophically inclined readers might find O'Brien's explanation perfectly sensible. Some of what Nietzsche has to say about the 'will to power' demands credulity, but in his more sensible moments he seems to understand it as a psychological mechanism manifest in animal life that explains a great deal of human behaviour. For example:

> Every animal – therefore *la bête philosophe*, too – instinctively strives for an optimum of favourable conditions under which it can expend all its strength and achieve its maximal feeling of power; every animal abhors, just as instinctively and with a subtlety of discernment that is 'higher than all reason', every kind of intrusion or hindrance that obstructs or could obstruct this path to the optimum.[22]

So understood, the will to power is 'the essence of life'.[23] For Nietzsche, it is not just totalitarians who long for power; we *all* do, as such a desire is endemic to humanity. O'Brien is no inhuman monster; he is all too human.

Appealing to Nietzsche in this context might normalize his explanation of the evil person's motives, but Nietzsche himself is best read as an evil-sceptic. Famously, Nietzsche contends that the concept of evil was introduced by the weak and the plebeian to characterize their more powerful oppressors, the product of their *ressentiment* – an especially virulent kind of resentment that emerges from a prolonged period of deprivation and inequality, from a 'cauldron of unsatisfied hatred'.[24] The powerful, by contrast, have no use for terms like 'evil' since they are actually able to avenge any injuries and because they are largely unconcerned with the weak and the plebeian. Partly because Nietzsche prizes the power of the strong and loathes the supposed virtues of the weak and partly because of its suspect origins, Nietzsche is plausibly read as encouraging us to abandon talk of evil.[25] And in any case, if everyone is possessed of the will to power, then it is hard to see why Party elite, like O'Brien, are evil but not the rest of us.

If the evil-realist does want to contend that O'Brien is evil, then we need some non-mythological conception of evil personhood that can make sense of his evil character given only the modest amount of information about him offered in the text. But even if this task can be achieved, *Nineteen Eighty-Four* suggests another different reason to embrace evil-scepticism, one grounded in Oceania's discourse about her adversaries.

The Abuse of Evil

Consider yet another pregnant passage from *Nineteen Eighty-Four*:

> Winston well knew [that] it was only four years since Oceania had been at war with Eastasia and in alliance with Eurasia. But that was merely a piece of furtive knowledge which he happened to possess because his memory was not satisfactorily under control. Officially the change of partners had never happened. Oceania was at war with Eurasia: therefore Oceania had always been at war

with Eurasia. *The enemy of the moment always represented absolute evil,* and it followed that any past or future agreement with him was impossible.

(*NEF*, p. 36, emphasis added)

Oceania's enemies are characterized as 'absolute evil' fairly often. The poster campaign intended to produce a frenzy of patriotism among the proles includes a photo of a Eurasian soldier portrayed as a 'monstrous figure' with an 'expressionless Mongolian face' (*NEF*, p. 156) who appears to be aiming a rifle at the viewer wherever she stands. During Hate Week, a Party orator bellows a lengthy list of 'atrocities, massacres, deportations, lootings, rapings, torture of prisoners, bombing of civilians, lying propaganda, unjust aggressions, [and] broken treaties' (*NEF*, p. 188) committed against Oceania. These are not just crimes but the very worst of crimes, the sort that only an evil enemy could perpetrate. During the Two Minutes Hate, Goldstein is identified as the 'primal traitor, the earliest defiler of the Party's purity' (*NEF*, p. 14) – defilement of that which was pure being a common means for conceiving of evil[26] – and the assembled react to his image with 'uncontrollable exclamations of rage' (*NEF*, p. 15). Surely conceiving of him as anything less than absolute evil is thoughtcrime.

Totalitarian states are not the only ones who employ the tactic of demonizing their enemies as evil, and talk of evil enemies is arguably just as noxious in the actual world and just as likely to mischaracterize adversaries and poison relationships. In this vein, Richard Bernstein complains about 'Vulgar Manichaeism', according to which evil 'comes to represent everything that one hates and despises, what one takes to be vile and despicable, which is to be violently extirpated'.[27] Roy Baumeister similarly worries about the pervasiveness of 'the myth of pure evil' according to which evil people are hostile outsiders unable to control their desires to inflict harm on us for their own sadistic pleasure.[28] Cole too worries that characterizing one's enemy as evil demands nothing less than their 'complete condemnation', a tactic that ensures 'the impossibility of communication and negotiation'.[29] Martha Nussbaum worries that characterizing enemies as evil extinguishes emotions like compassion and complex forms of personal love and replaces them with depersonalized forms of hatred, aggression, and fear, a result that she identifies as 'O'Brien's cherished goal'.[30] It is probably worth noting that the appendix to *Nineteen Eighty-Four* advises that Newspeak was designed explicitly 'to *diminish* the range of thought' (*NEF*, p. 313), not to expand the range of nuanced interpersonal dialogue.

The problematic thought being contemplated presently is not quite the normative one that one *shouldn't* try to negotiate, pacify, or otherwise reason with an enemy that one regards as genuinely evil. It is the psychological hypothesis that one *can't* negotiate, pacify, or otherwise reason with a genuinely evil enemy – at least, that it will be terribly difficult to do so. Arguably, as a matter of psychological fact, the more prone we are to conceive of someone as evil, the less likely we are to engage in sincere communication and the more likely we are to favour violent extirpation. The Two Minutes Hate is supposed to stir up mindless reactionary hostility and animus towards the subject of abuse, *exactly what should be expected* when others are characterized as evil. This result is not that problematic if only evil enemies are characterized as such; perhaps we *should* react with hostility and animus towards genuinely evil people. But *Nineteen Eighty-Four* vividly illustrates how talk of evil can be conscripted into the service of an unjust cause.

The argument for evil-scepticism sketched above doesn't make the case that evil people are metaphysically impossible or inconceivable. Rather, it turns on the thought that there are serious costs to calling others 'evil'. If the cost is too high – if, say, it escalates the likelihood and frequency of violent and hostile interaction – then we probably should abandon talk of evil altogether, a kind of victory for the evil-sceptic. This need not be understood as a strictly consequentialist argument. If we have moral obligations to maintain a virtuous character or to refrain from degrading ourselves, then we might have sufficient reason to abandon the toxic and poisonous language of evil. On more than one occasion, Orwell recalls something like Nietzsche's warning that 'he who fights against dragons becomes a dragon himself', a quotation that seems relevant at this moment in history.[31] If conceiving of or characterizing one's enemies as evil makes one more hateful and hostile, less compassionate and just, then perhaps we should demur from talk of evil to keep from becoming more like them.

How persuasive is this argument? It does suppose that we are capable of doing what it concludes we ought to do – that is, to extirpate 'evil' from our moral vernacular – and that might be more difficult than anticipated. I don't mean to suggest we are psychologically unable to resist the temptation to classify others as evil; some of our fellow human beings are perfectly able to do that. I do mean to suggest that we may *need* a superlative like 'evil' if we need an especially strong term for purposes of moral condemnation. There is arguably something morally untoward or disrespectful about expressing only weak or modest moral condemnation in certain moments as suggested in the following apt observation: 'call Hitler or the Holocaust evil and you are unlikely to arouse much disagreement. On the contrary: you will have better luck generating dissent if you refer to Hitler or the Holocaust merely as bad or wrong: "Hitler was a bad person, and what he did was wrong." As is often noted, such tepid language seems terribly inadequate to the moral gravity of this subject matter. Prefix your adjectives with as many "verys" as you like; you still fall short. Only "evil", it seems, will do.'[32]

The interesting concern here is not that characterizing Nazis as merely bad fails to accord with a popular understanding of them. Rather, the tepid language of mere badness is inadequate to describe them and inadequate for *moral* reasons. Arguably, classifying genuinely evil people as something less-than-evil fails to show due concern for their moral depravity or adequate concern for their victims. If no other term in English besides 'evil' conveys an adequate degree of moral disapprobation and if it is morally wrong to fail in this regard, then purging talk of evil from our moral vernacular will ensure that we abscond from some of our moral obligations. If sometimes only 'evil' will do, then this pragmatic argument for scepticism about evil people is blunted.

There can be no argument that talk of evil is prone to abuse, but the same could be said for most normative language, a fact noted by Orwell. *Animal Farm* (1945) does many things, but it certainly indicts various ways of conceptualizing and institutionalizing equality.[33] The natural differences between the farm animals – say, the innate cleverness of the pigs, the native stupidity of the hens and ducks, the gullibility of the sheep – render mere formal statements like 'All animals are equal' false as a matter of fact and useless as moral directives, a result that suggests that equality, as a condition of justice, requires more than formal equality of opportunity. But demanding a more robust guarantee of equal opportunity for equal welfare,[34] one that considers the specific needs and unchosen preferences of individuals, lends itself to seemingly unjust results. The suggestion that the pigs alone merit milk and apples – a claim 'proved by Science, comrades' (*AF*, p. 25) – is pretty clearly a cynical attempt to gain special advantage. But a seemingly unjust distribution of milk and apples might be exactly what is needed to ensure that the pigs also have an equal opportunity for equal welfare if their well-being really is uniquely tied up with the satisfaction of their unchosen preferences. For all that, Orwell clearly prized equality, and his affection for democratic socialism is surely based on a conviction that justice demands it. The possibility that talk of equality can be abused for corrupt purposes does not entail that we should purge 'equality' from our moral vernacular, much less that we should refrain from aspiring to realize it. So with talk of liberty, solidarity, and still more. Parity of reasoning suggests that the possibility that talk of evil can be abused for corrupt purposes does not entail that we should purge 'evil' from our moral vernacular, much less that we should refrain from aspiring to minimize and mollify the existence of those evils that so concerned Orwell.

Conclusion

I have suggested that *Nineteen Eighty-Four* includes a number of theses about evil. First, it supports some version of evil-realism: the horrors manifest in Oceania are not merely supposed to illustrate the simple badness of totalitarian regimes. Yet Orwell appears to be sceptical about the existence of evil people. The fairly implausible characterization of evil people offered in *Nineteen Eighty-Four* suggests that nothing but a mythological characterization of them is in the offing, a reason to doubt that there are any such people. Finally, the untoward consequence of describing others as 'evil', the tendency of such talk to frustrate the cultivation of virtue and nuanced reflection, is some reason to refuse to tolerate talk of evil at all. For my own part, I am inclined to share in Orwell's evil-realism, I suspect that the evil-realist has the resources to explain just what makes a character like O'Brien evil, and I doubt that his concerns about the abuse of evil discourse are adequate to purge 'evil', the term, from our moral vernacular, for reasons noted above.

Nineteen Eighty-Four raises still many questions about evil that merit serious philosophical reflection. What should we say about Winston at the end of *Nineteen Eighty-Four*? He has suffered the worst sort of abuses, but we are told unequivocally in the novel's final line that he loves Big Brother and that loving evil is evil in its own right.[35] Is Winston's betrayal of Julia evil? What should he have done? Honesty probably demands acknowledging that most of us would have fared just as poorly in Room 101. If his betrayal of her is evil, are we all capable of evil? What is the best response to evil? Winston and Julia both resist in their own way, but the consequences that they are forced to suffer are surely in excess of what morality can reasonably demand of us. Is it ever morally permissible, therefore, to cohabitate with evil or to tolerate its existence? Does O'Brien believe that he is in the right? What should we say about putative evil people who seem to sincerely believe that they are justified in their pursuits? Must totalitarian states be evil? Plato's *Republic*, famously characterized as totalitarian by Karl Popper, seems rather less bad than Oceania. Can democratic states be evil? Why not? Is there a unique category of political evil, something distinct from other kinds of evil? If politics and power are entwined, then the aphorism that power tends to corrupt is better understood as a dire warning. Is there any value to having knowledge of good and evil? Only Party members wind up in Room 101, while the proles, ignorant of such matters, can take comfort in the thought that they aren't being tortured.

None of these questions is easily answered, and it is an underappreciated virtue of *Nineteen Eighty-Four* that it compels us to reflect on them. *Nineteen Eighty-Four* is more than just Orwell's protest song against totalitarianism; it is a paradigmatic example of a philosophical novel, and one of its many virtues is its dogged tendency to command our philosophical attention and consideration. It compels us to question whether we really know what we think we know and how we might fight off the ghosts of scepticism. It invites us to entertain moral dilemmas and to think about what we would do if we were faced with the choices offered to Winston and Julia, among others. And, as I have been arguing, it bids us to answer any number of questions about evil. Iris Murdoch held that it is not easy to picture great evil in literature just as it is not easy for philosophy to deal with evil.[36] *Nineteen Eighty-Four* is one of a handful of literary works that stands as a counter-example to Murdoch's suggestion.

Notes

1 Peter Davison's textual note to the 1987 Secker and Warburg edition of *Nineteen Eighty-Four* – some of which is reproduced in *NEF*, pp. xl–xlii – does not suggest that this singular instance of capitalization was the product of editorial discretion or some scrivener's error and thus appears to be Orwell's deliberate product. See George Orwell, *Nineteen Eighty-Four* (1949), ed. Peter Davison (London: Secker & Warburg, 1987), pp. 327–41.

2 Luke Russell, 'Evil-Revivalism versus Evil-Skepticism', *The Journal of Value Inquiry*, 40.1 (2006), pp. 89–105, at p. 90.

3 Peter Brian Barry, *Evil and Moral Psychology* (New York: Routledge, 2013), p. 13.

4 *Ibid.*

5 Claudia Card, *The Atrocity Paradigm: A Theory of Evil* (Oxford: Oxford University Press, 2002), p. 28.

6 James Morrow, *Evil: An Investigation* (New York: Basic Books, 2003), p. 3.

7 Robert Ellwood, *Tales of Darkness: The Mythology of Evil* (New York: Continuum, 2009), p. 4.

8 Terry Eagleton, *On Evil* (New Haven, CT: Yale University Press, 2010), p. 17.

9 Richard Bernstein, *The Abuse of Evil: The Corruption of Politics and Religion Since 9/11* (Malden, MA: Polity Press, 2005), p. 1.

10 Susan Sontag, *Illness as Metaphor* (New York: Farrar, Straus, and Giroux, 1978), p. 85.

11 Bernstein, *The Abuse of Evil*, p. 4.

12 Peter Dews, *The Idea of Evil* (Malden, MA: Blackwell, 2008), p. 2.

13 Bernard Crick, '*Nineteen Eighty-Four*: Context and Controversy', in John Rodden (ed.), *The Cambridge Companion to George Orwell* (Cambridge: Cambridge University Press, 2009), pp. 146–59, at p. 153.

14 See David Chalmers, 'Does Conceivability Entail Possibility?', in Tamar Szabó Gendler and John Hawthorne (eds.), *Conceivability and Possibility* (Oxford: Oxford University Press, 2002), pp. 145–200 for a sophisticated discussion of these issues.

15 David Hume, *Dialogues Concerning Natural Religion*, ed. Richard H. Popkin (Indianapolis, IN: Hackett, 1980), p. 55.

16 Orwell's suggestion, shocking to some readers, that the 'fact is that there is something deeply appealing about [Hitler]' (CW, 12, p. 117) should be rather less shocking given that Orwell here makes his homicidal conviction clear.

17 Phillip Cole, *The Myth of Evil* (Edinburgh: Edinburgh University Press, 2006), p. 13.

18 Speaking to Christ, the Grand Inquisitor says: 'Tell me, were we right in doing so? Have we not, indeed, loved mankind, in so humbly recognizing their impotence, in so lovingly alleviating their burden and allowing their feeble nature even to sin, with our permission? Why have you come to interfere with us now? And why are you looking at me so silently and understandingly with your meek eyes?' See Fyodor Dostoevsky, *The Brothers Karamazov*, trans. Richard Pevear and Larissa Volokhonsky (New York: Farrar, Strauss, and Giroux, 1990), p. 257.

19 Richard A. Epstein, 'Does Literature Work as Social Science? The Case of George Orwell', in Abbott Gleason, Jack Goldsmith, and Martha C. Nussbaum (eds.), *On 'Nineteen Eighty-Four': Orwell and Our Future* (Cambridge, MA: Princeton University Press, 2005), pp. 49–69, at p. 66.

20 Bernard Crick wonders aloud: 'Are we meant to think that O'Brien in *Nineteen Eighty-Four* has revealed a secret that the Inner Party stand for nothing except possession of power? Or are we meant to think that such a belief is absurd and part of the "satire", he was to call it, of the book?' (*George Orwell: A Life* (Boston: Little, Brown and Company, 1980), p. 322). Later, after describing *Nineteen Eighty-Four* as a 'flawed masterpiece', Crick suggests that 'we need to know whether he really believes that total power needed no ideology other than power for its own sake (a bleak pessimism indeed) or whether that view is satire on the power-hungry' (p. 399).

21 Adam Morton, *On Evil* (New York: Routledge, 2004), p. 93.

22 Friedrich Nietzsche, *On the Genealogy of Morals and Ecce Homo*, ed. Walter Kaufmann and R. J. Hollingdale (New York: Vintage, 1989), p. 107.

23 *Ibid.*, p. 79.

24 *Ibid.*, p. 40.

25 Peter Brian Barry, *The Fiction of Evil* (New York: Routledge, 2016), pp. 54–60.

26 Paul Ricoeur, *The Symbolism of Evil*, trans. Emerson Buchanan (Boston: Beacon Press, 1967).

27 Richard Bernstein, *Radical Evil: A Philosophical Interrogation* (Cambridge: Polity, 2002), p. 3.

28 Roy Baumeister, *Evil: Inside Human Violence and Cruelty* (New York: Freeman, 1997), p. 17.

29 Cole, *The Myth of Evil*, p. 236.

30 Martha C. Nussbaum, 'The Death of Pity: Orwell and American Political Life', in Gleason, Goldsmith, and Nussbaum (eds.), *On 'Nineteen Eighty-Four'*, pp. 279–99, at p. 281.

31 Gordon Bowker notes two instances in which Orwell invokes this passage and credits it to Nietzsche (*George Orwell* (London: Abacus, 2003), pp. 237, 320). One such instance occurs in a review of G. L. Steer's *The Tree of Gernika* and Arthur Koestler's *Spanish Testament* in *Time and Tide*, 5 February 1938 (CW, 11, p. 113), and another in Orwell's 'As I Please' column for 8 September 1944 (CW, 16, p. 387). Orwell probably has in mind Aphorism 146 of *Beyond Good and Evil*, where Nietzsche says: 'Whoever fights monsters should see to it that in

the process he does not become a monster' (*Beyond Good and Evil: Prelude to a Philosophy of the Future*, trans. Walter Kaufmann (New York: Vintage, 1989), p. 89). Thanks to Nathan Waddell for helpful guidance here.

32 Daniel Haybron, 'Moral Monsters and Saints', *The Monist*, 85.2 (April 2002), pp. 260–84, at p. 260.

33 David Dwan, *Liberty, Equality, and Humbug: Orwell's Political Ideals* (Oxford: Oxford University Press, 2019), especially pp. 81–100.

34 G. A. Cohen, 'On the Currency of Egalitarian Justice', *Ethics*, 99.4 (July 1989), pp. 906–44.

35 Thomas Hurka contends: 'If x is intrinsically evil, loving x for itself is also intrinsically evil' (*Virtue, Vice, and Value* (Oxford: Oxford University Press, 2001), p. 16). David Lewis offers the different but still relevant suggestion that 'it is evil to admire someone who is evil' ('Divine Evil', in Louise M. Antony (ed.), *Philosophers Without Gods: Meditations on Atheism and the Secular Life* (Oxford: Oxford University Press, 2007), pp. 231–42, at p. 239).

36 Iris Murdoch, *Metaphysics as a Guide to Morals* (New York: Allen Lane, 1992), pp. 101, 290.

PART IV

Media

13

DANIEL BUCKINGHAM

Nineteen Eighty-Four on Radio, Stage, and Screen

'Posterity will never even hear of you': The Challenge of Change and Replication

'Lux Toilet Soap care', we are told during the course of Lux Radio Theatre's 1955 radio adaptation of *Nineteen Eighty-Four* (1949), 'makes a wonderful difference in my skin. It makes skin look softer, dewier. You'll find it'll make you lovelier, too.'[1] Actress Mary Murphy's sprightly, reassuring soap endorsement occurs, not at the beginning of the broadcast, but moments after Julia's heart-wrenching cry at the prospect of imminent torture and probable death due to Charrington's betrayal. This juxtaposition captures arguably the most significant aspects of any discussion regarding adaptations of *Nineteen Eighty-Four*: the substantial commercial advantages Orwell's final novel brings, and the qualities of the novel which have helped to maintain its popularity. As Suzanne Speidel has recently noted, 'adaptation critics, such as Deborah Cartmell, Linda Hutcheon, and Brian McFarlane, are accustomed to citing commercial interests as a key motivation for the act of adapting [...] [and] this has rarely been so conspicuously declared than in the adaptations of Hollywood movies, which were a staple element of broadcasting schedules during US radio's "golden age".'[2]

Speidel writes in reference to the Lux Radio Theatre, noting its capacity to blend 'adaptations and commercials into single-entertainment packages for listeners and buyers, with Hollywood narratives segueing into advertisements for washing detergents, make-up, cigarettes and soap'.[3] These advertisements are on very sound footing: as Crispin Aubrey commented in 1983 – the backdrop for the production of Michael Radford's iconic film adaptation – the novel was still at that time selling as much as an 'above average current bestseller', and it is entirely plausible to suggest that an adaptation of the novel might be driven, at least in part, by a desire to share in the financial advantages its name brings.[4]

By accentuating the commercial interests at the heart of the eleven adapta-tions of *Nineteen Eighty-Four* addressed in this chapter, we can better chart the reasons for the novel's continued popularity and influence, discussing the ways in which that popularity persists and, by extension, the common practice of continually bringing Orwell's novel to bear on our own circum-stances. The depth to which Orwell's name (and its association with his famous dystopia) has sunk into our cultural milieu scarcely needs comment: even the most perfunctory internet search for recent uses of the term 'Orwellian' provides, from mainstream media outlets, a huge number of topics ranging from a pub in Islington;[5] the political appointments made by Boris Johnson;[6] and Roger Hargreaves's *Mr Men*.[7] For Julie Sanders, adap-tation can be understood to be at least partially driven by a desire 'to make texts "relevant" or easily comprehensible to new audiences and readerships via the process of proximation or updating'.[8] The implicit desire for adapta-tions to capture the sense of relevance the novel continues to enjoy fuels much of our discussion.

While Sanders's comment has broad applications, there are issues asso-ciated with *Nineteen Eighty-Four* which mark its quest for relevance as particularly noteworthy. Orwell's overtly 'satirical'[9] tale of totalitarian dom-ination suffers from contextual limitations born of Orwell's status as 'pri-marily a political writer'.[10] Adaptation is a process whereby a text is 'transplanted', as Dennis Cutchins notes, 'through time'.[11] As such, these works must contend with satire's 'ephemerality':[12] it is, to some extent, tied to its context, and its longevity suffers at the hands of what Northrop Frye might call 'fluctuating' standards, targets, and events.[13] For some critics, *Nineteen Eighty-Four* is no exception: it is, as Jeffrey Meyers suggests, very much a product of its time.

> The most common cliché of Orwell criticism is that *1984* (1949) is a 'nightmare vision' of the future. I believe, on the contrary, that it is a very concrete and naturalistic portrayal of the present and the past, and that its great originality results more from a realistic synthesis and rearrangement of familiar materials than from any prophetic or imaginary speculations.[14]

Meyers captures the essential tension at the heart of any adaptation of *Nineteen Eighty-Four*. The novel is rooted in historical particulars. The adaptations which form the core of this chapter's discussion, then, must employ – to use Sanders's phrase – 'proximation or updating' in order to combat the transience of Orwell's 'portrayal of the present'. Simultaneously, however, these works cannot be too distanced from their source text: heavy deviation from the novel risks losing its financial clout. We can modify Sanders's suggestion by turning to Linda Hutcheon's characterization of adaptation as a process which benefits from both 'change' and 'successful replication'.[15] Bearing in mind our chief assumption – that, for commercial reasons, an adaptation of this novel is well advised to manufacture or to accentuate a sense of the novel's continued relevance – we can use Hutcheon's formulations as organizing principles. What do these adaptations change? What do they replicate?

Returning to the 1955 Lux adaptation, the proximity of a commercial to Julia's cry of fear provides a clue as to which aspects of the novel might be fruitfully replicated. A more prominent clue may be found in the announcer's reminder, prefacing the broadcast, of the notoriety associated with the previous year's BBC television adaptation starring Peter Cushing (the first of four actors who have portrayed both Winston Smith and Doctor Who). Moral outrage associated with this production led to a motion in the House of Commons strongly condemning its 'sexual' and 'sadistic' aspects.[16] The announcer's explicit reference to this controversy, much reported in 'the Australian media', bears out David Ryan's assertion that the panic surrounding adaptations of the novel 'encouraged' Lux Radio Theatre's Australian broadcaster to produce the 1955 radio play.[17] Sex and violence, in short, are provided in no small measure in *Nineteen Eighty-Four*, and we may surmise that these qualities, associated by the novel itself with popularity, are significant to any adaptor wishing to replicate the popularity of the source material. In the following discussion, this avenue allows us to explore some of the complexities surrounding Orwell's snobbishness towards middlebrow mass media.

Adaptation is often associated with the popular and has been derogated as a 'middlebrow' process. By taking as our subject the romance and thrills adaptations frequently replicated from the novel, we shall be better able to chart the ambivalence and inconsistency of the relationship between Orwell and commercial mass media. Through adaptation, we are able to foreground money as a motive while placing that motive in the context of our continued responses to the novel today. Christoph Ehland and Cornelia Wächter have argued that the middlebrow is 'conducive to escapist consumption *and* include[s] challenges to the established order. It frequently contains invitations to question dominant ideologies, which the reader can but need not accept.'[18] Many adaptations adhere to these critical principles by extracting subtleties from 'escapist' explosions and lovemaking – qualities the novel itself unselfconsciously derides as part of the oppressive, placatory 'prolefeed' (*NEF*, p. 320) produced by the Party. As such, an implicit critique emerges which challenges Orwell's snobbery even as it champions his prescience by depicting, in a gesture towards his continued relevance, a world in which prolefeed is in use.

If these middlebrow, popular aspects of the novel are vital to its replication, the changes commonly incurred in replication are no less significant. As contexts change, depictions of the technology of Airstrip One have evolved to better gesture towards the world as it appeared during the respective years of each adaptation's production. Moreover, as I shall discuss at greater length, these adaptations go so far as to implicate the very media through which they communicate as examples of the technology of indoctrination and oppression. As such, the changes and replications charted in this chapter share a sense of complicity with the malignant forces Orwell describes. Consider, for example, the following passage from the novel, in which Winston Smith, on the verge of writing in his diary, contemplates the futility of his looming action. 'How', Winston asks, 'could you communicate with the future? It was of its nature impossible. Either the future would resemble the present, in which case it would not listen to him: or it would be different from it, and his predicament would be meaningless' (*NEF*, p. 9). Unsurprisingly, this is not a passage which makes its way into many of the eleven adaptations addressed in this chapter. This gesture towards pointlessness is incompatible with adaptation's implicit dependence on a meaningful afterlife. However, one adaptation – the 2013 stage version of *Nineteen Eighty-Four* – does include this passage. A narrator-like character repeats Winston's sentiment with all the ineffectuality expressed in the novel. In a notable moment of modification, however, the Host prefaces this brief admission of fruitlessness with the word '[d]oublethink'.[19]

The novel itself goes to great lengths to define doublethink as 'to hold simultaneously two opinions which cancelled out, knowing them to be contradictory and believing in both of them' (*NEF*, p. 37). In this instance, the stage adaptation asks us to accept, at once, that Winston's story is a pointless irrelevance, that we exist in a future either too different or too similar for the novel to matter, and yet that it is worthy of adaptation and should have new life breathed into it. The subtlety of this position is not necessarily noticeable at first glance. Not only does this adaptation justify its existence without compromising some of the core preoccupations of the novel, but – perhaps more significantly – it also casts us, the audience, as people susceptible to the process of doublethink. Invoking the authority of the novel's own precepts, this adaptation manufactures a sense of the novel's, and therefore the adaptation's own, importance and pertinence by attributing to its audience the qualities of the oppressed occupants of Airstrip One. We must surrender our faculties to doublethink, the line implies, in order to accept this stage production; indeed, surely, the reader familiar with *Nineteen Eighty-Four*'s 'unbearably gloomy' tone must have surrendered to this kind of doublethink in order to have bought a ticket.[20] This is one of several examples of what can be understood as an attempt to create and to enforce a world in which *Nineteen Eighty-Four* remains pertinent and profitable.

From Telescreens to Radio Cameras

One of the more insidious ways in which adaptations of Orwell's novel manufacture or accentuate a sense of their continued relevance lies in their representations of the various technologies present in *Nineteen Eighty-Four*. As Abbott Gleason and Martha Nussbaum note, 'Orwell did not lose his power with the collapse of the Soviet system. Indeed, the new era of ever-vigilant technology seemed to give a new relevance to his ideas, just when their specific political occasion had apparently vanished.'[21] The connection between technology and a sense of relevance is often exploited: in a recent adaptation of *Animal Farm* (1945), the director overtly refers to his decision to go 'further than Orwell by making inventive use of technology and media'.[22] Though the present day lacks the aftermath of atomic war or pyramidal Ministry buildings, the ubiquitous presence of 'screens' (as the stage adaptation, to which in a moment we shall return, puts it) in our lives marks an uninterrupted thread between 1949 and the present day.[23] And, indeed, my intention is not to suggest that there is no justifiable cause for drawing parallels between *Nineteen Eighty-Four* and the present in every case: it is difficult to deny that a world of disinformation via social media and surveillance via voice assistants and webcams provides an overt – if not obvious – line of connection between Orwell's novel and the present day.

It is important, however, to address the techniques used in these adaptations to encourage association between the novel and the present: such is the novel's influence, associations of this kind are valuable exercises in reminding ourselves that, to some extent, our desire to bring the novel to bear on our own circumstances is not a given, but can be considered the product of the kinds of interventions of which adaptations are capable. There is a clear distinction, moreover, between those adaptations which were produced prior to the year 1984, and those produced on or after that date. A sense of continued applicability to the historical particulars of Orwell's time was in grasping distance of the pre-1984 adaptations, sharing, as they did, a broad context with Orwell's novel which allowed them to address an audience largely familiar with the post-war period in which Orwell wrote. The 1949 radio adaptation starring David Niven, produced in the same year as the novel's publication, begins with an announcer commenting that '[i]n his current and very widely discussed novel, Mr. Orwell has projected the totalitarian techniques abroad *in the world today* to their terrible extreme',[24] while David Ryan describes the 1954 teleplay as a 'contemporaneous, site-specific staging' of Orwell's vision of the 'UK in the immediate post-war years'.[25] Moreover, these works are better able to capitalize on the associations between the novel and prophecy, their appeal enhanced by the compellingly morbid prospect of Orwell's imagined world possibly coming to pass. These adaptations frequently employ narration as framing devices to underscore the latter point: the 1956 film begins, for example, with '[t]his is a story of the future', 'the immediate future'. It ends on a similar note, emphasizing the possibility of this future coming to pass while preserving a sense of warning: '[t]his, then, is a story of the future. It could be the story of our children, if we fail to preserve their heritage of freedom.'[26] The 1953 radio play goes so far as to overtly describe the production as 'a kind of prophetic reporting of the future'.[27] Peddling prophecy and warnings, then, is a technique through which early adaptations were able to stress their continued significance: the year 1984 had not yet come to pass, and Orwell's predictions may yet be realized.

Though the 1956 film is not, as Ryan points out, 'well liked',[28] its tele-screens demonstrate earlier adaptations' reliance on shared context as opposed to reflecting real-world technological change in order to promote a sense of pertinence. In the novel, telescreens are described as 'oblong' (*NEF*, p. 3). In this film, however, some telescreens – most prominently the one overseeing Winston's apartment – are shaped in a manner irresistibly reminiscent of an eyeball. This interpretation of the telescreen communicates Orwell's preoccupation with such technologies, not as universally malevolent, but as implements of totalitarian surveillance: as Christopher Roper notes, 'the telescreen is largely a metaphor for depersonalized Stalinism and Fascism', and its metaphorical status is here emphasized by the distinctive shape of a human eye which symbolizes surveillance.[29] Crucially, these eyeball-shaped devices bear little resemblance to the predominantly square real-life televisions of the 1950s. By comparison, the 2013 stage adaptation deliberately aligns the telescreens of the novel with the 'television' referenced during the opening scene of the play.[30]

It is not only in parallels to real-world technology, however, that more recent adaptations make their case for continued pertinence. In a subtle, counter-intuitive move, the film and radio adaptations produced during or after the year 1984 have implicated the technology which comprises the medium in which they operate. They do this to make the case for a sense that Orwell's world has, in some respects, come to pass. This observation is best expressed by way of comparison. In the 1965 radio adaptation starring Patrick Troughton, a curious departure from the novel occurs. After his clandestine meeting with O'Brien, this version of Winston is not given *The*

Theory and Practice of Oligarchical Collectivism in the form of a book. Rather, he is told to tune in to a secret radio frequency and invited simply to listen to a recording of it.[31] This cannot be simply due to the constraints of the medium. There are many possible ways to allow the audience access to Goldstein's words while retaining its form as a book: Troughton's Winston could simply read aloud, as Niven's Winston does; we could gain access to his thoughts, which happens in other parts of the 1965 production; or a narrator could take over. Or, to follow the example of the 1953 televised production, Goldstein's work could have been omitted altogether.[32] Why, then, is Goldstein's book adapted, just as Orwell's novel is adapted, for radio? Perhaps because, in its pre-1984 context, this adaptation stands to gain from capitalizing on Orwell's novel as a warning, as an important contribution to what David Brin would come to describe as 'self-defeating prophecy'.[33] Radio can thus be represented as a symbol of hope.

By comparison, the 2013 radio adaptation, starring another Doctor Who (Christopher Eccleston), adopts a different approach. Produced nearly three decades after Orwell's doom-laden date, 'warning' is naturally an unpersuasive platform from which to gesture towards continued pertinence: such warnings depend, as Bernard Crick remarks, on 'plausibility in the circumstances of the day'.[34] However, this version is able to make use of its medium – albeit in a counter-intuitive manner – in order to produce its own brand of pertinence. In a very early scene in this adaptation, we learn of the superior 'new radio cameras' which make multiple appearances throughout, including the clandestine lovers' meeting between Winston and Julia outside London.[35] Indeed, the packaging for the CD of this adaptation features a picture of a radio tower broadcasting through loudspeakers, as opposed to more recognizable images like Big Brother or a telescreen. In short, this adaptation is able to justify its existence by reminding us that the malign technology Orwell invokes is akin to the very technology through which we hear it.

Michael Radford makes use of this tension in his own adaptation. A filmgoer in 1984 would have found themselves in precisely the position of John Hurt's Winston and his fellow Party members as they watched Winston watching propaganda films in a crowded cinema. This is described only at second hand in the novel, yet Radford chooses to heavily accentuate cinema's capacity for indoctrination. At first glance, this would appear counter-intuitive: why represent the medium through which one is relaying this novel as a medium complicit in the novel's primary target of censure: totalitarian oppression? The answer is that this, of course, is the perfect way to communicate a sense of continued pertinence that stretches beyond the year 1984. Just as radio cameras make radio complicit with the Party, so, here, does the medium of cinema offer the audience a visceral sense of vulnerability to manipulation. The film justifies its existence by casting a malevolent shadow over itself.

An important interpretive question to answer, at this point, is: What are the stakes in recognizing these attempts to promote a sense of pertinence? In their representations of Orwell's imagined technology, these adaptations run the risk of proliferating a potential misinterpretation of Orwell's novel: that he was simply against technology. As Brin reminds us:

> Orwell's books are often cited as warnings against science and technology [. . .] a terrible misinterpretation. [. . .] The central lesson [. . .] is that technology can be abused when it is monopolized by a narrow, secretive, and self-deceiving elite, absent any accountability or outside criticism. Almost any modern scientist would call this obvious.[36]

Brin's reading is persuasive. Orwell's telescreen is as strongly associated with the malign powers of technological surveillance as O'Brien's metaphorical boot (*NEF*, p. 280) is associated with the violence of oppressive totalitarianism. But it does not follow, from this admittedly powerful image, that Orwell was anti-footwear. Adaptations are eminently capable, in their capacity as interpretations, of shaping our readings of these issues. Indeed, the 1949 adaptation made this notion viscerally apparent by including an intermission featuring a 'commentary' on the work by author James Hilton. As Hutcheon notes, '[n]ow that I know what an enemy orc or a game of Quidditch (can) look like (from the movies), I suspect I will never be able to recapture my first imagined versions again'. The alterations made through the process of adaptation, she goes on, 'make for permanent change'.[37] By shifting emphasis away from Orwell's allegorical use of technology in order to justify its existence in later periods, adaptation risks the novel becoming, as Crick warns, 'misread if not read in the context of its time'.[38]

If there is a degree of indelibility surrounding the effects an adaptation can have on subsequent readers of a work – particularly when, as Sarah Cardwell observes, one of the perceived roles of adaptation is precisely to send readers back to the book[39] – we must examine, critically, what kind of impact these machinations may have. In the 2013 stage play, O'Brien crows over Winston while torturing him: '[t]he people', he tells Winston, 'are not going to revolt. They will not look up from their screens long enough to notice what's really happening.'[40] At the beginning of the play, in which we find a family who represent the contemporary reader offering their thoughts on the meaning of *Nineteen Eighty-Four*, a sequence occurs in which the iconic musical motif associated with the novel – 'Oranges and Lemons' – 'changes' in quality 'to that of a mobile phone ringtone', after which the family 'are all absorbed by checking their phones'.[41] As such, we can understand O'Brien's comment about looking up from screens – an anachronism when considered purely in the context of Orwell's time – is a reference to the smartphone screens ubiquitous in today's society. But that precise ubiquity betrays the potentially reductive nature of any attempt to base an adaptation's continued relevance upon a misreading of Orwell's attitude towards technology. Adaptation, to quote Sanders again, is capable of 'amplifying' aspects of its source.[42] Amplifying technological perniciousness in *Nineteen Eighty-Four* essentially magnifies Orwell's lack of knowledge of, and interest in, current and future technological change, as Roper has it.[43] Yet the resultant and enduring image encouraged by this stage adaptation encompasses all smartphones or computer screens upon which one might be doing anything at all – including, indeed, reading *Nineteen Eighty-Four*. Perhaps, in this bid for relevance, some adaptations lose what Christopher Hitchens calls, in the omission of Orwell's context, an 'extra dimension'.[44]

'One Man and One Woman Dare to Love': Sex, Thrills, and Popularity

It would be reductive in turn, however, to suggest that this sense of complicity between the Party's ideology and adaptations depicting it are without merit. Adaptation is a form of criticism, and its amplifications can bring critique to bear on the weaknesses of its source.[45] When, to use a previous example, Radford's cinema sequence implicates the film as a potential instrument of manipulation, the audience is, by extension, cast as the manipulated party. Many adaptations encourage a sense of identification, a sense of shared fate, between the audience and Winston Smith: in the 1949 radio play, the narrator speaks in the second person, and the 'you' constantly addressed throughout gives the impression of addressing the audience as much as Niven's Winston. Similarly, the 1954 teleplay invokes the novel's already disturbing passage in which we learn that O'Brien, '[b]y sharing a small act of thoughtcrime', had turned himself and Winston 'into accomplices' (*NEF*, p. 165). We, the audience, become accomplices to Winston's thoughtcrime when he says 'two plus two equals four' directly to camera. This moment is then paid off later, when Charrington's ominous 'here comes a chopper to chop off your head' is also said to camera, placing the audience very firmly in Winston's shoes. Radford's film, however, goes one further. If his cinema sequence tacitly casts the audience as members of the oppressed, O'Brien later offers a more specific classification for us. Having been captured by the Thought Police, Winston and Julia are subjected to a form of torment not depicted in the novel: O'Brien calmly informs the couple that the footage and photographs of their lovemaking will be 'recycled for prole use'.

In transforming the rebellious act of sexcrime into pornography, this line invokes the portion of the novel which deals with entertainment as a means of placating the proletariat, or 'prole':

> the Ministry had not only to supply the multifarious needs of the Party, but also to repeat the whole operation at a lower level for the benefit of the proletariat. [...] Here were produced rubbishy newspapers containing almost nothing except sport, crime and astrology, sensational five-cent novelettes, films oozing with sex, and sentimental songs which were composed entirely by mechanical means on a special kind of kaleidoscope known as a versificator. There was even a whole sub-section – *Pornosec*, it was called in Newspeak – engaged in producing the lowest kind of pornography, which was sent out in sealed packets and which no Party member, other than those who worked on it, was permitted to look at. (*NEF*, pp. 45–6)

Having obliquely cast the audience as those susceptible to manipulation, Radford's film now concretizes this tacit assertion. If, as O'Brien states, we can consider watching Winston and Julia's lovemaking as mere pornography, designed simply to keep the people placid and incapable of revolt, then, surely, the audience's own witnessing of that lovemaking belongs to the same category. The adaptation casts its viewers as proles, absorbing a film, as prolefeed is described in the novel, 'oozing with sex' (Ryan describes the film as 'sexually charged').[46] O'Brien's line, in which the viewer is cast as a prole through watching prolefeed-like pornography, should not be read simply as an example of Orwell's predictions coming true. Certainly, Crick does suggest that '[t]he actual development of mass television today would have been added grist to Orwell's satiric mill, prolefeed indeed'.[47] But this adaptation, even as it appears to adhere to a commercially necessary ratification of Orwell's predictions, also offers a direct challenge to Orwell himself. The satirist's well-documented horror at discovering his publishers were attempting to market *Nineteen Eighty-Four* 'as though it were a thriller mixed up with a love story'[48] clashes heavily and fruitfully with the marketing material for Radford's film, including a voiceover which makes much of this story about 'a man and woman who dared to love' against a backdrop of explosions and helicopters.[49]

The 2015 ballet undergoes a comparable process. At key moments throughout the work, transgression and disobedience are represented by means of characters turning to face the audience. During a sequence depicting the Two Minutes Hate, while all of Winston's colleagues have their backs to the audience, Winston turns to watch Julia do her own dance, distinct from the uniform movements of the other workers and thereby signalling their shared nonconformity.[50] Crucially, however, the audience must necessarily face the same direction as the workers, imposing on us a sense of inescapable conformity and, of course, an inability to participate in the onstage action of the Outer Party: imposing upon us the state of the prole. This sentiment is taken to extremes in the 2013 stage adaptation. In a particularly harrowing moment, when the rat cage is lowered onto Winston's head and the fourth wall is broken, the character begins to exhort the audience, shouting: 'HOW CAN YOU JUST SIT THERE? GET UP! DO SOMETHING'. Once again, the audience are cast as proles. In the novel, Winston repeatedly suggests that the proles, if only they can become aware of their collective strength, will be able to overthrow the Party just as a horse can shake off flies from its body.[51] The members of the theatre audience can, if they choose to, do just the same: they do not.

By justifying their existence through identifying the audience as potential proles capable of being indoctrinated by popular entertainment, some adaptations are able to breathe new life into the novel's own complicated relationship with popular culture. As Neil Sinyard notes,

> [a]lthough Orwell's critical accounts of aspects of popular culture such as comics, picture postcards and crime fiction were to facilitate the acceptance of contemporary cultural studies as a serious academic subject in Britain [...], he remained suspicious of the mass media in general and cinema in particular: it was the modern opium for the masses.[52]

Certainly, Orwell was aware of the 'commercial necessity' of filmmaking's need to 'appeal to a public of millions'.[53] But when we return to *Nineteen Eighty-Four*'s description of the mindless 'prolefeed' used as a tool for totalitarian oppression, it's hard not to notice – particularly in light of the pornographic overtones deliberately evoked in Radford's film – that the characteristics Orwell condemns with the epithet 'rubbishy' are, to varying degrees, present in his own novel. Crime, sex, sensation, and even 'sentimental songs' occur throughout *Nineteen Eighty-Four*, and the fact that film and radio – both potential disseminators of the kind of insidious manipulation the author despised – can amplify these qualities while retaining, with a considerable amount of fidelity, the dimensions of the adapted source work raises fruitful questions. To what extent does Orwell's novel itself constitute 'prolefeed'? This is a question best asked when adaptations, adopting the very commercial stances Orwell acknowledges in his day, implicitly assign to their audiences the status of prole. Sinyard describes Orwell's view of cinema as 'surprisingly snobbish', but his most significant novel has proven exceptionally amenable to cinematic adaptation which faithfully depicts the sex and thrills of prolefeed. The aforementioned moral uproar caused by the depiction of violence in the 1954 teleplay is comparable to today's occasional moral condemnation of violent video games: a surprising association to be made with a text now routinely studied in secondary schools.

It is, perhaps, appropriate that adaptation – a practice often derogated through use of the epithet 'middlebrow'[54] – should approach Orwell's 'rubbishy' elements in such a way as to emphasize the middlebrow aspects of Orwell's work even as it implicitly critiques his snobbery. As Ehland and Wächter have recently suggested, 'middlebrow writing may at the same time be conducive to escapist consumption *and* include challenges to the established order. It frequently contains invitations to question dominant ideologies, which the reader can but need not accept.'[55] A sense of complicity with Big Brother may be unpersuasive when applied to evolving technologies, but this interpretation paves the way towards observing techniques which play with this understanding of popular works. These adaptations demonstrate, through their necessary insistence upon continued relevance to the world of today, that the 'putrid "escape" stuff' (*CW*, 10, p. 499), as Orwell put it, that comprises aspects of popular culture is very much present in *Nineteen Eighty-Four* and in the twenty-first century, while unravelling Orwell's associated dismissal of such forms and media. Raymond Williams argues in his 1975 criticism of Orwell that a weakness of the novel is its 'insulting' depiction of the proles: he says that Orwell does the working classes a disservice by representing them in such reductive and unflattering terms, suggesting that the Party's view of them as sub-human or animalistic is a sentiment Orwell comes dangerously close to sharing.[56] However, through adaptation's powers of amplification and critique, so capable of fanning the flames of misinterpretation as we have seen, we may also detect the capacity for a more nuanced approach to Orwell's work and popularity. When we are simultaneously asked to criticize the technology of our society and to accept our roles as unthinking proles; when we are asked to perform doublethink while feeling uncomfortable with the notion of doublethink; when these adaptations faithfully retransmit Orwell's censure of 'rubbishy' sex and violence while marketing themselves as sexually charged vehicles for explosive helicopter attacks; when, in short, they ask us to consider the full, nuanced expanse of Orwell's middlebrow qualities, paying homage to an author of unquestionable significance while fundamentally questioning his own biases and hypocrisy: these adaptations are proof positive that his work is the epitome of Ehland and Wächter's description of a text that can be both escapist consumerism and a challenge to dominant ideologies at the same time.

Notes

1 Vincent Price, *Nineteen Eighty-Four*, radio broadcast (Sydney: Lux Radio Theatre, 1955).
2 Suzanne Speidel, 'Lux Presents Hollywood: Films on the Radio during the "Golden Age" of Broadcasting', in Dennis Cutchins, Katja Krebs, and Eckart Voigts (eds.),

The Routledge Companion to Adaptation (London: Routledge, 2018), pp. 265–77, at p. 265.

3 *Ibid.*, p. 265.

4 Crispin Aubrey, 'The Making of *1984*', in Crispin Aubrey and Paul Chilton (eds.), *'Nineteen Eighty-Four' in 1984: Autonomy, Control and Communication* (London: Comedia Group, 1983), pp. 7–14, at p. 7.

5 Ed Cumming, 'The Compton Arms: Orwellian Dream or Nightmare, Depending on How You Look at it', *Independent* (9 August 2019) [www.independent.co.uk /life-style/food-and-drink/reviews/compton-arms-restaurant-review-orwellian-dream-nightmare-a9045001.html] (accessed 8 November 2019).

6 Reiss Smith, 'Jacob Rees-Mogg Joins Boris Johnson Cabinet: "An Orwellian Nightmare"', *Pink News* (25 July 2019) [www.pinknews.co.uk/2019/07/25/ jacob-rees-mogg-cabinet/] (accessed 08 November 2019).

7 Emily Bear, 'The Orwellian Horror of the Mr Men Books', *The Spectator* (3 August 2019) [www.spectator.co.uk/2019/08/the-orwellian-horror-of-the-mr-men-books/] (accessed 8 November 2019).

8 Julie Sanders, *Adaptation and Appropriation*, 2nd edn (London: Taylor & Francis, 2016), p. 3.

9 Robert A. Lee, *Orwell's Fiction* (London: University of Notre Dame Press, 1970), p. 147.

10 John Rossi and John Rodden, 'A Political Writer', in John Rodden (ed.), *The Cambridge Companion to George Orwell* (Cambridge: Cambridge University Press, 2007), pp. 1–11, at p. 1.

11 Dennis Cutchins, 'Reception', in Cutchins, Krebs, and Voigts (eds.), *The Routledge Companion to Adaptation*, pp. 243–4, at p. 243.

12 Evan R. Davis and Nicholas D. Nace, 'Introduction', in Davis and Nace (eds.), *Teaching Modern British and American Satire* (New York: The Modern Language Association of America, 2019), pp. 1–36, at p. 4.

13 Northrop Frye, 'The Nature of Satire', *The University of Toronto Quarterly*, 14.1 (October 1944), pp. 75–89, at p. 78.

14 Jeffrey Meyers, *A Reader's Guide to George Orwell* (London: Thames and Hudson, 1975), p. 144.

15 Linda Hutcheon, *A Theory of Adaptation*, 2nd edn (Abingdon: Routledge, 2013), p. xxvi.

16 David Ryan, *George Orwell on Screen: Adaptations, Documentaries, and Docudramas on Film and Television* (Jefferson, NC: McFarland and Company, 2018), p. 30.

17 *Ibid.*, p. 34.

18 Christoph Ehland and Cornelia Wächter, 'Introduction: "... All Granite and Female Fiction"', in Ehland and Wächter (eds.), *Middlebrow and Gender, 1890–1945* (Boston: Brill Rodopi, 2016), pp. 1–18, at pp. 3–4.

19 Robert Icke and Duncan Macmillan, *1984* (London: Oberon Books, 2013), pp. 12–13.

20 Lee, *Orwell's Fiction*, p. 128.

21 Abbott Gleason and Martha C. Nussbaum, 'Introduction', in Abbott Gleason, Jack Goldsmith, and Martha C. Nussbaum (eds.), *On 'Nineteen Eighty-Four': Orwell and Our Future* (Princeton, NJ: Princeton University Press, 2005), pp. 1–10, at p. 1.

22 Tom Ue, 'Orwell's *Animal Farm* for the Twentieth Century', *Journal of Adaptation in Film & Performance*, 11.2 (October 2018), pp. 217–25, at p. 222.

23 Icke and Macmillan, *1984*, p. 83.

24 Milton Wayne, *George Orwell's 1984* (Hollywood: NBC University Theatre, 1949).

25 Ryan, *George Orwell on Screen*, p. 22.

26 Ralph Gilbert Bettison and William Templeton, *1984*, DVD, dir. Michael Anderson (Los Angeles: Columbia, 1956).

27 Richard Widmark, *1984*, CD (New York: NBC, 1953).

28 Ryan, *George Orwell on Screen*, p. 53.

29 Christopher Roper, 'Taming the Universal Machine', in Aubrey and Chilton (eds.), *'Nineteen Eighty-Four' in 1984*, pp. 58–70, at p. 58.

30 Icke and Macmillan, *1984*, p. 13.

31 Patrick Troughton, *Nineteen Eighty-Four* (London: BBC Home Service, 1965).

32 William Templeton, *1984*, dir. Paul Nickell (New York: CBS, 1953).

33 David Brin, 'The Self-Preventing Prophecy; or, How a Dose of Nightmare Can Help Tame Tomorrow's Perils', in Gleason, Goldsmith, and Nussbaum (eds.), *On 'Nineteen Eighty-Four'*, pp. 222–30.

34 Bernard Crick, '*Nineteen Eighty-Four*: Context and Controversy', in Rodden (ed.), *The Cambridge Companion to George Orwell*, pp. 146–59, at p. 148.

35 Jonathan Holloway, *Nineteen Eighty-Four*, CD, dir. Jeremy Mortimer (London: BBC Audio, 2013).

36 Brin, 'The Self-Preventing Prophecy', pp. 224–5.

37 Hutcheon, *A Theory of Adaptation*, p. 29.

38 Crick, '*Nineteen Eighty-Four*: Context and Controversy', p. 146.

39 Sarah Cardwell, *Adaptation Revisited: Television and the Classic Novel* (Manchester: Manchester University Press, 2002), p. 38.

40 Icke and Macmillan, *1984*, p. 83.

41 *Ibid.*, pp. 15–16.

42 Sanders, *Adaptation and Appropriation*, p. 9.

43 Roper, 'Taming the Universal Machine', p. 58.

44 Christopher Hitchens, 'Why Orwell Still Matters', in Rodden (ed.), *The Cambridge Companion to George Orwell*, pp. 201–7, at p. 203.

45 Hutcheon, *A Theory of Adaptation*, p. 3.

46 Ryan, *George Orwell on Screen*, p. 12.

47 Crick, '*Nineteen Eighty-Four*: Context and Controversy', p. 153.

48 *Ibid.*, p. 147.

49 Michael Radford, *1984 Theatrical Trailer*, DVD, dir. Michael Radford (Los Angeles: Twentieth-Century Fox, 1984).

50 Jonathan Watkins, *1984* (London: Riverside Studios, 2016).

51 Icke and Macmillan, *1984*, p. 80.

52 Neil Sinyard, *Filming Literature: The Art of Screen Adaptation* (Abingdon: Routledge, 2013), p. 55.

53 *Ibid.*, p. 56.

54 Hutcheon, *A Theory of Adaptation*, p. 2.

55 Ehland and Wächter, 'Introduction', pp. 3–4.

56 Raymond Williams, *Orwell* (London: Fontana, 1971), p. 78.

14

JAMIE WOOD

Making *Nineteen Eighty-Four* Musical
Pop, Rock, and Opera

An Organic Music

Arriving on Richard Branson's boat to discuss the score for Michael Radford's *1984* (1984), David Bowie announced that he intended 'to do "organic music"'. Bemused, the film's backers sent him packing; no one understood what 'organic music' might mean, and, in any case, how could it help an under-funded movie that was already over budget? Instead, the financiers opted for the Eurythmics' synthesizers without telling Radford, who in turn commissioned Dominic Muldowney's orchestral touch.[1] Bowie was no stranger to rejection. Sonia Orwell had spurned his plan for a rock musical based on the novel, according to Bowie, because she had reservations about the very possibility of musical adaptation. Instead, he was forced to quickly transform the project into the slightly unhinged *Diamond Dogs* (1974).[2] It is one of those genealogical oddities that those most responsible for the preservation of Orwell's legacy prevented one of his most sensitive readers from a crucial critical contribution.[3] Bowie was onto something, but what?

It is easy to read *Nineteen Eighty-Four* (1949) without noticing just how musical Oceania is. A martial beat pours constantly from its telescreens, its voices stick in Winston's 'brain like jagged splinters of glass' (*NEF*, p. 106). This is an industrial electronica, 'brassy' and 'squalling' (*NEF*, p. 106), 'tinny' (*NEF*, p. 80), relieved only by the patriotic bars of 'Oceania, 'tis for thee' (*NEF*, p. 28). The Hate Song is 'endlessly plugged on the telescreens', 'a savage, barking rhythm' – not a music at all, Winston thinks (*NEF*, p. 155). Set against this dystopian drum'n'bass are those folk rhythms that repeatedly punctuate the narrative, reminders of authentic experience handed on from generation to generation. We hear it in the cells of the Ministry of Love with the brief recollection of Rudyard Kipling's 'McAndrew's Hymn' (1894; see *NEF*, p. 242). The relics in the junk shop drag 'from the corners of [Winston's] memory [...] fragments of forgotten rhymes' (*NEF*, p. 158), what we know

213

to be, from the handful of images he can recall, 'Sing a Song of Sixpence', 'The House that Jack Built', and 'Who Killed Cock Robin'. Charrington, Julia, and O'Brien, in their own peculiar and perverse ways the objects of Winston's love, put 'Oranges and Lemons' back together for him.[4] This act of mending reaffirms the power of the communal tradition, but the unuttered final line of 'Oranges and Lemons' foretells the certainty, not merely the possibility, of Winston's death: 'Chip chop chip chop the last man is dead'.

I imagine Bowie had a different kind of music in mind. We hear it three times in the novel. First, in the song of the thrush that captivates Winston in '"the Golden Country"': 'It was as though it were a kind of liquid stuff that poured all over him and got mixed up with the sunlight that filtered through the leaves. He stopped thinking and merely felt' (*NEF*, pp. 129–30). Second, in the washerwoman's song 'float[ing] upward with the sweet summer air' (*NEF*, p. 148) from the depths of her 'monstrous' (*NEF*, p. 144) body. Her music, like the bird's, seems to come out of the body's deepest recesses. 'Deep-lunged' (*NEF*, p. 227), it seems it would flow ceaselessly were it not for the clothes pegs, the symbols of labour that 'cork' (*NEF*, p. 144) and 'gag' (*NEF*, p. 209) her mouth. And third, there is the 'peculiar, cracked, braying, jeering note' (*NEF*, p. 80) of 'Under the spreading chestnut tree'.[5] Resting somewhere between euphoria and pain, Winston calls it 'a yellow note' (*NEF*, p. 80).

Crucially, all three relate to epiphany. The thrush frees Winston from sexual impotence: '*Now*' (*NEF*, p. 131), he whispers to Julia; it silences the ego and gives access to pure affect. The song thrush gifts Winston the hard-on he craves. When Winston finally connects this song to the washerwoman's, he accepts that he and Julia 'are the dead', a position affirmed by the 'iron voice' (*NEF*, p. 230) of the disc jockey behind the telescreen. The 'yellow note' is a reminder of betrayal, *of* Jones, Aaronson, and Rutherford, and *by* Julia. But it is also a reminder, even after the trauma of Room 101, of the perpetual, albeit faint, possibility that Winston's love remains untouched.

Orwell, Music, and Technology

But is it possible that Bowie, or indeed any other musician, could capture this in music? Is there even the possibility that music can inform here, or is it fated to merely strip bare the novel's critical content in the very act of making entertainment? The problem is that Orwell's organicism is *a cappella*: it is in the style of the church, not the stage. It prefers the purity of natural sound to technological mediation; it supposes that the voice is an instrument of music making that ranks above all other instruments.[6] It has a certain religiosity that fetishizes aura and loathes repetition. This would be a perfect object for

Marxism's critique of high modernism's model of emotional and psychical depth expressing itself through the peculiarities of individual style.[7] It reminds us of Orwell's recurrently conflicted position in relation to that aesthetic, of the uneasy coalescence of past, present, and progress in his work.

'Pleasure Spots' (1946), an essay Orwell published shortly before the writing of *Nineteen Eighty-Four* on Jura, sets out the problem. Taking as his subject an article clipped from a 'shiny magazine', he mocks one dreamer's vision for the pleasure resorts of the near future. Permanently sunlit arenas cosseted by sliding roofs; restaurants, bars, lagoons, wave pools, skittle alleys; giant underlit dance floors with, according to the *précis*, 'music seeping through hundreds of grills connected with a central distributing stage, where dance or symphonic orchestras play or the radio programme can be caught, amplified, and disseminated' (*CW*, 18, pp. 29–30). This is a sonic capitalist nightmare in which music is the hallmark of a consumer-centric Xanadu. Orwell sees the great British holiday camp as a hedonistic paradise, a site designed for the rest of the labouring body becomes a cell in which the body is cut off from the sublime:

> The music – and if possible it should be the same music for everybody – is the most important ingredient. Its function is to prevent thought and conversation, and to shut out any natural sound, such as the song of birds or the whistling of the wind, that might otherwise intrude. The radio is already consciously used for this purpose by innumerable people.　　　(*CW*, 18, p. 31)

This is a utopia seen as regression, a return to the 'continuous rhythmic throbbing' (*CW*, 18, p. 31) of the womb, a movement away from the depths of genuine emotion, a retreat from community and from social responsibility. This is a form of mechanical reproduction that destroys consciousness because it drives mankind into self-absorbed complexity, stupefying wonder, leaving the animal less human.

Here, Orwell makes music the primary vehicle for American soft power, makes it responsible for the levelling out of all social and aesthetic criteria that so concerned him in these years.[8] This is the fear of 'dumbing-down' that drives the 'satiric rage' in *Nineteen Eighty-Four*.[9] This is the Orwell that chips away at mass media's 'mechanising process' in 'The Prevention of Literature' (1946), the half of him that feared the 'subordinat[ion]' of 'individual style', the 'chopp[ing]' of raw material, the 'readymade', the operation of an 'algebraical formula' (*CW*, 17, p. 378). It is the Orwell who invented the 'versificator' (*NEF*, p. 46), the one who saw popular culture as '*prolefeed*' (*NEF*, p. 320), the man appealing to the spontaneity of consciousness as bulwark against a 'topography of incipient totalitarianism'.[10]

Orwell was writing at a time when the music industry was on the brink of radical change, driven, ironically given his pre-war obsession with the waning of sexual potency, by the boomer generation. Robert Marley, Dolly Parton, Farrokh Bulsara, David Jones, Reginald Dwight, and Brian Eno were all born during the writing of *Nineteen Eighty-Four*. This new youth market (leisure-oriented and monied) forced the mass-market approach of the lyricists in Tin Pan Alley to pay heed to what was already emergent within Big Band culture, a stratification of music according to age and taste catering to an audience focused on artistic intention and authenticity as well as on the tune.[11] Orwell rightly sensed that this unparalleled moment of industrialization in the history of music would be enabled by the new technologies of distribution and amplification, especially the introduction of the microphone, which opened up new emotional intimacies between singer and audience.[12] Roy Brown released 'Good Rocking Tonight' in June 1947, the finely grooved LP followed in 1948, and the 45 rpm or vinyl single a year later. Beneath Orwell's pleasure dome, rock'n'roll was taking shape.

There is then a fundamental problem in thinking about *Nineteen Eighty-Four* and popular music. After all, music survives the novel; it is the source of those powerful epiphanies that arise despite intolerable circumstance. This suggests the potential for musical adaptation to resist reduction to prolefeed and, instead, to exist as a dynamic or kinetic art form, one capable of undermining the very automatism that Orwell feared.[13] The multiple possibilities offered by the interaction of style, rhythm, beat, melody, hook, sample, instrumentation, and arrangement with fashion, taste, and technology set up the possibility of perpetual adaptation rather than the encircling of imagination.[14] In short, we can see a path along which popular music might be able to walk in order to meet those classically Orwellian demands: collective memory, mutual trust, and plain language.

On the other hand, the novel's attitude to technological change makes it an object against which popular music ought to work. After all, Winston suspects that his betrayer, Charrington, was 'perhaps a musician' (*NEF*, p. 97) in a former life. Orwell's demand that music be unmediated fundamentally ruptures his relationship to an industry that only exists through a series of distancing effects that intercede between a sound wave and the cochlea. There must always be valves, transistors, needles, or copper wire in the way of modern music; it must always come from some version of the telescreen. Notably, when the thrush sings it initially prods Winston's anxiety: could there be a microphone hidden somewhere nearby, with 'some small, beetle-like man' (*NEF*, p. 130) listening covertly? This is the Orwell confirming the idea that the music of the Other is always *too* loud, repetitive, and chaotic. But it is also the Orwell seeing the doublethink at the heart of the rock'n'roll project. For the history of popular music is simply one new underground after another, each shift constructed as an act of betrayal, the infringement of the boundaries of authenticity, the gravitational succumbing to the marketplace. Youth rebellion sits awkwardly cheek by jowl with sold-out stadia tours and mass merchandising. Its nature as industrialized artefact must jeopardize music's claim on epiphany.

What kind of ground then is *Nineteen Eighty-Four*? Take as example the work of two post-punk bands working on both sides of the Atlantic at the same time, The Fall and the Feederz. Mark E. Smith's snarling cynicism labels Orwell – that is the curmudgeon, the latter-day Luddite in Orwell, the Orwell that works by opposition *to* rather than support *of* – a fascist precursor in 'Who Makes the Nazis?' (1982). Frank Discussion, however, returns to a model of Orwell-as-prophet, the man who foresaw rule-bound elders squatting on the young: 'They waste their fucking lives but they still have the nerve to try to manage your life,' he gasps on '1984' (1984). Is the novel the answer to the problem or a manifestation of it? Is an 'organic music' then even theoretically possible?

The Four Ages of Rock'n'Prole

It may well be that in the very contradiction there lies the possibility. Indeed, the steady flow of attempts to make *Nineteen Eighty-Four* musical is remarkable. 'Rock'n'prole', to give this body of work a label, has become its own sub-genre (see Figure 14.1). The playlist accompanying this chapter currently runs to over three hundred tracks, twenty-two hours of material.[15] There are undoubtedly many more. Of course, many of these tracks do little more than reflect the absorption of Orwell's terminology into common usage. They are neither adaptation nor appropriation; they neither offer nor intend to engage with their source through transposition, commentary, or analogy.[16] This is *Nineteen Eighty-Four* as a meme that allows a malleable *us* to be set up against a protean *them*. Nonetheless, there is still information here, and the aggregate metadata allows us to mine some interesting observations about this sub-genre's history and its creators.

Generally thought to originate in the psychedelic rock movement of the 1970s, rock'n'prole can in fact be traced back much further to Sheldon Allman's 'Big Brother', one of a series of dystopian narratives on *Folk Songs for the 21st Century* (1960). Certainly tongue-in-cheek, but Allman's suspicion of technology ('And when you watch that TV screen remember it works both ways') is an early marker of an industrialized state hell-bent on spaceflight. Thereafter, from the hippie vibe of Tim Buckley (1967) to

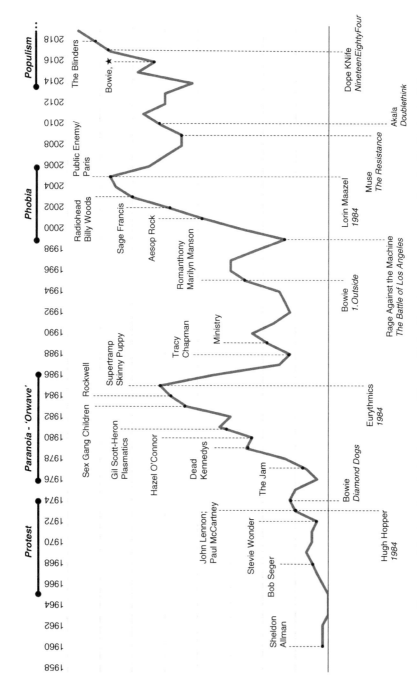

Figure 14.1 Number of musical references to *Nineteen Eighty-Four* (moving average based on *Rock'n'Prole* playlist)

competing back-to-back tracks by ex-Beatles John Lennon and Paul McCartney in the autumn of 1973, *Nineteen Eighty-Four* marked a growing sense of intellectual protest aimed at the uses and abuses of American power. Bob Seger's '2+2=?' (1968) took up the symbolic alignment of an emergent neoliberalism with Ingsoc in its anger at the Vietnam draft. The unanswered question in the song's title reminds us of the doublethink inherent in making war: 'in philosophy, or religion, or ethics, or politics, two and two might make five, but when one [is] designing a gun or an aeroplane they [have] to make four' (*NEF*, p. 206). Spirit (1969) and Rare Earth (1971) both called youth to resistance. Stevie Wonder (1972) linked state oppression to black politics, optimistically forecasting that the seeds of destruction lie in the state's corruption. From the freak of The Mothers of Invention (1966) to the early heavy metal of Black Sabbath (1973) and the Californian rock of the Eagles (1974), the novel moved quickly to the centre of counterculture.

In anticipation of 'Orwell's Year' (Golden Earring, 1984), rock'n'prole eventually returned to surveillance, its ur-theme, with a paranoia so persistent that we now recognize it as its own sub-genre, 'Orwave'.[17] The Beat (1980), Daryl Hall/John Oates (1981), Judas Priest and The Alan Parsons Project (1982), The Police and Rockwell (1983), Elton John (1984): suddenly, the scopic imagery exploded as everyone feared they had become the object of voyeurism. Hazel O'Connor (1980) was determined to track down 'B- B- Big Brother' and 'kick him in the 'ah (sh) ah (sh) ah (sh) ah (sh) arse'. The first woman to sing the novel, behind O'Connor's jokey chorus and catchy tune lurks a much deeper call to violence. Coming from the repressed 'scum' rather than the intellectual Outer Party, it is aimed at the amorphous *they* pulling the strings somewhere behind the scenes. Supertramp's epic 'Brother Where You Bound' (1985), which interlaces O'Brien's sampled voice with a stripped down 'Internationale', snatches of 'Oranges and Lemons', and loops of Cold War newsreel, refuses to make light of the dictator's arrival: 'There's a red cloud hanging over us / And it's so big and it's gonna burst / All you people with your heads in the ground / Hey brother, where you bound?' As Oingo Boingo (1983) neatly put it: '(wake up), it's 1984'. Pop had incorporated the novel as a prophecy leading to a felt reality rather than as a warning against a future possibility.

These positions reflect the extent to which punk had radically remoulded the amphetamine-fuelled optimism of prog protest into a generalized anti-authoritarian rage aimed at both the empowered and its own powerlessness. This would culminate in that sense of urban disaffection best captured by the confused politics of the British Oi! subculture coinciding with the arrival of Thatcherism. For The Clash (1977), the Dead Kennedys (1979), The 4-Skins (1981), and Crass (1982), and for those mods (The Jam, 1977) and metalheads (Samson, 1979) working with similar ideas, Big Brother had gone underground. By shifting his apparatus to a more nefarious 'power in the darkness' (TRB, 1978), protest seemed increasingly impotent, especially as deregulation and monetarism combined to set the stage for the closed realm of business to surreptitiously accede power. Tom Robinson's mock-British establishment figure demanding in BBC English 'freedom from the reds and the blacks and the criminals, prostitutes, pansies and punks' remains a powerful counter-symbol of a country scarred by prejudice. XTC's 'Making Plans for Nigel' (1979) speaks to how youth culture had absorbed and generalized Oceania's authoritarianism into a pervasive sense of stifling oppression.

It is unsurprising that rock'n'prole fell into comparative abeyance after 1985, exhausted by its own mania. It would re-emerge with the approach of a new millennium, a moment marked by Rage Against the Machine's *The Battle of Los Angeles* (1999). A powerful critique of the neoliberalist hegemony that had appeared in punk's wake, Zack de la Rocha's relentless melange of punk, rap, and thrash captured the growing concern that these ideologies had become so entrenched they seemed both inevitable and choiceless.[18] The album's call to 'Testify', to hear the 'Voice of the Voiceless', heeded *Nineteen Eighty-Four* as both a warning and a call to action. In short order, Coldplay (2000), Muse (2001), and Bad Religion (2004) used Orwellian motifs to expose the abusive powers granted to the Oceanic states in the Regulation of Investigatory Powers Act (2000) and the PATRIOT legislation (2001). In *Labor Days* (2001), Aesop Rock turned to *Nineteen Eighty-Four* to think through modern wage slavery. Neil Young (2006) used it against the Iraq War; Anti-Flag (2001) to highlight the invasion of Panama. Sage Francis's conscious 'Hey, Bobby' (2002) intertwines doublethink with a return to pre-Electric Dylan's 'Masters of War' (1963), creating a powerful indictment of presidential abuse: 'Don't forget what two plus two equals. Don't let them upgrade your math.' Radiohead's '2+2=5' (2003), originally subtitled 'The Lukewarm' after Dante, takes the same formula and casts those who refuse the call to action into the burning inferno: 'You have not been payin' attention.'

Subsequently, Orwell's novel has remained a constant source of inspiration. Rock'n'prole has now found a fourth life as a metacritique of the populism appearing in the wake of financial crisis and communication revolution. The hackneyed anti-capitalist line is still evident in tracks such as Muse's 'The Globalist' (2015). But this is a body of music starting to follow a more personal path, noticeably at the experimental fringes in the work of bands such as clipping (2016), Hostile Array (2018), and mewithoutYou (2018). On his new project with Tobacco, Malibu Ken

(2019), Aesop Rock puts together rap and electronica to summon up the novel as if it were an occult spirit ('wake up the Orwell in me') in order to think through the horrific story of a teenage murder. Ghostemane (2018) combines rap with metal around a chilling repetition of Ingsoc propaganda to riff on emotional isolation through occult and suicidal imagery. Zheani (2019) transforms thoughtcrime – 'I see I belong on my knees' – into a powerful feminist critique of sadism. These interventions have taken rock'n'prole in a more confessional direction, away from protest and into affect and the deeper mysteries of the novel.

But we ought to pause here to register just how patriarchal this history is. Roughly 90 per cent of its composers, writers, lyricists, and lead performers are men. The skew is too great for this to be merely a function of the industry's bias. We might be unimpressed by the depth of contributions by Lisa Stansfield (1983) and Girls Aloud (2004), but these are rarities. In general, women do not make this novel musical; they do not sing it or strum it either. There are only a handful of tracks written by women on *Rock'n'Prole*, only two dozen vocalists, and for every woman band member on the list there are over twenty men. This is deeply problematic, especially when we consider what ought to have been the powerful and early feminist influence of Wendy O. Williams on the Plasmatics' *Beyond the Valley of 1984* (1981). But the same problem is true of race. There are barely twenty black artists, and whilst hip-hop is the fifth most recurrent style, white rappers perform more than half the tracks. There is only one black woman on the list, Tracy Chapman with 'Why?' (1988). She alone focuses on that central unanswered question in *Nineteen Eighty-Four*, not the '*how*' of power and its terror apparatus, but its '*why*' (NEF, p. 226), the why that still eludes answer, '*why* should human equality be averted?' (see NEF, p. 225).

This bias is evident from the stylistic dominance of punk subculture within rock'n'prole (Figure 14.2). Punk labels such as Alternative Tentacles and Fat Wreck Chords (founded by members of the Dead Kennedys and NOFX) dominate the list of independent publishers. The collagist Winston Smith (born James Morey) designed the cover for the Kennedys' EP *In God We Trust, Inc.* (1981) and the album *Give Me Convenience or Give Me Death* (1987). We find bands in the harder rock genres plundering the novel for names: Combat 84, facecrime, The Thought Criminals, Jr. Anti-Sex League, Two Minutes Hate. Using a representative sample, over 70 per cent of the tracks take state power as their main theme. Song titles referencing 'hate', lyrics that fetishize Ingsoc slogans, and samples of O'Brien's voice tend to recur. Women's experience in the novel is threadbare, but even when Annie Lennox (Eurythmics, 1984) sings 'Julia', she does so from Winston's

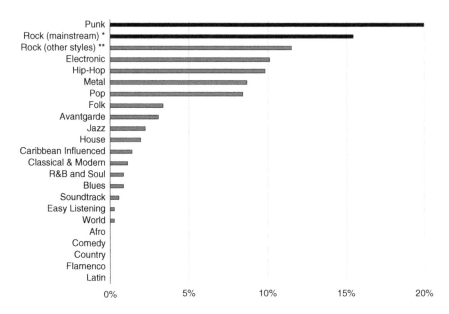

* Alternative. Classic, Hard, Indie, Rock & Roll, Soft
** Art, Garage, Glam, Goth, Grunge, New Wave, Post-Punk, Prog, Psychedelic,
  Post-Rock, Space, Stoner, Symphonic

Figure 14.2 *Rock'n'Prole*: analysed by major genre/style

perspective.[19] These add up to confirm a certain stereotype. The average rock'n'prole band is three white guys from some industrial heartland. Their sound skews to the industrial end of electronic, the death and grindcore ends of metal, the hardcore end of punk.[20] Disenfranchised, angry, and lonely; recurrently fascinated and repulsed by torture; suspicious of a vast conspiracy. Large parts of *Rock'n'Prole* represent an achingly dull confirmation of Milan Kundera's point that *Nineteen Eighty-Four* was just ideology in a Secker & Warburg wrapper.

Part of the problem here is a matter of form: the average track time on the *Rock'n'Prole* playlist is just four minutes. It is difficult to adapt a novel with a strophic structure and repetitional versification that allows for little variation other than a middle eight.[21] Hence the notable recurrence of the 'experimental *Nineteen Eighty-Four* concept album' as a weathervane of rock'n'prole's shifting currents. Beginning with jazz, psychedelic rock, and punk hybrids from Hugh Hopper (1973) and David Peel & The Lower East Side (1983), through the synth-prog of Anthony Phillips (1981) to the space-age stirrings of Ed Starink (1991) and Bobby Previte (2006), it has taken new shape in techno (Rødhåd, 2012), noise (Zbigniew Karkowski's 2013 setting of the BBC's teleplay of the novel), and glitch (Marco Malasomma, 2018). Fragile, evanescent, and often beautiful, these works take us into very private and emotive responses to the novel, often without resorting to a film sample to set mood and context.

This is not the case with Lorin Maazel's operatic version of the novel, *1984*, first staged in a partially self-funded production in May 2005. This ought to be a form more suited to Orwell's organicism, but it succumbs to the very sentimentalism he deplored. For Maazel, this is above all a 'heartbreaking love story', a classic boy-meets-girl affair under dystopian conditions.[22] That reduction helps to explain the limpness of the libretto and a sweeping love duet that might easily have taken its place in James Cameron's *Titanic* (1997). In any case, the idiosyncrasies of the adaptation are so jarring that they serve to repeatedly distract us from meaning. Lawrence Brownlee is cast as Syme, an African-American in the Outer Party, delivering what Maazel stereotypes as the rap of Newspeak.[23] The 'Physical Jerks' (*NEF*, p. 34) scene is granted five minutes, principally appearing to allow the introduction of a new technique into the history of operatic performance: a moment in which the telescreen cuts over the stage and orchestra who carry on performing silently. This is *Nineteen Eighty-Four* used, not for the first time, as a prefabricated container for a message that took its shape elsewhere.

Queering Winston

But there are exceptions to these broad rules; there are tracks which show us how strange this novel is, unlocking it as a novel from its status as treatise, returning us to its profound engagement with what it means to be human. I have grouped these tracks into an alternative playlist, *Alt-'84*: fifty key adaptations, a collaborative rock opera from the annals of rock'n'prole, a re-telling of each of the novel's key scenes.[24]

Tracks such as Pink Floyd's 'Goodbye Blue Sky' (1979), The Jam's 'Tales from the Riverbank' (1981), and Saint Etienne's 'Finisterre' (2002), for example, create powerful analogies for the English pastoralism that constitutes Winston's dreamscape, interweaving images of London, the Blitz, and the 'Golden Country'. 'Cygnet Committee' (1969), Bowie's earliest reference to the novel, is a detailed deconstruction of the inevitable failure of revolutionary agitprop. It is a theme made manifest on '1984/Dodo' (1973) by his horrified attraction to the perpetual possibility of personal exposure through the casual betrayal of Parsons by his own family. On 'Coinsequences' (2005), Public Enemy and Paris use Newspeak ('the consequence of coincidences all add up') to rhetorically question why America's black population seems so 'shit out of luck' when it comes to historical circumstance. Ministry's 'Faith Collapsing' (1989) comes closest to capturing Oceania's electronic music and the 'savage, barking rhythm' of the Hate Song. The novel's dystopian menace becomes a hellish industrial drum beat that offers no escape. At the centre of Akala's extended meditation on the novel, *Doublethink* (2010), is a soaring recreation of O'Brien forcing Winston to look at his broken body in the mirror of the torture chamber: 'The only way we can ever change anything is to look in the mirror and find no enemy.' On *Camouflage* (2003), billy woods, the most prolific rock'n'proller, besting even Bowie, sets the novel to create a terrifying vision of a dark and claustrophobic modern America. woods, the son of a literature professor and Rhodesian revolutionary, has returned hip-hop to the underground, building his career around the concept of hiding from public surveillance.

But what really marks out *Alt-'84* are the signs of a recurrent turn to the novel in order to think through issues related to affect, gender, and sexuality. The performative aspects of popular music obviously fit it to exploration of these issues. But we must note that there is something peculiar about Orwell's use of gender in relation to music that lends itself to this examination. On the one hand, the mechanical music in 'Pleasure Spots' is clearly feminine: it detracts from the supposedly serious business of 'solitude, creative work and the sense of wonder' (*CW*, 18, p. 32).[25] Orwell keenly tells us his clipping was 'written by a female journalist' (*CW*, 18, p. 29). And yet on the other hand, Oceania's music is obviously masculinist, springing from an elemental vocabulary of glass, brass, tin, and iron. To complicate matters, when the telescreens sing, women do the singing (*NEF*, p. 106). As with the gym instructress, we sense that Orwell saw the female convert to fascism as far more terrifying than her male peer.

Orwell's 'organic music' starts then from an odd base. It is notoriously difficult to identify the female from the male thrush. In this case, there is the suggestion of masculinity: Winston's thrush has 'no mate, no rival' (*NEF*, p. 130), and it is the second of May (*NEF*, p. 123), well after mating season. Its markings suggest this vocalist is *Turdus philomelos*. A keen ornithologist, Orwell would have known its song was remarkable for regularity rather than the 'astonishing variations' (*NEF*, p. 130) noted by the lovers.[26] The bird is here partly as metaphor: to perform, to lament the rape, mutilation, and trauma of its mythological namesake, to evoke 'The Darkling Thrush' (1900) as a register of epochal social decline. Similarly, the washerwoman is that exceedingly rare thing, a 'powerful contralto' (*NEF*, p. 144). This is where Bowie's key begins on 'Sweet Thing' (*Diamond Dogs*). These are the operatic roles reserved for *travestis*, originally written for *castrati*. With her 'brawny red forearms' (*NEF*, p. 144) and a body from whose 'mighty loins a race of conscious beings must one day come' (*NEF*, p. 230), Orwell's singer is androgynous in a way that her precursors, the drain-pipe cleaners, Mrs Parsons, and the slum girl of *The Road to Wigan Pier* (1937), are clearly not. Orwell's 'organic music' seems to seek signification from the body's inner depths, endocrinological, a fleshy encoding prior to language, the amygdala made vocal.

I do not want to make the claim that Orwell was an early gender theorist. On the contrary, he was of his times, confused about race and gender, essentially an essentialist. But such confusion creates a rupture in the surface of the text. Winston can be queered. The theme first appears in Bowie's work in the 'Sweet Thing' suite, which takes Winston into a rotten, cocaine-fuelled version of the prole slums. Bowie's shift from deep growl to high pitch seamlessly blends together pieces of *Nineteen Eighty-Four*'s women through the image of its prostitute. Placebo's 'The Bitter End' (2003) faithfully uses the novel's love story, and the eventual betrayal of that love, as the frame for understanding how to avoid the scarring of a broken relationship. Muse's *The Resistance* (2009), although ostensibly focused on its own dystopia, finds its centre in 'Undisclosed Desires', returning to the often ignored violence within Winston as an attempt to understand the peculiarities of desire, its relationship to power, and the permanent possibility of totalitarianism within the human soul. In 'The Centre Bullet' (1985), EBM pioneers Skinny Puppy sample from the novel's reflections on the primacy of feeling to consider whether affect can survive the torturer's arsenal. There is no finer tribute to the novel's ambivalence.

Several musicians play with the novel's emphasis on sexual space. In Romanthony's house classic 'Ministry of Love' (1995), '"the place where there is no darkness"' (*NEF*, p. 27) is transformed into an erotically charged dance paradise. In the wake of the Pythonesque attempt to regulate repetitive beats in the Criminal Justice and Public Order Act (1994), here the deserted belfry returns to the warehouse roots of Chicago house culture. It becomes a temporary autonomous zone, a new kind of cell away from the eyes, microphones, and batons of the police.[27] On *1.Outside* (1995), Bowie introduces Algeria Touchshriek, a 'broken man' with a spare room to lease above a shop that 'sells egg shells off the seashores and empty females'. He is a thinly veiled Charrington, spying on the lovers, a grotesque who acts to remind us of the tyrant's henchmen. Theirs is a voyeuristic, masturbatory, and sadistic spirit that takes root in their proprietorial need to hoard.

On 'Girl Loves Me' (2016), a track orchestrated for release days before his imminent death, Bowie is in the Chestnut Tree Café as the doomed Winston, privately mixing *nadsat* argot with Polari slang to explore the passing of time, the emptying out of love for boys and girls. Douglas Dare's 'Doublethink'

(2016) painfully exposes relationship breakdown and the challenges of coming out to his father. In 'Sebastiane' (1983), Sex Gang Children place Derek Jarman's homoeroticism alongside the shocking elements of Winston's desire for Julia: 'He would flog her to death with a rubber truncheon. He would tie her naked to a stake and shoot her full of arrows like Saint Sebastian. He would ravish her and cut her throat at the moment of climax' (*NEF*, p. 17). This is a Winston Smith that still needs critical exploration.[28]

When we try listening to this work in this way, as if it were a continuous cultural statement, a crowdsourced concept album, we can start to see its real value as adaptation. There is no single monumental adaptation of the novel in music. How could there be? But taken in aggregate, we have a music that has become an 'immense communication network', one granting us access to the very collective world Orwell sought.[29] *Nineteen Eighty-Four* is primarily a biting satire of hierarchy. But it is also a variation on the *ghazal*, an agonized, almost wailing love poem set to music. This was a novel written out of that powerful love between a father and his son, between a lover and a lost partner. It was a message made urgent by the author's foreknown death. This was no dead letter: *Rock'n'Prole* tells us how much Orwell's novel has changed humanity. But *Alt-'84* tells us how much of his love song still needs to be heeded.

Brief chronology of Rock'n'Prole: release date, artist, track (Album/EP)

Protest, Pacifism, Resistance

1960	Sheldon Allman	'Big Brother' (*Folk Songs for the 21st Century*)
1966	The Mothers of Invention	'Who Are the Brain Police?' (*Freak Out!*)
1967	Tim Buckley	'Goodbye and Hello' (*Goodbye and Hello*)
1968	The Bob Seger System	'2+2=?' (*Ramblin' Gamblin' Man*)
1969	David Bowie	'Cygnet Committee' (*David Bowie* aka *Space Oddity*)
	Spirit	'1984'
1971	Rare Earth	'Hey, Big Brother'
1972	Stevie Wonder	'Big Brother' (*Talking Book*)
1973	David Bowie	'1984/Dodo' (rec. October 1973; rel. *Sound +Vision*, 1978)
	John Lennon	'Only People' (*Mind Games*)
	Black Sabbath	'Who Are You?' (*Sabbath Bloody Sabbath*)
	Paul McCartney and Wings	'Nineteen Hundred and Eighty Five' (*Band on the Run*)
	Hugh Hopper	*1984*
1974	Eagles	'On the Border' (*On the Border*)
	Bowie	*Diamond Dogs*

Continued

Paranoia and 'Orwave'

1977	The Clash	'1977' (B-side, 'White Riot')
	Kansas	'Sparks of the Tempest' (*Point of Know Return*)
	The Jam	'Standards' (*This Is the Modern World*)
1978	Elvis Costello & The Attractions	'Night Rally' (*This Year's Model*)
	The Rutles	'Hold My Hand' (*The Rutles*)
	Tubeway Army	'The Dream Police' (*Tubeway Army*)
	TRB	'Power in the Darkness' (*Power in the Darkness*)
1979	Dead Kennedys	'California Über Alles'
	Samson	'Big Brother' (*Survivors*)
	XTC	'Making Plans for Nigel' (*Drums and Wires*)
	Cheap Trick	'Dream Police' (*Dream Police*)
	Pink Floyd	'Goodbye Blue Sky' (*The Wall*)
1980	The Beat	'Mirror in the Bathroom' (*I Just Can't Stop It*)
	Hazel O'Connor	'Big Brother' (*Breaking Glass*)
1981	Plasmatics	'Pig Is a Pig' (*Beyond the Valley of 1984*). See also '12 Noon' (*Metal Priestess*, 1981)
	Rick Wakeman	*1984*
	Daryl Hall, John Oates	'Private Eyes' (*Private Eyes*)
	The Jam	'Tales from the Riverbank' (*The Jam*)
	Dead Kennedys	'We've Got a Bigger Problem Now' (*In God We Trust, Inc.*)
	Anthony Phillips	*1984*
	Gil Scott-Heron	'"B" Movie' (*Reflections*)
	The 4-Skins	'1984' (*From Chaos to 1984 (The 4-Skins Live)*)
1982	The Fall	'Who Makes the Nazis?' (*Hex Enduction Hour*)
	The Alan Parsons Project	'Eye in the Sky' (*Eye in the Sky*)
	Judas Priest	'Electric Eye' (*Screaming for Vengeance*)
	Crass	'Nineteen Eighty Bore' (*Christ – The Album*)
1983	Oingo Boingo	'Wake Up (It's 1984)' (*Good for Your Soul*)
	The Police	'Every Breath You Take' (*Synchronicity*)
	Sex Gang Children	'Sebastiane' (*Song and Legend*)
	Ozzy Osbourne	'Rock 'N' Roll Rebel' (*Bark at the Moon*)
	Rockwell	'Somebody's Watching Me' (released 14 December 1983)
	David Peel & The Lower East Side	*1984*
	Lisa Stansfield	'The Thought Police' (B-Side, 'Listen to Your Heart')
1984	Elton John	'Restless' (*Breaking Hearts*)

Continued

	Eurythmics	*1984 (For the Love of Big Brother)* soundtrack (also, *1984* score)
	Dominic Muldowney	*Nineteen Eighty-Four (The Music of Oceania)* (*1984* alternative score)
	Feederz	'1984' (*Ever Feel Like Killing Your Boss?*)
	Golden Earring	'Orwell's Year' (B-side 'When the Lady Smiles')
1985	Supertramp	'Brother Where You Bound' (*Brother Where You Bound*)
	Skinny Puppy	'The Centre Bullet' (*Bites*) (also as The Tear Garden, 'The Center Bullet', 1986)
1988	Tracy Chapman	'Why?' (*Tracy Chapman*)
1989	Ministry	'Faith Collapsing' (*The Mind Is a Terrible Thing to Taste*)
1991	Ed Starink	'Suite "1984"' (*Retrospection*)
1993	Propagandhi	'Head? Chest? Or Foot?' (*How to Clean Everything*)
1994	Manic Street Preachers	'Faster' (*The Holy Bible*)
1995	David Bowie	*1.Outside* (aka *The Nathan Adler Diaries: A Hyper Cycle*)
	Marilyn Manson	'Irresponsible Hate Anthem' (*Dead in Chicago 1995*); official release on *Antichrist Superstar* (1996)
	Romanthony	'Ministry of Love'

Fear and the Millennium

1997	Radiohead	'Karma Police' (*OK Computer*)
1999	Rage Against the Machine	*The Battle of Los Angeles*
	Marilyn Manson	'Disposable Teens' (*Holy Wood (In The Shadow of the Valley of Death)*)
2000	Coldplay	'Spies' (*Parachutes*)
2001	Anti-Flag	'The Panama Deception' (*Underground Network*)
	Muse	'Citizen Erased' (*Origin of Symmetry*)
	Aesop Rock	*Labor Days*
2002	Sage Francis	'Hey, Bobby' (*The Makeshift Patriot EP*)
	Saint Etienne	'Finisterre' (*Finisterre*)
	Pulp	'Last Day of the Miner's Strike' (*Hits*)
2003	Placebo	'The Bitter End' (*Sleeping with Ghosts*)
	Radiohead	'2+2=5 (The Lukewarm.)' (*Hail to the Thief*)
	billy woods	*Camouflage* (reissued 2008)

Continued

2004	Incubus	'Talk Shows on Mute' (*A Crow Left of the Murder . . .*)
	Bad Religion	*The Empire Strikes First*
	Manic Street Preachers	'1985' (*Lifeblood*)
	Girls Aloud	'Big Brother' (*What Will the Neighbours Say?*)
	Anaïs Mitchell	'1984' (*Hymns for the Exiled*)
	billy woods	'Mind Control' (feat. Vordul Mega) (*The Chalice*)
2005	Lorin Maazel	*1984*
	Public Enemy Featuring Paris	'Coinsequences' (*Rebirth of a Nation*)
2006	Bobby Previte	*The Coalition of the Willing*
	Neil Young	'Living with War' (*Living with War*)
	The Haunted	'The Program' (*The Dead Eye*, special collector's edition)
2008	Nas	'Sly Fox' (*[Untitled]*)
2009	Paris	'Martial Law' (Various: *Paris Presents: Hard Truth Soldiers Vol 2*)
	Muse	*The Resistance*
	Thrice	'Doublespeak' (*Beggars*)
2010	Super Chron Flight Brothers	'Emmanuel Goldstein' (feat. Bigg Jus) (*Cape Verde*)
	Akala	*Doublethink*
	Computer Magic	'Victory Gin' (*Hiding from More of Our Time EP*)
2012	billy woods	'Human Resources' (*History Will Absolve Me*)
	Rødhåd	*1984*
	The Offspring	'The Future Is Now' (*Days Go By*)

Crisis, Populism, Confession

2013	billy woods	'Pro Wrestling' (*Dour Candy*)
	The Used	'Iddy Biddy' (*The Ocean of the Sky*)
	Zbigniew Karkowksi	*The Last Man in Europe* (recorded live October; released 2016)
2015	Muse	'The Globalist' (*Drones*)
	Cult of the Damned	'Cult of the Damned' (*Cult of the Damned*)
2016	David Bowie	'Girl Loves Me' (★ *[Blackstar]*)
	Clipping.	'Interlude 01 (Freestyle)' (*Splendour & Misery*)
	Douglas Dare	'Doublethink' (*Aforger*)
2017	Dope KNife	*NineteenEightyFour*
	STREET LIGHT	'Brother' (*Run for Your Life*)
2018	Hostile Array	'Newspeak' (*Hostile Array*)

Continued

	The Blinders	*Columbia*
	mewithoutYou	'Julia (or, "Holy to the LORD" on the Bells of Horses)' (*[Untitled]*)
	Ghostemane	'Gatteka' (*N/O/I/S/E*)
	Marco Malasomma	*Jura*
2019	Aesop Rock and Tobacco Are Malibu Ken	'Acid King' (*Malibu Ken*)
	Zheani	'Thought Criminal' (*Eight*)

Note: Within individual years, ordered by month of album release where identifiable (otherwise alphabetically).

Notes

1 David Ryan, *George Orwell on Screen: Adaptations, Documentaries, and Docudramas on Film and Television* (Jefferson, NC: McFarland & Company, 2018), pp. 152–3.
2 On the impact of anarchy, cocaine, and totalitarianism, see Dorian Lynskey, *The Ministry of Truth: A Biography of George Orwell's 1984* (London: Picador, 2019), pp. 218–22. For a chronological listing of the tracks and albums referenced in this chapter, see the table at the end of this chapter.
3 On Orwell and popular music, see D. J. Taylor, *On 'Nineteen Eighty-Four': A Biography* (New York: Abrams Press, 2019), pp. 145–7.
4 Roud Folk Index numbers 13191, 20584, 494, and 13190, respectively.
5 This song's status is highly ambivalent in the novel. It was a community action song in those boys' camps set up by the future George VI in the 1920s, but originally derived from a line of English folk songs that included 'Go No More a Rushing' (Roud 330), possibly a dance tune. See Frank Howes, *Folk Music of Britain – And Beyond* (1969; Abingdon: Routledge, 2016), pp. 116–17. The tune speaks of betrayal probably because Orwell sensed that the fake scout folk of the 1930s had betrayed *it*.
6 Roy Shuker, *Popular Music: The Key Concepts*, 4th edn (Abingdon: Routledge, 2017), p. 3.
7 Fredric Jameson, *Postmodernism, or the Cultural Logic of Late Capitalism* (London: Verso, 1991), pp. 6–16.
8 Dick Hebdige, *Hiding in the Light: On Images and Things* (1988; London: Routledge, 2002), pp. 50–52.
9 Bernard Crick, '*Nineteen Eighty-Four*: Context and Controversy', in John Rodden (ed.), *The Cambridge Companion to George Orwell* (Cambridge: Cambridge University Press, 2007), pp. 146–59, at p. 147.
10 Philip Bounds, *Orwell and Marxism: The Political and Cultural Thinking of George Orwell* (New York: I. B. Tauris, 2009), pp. 79–80.
11 Keir Keightley, 'Reconsidering Rock', in Simon Frith, Will Straw, and John Street (eds.), *The Cambridge Companion to Pop and Rock* (Cambridge: Cambridge University Press, 2001), pp. 109–42, at pp. 110–13.

12 Paul Théberge, '"Plugged In": Technology and Popular Music', in Frith, Straw, and Street (eds.), *The Cambridge Companion to Pop and Rock*, pp. 3–25, at pp. 5–6.

13 Julie Sanders, *Adaptation and Appropriation* (Abingdon: Routledge, 2006), pp. 23–4.

14 Mike Ingham, 'Popular Song and Adaptation', in Thomas Leitch (ed.), *The Oxford Handbook of Adaptation Studies* (Oxford: Oxford University Press, 2017), pp. 324–39, at p. 328.

15 See Spotify, *Rock'n'Prole* [http://bit.ly/rocknprole] (accessed 30 October 2019). Release date order.

16 On these modes see Ingham, 'Popular Song and Adaptation', pp. 325–6.

17 See 'George Orwave', *Beyond Yacht Rock Podcast*, 18 (13 May 2016) [http://bit .ly/georgeorwave] (accessed 30 October 2019).

18 See Mark Fisher, *Capitalist Realism: Is There No Alternative?* (Ropley: Zero Books, 2009).

19 See also Rick Wakeman (1981) and mewithoutYou (2018).

20 On the gendering of rock style see especially Robert Walser, *Running with the Devil: Power, Gender, and Madness in Heavy Metal Music* (Middletown, CT: Wesleyan University Press, 1993) and Simon Reynolds and Joy Press, *The Sex Revolts: Gender, Rebellion, and Rock 'n' Roll* (Cambridge, MA: Harvard University Press, 1995).

21 Ingham, 'Popular Song and Adaptation', p. 335.

22 Lorin Maazel, '*1984*: An Opera for Today' [booklet]. Lorin Maazel, *1984*, Royal Opera House Covent Garden, cond. Lorin Maazel [on DVD-ROM], p. 11–13, at p. 11.

23 Lorin Maazel, 'Bonus Feature: 1984 – An Introduction by Lorin Maazel', on Maazel, *1984* [Disc 2, DVD-ROM].

24 Spotify, *Alt-'84* [http://bit.ly/alt84] (accessed 30 October 2019). Open to collaboration.

25 Laura Frost, *The Problem with Pleasure: Modernism and Its Discontents* (New York: Columbia University Press, 2013), p. 19.

26 For Orwell's ornithology, see 'Domestic Diary' (CW, 19, p. 465).

27 See Hakim Bey, *T.A.Z.: The Temporary Autonomous Zone, Ontological Anarchy, Poetic Terrorism*, 2nd edn (Brooklyn, NY: Autonomedia, 2003).

28 See Jamie Wood, 'George Orwell, Desire, and Encounters with Rural Sex in Mid-Century England', *College Literature*, 45.3 (Summer 2018), pp. 399–423.

29 Simon Frith, 'The Popular Music Industry', in Frith, Straw, and Street (eds.), *The Cambridge Companion to Pop and Rock*, pp. 26–52, at pp. 27–8.

15

ISABELLE LICARI-GUILLAUME*

Nineteen Eighty-Four and Comics

Contrary to many classics of modern literature, *Nineteen Eighty-Four* (1949) has never been adapted into comics[1] – more precisely, there are no published comics[2] of that title that strive to provide a faithful adaptation of Orwell's narrative. Conversely, if we move beyond the discourse of fidelity and understand 'adaptation' in a looser sense, as Linda Hutcheon does, it becomes clear that a large number of comics follow the pattern of 'repetition without replication'.[3] In this sense, acknowledgements of Orwell's influence within the medium of comics are numerous and can take a variety of forms.

Some of them, like Ted Rall's *2024: A Graphic Novel* (2001), are presented as explicitly Orwellian re-imaginings that play with the structure and themes of the adapted text. Others, like Alan Moore's *V for Vendetta* (1982–1989, with David Lloyd) and *The League of Extraordinary Gentlemen: Black Dossier* (2007, with Kevin O'Neill), conjure up Orwell's intertextual presence, both as political text and as literary classic. Finally, many of them deal with the pop-cultural substrate of *Nineteen Eighty-Four* as a set of characters and concepts (such as Big Brother, Room 101, and Newspeak) that can be reconfigured within different generic contexts, in a postmodern era where intertextual allusion has become standard practice. This last category includes works such as Grant Morrison's *The Invisibles* (1994–2000) and Warren Ellis's *Transmetropolitan* (1997–2002).[4]

As Asami Nakamura has shown, Orwell's correspondence and public statements about *Nineteen Eighty-Four* are shaped by the belief that 'the author is the ultimate holder' of meaning.[5] If this were true, then the adaptor's ideal role would be one of 'subservience' – a term used by traductologist Daniel Simeoni to refer to the sociological ethos of literary translators – and 'invisibility' – as theorized by Lawrence Venuti, also in the context of translation.[6] This is clearly not the position favoured by the comics writers and artists under study. Rall, Moore, O'Neill, and the others mentioned above use and interpret the adapted text along a continuum that goes from tight rewriting to loose allusion – but in all cases they remain eminently visible as authors.

Although adaptation studies have now largely outgrown the fidelity paradigm, it remains especially resonant in the context of comics that adapt literary classics, because of the respective cultural positions of these two media. Indeed, the 'literary' character of certain comics has often been used as a way to legitimize comics more broadly as a form. In the 1940s, comics adaptations of famous novels were a way to 'respond to the concerns of parents'[7] over the supposed noxiousness of the medium, while DC's Vertigo comics in the 1990s and 2000s were noted for their maturity and the literariness of their writing.[8] By the same token, the term 'graphic novel' was notoriously used as a marketing ploy by Will Eisner, in order to sell his comics to a mainstream publisher.[9] In other words, as we consider the legacy of *Nineteen Eighty-Four* in the comics medium, we should pay close attention to how this legacy is treated by comics creators with regard to Orwell's status as a canonical author. The passage from one medium to another also entails a change in the system of signs that is used to convey meaning – indeed, we move from written text to comics, a medium that combines words and images arranged in sequential order. This makes for a complex adaptive system whose possibilities range from direct quotation to visual allusion to much looser forms of reference. And as Orwellian ideas are given visual shape and form, we must bear in mind the role of the artist's graphic style in the process of appropriation.

In this chapter I argue that the politics of homage and adaptation displayed in the comics mentioned above are intrinsically tied to a broader consideration of comics' relationship to literature, its older and supposedly more respectable counterpart. Adapting a classic can be a means of claiming legitimacy; but appropriating it and integrating it in a different narrative system can, in turn, constitute resistance to cultural homogeneity and orthodox readings. This is particularly relevant in the context of a novel that is about challenging political and cultural power. What is more, such appropriations are carried out through a 'transmutation'[10] or 'transcoding'[11] into visual narratives which aptly echo *Nineteen Eighty-Four*'s constant preoccupation with screens, images, and visibility.

Airstrip One Revisited: Ted Rall's 2024

The first comics narrative under scrutiny is Ted Rall's *2024: A Graphic Novel*, which was published in 2001 by NBM. It is, in the words of the author, who is primarily known as a creator of political cartoons and nonfiction, an 'homage to / parody of / updating of' Orwell's novel.[12] In terms of structure, the text closely follows Orwell's division into three sections, and many sentences parallel the novel – for example, 'It was a bright cold day in April' (*NEF*, p. 3) becomes 'it was a bright hot day in April'.[13] Therefore, Rall's ideal reader is one who is closely familiar with Orwell's text and will identify not only the book's most popular themes and ideas but also its textual echoes. This is consistent with the cultural status of *2024*, whose subtitle, *A Graphic Novel*, emphasizes its proximity with literature and reinforces the distinction between 'comics' (mainstream comic books or, in Rall's case, press drawings) and 'graphic novels', which are expected to be longer and more complex. NBM's comics imprint, 'ComicsLit', similarly posits a difference between mainstream comics and those that are 'literary' (i.e. not published by a specialized house). Materially, the book exhibits traits associated with 'quality' publications, especially its heavy stock paper and its black-and-white format, all of which participate in a strategy of cultural distinction that gestures towards a knowledgeable readership.

The story of *2024* is set in New York, which is now part of Canamexicusa, the Pan-American superstate that wages economic war with the EC (Europe) and the South Asian free trade alliance. In this post-capitalist form of corporate government, all power is wielded by private companies and the state exists only to cater to the market's needs. *2024* is an intensely cynical take on Orwell, in which the characters' motivations are much more ambiguous than in *Nineteen Eighty-Four*; their goal is not to reclaim individual freedom but to rise as the new elite and thus to 'land the ultimate promotion' (*2024*, p. 65). Although most of Orwell's iconic creations have equivalents in Rall's book (Room 101 becomes Channel 101, for example), it is quite significant that there is no Big Brother. In the last panel of *2024*, the caption ends in a ternary rhythm: 'He loved his life. He loved everything. He loved *himself*' (*2024*, p. 96, emphasis added) – the sentence echoes Orwell's 'He had won the victory over himself. He loved Big Brother' (*NEF*, p. 311), and suggests that, in our modern world, the cult of an authoritarian leader is less threatening than the cult of the individual in consumer society. This effort to 'update' Orwell's political thought is visible in Rall's equivalent for doublethink, 'Neopostmodernism', which presents a distorted vision of 1970s postmodernist theory by positing that the instability of language effectively prevents thought and knowledge. More pointedly, as the narrator explains that 'humanity had arrived at the highest stage of development: anarcho-capitalism and subsidiary government. *History had ended* in 1991' (*2024*, p. 18, emphasis added), Rall seems to echo Francis Fukuyama's famous view that we have reached the 'end of history' brought about by 'the total exhaustion of viable systematic alternatives to Western capitalism'.[14] Fukuyama describes a world where 'the willingness to risk one's life for a purely abstract goal' is gone, replaced with 'the endless solving of technical problems', which is an accurate depiction of the future as imagined by Rall.[15] Whereas *Nineteen Eighty-Four* suggests that ideological resistance against totalitarianism is doomed to fail, 2024 doubts whether such resistance is possible in the first place.

Rall's style relies on very simple depictions of his characters (Figure 15.1) – faces are only ever seen in quarter profile, and consist most of the time of two dots for eyes, a prominent nose, and a mouth that is only visible if it is open. The range of emotion is limited, in keeping with the Neopostmodern condition of the characters: 'ironic detachment has killed sentimentality, and without cheesy sentimentality there's no point feeling sentiment' (2024, p. 62). When there is emotion, it is conveyed first and foremost through emanata (sweat drops, exclamation marks, question marks) and/or expressive variations in the background, with the use of focus lines (2024, p. 86) or

Figure 15.1 2024 (page 19, panels 1–4). ©Ted Rall. Used with permission

highly contrasting explosion shapes. This minimalism has two effects: first, it forces the reader to rely heavily on texts to follow the story, thus foregrounding textual connections with *Nineteen Eighty-Four*.[16] Second, it fosters a sense of distance from characters who appear largely mechanical: in 2024, Winston's face hardly ever changes, whether he is about to be tortured by O'Brien (2024, p. 89) or having sex with Julia (2024, p. 56). In the second instance, his detachment is even mirrored by the understatement in the thought bubble, which reads 'Hey – I don't hate sex!' Similarly, although the narrative often sticks close to Winston's point of view in order to account for his thoughts, it occasionally reverts to the narrator's external point of view (zero focalization) and a rather snarky tone that prevents empathy and instead underlines Rall's criticism of the unthinking consumer ('back at the love pad [...] Winston and Julia exchanged *their usual sophistries*'; 2024, p. 70, emphasis added).

The lack of information conveyed by the pictures, as well as the overabundance of contradictory textual cues, result in a sense of erasure and loss of stable meaning about the broader issues of this world – which is the point of the Neopostmodern era denounced by Rall. While Orwell eventually provides his reader with a key to the diegetic world in the form of excerpts from Goldstein's fictional book, Rall declines to do so in two separate instances: first when O'Brien gives Winston 'the url for a secret channel [where he] will find answers to the major questions of our time' (2024, p. 67), which Winston immediately misplaces; and then when Winston, randomly typing URLs into his web browser, finds himself on the very same page and proceeds to read a few lines, only to get distracted by another hyperlink (2024, p. 69), so that the reader never gains any access to this text beyond its title ('Why Everything Sucks: the Deconstruction of Neopostmodernism'). This absent book and Winston's *blasé* attitude are correlated with the demise of traditional print culture: 'before – before when? – history had been revised. But the demise of print meant that electronic archives could be edited with a few keystrokes, or simply deleted' (2024, p. 16). In 2024, the rise of web TV and the loss of books have permanently damaged the characters' attention spans, so that they endlessly chase light entertainment. But there is another ability that Winston has lost; indeed, as he daydreams about his stepmother, we learn that 'she'd taught him how to draw, but he'd forgotten his skills after the demise of trees had eliminated paper' (2024, p. 19). In a comic book this is bound to be read metatextually – but the fact that Rall is first and foremost a political cartoonist further suggests that the material loss of paper is the root of Winston's inability to think critically about politics. Such emphasis on materiality is reminiscent of Winston's fascination for his journal in Orwell's novel, but it is also a recurrent feature in the other comics I am considering.

On his website, Rall states that 2024 is one of his 'personal favorites, but also [his] worst-selling book'.[17] This lack of recognition might be a consequence of the need to read 2024 first and foremost as a political comment on *Nineteen Eighty-Four*, which requires the reader to be familiar with Orwell's text in order for its parodic nature to be grasped. Read in isolation, 2024 is about a character who ends up exactly where he started: as a self-satisfied egotistical product of consumer society, with few aspirations and fewer reasons to rebel. Winston's lack of concern for Julia,[18] for example, is only comical when contrasted with his dedication to her in Orwell's novel – otherwise, it may seem to destabilize the 'truth-of-coherence'[19] in Rall's book. In other words, in 2024 the process of adaptation itself is key to the successful interpretation of the narrative; conversely, in the comics I am going to examine next, *Nineteen Eighty-Four* is one of several intertexts that are implicitly or explicitly conjured up.

Nineteen Eighty-Four in Moore's *Oeuvre*

We now turn to the study of two comics scripted by Alan Moore, which again must be considered in their context of production. Unlike Rall's career, most of Moore's is defined by his proximity to the American mainstream comic book industry, leading to a comics *oeuvre* that is both transatlantic (Moore is an Englishman) and fraught with issues of legitimacy, cultural status, and what Jochen Ecke terms the 'conflicts of authorization':[20] while many mainstream companies in the 1980s offered 'work-for-hire' contracts under which creators did not hold copyright for their work, Alan Moore fought to promote his own authorial status and is still considered one of the most important comics writers of the last decades. The two books that are most influenced by *Nineteen Eighty-Four* appear widely apart in Moore's career. *V for Vendetta*, one of his earliest series, was begun in 1982, while *The League of Extraordinary Gentlemen: Black Dossier* dates from 2009. Both texts treat Orwell as one of several major influences.[21]

Begun in 1982 in *Warrior*, a British magazine, and finally completed in 1989 with DC Comics after a long publication hiatus,[22] *V for Vendetta* is a nightmarish vision of Britain's imminent future. In the world of *V*, a Labour victory in 1982 led to the removal of American missiles from British soil – causing Britain to be spared in the nuclear bombings of the Third World War that destroyed the rest of Europe. However, as the war abated, fascism seized the country. Jews, homosexuals, people of colour, and political dissenters were sent to detention camps and exterminated by the ruling party,

Norsefire. Years later, a former inmate of those camps, known only as codename V, sets out to destabilize the regime and to bring about anarchy. Another who shares his goal is Eve, a young woman who undergoes the same torture he did, and who will eventually assume his mantle after his death. This political premise is grounded in the rise of Thatcherism as witnessed by Moore and Lloyd, two creators with left-wing sympathies (Moore in particular is a self-described anarchist, and has been involved in anti-Nazi activism). As Maggie Gray explains, Thatcher's emphasis on 'law and order', her endorsement of widespread social surveillance, her xenophobic approach to immigration (as early as 1978), and ten years later her support of Section 28, which forbade local authorities from 'promoting homosexuality', all fuelled the Left's anxiety about the imminence of a fascist police state.[23]

Moore follows Orwell's strategy of setting his story in the near future in order to foreground contemporary concerns. However, the art style developed by David Lloyd owes less to traditional science-fiction artwork and more to the noir aesthetics of the 1930s[24] – this fosters a sense of chronological confusion, much in keeping with the fact that although *V for Vendetta* is set in the future, the story depicts living conditions that evoke the past of wartime and post-war England (rationing, the acquisition of goods on the black market, and so forth). From the outset, it is clear that *Nineteen Eighty-Four* was a major influence on both creators, something visible in *V for Vendetta* through the omnipresence of posters and slogans ('strength through purity / purity through faith'); the reliance on technology to enforce constant surveillance; and the power of songs and folk culture as instruments of cultural resistance – although in this case 'Oranges and Lemons' is replaced with 'The Fifth of November'.

In *V for Vendetta*, privacy and autonomy are hindered by the various instruments of surveillance put in place by Norsefire. To speak in Foucauldian terms, 'visibility is a trap', and the screens and cameras used in the book conjure up the model of the panopticon, whereby a central authority can watch any individual at any given time.[25] This is reinforced graphically by Lloyd's uses of intense contrast, with no grey areas. When representing strongly lit faces or objects, Lloyd tends to omit the external outline completely – as would happen in overexposed photographs (for a particularly clear example, see *V for Vendetta*, p. 122, panel 1). And this visual 'overexposure' is linked to the character's vulnerability to surveillance. Such vulnerability resonates with the development of CCTV in the 1980s, when *Nineteen Eighty-Four* 'became the key reference point for the dystopian structure of feeling surrounding state strategies of mass surveillance and panoptic social control'.[26] What is more, in the specific context of sequential graphic narratives, the issue of visibility is perpetually foregrounded, as the medium by its nature allows readers to see everything at once – all the panels are visible on the page and the reader can leaf through the narrative at will. Hence, perhaps, the attraction of Orwellian intertexts within a visual medium.

Moore's biggest departure from Orwell is that, in *V for Vendetta*, the rebellion does succeed, if not to destroy the regime completely, then at least to destabilize it. While in *Nineteen Eighty-Four* Winston and Julia's love for each other is eventually taken away from them, V and Eve retain their free will, even under torture. It is the last 'inch' of freedom they have, 'the only thing in the world worth having' (*V for Vendetta*, p. 160). This 'inch' is metaphorical, but it also alludes to the female body and to sexuality. Valerie, the former prisoner who inspired both V and Eve to fight for their freedom, is remembered through letters written with a smuggled pencil that she 'hid [...] inside [her]' (*V for Vendetta*, p. 154). Similarly, for Eve, who narrowly escapes rape at the hands of the Party in book one, reclaiming bodily autonomy and the right to privacy becomes a means of resistance, in a way that is highly resonant with Winston's view that Julia's sexuality 'was the force that would tear the party to pieces' (*NEF*, p. 132). Thus, in *V for Vendetta*, intertextual references to *Nineteen Eighty-Four* deal mainly with the political discourse of the book. By contrast, *Black Dossier* tackles its literary legacy, setting up a complex network of allusions within which Orwell's novel is given a place of choice among British classics.

Black Dossier is an autonomous story set in the world of Moore and O'Neill's *League of Extraordinary Gentlemen*, which incorporates many works of fiction from nineteenth- and twentieth-century literature. The 'league' of the title is a special operations team led by Mina Murray (Mina Harker from *Dracula*) that includes Allan Quatermain and Dr Jekyll, among others. While the first two volumes of the series are set in the Victorian era, *Black Dossier* takes place in 1958, which in this world's timeline marks the end of Ingsoc rule; Big Brother came to power in 1945 and was replaced in 1952 by O'Brien, who renamed the party 'New Ingsoc' (presumably a jab at Tony Blair's New Labour) and restored the Conservatives' role as official opposition. Many objects represented in the frames of *Black Dossier* directly reference the world of *Nineteen Eighty-Four*, from Victory gin and cigarettes to Goldstein's book (*Black Dossier*, p. 8).

As is often the case in *League*, characters from different literary sources are conflated into one single figure; here, Big Brother happens to be Harold Wharton, a character from the Greyfriar School stories written by Frank Richards (Charles Hamilton). The joke is that Orwell wrote an essay about Hamilton's work, 'Boys' Weeklies' (1940), in which he calls Hamilton's writing 'artificial' and 'repetitive' (*CW*, 12, p. 59), and criticizes the timeless, sanitized representation of public school life and its 'supposed "glamour"' (*CW*, 12, p. 62). Moreover, casting Orwell's totalitarian leader as a former public schoolboy is a way to address social reproduction and the class divide in Britain, past and present. This is also consistent with Moore's willingness to put on an equal footing literary classics (Orwell) and popular transmedia narratives (Richards). In Mark Singer's words, '*League* gleefully collapses the social distinctions between high and low culture just as surely as it ignores the authorial boundaries between the texts themselves.'[27]

In the comic, Mina and Allan set out to retrieve the eponymous Black Dossier, which is a collection of documents assembled over the years by Ingsoc to gather intelligence on the members of the League. The contents of the dossier are embedded within the main narrative and include pastiches ranging from lost Shakespearean drama to Pornsec Tijuana Bibles.[28] In other words, the plot is driven by the need to salvage material evidence from the past. Like in *V for Vendetta*, where V rescues books and music from destruction, salvaging material culture becomes a means of resistance, allowing the League to eventually discover a broader conspiracy. The materiality of the archive is foregrounded by its direct inclusion in the narrative, so that, like the characters, the reader can actually hold the Black Dossier in her hands. The first page of this book-within-a-book features a warning written in parodic Newspeak listing the crimes one commits by reading this dossier. The playful sentence 'Now look. Now Don't. Now Look. Now don't' (*Black Dossier*, p. 16) simultaneously forbids and invites the act of seeing; the alternation between seeing and not seeing also mirrors the reading process of a comic book, where continuous processes are only shown in discrete images.

In fact, material evidence contaminates the entire *League* series, as the stories themselves are framed by various documents from the past, either real (like the infamous 'Marvel douche' advert that led to vol. 1, issue 5 being recalled) or fabricated by O'Neill (like the fictitious Ingsoc identity card which appears at the beginning of *Black Dossier*, and which is both a signifier of Orwellian surveillance and a reference to the real-life controversy over the introduction of identity cards in Britain). But materiality is also a source of pleasure; like Winston and Julia with Goldstein's book, Mina and Allan delight in reading the Dossier in bed. Some fans of the series have even suggested that the room where they do so might actually be the same room Winston rents, based notably on the presence of 'Mrs C.', whose physical description matches that of the singing prole in *Nineteen Eighty-Four* (and whose name may be a reference to Mr Charrington).[29]

Orwellian Appropriations and Genre Narratives

As one of the most prominent comics creators of his time, Moore has had a profound influence on the comics industry on both sides of the Atlantic, and most conspicuously on DC's Vertigo imprint, which has tried to replicate many of Moore's innovations. In the last part of this chapter, I intend to deal with the way Orwell's premise is borrowed, adapted, and appropriated by Moore and by later Vertigo creators within the framework of specific narrative genres, focusing largely on issues of power, surveillance, and resistance.

First, and perhaps most straightforwardly, Orwellian intertext is used as a critique of the superhero genre, which has dominated American comics since the 1960s. While this genre is obviously preoccupied with issues of power, it also questions the writing and re-writing of history: since all the stories featuring a given character are expected to form a consistent whole, it is not uncommon for certain events to be written out of the continuity. Superheroes in their classical incarnation are protectors of the *status quo* who operate outside the realm of law, and for this reason they have been seen as conservative and sometimes as fascistic figures. This is already addressed in *V for Vendetta*, where 'Moore inverts the historical ideological role of the superhero' and plays with the expectations of the genre (notably the tropes of superhuman abilities and the hidden identity, which in V's case is never revealed).[30] In the narrative, V's role likens him to a villain – he is the agent of change rather than of order, and a character who will not hesitate to resort to extreme violence (contrasted with Eve's refusal to kill). V elaborates on Orwell's politics by suggesting that although hope does lie in the 'proles' (since it is up to the Londoners to actually finish the rebellion started by V), they may still need some kind of charismatic leader to lead the way.

Such questioning of the means and ends of political rebellion is also clearly visible in Grant Morrison's *The Invisibles*. The book features a team of marginalized rebels belonging to the various categories of people most at risk in totalitarian regimes – Boy is black, King Mob is of Polish descent, Fanny is queer, and so forth. Like V, they are charismatic antiheroes whose willingness to kill is problematized over the course of the story. They are pitched against the supernatural forces of order and conformity, the Outer Church, that secretly pull the strings of the government. The underground organization to which they belong, aptly named the Invisibles, resembles the Brotherhood in *Nineteen Eighty-Four* insofar as its agents never meet the entire organization and work in small units for safety (*NEF*, p. 183; *Invisibles*, book 1, p. 140). At the end of the fourth issue, as Dane is initiated into the organization, a blackboard states 'Big Brother is watching you /

Learn to become invisible' (*Invisibles*, book 1, p. 122), thus concretizing the reference to Orwell.

Over the course of *The Invisibles*, two of the protagonists are imprisoned in a facility designed to torture them into submission. The story begins with Dane being sent to a redress camp for rebellious teenagers, antiphrastically called 'Harmony House', where he barely escapes the surgical procedure meant to render him truly obedient. The dialogue here is an open pastiche of Orwell – simply compare 'we have mummified the living here. Removed all their anger and frustration, all their feelings; left them hollow and dry' (*Invisibles*, book 1, p. 40) with 'Everything will be dead inside you. Never again will you be capable of love, or friendship, or joy of living [...]. You will be hollow' (*NEF*, p. 269).

There's a second torture scene, this time at the hands of Sir Miles, a British aristocrat and a servant of the Outer Church. As he tries to break King Mob's will and force him to accept the views of his oppressor, both his methods and his pretence at benevolence again echo O'Brien's: 'How many fingers do you see?'; 'It is not enough to *see*. It is not enough to say that you see. You must *believe*' (*Invisibles*, book 3, p. 63, original emphasis). The axiomatic two plus two equals five is literalized on the page as Sir Miles holds up a hand that now has *five* lifted fingers and a folded thumb. The decision suddenly to break the rules of anatomy in a story that had so far relied on Phil Jimenez and John Stokes's detailed, realistic treatment of bodies places the reader in the situation of one who *already sees* reality the way Miles wants. This can be read as a metatextual reference to the reader's position as someone who, like Big Brother, is always watching the characters, perversely enjoying the unfolding scene. But here the reader's point of view is also that of King Mob himself, which hints instead at the possibility of rebellion and resistance, and the necessity to choose a side.

The ambiguity of the reader's stance is reinforced by the way Sir Miles describes Orwell's novel: 'I take it you are familiar with Orwell's *1984*; political pornography drooled over by those who talk of freedom yet thrill to depictions of absolute control. Let me show you how far beyond those ideas we have gone' (*Invisibles*, book 3, p. 62). In this sentence, 'those who talk of freedom' might just be a reference to the readers who are currently 'thrilling to depictions of absolute control' yet still root for the freedom fighters. Morrison simultaneously questions cultural hierarchies (by likening a canonical novel to pornography) and encourages the reader to question the underlying politics of (super-) hero narratives.

Finally, *Nineteen Eighty-Four*'s anticipatory narrative is also frequently reinvested within an SF framework, where it becomes a shorthand for totalitarian dystopias. *1984* was the title of a science-fiction comics magazine published from 1978 to 1983 by Jim Warren (though the Orwell estate required that the name be changed to *1994* in 1980). In Britain, science fiction has been one of the dominant comics genres through the 1980s and 1990s, as attested by the permanence of the anthology *2000AD*, which is still in print today. Thus, many of the British writers who (like Alan Moore, Grant Morrison, and Warren Ellis) worked extensively for American publishers were heavily influenced by science fiction, and within this framework they often resorted to Orwellian themes and motifs. In particular, adapting Orwell in the late twentieth century means taking into account rapid developments in technology, not only to denounce its present use (as with *V for Vendetta*'s CCTV) but also to speculate about its future. In this regard, a forerunning and hugely popular title is Warren Ellis and Darick Robertson's *Transmetropolitan*, which was serialized from 1997 to 2002. Interestingly, the series shares some features with Rall's *2024*, notably its setting in an unnamed 'city' that can be identified as New York, and its depiction of libertarian capitalism gone mad.

The world of *Transmetropolitan* is swamped with images; light-emitting screens and displays are omnipresent and emit both ways, which allows private companies to generate buying impulses in consumers. Society seems stuck in an eternal present and is 'actively against the constant reminder of the past'.[31] However, Ellis's choice to have a truth-obsessed journalist as his main character makes it clear that history is not as malleable as it is in *Nineteen Eighty-Four* – it can be recorded and documented, textually (through newspaper articles) or visually (notably through the character of Mary, a photographer, whose pictures will serve as crucial evidence at the end of the story). Thus, like *The Invisibles*, *Transmetropolitan* is a story led by charismatic anti-heroes who will go to extreme lengths in order to preserve free thought and free expression. Both narratives display an awareness of comics' history as a 'low', often counter-cultural medium, and this leads them to re-configure modes of rebellion in order to envision a world in which resistance is possible, and even often successful.

These series are also staples of the Vertigo imprint developed by DC Comics between 1993 and 2019. And in this regard, Orwellian references are part of a broader aesthetic project, one actively encouraged by the imprint's curator, Karen Berger: the creation of a tight intertextual network uniting these comics with literary classics has been a way to woo a different readership, to assert the status of comics writers as authors,[32] and more generally to raise the profile of comic books within the mainstream cultural industry.

Conclusion

The comics discussed in this chapter deal with their Orwellian legacy in many different ways, often combining a form of reverence for this beloved classic of literature and a frankly iconoclastic approach, in keeping with the medium's counter-cultural roots. Ted Rall's 2024 is the most striking comic in this regard, as it rewrites Orwell's story with an eye to the political developments of the late twentieth and early twenty-first centuries. But Rall's narrative also foregrounds several elements that resonate with the nature of the comics medium itself, by focusing on visibility, surveillance, and the materiality of books (be they comic books or prose novels) as vehicles for human ideas and aspirations. These themes resurface in most of the comics I have considered; sometimes, as in *V for Vendetta* and *The Invisibles*, they are used to engage the reader, asserting the need to resist dehumanizing state surveillance and oppression. In other instances, as is notably the case in Alan Moore's *League of Extraordinary Gentlemen*, they address the pleasures of reading and writing, drawing and viewing, and invite us to reflect on the nature of fiction. The familiar characters and concepts invented by Orwell take on new guises as they are brought into resonance with some of the most idiosyncratic genres and themes of American and British comics. They support a political reading of the moral ambiguities behind heroic or superheroic figures, and resonate with the anticipatory mode of anti-authoritarian science fiction, a genre deeply indebted to Orwell. Finally, using and abusing the work of a canonical author are means to reflect on the cultural status of comics writers and artists, and on the role that comics play in contemporary culture. Ultimately, Orwellian intertexts allow creators to assert their own creative voices by rewriting *Nineteen Eighty-Four*, while also questioning their respective positions on the scale of cultural respectability. This allows us to think of adaptation as a two-way process; it's about what comics do to Orwell, but also, in part, about what Orwell does to them.

Notes

* The author would like to thank Ted Rall, who generously granted permission to reproduce his work in the present volume.

1 Throughout this article, 'comics' refers to the medium itself. I will not be using the term 'graphic novel', because it is problematic in ways that go beyond the scope of this article. For more on the debate on terminology, see Barbara Postema, *Narrative Structure in Comics: Making Sense of Fragments* (Rochester, NY: RIT Press, 2013), p. xi.

2 A webcomic by Canadian artist Frédéric Guimont appeared around 2007 at 1984comic.com. It was discontinued after two chapters. The website is now offline

but can still be seen via WayBackMachine (the exact opposite of a memory hole): [https://web.archive.org/web/20110707060959/http://1984comic.com/pdf/1984comic_chapter_02.pdf] (accessed 15 October 2019).

3 Linda Hutcheon, *A Theory of Adaptation* (New York: Routledge, 2006), p. 7.
4 Grant Morrison (w [writer]) *et al.*, *The Invisibles*, books 1–7 (New York: DC/Vertigo, 1996–2002). Henceforth abbreviated as *Invisibles*. The series was first published in monthly issues between 1994 and 2000 by DC/Vertigo. Warren Ellis (w), Darrick Robertson (p [penciller], i [inker]), *et al.*, *Transmetropolitan*, books 1–10 (New York: DC/Helix/Vertigo, 2009–2011). Ellis's series was first published in monthly issues between 1997 and 2002 by Helix and DC/Vertigo.
5 Asami Nakamura, 'Adapting George Orwell's *Nineteen Eighty-Four*', *The Luminary*, 6 (2015), n.p. [www.lancaster.ac.uk/luminary/issue6/issue6article4.htm] (accessed 06 November 2019).
6 See Daniel Simeoni, 'The Pivotal Status of the Translator's Habitus', *Target*, 10.1 (1998), pp. 1–39 and Lawrence Venuti, *The Translator's Invisibility: A History of Translation*, 2nd edn (London: Routledge, 2008).
7 Jean-Paul Gabilliet, *Of Comics and Men: A Cultural History of American Comic Books* (Jackson: University Press of Mississippi, 2010), p. 27.
8 Julia Round, '"Is This a Book?": DC Vertigo and the Redefinition of Comics in the 1990s', in Paul Williams and James Lyons (eds.), *The Rise of the American Comics Artist: Creators and Contexts* (Jackson, MS: University Press of Mississippi, 2010), pp. 14–30.
9 Will Eisner, 'Keynote Address, Will Eisner Symposium', *ImageTexT: Interdisciplinary Comics Studies* (2004), n.p. [http://imagetext.english.ufl.edu/archives/v1_1/eisner/] (accessed 06 November 2019).
10 Federico Zanettin (ed.), *Comics in Translation* (Manchester, UK and Kinderhook, NY: St. Jerome Publications and InTrans Publications, 2008), p. 11.
11 Hutcheon, *A Theory of Adaptation*, p. 7.
12 Ted Rall, '2024: A Graphic Novel' (1 May 2001), n.p. [http://rall.com/2001/05/01/2024-a-graphic-novel] (accessed 06 November 2019).
13 Ted Rall (w, p, i), *2024: A Graphic Novel* (NBM, 2001), p. 9. Henceforth abbreviated as *2024*.
14 Francis Fukuyama, 'The End of History?', *The National Interest*, 16 (1989), n.p.
15 *Ibid.*
16 In private correspondence with the author (3 July 2019), Rall stated that he is the kind of cartoonist who 'come[s] up with the words first and then figure[s] out what artwork services that dialogue or caption', which might explain the prominence of text in his work.
17 Rall, '2024: A Graphic Novel' (available at https://rall.com/2001/05/01/2024-a-graphic-novel).
18 After the explosion, when he believes her to be dead, his only thought is 'fuck! I'll be stuck filling out forms for hours!' (*2024*, p. 51).
19 Hutcheon, *A Theory of Adaptation*, p. 14.
20 Jochen Ecke, *The British Comic Book Invasion: Alan Moore, Warren Ellis, Grant Morrison, and the Evolution of the American Style* (Jefferson, NC: McFarland & Company, Inc., 2019), p. 161.
21 Alan Moore (w) and David Lloyd (p, i), *V for Vendetta* (New York: DC Comics, 1990). Henceforth abbreviated as *V for Vendetta*. Alan Moore (w) and Kevin

O'Neill (p, i), *The League of Extraordinary Gentlemen: Black Dossier* (New York: DC/Wildstorm, 2008). Henceforth abbreviated as *Black Dossier*.

22 In this article, all references are to the *V for Vendetta* collection published by DC, which is the one most likely available to readers. However, it is important to bear in mind the series's complex publication history.

23 See Maggie Gray, '"A Fistful of Dead Roses ... " – Comics as Cultural Resistance: Alan Moore and David Lloyd's *V for Vendetta*', *Journal of Graphic Novels & Comics*, 1.1 (2010), pp. 31–49, at p. 36.

24 This might be less obvious in the coloured version put together by DC than in the original black and white. In the postface to the book, Moore talks of his initial desire to set the story 'in a realistic thirties world' but had to abandon the idea when David Lloyd informed him that 'if he was called upon to draw one more 'twenty-eight model Duesenberg he'd eat his arm' (*V for Vendetta*, p. 270).

25 Michel Foucault, *Discipline and Punish: The Birth of the Prison*, trans. Alan Sheridan, 2nd edn (New York: Vintage, 1995), p. 200.

26 Gray, '"A Fistful of Dead Roses ... "', p. 36.

27 Marc Singer, *Breaking the Frames: Populism and Prestige in Comics Studies* (Austin, TX: University of Texas Press, 2018), p. 100.

28 Tijuana bibles were small pornographic pamphlets produced in the United States from the 1920s to the 1960s. Here they are attributed to Ingsoc's department of pornography (Pornosec, in the original), where Julia works in *Nineteen Eighty-Four*.

29 Jess Nevins, 'Annotations to the Black Dossier' (2018) [http://enjolrasworld.com /Jess%20Nevins/Black%20Dossier/dossier.html] (accessed 06 November 2019).

30 Gray, '"A Fistful of Dead Roses ... "', p. 40.

31 Sean Witzke, 'The Future is Inherently a Good Thing: Is the World of *Transmetropolitan* Utopian or Dystopian?', in Chad Nevett (ed.), *Shot in the Face: A Savage Journey to the Heart of Transmetroplitan* (Sequart Research and Literacy Organization, 2013), pp. 7–14, at p. 12.

32 See Isabelle Licari-Guillaume, 'Ambiguous Authorities: Vertigo and the Auteur Figure', *Authorship*, 6.2 (2017), n.p. [www.authorship.ugent.be/article/view/7700] (accessed 06 November 2019).

16

SORAYA MURRAY*

'In this game that we're playing'
Nineteen Eighty-Four *and* Video Games

At roughly the midpoint of George Orwell's dystopian fiction *Nineteen Eighty-Four* (1949), during a fleeting moment of respite from his nightmarish existence, protagonist Winston declares to his secret lover: 'In this game that we're playing, we can't win. Some kinds of failure are better than other kinds, that's all' (*NEF*, p. 142).

The game of which Winston speaks involves attempting to navigate a totalitarian system, wherein no conceivable winning scenario is possible. Full devotion to the 'Ingsoc' Party and its leader 'Big Brother' is compulsory down to the thought, to the minute expression or gesture, to minor aesthetic indulgence, and even to the very notion of a private act. The state, embodied in the figure of Big Brother, sees all. The internalization of the law is so complete that most citizens police themselves, the rest police each other, and any infraction is tantamount to sedition. Exerting one's individuality brings certain death, eventually. Winston and his lover Julia know it, but they pursue their free will in each other's fleeting company.

Traces of Orwell's critiques of totalitarian society, in both blunt and subtle forms, exist throughout video games. Major themes of dystopia, surveillance culture, technologies of control, authoritarianism, and the oppression of a large underclass exist in innumerable video game narratives and environments. Some of these are inspired by and refer directly to *Nineteen Eighty-Four*, while others more obliquely borrow its themes and concerns. Games like the *BioShock* series (2007–), *Remember Me* (2013), the *Watch Dogs* series (2014–), *We Happy Few* (2018), *Orwell* (2016–), *Inside* (2016), and *Papers, Please* (2013) are among the more innovative and thoughtful video games addressing these issues. Do these simulations encourage critical thought around the eventuality of totalitarianism, of which Orwell warned? Or are these games merely systems in which to practise a kind of entrapment, in which so-called freedom may be practised within a medium that is exceedingly ordered in its very constitution? Through the stories games tell, as well as in the very form of video games, is it even possible to truly stimulate a model of criticality? This chapter proposes that the critical influence of *Nineteen Eighty-Four* exists not only in video game narratives and the constitution of their navigable spaces but also in their wide variety of strategies, rule-based systems, rhetorical capacities, ethical problematics, and – critically – their effective deployment of failure to provoke thought in players.

Nineteen Eighty-Four

Orwell's novel details an alternative dystopian reality in which the world has been reduced to three great superpowers which engage in ceaseless war: Oceania, Eurasia, and Eastasia. The story follows Winston Smith, a subject of the government of Oceania, a totalitarian society dominated by the Party and its dictator, Big Brother. As the embodiment of the Party, Big Brother is purportedly protector and guide, but in fact functions as an all-seeing eye that dominates the culture in a draconian fashion, subjugating all under his gaze. This is emblematized in Big Brother's visage, which is exhaustively reproduced on Oceania's coins, books, stamps, banners, and packaging; his eyes seem to follow citizens everywhere. More pointedly, two-way 'telescreens' surveil behaviour and feed everyone a constant stream of Party ideology. Winston eventually learns that Big Brother is not a person but an idea embodied in an image, which is used to galvanize the authority of the Party. The notion that 'Big Brother is Watching You' – as Oceanic propaganda informs its citizens – organizes all logic around Party ideals, to the point of breaking all human bonds except those which serve the state. Social control extends to the relationships between people in terms of love, friendship, and fidelity: children spy and inform on their parents; marriage is mechanical and intended for reproduction, not love. Pleasure has been beaten out of the living, and only those closest to the leadership of the Party are offered anything more than base existence and a grey life of endless labour. It is a model of total repression, in which, as Winston puts it: 'Nothing was your own except the few cubic centimetres inside your skull' (*NEF*, p. 29).

Orwell places great emphasis on detailing how systemic rule-based control is exerted over society. The will of Big Brother is administered through Oceania's four ministries: the Ministry of Truth (addressing all avenues for information and thought), the Ministry of Peace (addressing war), the Ministry of Love (addressing law and order), and the Ministry of Plenty (addressing economic affairs). A low-level employee, Winston busies himself in the Ministry of Truth, squirrelled away in a cubicle at the Records Department, manipulating news of the present and the past so that it always aligns with the Party's agenda. Of keen importance in this narrative is the manipulation of language as a means to control thought. This is so central an idea for Orwell that he dedicates an entire appendix to the concept of 'Newspeak', which is described as 'the official language of Oceania' (*NEF*, p. 5) and to whose principles more than a dozen pages are dedicated. With Newspeak, terms like *crimethink* (any thought against the party ideology), *sexcrime* (sexual immorality), *facecrime* (non-compliant facial expressions in public), and *ownlife* (individualism and eccentricity) are engineered as a system to foreclose the very possibility of formulating a thought outside of Party orthodoxies:

> The intention was to make speech, and especially speech on any subject not ideologically neutral, as nearly as possible independent of consciousness. [...] a Party member called upon to make a political or ethical judgment should be able to spray forth the correct opinions as automatically as a machine gun spraying forth bullets. His training fitted him to do this, the language gave him an almost fool-proof instrument, and the texture of the words, with their harsh sound and a certain willful ugliness which was in accord with the spirit of Ingsoc, assisted the process still further. (*NEF*, pp. 321–22)

All so-called Oldspeak is slowly being revised into Newspeak, and Orwell captures well the intellectually binding transformation of language taking place, and how eventually any way of being that is outside of Ingsoc ideology would be 'nameless and therefore unimaginable' (*NEF*, p. 324). Orwell intricately maps the ways that thought, human connection, and particularly sexual impulses are rerouted into 'war-fever and leader-worship' (*NEF*, p. 139). Through his detailed attention to the function of language and its connection to the regulation of thought, Orwell reveals the ideological strictures and value systems that are embedded in linguistic rules, and the way those rules ultimately engage in world-making.

Video Games as Rule-Based Systems

One of Orwell's most urgent concepts addresses how language can define the terms or rules around which a whole sense of world-making comes into existence. This intersects meaningfully with a major line of thought around the implicit qualities of video games as a medium. Video games consist of rule-based systems. The combinations of rules within a system result in a simulation with which the player engages. From the study of play even prior to video games, rules have been thought of as central to games. Roger

Caillois, in his introduction to *Man, Play, and Games*, wrote in 1958 that '[a]ny game is a system of rules. [...] They cannot be violated on any account, or else the game ends right away and is destroyed by the same fact.'[1] Many have argued that video games should be primarily understood as rule-based systems, and therefore properly studied not as narratives but as games, in terms of Caillois's 'systems of rules'. For example, the pioneering game scholar Jesper Juul famously argued for an approach to games in which they are understood as rule-based, formal systems, but eventually softened his position on games to a view in which they combine rules and fictional worlds.[2] Katie Salen and Eric Zimmerman define a game as 'a system in which players engage in an artificial conflict, defined by rules, that results in a quantifiable outcome'.[3] These positions are part of a long debate about how video games should be understood and studied. But for the purposes of this chapter, what is key to remember is that, as Rolf H. Nohr puts it, '[t]ogether, rules create the impression of a hermetically sealed autonomous world. [...] Rules have a way of erasing that which lies beyond the field of play, just as it normalizes actions within the game space.'[4] Or as Pat Harrigan has more pointedly declared: 'A game design is an argument.'[5]

If this is the case, then video games propose a version of the world through their simulations, and create the conditions under which it is possible to move within them. The utopias and dystopias in games embed players in systems they can experiment with, and in which they can contemplate their relationship to the ideals that have given rise to such spaces.[6] Like Orwell's Newspeak, the rule systems within video games set the terms in which the worlding of the game occurs. For example, in a game categorized as a 'shooter' it is likely that most of the core mechanics would be bent towards twitch-reflexes, an adversarial relation to other entities, and an understanding of space orientated towards optimizing strategic positioning. Alternatively, in a game emphasizing exploration and puzzle-solving, a relationship to space might be more open and inquisitive, encourage experimentation, and de-prioritize twitch-reflexes.

Video games' world-making properties have, likewise, long been considered central to the unique qualities of the medium.[7] Janet Murray, in her ground-breaking text *Hamlet on the Holodeck* (1997), foregrounds traversable space as a key asset of digital media.[8] Lev Manovich identifies eminently navigable space as a 'key form' of new media.[9] And Espen Aarseth argues: 'The defining element in computer games is spatiality. Computer games are essentially concerned with spatial representation and negotiation, and therefore a classification of computer games can be based on how they represent – or, perhaps, *implement* – space.'[10] Henry Jenkins proposes 'an understanding of game designers less as storytellers and more as narrative architects'.[11]

In his 'Game Design as Narrative Architecture' (2006), Jenkins describes game consoles as 'machines for generating compelling spaces'.[12] These spatial stories, Jenkins argues, 'are pushed forward by the character's movement across the map', and telling these stories well becomes about 'designing the geography of imaginary worlds, so that obstacles thwart and affordances facilitate the protagonist's forward movement towards resolution'.[13] Games as rule-based systems make space for certain kinds of engagements, while limiting or entirely foreclosing upon others. Video games present persuasive worlds that suggest certain things to the player about the nature of their relations within them. As a result, video games tread into discussions of ethics and have powerful rhetorical functions.[14] As with Newspeak, games communicate not only ideas but also values and ethics.

Video games require engagement; the player is expected to make decisions which, in the best games, have consequences. This creates the conditions for simulations that, as Miguel Sicart argues, can be especially useful for stimulating ethical self-inquiry in the player.[15] Video games, he asserts, require a degree of complicity in the player, and therefore what we play and the experiences we have while playing matter. Sicart suggests that we play by mobilizing our ethics as well as our skills, and that careful design choices can encourage players to consider their actions from a moral perspective.[16] Particularly in the case of being presented with more than playing as simply a 'good' or 'evil' character, being faced with the choice between a bad option and a worse one – what he calls a 'wicked problem' – can engender ethical self-inquiry.[17] Many of the best video games that explore Orwellian themes are potent because of the friction that results from engaging with systems that ultimately deny the player's ability to distance themselves from the moral complications of their choices. This is where the notion of how we might play, even though we may inevitably fail, takes on moral significance. Part of what is subtly communicated in Winston's musing on the 'game that we're playing' is that its rules not only virtually guarantee failure but set the terms by which a player must submit to the rules in order to play at all. In the next section of this chapter, several key games that exhibit the influence of Orwell's *Nineteen Eighty-Four* will be discussed, particularly in terms of their implication of the player as complicit in ethically difficult contexts.

Nineteen Eighty-Four and Video Games

While dystopian authoritarian cultures surely proliferate as the setting for many video games, this is not necessarily the most crucial way in which the influence of Orwell's *Nineteen Eighty-Four* can be detected. As suggested above, it is more precisely in the articulation of a relation between authoritarianism, the weaponization of language, and excessive bureaucratization that the uniqueness of Orwell's vision lies. One of the most well-known and beloved examples of a dystopian world in video games is *BioShock* (2007), a first-person perspective shooter developed by 2K Boston (previously Irrational Games) and published by 2K Games. The game's creative director Ken Levine specifically mentions the literature of Ayn Rand and George Orwell as influences upon it.[18] Widely regarded as one of the best video games of all time, *BioShock* was also one of the highest selling of its period, and certainly one with continuing relevance to anyone interested in video game culture. Set in 1960, *BioShock* explores a defunct undersea utopia built in the 1940s by Andrew Ryan, a corporate billionaire. Ryan has created a utopian haven for the individualist, in keeping with the philosophical tenets of objectivism popularized by the works of Ayn Rand, particularly *The Fountainhead* (1943) and *Atlas Shrugged* (1957).[19] The main playable character, Jack, enters the defunct art deco underwater city of Rapture. In this retro-futuristic space, citizens were to pursue extreme self-realization and individualism, as a manifestation of the egoism of its leader's philosophy. Of course, it has not gone well. In the present day of the game, the utopian society is destroyed, and scantly populated by survivors of a civil war that decimated most of Rapture. Among those left behind are genetically modified and deformed 'Splicers'. Wandering this dystopia, it is up to the player to discern the truth of how Rapture fell.

One of the original interventions of *BioShock* that set it apart from games of its time was its sustained engagement with philosophical ideas, but also how players were implicated in ethically vexed actions through their in-game actions. Part of this was achieved by the upending of a sense of player autonomy, or free will. Within the narrative – and even for the player themselves – moral ambiguity, hypnotic mind control, and deception play a key role. This is smartly introduced through the narrative use of the repeated phrase 'Would you kindly', a critical hypnotic suggestion trigger revealed deep within the game. Jack (the playable character) falsely believes in his own free will and autonomy, while in fact the trigger phrase is used to drive actions and outcomes at key moments. Though the specific scenarios are very different from *Nineteen Eighty-Four*, the game recalls the novel's idolized and elusive autocratic leader, its focus on brainwashing, its bleakness, its attention to the crushing denial of free will, and its general focus on the connection between language and the parameters of what may be thought. In this respect, 'Would you kindly?' recalls the Ingsoc Newspeak catchphrases designed to suppress and corral free thinking.

In *Papers, Please* (2013), developed by Lucas Pope and published by 3909 LLC, a player takes the role of a border inspector in the fictive

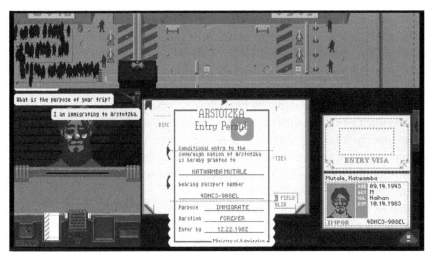

Figure 16.1 *Papers, Please* (2013), developed by Lucas Pope and published by 3909 LLC.
Screenshot by Benjamin Tran for the author

Soviet Union-esque nation of Arstotzka. The game is set in 1982 and its aesthetics reflect the rendering capacities of games during that time (Figure 16.1): flat and blocky sixteen-bit imagery, with a click-and-drag interface. After winning the labour lottery, the player character is made responsible for checking the immigration papers of potential visitors and discerning, on the basis of the limited information presented, whether to accept them. The screen displays a view of the checkpoint, and beneath it an image of the migrant attempting to pass the border, as well as the paperwork they are presenting. Some are refugees fleeing war-torn countries, others wish to enter with a work permit, some are sex workers, and others are potential enemies of Arstotzka. One never has all the information necessary to make a fully informed decision. But one must work quickly to decide, because the day's labour is timed. Processing more people brings more credits, but of course the regulations change and grow incrementally more complicated. Overlook too many discrepancies in documentation and credits are potentially lost. Credits lost have an impact on the player's ability to provide shelter, food, heat, and medicine for their family members. The actions expected in gameplay simulate mundane dehumanizing procedure, what Pope himself characterizes as 'Orwellian communist bureaucracy'.[20] Sicart in his analysis of *Papers, Please* observes: 'The dull routine of these choices, such as the daily work of a border control guard, is bound up in rules and procedures, which can further remove the participant from feeling culpable. The emotional impact of *Papers, Please* is largely a result of this design.'[21]

A player immediately feels themselves a cog in a machine that is inhumane in its procedural functioning, and in which it is increasingly hard to make good choices. The game purposefully grinds the player down over thirty-one in-game days of play through the use of repetition, protocols, and instrumental rationality.[22] The rules of the game in *Papers, Please* are carefully curated to convey how authoritarian power bears down on the lowly bureaucrat, and how enforcement of the totalitarian regime comes as a result of a thousand small, often poorly informed decisions that add up to larger consequences. This endows the game with a rhetorical force. In disallowing the possibility of playing in an ethically fulfilling way, *Papers, Please* interrupts the ability to play for 'fun', or to achieve a satisfying win state.

Unlike the independent game *Papers, Please*, the AAA mainstream title *Remember Me* (2013) creates a richly traversable world in which the player is bound to be a glitch in the system, and to work against the repressive rules of an advanced hyper-capitalist, corporatized police state.[23] It is a third-person perspective (Figure 16.2), science-fiction action adventure set in a cyberpunk future, in which the commodification of memories has generated a dystopian reality driven by a memory economy. The game was developed by the French DONTNOD Entertainment, and published by Capcom. Set in Neo-Paris in 2084, the playable character is an elite memory 'hunter' named Nilin who has the power to hack, manipulate, and delete the memories of others. The problem is that she is imprisoned, her memory has been erased, and she no

Figure 16.2 *Remember Me* (2013), developed by DONTNOD Entertainment and published by CAPCOM. Image ©CAPCOM U.S.A., INC.

longer has any clear sense of her role in this carceral nightmare. Nilin must navigate a dismal scenario in which a revolution in smart-tech has given rise to an extreme surveillance society whose primary economy consists of the encoding, commoditization, and exchange of memories. DONTNOD characterizes their possible world as one where the 'last remnants of privacy and intimacy have been swept away in what appears to be a logical progression of the explosive growth of social networks at the beginning of the 21st century'.[24] The Sensen memory technology has been developed by a megacorporation called Memorize, and its control has created corruptive effects that the player's character is driven to uncover, along with her own true identity and relationship to the corporation. Edge, her elusive ally and leader of the anti-Memorize resistance group, the 'Errorists', has nebulous aims, and Nilin is never sure whom to trust, or what is real. In retrospect, Nilin's disorientation prefigures the reality of 'alternative facts' and the political struggle to strategically mobilize competing notions of the real. However, the game was, in its own moment, on the pulse of complicated ethical questions issuing around the rise of social media networks like Facebook, Instagram, Snapchat, and Twitter, all of which emerged – seemingly unchecked – as powerful forces that shape political realities and galvanize a 'post-truth' era.

Notably the time period in which the game is set, 2084, is intended by the lead designer, Jean-Max Moris, to signal Orwell's *Nineteen Eighty-Four*:

> The book depicts a very vertical authoritarian society, the kind of society which is now pretty much non-existent in Western Europe and North America. But we believe a new insidious, horizontal form of control has emerged. Since the revolution of instant content sharing, people have been uploading more and more of their personal data onto social networks. What is being done with all that data, most people don't care to know, because the 'cool' benefits outweigh the perceived threat to individual freedom.[25]

Over the course of the game, the ethical implications of memory manipulation, the new social hierarchies that have emerged from the memory economy, and the pernicious by-products of advanced memory culture come to the fore. These culminate in a nefarious social cleansing plot against the most devastated victims of the Sensen technology, and a rude awakening as to the nature of the 'revolutionary' counsel Nilin has chosen to follow. In keeping with Sicart's ideas about ethical difficulty in games, the outcomes leave the player short of feeling like a conventional video game hero.

Anxieties about surveillance culture as exemplified in *Remember Me* are a dominant theme widely explored in mainstream video games, such as the hacker-themed *Watch Dogs* series. A third-person action-adventure video franchise developed by Ubisoft Montreal and published by Ubisoft, and originally released in 2014, the game plunges the player into what reads as a technothriller. While each game's specific narrative varies, players must use their character's hacking skills in intrigues that explore common anxieties around the powers of advanced computation and digital surveillance culture. *Watch Dogs* feels less troubled about the nefarious dimensions of the networked society. And at times the game even seems to invest in power fantasies about commanding powerful technologies, even while it purports to critique them.

Among the games that harness the more potent rhetorical capacities of the medium is *Orwell: Keeping an Eye on You* (2016), which is especially relevant for its direct homage to *Nineteen Eighty-Four*. An episodic simulation game developed by the indie German designers Osmotic Studios, and published by Fellow Traveller, *Orwell* immerses the player in an alternative present in which an authoritarian government called The Party has risen to power in 2009. Led by Prime Minister Blaine on the strength of his promise of a Safety Bill, which The Party was able to pass in 2012, The Nation has become a control society with total digital surveillance capacities and hyper-nationalist values.

In the role of an outside agent tasked with monitoring subjects as an 'Investigator' for The Nation, players attempt to create a profile for suspected individuals, poring over the details of their personal data in a covert surveillance system called Orwell (Figure 16.3). The system functions as

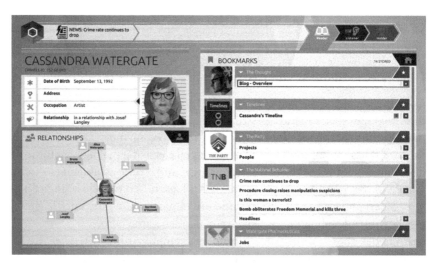

Figure 16.3 A view of the interface for *Orwell: Keeping an Eye on You* (2016), developed by Osmotic Studios and published by Fellow Traveller. Image courtesy of Osmotic Studios. Used with permission

a security programme that utilizes information retrieval from personal blogs, chats, news, and other resources, along with human-driven suspect profiling. Through frequent contact with an 'Adviser' (named Symes, after Winston's disappeared acquaintance Syme from the novel), you are trained to share the appropriate 'Datachunks' with higher-ups, to aid with anti-terrorism efforts against The Nation. The so-called Orwell Ethical Codex delegates the gathering of information to Investigators, and the execution of actions based on uploaded Datachunks to Advisers. The game's division of labour emphasizes the dimension of human discernment involved in surveillance by creating the conditions under which sending the wrong Datachunks may result in false positives with devastating results. There is a strong focus on social media and on technologically mediated conversations which can easily be surveilled, and on the prospect of doing this for the greater good. The player must decide which information is pertinent – which often involves conjecture. What becomes interesting is how quickly one slips into the goal-orientation of combing through the minutiae of strangers' lives, and ascribing meanings to those details. Playing feels only slightly dissimilar from scouring a Facebook profile, and surely the use of a similar blue, grey, and white colour scheme is no accident. The polygonized aesthetic has a distancing effect that encourages dispassionate consideration of systems that players might normally leave unexamined.

In the game, a terror attack in Freedom Plaza occurs in the capital city of Bonton, and the player is set to work scrolling through windows of information to harvest clues about potential perpetrators. Two things become immediately clear: first, there are stakes involved in what gets uploaded to the system; second, it is impossible to definitively know which details might be the most important. Opposition to the authoritarian Nation comes in the form of Thought, a supposedly peaceful group headed by Abraham Goldfels. In reference to *Orwell*, the critic Colin Campbell notes that it 'offers some stark lessons in the way we all present ourselves online, to the various congregations we expose ourselves to, from family, friends and potential lovers, to employers and the government'.[26] Indeed, the clear, innocuous-looking interface and rational tasks of data mining belie a more pernicious system, in which elements of one's data profile may become ammunition to be used against a subject of investigation. Before long, one begins to ponder the amorality of the system, and the fact that another 'Investigator' is likely mining the player's data, as well.

Likewise, *Orwell*, according to Katherine Cross,

puts the lie to the utopian ideal of 'sousveillance', the idea that ordinary people can avail ourselves of techno-snooping tools to act as a check on the powerful. Our judgment is no less fallible, no less prone to heedless destruction. Our dystopian future may not be the uniformed powerful against the masses per se, but the masses being drafted into oppressing each other using the tools of online surveillance.[27]

The oppressive dimensions of big data, as with the critique present in other games like *Remember Me* and the *Watch Dogs* series, would be extended here, but with a heavy emphasis on player complicity. In this sense, *Orwell* functions similarly to *Papers, Please* in its bureaucratic orientation and in the way it frustrates the player's ability to make fully informed decisions. Both games needle the player by making sure they never have everything necessary to really know the full consequences of their actions, while also forcing them to make decisions about the data they have before them. In its vision that combines nationalism and digital surveillance culture, *Orwell* effectively proposes a dystopian world that is a subtly different version of our own.

Inside (2016), a minimal, elegant design by the Danish company Playdead (Figure 16.4), uses form to eloquently convey a similar critique of authoritarian repression, but from the vantage point of the imperilled body, rather than the hyper-bureaucratic information society. The puzzle-platformer is a side-scrolling adventure that slowly unfurls a vast dark world of hard edges, robotic technologies, and inhumane spaces. Players are tasked with steering a small boy in a red shirt safely through a series of obstacles and

Figure 16.4 *Inside* (2016), designed and published by Playdead. Screenshot by Benjamin Tran for the author

dangers. Greyish, conformist, and slumped-over humans reminiscent of the workers in the film *Metropolis* (1927) make the playable character stand out as a dab of colour against the massive, perpetually gloomy environment. Alienating sites of total control, machines of mysterious purpose, cold experimentation facilities, and mind-control devices convey a sense of systemic domination. Moving stealthily, the boy must use his wits to solve puzzle-like challenges and keep his forward momentum. He is a spark of life, but endangered in a hostile world because of his failure to blend in. The aesthetic effect achieved by imaging a diminutive figure against a looming space suggests a fragile entity to be protected, and enhances the stakes of navigating his world carefully. In its long view of a totalitarian vision, the video game is extraordinary for the concentrated affective intensity it achieves without any dialogue, facial expressions, or didactic statements.

Similarly potent in its conveying of precarious living under hegemony is *We Happy Few*, an action-adventure survival game developed by Compulsion Games and published by Gearbox Publishing in 2018. The game's irreverent, satirical vision (Figure 16.5) presents an alternate reality in which Germany won the Second World War because the United States refused to participate in the conflict. Set in Wellington Wells, a fictive retro-future English city in 1964, the game images a society in full denial of its unpleasant past. Compulsory happiness is enforced in all aspects of society. Propaganda murals remind citizens: 'Happy is the country with no past'.

Figure 16.5 *We Happy Few* (2018), developed by Compulsion Games and published by Gearbox Publishing. Screenshot by Benjamin Tran for the author

Television personality 'Uncle Jack' spouts his ceaseless ideology on the television and radio to reinforce the will of the authoritarian regime. Citizens are kept perpetually cheerful through a freely available hallucinogen called Joy, which provides an artificial high, and staves off both the ugly truth of their complicity in a wartime horror and the true misery of their present reality. There is a crushing social pressure to wear grinning white masks which shape the face muscles into a smile, to prevent what, in Orwell's Oceania, would be a facecrime. As three separate characters who – for very separate reasons – can no longer conform (i.e. crimethink), they begin to stand out as 'Downers' who threaten the authoritarian order. By refusing to take Joy, characters experience how the rotting truth reveals itself through the technicolor city's façade. They are policed as nonconformist by their fellow citizens, resulting in mob aggression, public beatings, forced Joy treatments, and worse by the local authorities. 'Get Happy!' they all shout, while meting out their corporal punishments.

The game feels like Orwell's *Nineteen Eighty-Four* combined with dystopian films about extreme repression, such as Stanley Kubrick's *Clockwork Orange* (1971) and Terry Gilliam's *Brazil* (1985). Nods to Orwell's novel circulate in the whole scenario of a society of people that inform on each other for any infraction of nonconformity. A shadow of Winston is particularly evident in the narrative of the first playable character, Arthur Hastings. Players are introduced to him in his role as a media censor, his hands moving smoothly between a pneumatic tube dispenser and a red 'Redactor' device which he uses to edit newspaper articles to suit the ideology of Wellington Wells. Like Winston, Arthur is a cog in the machine, until he sees something that jogs a painful memory which contradicts the party line. And like Winston, Arthur cannot force the contradiction out of his mind. Arthur quips at the beginning of the game, 'Do you think the canister wonders what life's like outside the tube? Of course he'd have to break the tube to get out, but that'll break it for everybody.' The slippage of language in which Arthur ascribes a male pronoun to the pneumatic canister suggests his identification with its condition. Its claustrophobic first-person perspective and heavy emphasis on scavenging for basic necessities suggests the cost of becoming an outcast. *We Happy Few* simulates the degree to which people are willing to go to preserve their illusions, and to delude themselves with alternative facts, for the sake of evading accountability and consequences. It simultaneously gestures to the dangerous but liberating dimensions of failure which, in the case of both Winston and Arthur, consists of finally seeing things for what they are.

The Revolutionary Potential of Failing the Game

The inevitable question arises: Does Winston's inability to successfully conceal himself constitute failure? In this game that he is playing, what constitutes a win state? And should there be potentials imagined other than successfully adhering to the rule-based systems of his dystopian society? In his acts of protest, Winston plays 'incorrectly' in the sense of not adhering to the rules of the authoritarian game to which he is subject. These are small acts at first: the procurement of real paper and a proper pen, the impulse to write down an idea of his own, the will towards privacy, the fleeting desire to hold on to a fragment of truth in the face of its erasure. But this snowballs into more blatant failures to adhere to Big Brother's law: the craving for human connection, his political acts of lovemaking, his increasingly anti-authoritarian thoughts, the purchase of something he deems beautiful, and his (albeit fleeting) force of will under the duress of torture.

Playing the game is, in some sense, submitting to the terms of the game. A player can bend them a bit, or exploit imperfections or contradictions, or find back doors, but partaking seems to implicitly include adherence to its rules. However, hidden in Winston's utterances about degrees of failure is the seed of a kind of protest. Judith 'Jack' Halberstam has theorized the notion of failure as something not merely to be overcome, but as a tool for breaking with dominant heteronormative patriarchal values. Halberstam writes: 'The queer art of failure turns on the impossible, the improbable, the unlikely, and the unremarkable. It quietly loses, and in losing it imagines other goals for life, for love, for art, and for being.'[28] Bonnie Ruberg has applied this theorization specifically to player engagements with video games, asking questions like: What if we choose to play incorrectly? What if we refuse to play altogether? What if we let ourselves 'be slowly and beautifully beaten', and, in doing so, subvert preconceived ideas about adhering to the rules? What new possibilities open up then?[29] Ruberg writes:

> If we adjust Halberstam's language for games, we can read normative 'advancement' as advancement through levels (or a refusal to advance), and 'capital accumulation' as in-game points accumulated (or ignored, wasted). 'Nonreproductive lifestyles' becomes the squandering of extra lives, the abandonment of hard-fought unsaved games. The queer takes on the guise of the bad subject, the bad player who rejects the regulating logic of the game and '[stalls] the business of the dominant', the cheater who exercises her unsanctioned agency[.][30]

This theorization dislocates the conventional presupposition that failure is to be avoided or that it is inherently self-destructive, and opens up possibilities for failure as a site of agency, and a means with which to negotiate relations to powerful forces dominating one's life.

While Halberstam's and Ruberg's theorization pertains to queerness and society, its logic has further-reaching ramifications applicable to other forms of repression, such as those modelled in *Nineteen Eighty-Four*. Winston's gestures, then, push against the presumed objective that he should become the perfected subject of Oceania. In his playing of the game which he is preordained to lose, Winston bucks a system of repression by embracing failure, and in doing so he finds a way to carve out a provisional space for himself outside the normative expectations of his society. This is not to diminish the profound cost extracted from him, in body and mind. But it is important to remember that for a brief time, despite the overbearing and pervasive control culture in which he exists, Winston attains his own personhood.

Salen and Zimmerman describe a game as 'a space of possibility' in which players can explore.[31] This functions similarly to speculative fiction, in which possible futures may be safely hypothesized and played out. Or, in some cases, present realities can be re-contextualized into the realm of fantasy or speculative fictions, in order to create literary models to be considered from a distance. What unifies the games above, which reflect the influence of Orwell's *Nineteen Eighty-Four*, is the mobilization of moral complication and even failure as a tool to stimulate ethical self-inquiry in the player. *BioShock*, *We Happy Few*, *Orwell*, *Remember Me*, *Inside*, and *Papers, Please* all complicate player expectations in some way, by questioning what it means to agree to play by the rules. The most stinging of these games do more than simply appropriate narrative elements or settings from Orwell's vision; they persuade by troubling player expectations of success or heroism, and by opening up a conversation about failure to 'play the game' as a site of agency within a repressive system.

By limiting options, or by withholding information, these games frustrate the player's ability to fully succeed or come to a morally comfortable resolution. Players engage with systems that ultimately won't exactly let them off the hook, which gives rise to a productive discontent. This discontent opens up the possibility of thinking beyond the rules, or of engaging in a critique of them as constituting a system that doesn't satisfy. In this regard, the terms of these rule-based systems point to their own limits, stimulating players to imagine other possible alternatives. To be sure, in these systems with which we play, some kinds of failure are better than others.

Notes

* The author wishes to thank Benjamin Tran for his assistance in game image capture, as well as Derek Conrad Murray, Nathan Waddell, and the external readers for their feedback during the development of this chapter.

1 Roger Caillois as translated in Bernard Perron, 'Conventions', in Mark J. P. Wolf and Bernard Perron (eds.), *The Routledge Companion to Video Game Studies* (New York, NY: Routledge, 2014), pp. 74–82, at p. 74. See also Roger Caillois, *Man, Play, and Games*, reprint edn (Urbana: University of Illinois Press, 2001). Originally published in French in 1958.

2 Jesper Juul, *Half-Real: Video Games between Real Rules and Fictional Worlds* (Cambridge, MA: MIT Press, 2005).

3 Katie Salen and Eric Zimmerman, *Rules of Play: Game Design Fundamentals* (Cambridge, MA: MIT Press, 2003), p. 80.

4 Rolf F. Nohr, 'Tetris: Rules', in Matthew Thomas Payne and Nina Huntemann (eds.), *How to Play Video Games* (New York: New York University Press, 2019), pp. 21–9, at p. 25.

5 Patrick Harrigan, 'Game History as Public Debate', *ROMchip: A Journal of Game Histories*, 1.1 (1 July 2019) [http://romchip.org/index.php/romchip-journal/article/view/75] (accessed 7 November 2019).

6 For discussion of this, see Marcus Schulzke, 'The Critical Power of Virtual Dystopias', *Games and Culture*, 9.5 (2014), pp. 315–34.

7 Mark J. P. Wolf, *Building Imaginary Worlds: The Theory and History of Subcreation* (New York: Routledge, 2012).

8 Janet Horowitz Murray, *Hamlet on the Holodeck: The Future of Narrative in Cyberspace* (New York: Simon and Schuster, 1997). See especially pp. 79–83.

9 Lev Manovich, *The Language of New Media*, reprint edn (Cambridge, MA: The MIT Press, 2002), p. 252.

10 Espen Aarseth, 'Allegories of Space: The Question of Spatiality in Computer Games', in *Cybertext Yearbook 2000* (Jyvaskyla, Finland: Research Centre for Contemporary Culture, 2001), pp. 152–71, at p. 154.

11 Henry Jenkins, 'Game Design as Narrative Architecture', in Noah Wardrip-Fruin and Pat Harrigan (eds.), *First Person: New Media as Story, Performance, and Game* (Cambridge, MA: The MIT Press, 2006), pp. 118–30, at p. 121. See also Henry Jenkins, '"Complete Freedom of Movement": Video Games as Gendered Playspace', in Justine Cassell and Henry Jenkins (eds.), *From Barbie to 'Mortal Kombat': Gender and Computer Games* (Cambridge, MA: MIT Press, 2000), pp. 330–63, and Henry Jenkins and Kurt Squire, 'The Art of Contested Spaces', in Lucien King (ed.), *Game on: The History and Culture of Video Games* (London: Laurence King Publishing, 2002), pp. 65–75.

12 Jenkins, 'Game Design as Narrative Architecture', p. 122. See also Jenkins, '"Complete Freedom of Movement"'.

13 Jenkins, 'Game Design as Narrative Architecture', pp. 124–5.

14 Ian Bogost, *Persuasive Games: The Expressive Power of Videogames* (Cambridge, MA: The MIT Press, 2010).

15 See Miguel Sicart, *The Ethics of Computer Games* (Cambridge, MA; London: MIT Press, 2011) and *Beyond Choices: The Design of Ethical Gameplay* (Cambridge,

MA: MIT Press, 2013). See also Mary Flanagan and Helen Nissenbaum, *Values at Play in Digital Games* (Cambridge, MA: The MIT Press, 2014).

16 Sicart, *Beyond Choices*, p. 29.

17 *Ibid.*, pp. 111–26.

18 Douglass C. Perry, 'The Influence of Literature and Myth in Videogames', *IGN*, blog (18 May 2006) [www.ign.com/articles/2006/05/18/the-influence-of-literature-and-myth-in-videogames?page=1] (accessed 7 November 2019).

19 Elizabeth Nyman and Ryan Lee Teten, 'Lost and Found and Lost Again: Island Utopias and Dystopias in the *BioShock* Series', *Games and Culture*, 13.4 (2018), pp. 370–84, at p. 376.

20 Andrew Webster, 'Immigration as a Game: "Papers, Please" Makes You the Border Guard', *The Verge* (14 May 2013) [www.theverge.com/2013/5/14/4329676/papers-please-a-game-about-an-immigration-inspector] (accessed 7 November 2019).

21 Miguel Sicart, '*Papers, Please*: Ethics', in Payne and Huntemann (eds.), *How to Play Video Games*, pp. 149–56, at pp. 151–2.

22 For an excellent discussion of video games and instrumental rationality, see Paolo Pedercini, 'Videogames and the Spirit of Capitalism', blog, *Molleindustria* (14 February 2014) [www.molleindustria.org/blog/videogames-and-the-spirit-of-capitalism/] (accessed 7 November 2019).

23 The term 'AAA' (also 'triple-A') refers to mainstream, large-budget video games.

24 DONTNOD, 'Remember Me DONTNOD Entertainment – Video Game – Jeu Vidéo', official game site, Dontnod.Com (blog), 2011 [www.dont-nod.com/category/projects/rememberme-en/] (accessed 7 November 2019).

25 Kirill Ulezko, 'Jean-Max Moris: "In *Remember Me* We Invite the Player to Join Nilin on Her Voyage of Self-Discovery"', *Gamestar* (2013) [http://gamestar.ru/english/remember_me_interview_eng.html] (accessed 7 November 2019).

26 Colin Campbell, 'A Game about Freedom of Speech', *Polygon* (22 August 2016) [www.polygon.com/features/2016/8/22/12543862/orwell-game-political-games] (accessed 7 November 2019).

27 Katherine Cross, 'Believing Is Seeing: *Orwell* and Surveillance Sims', *Gamasutra* (15 September 2016) [www.gamasutra.com/view/news/281291/Believing_is_seeing_Orwell_and_surveillance_sims.php] (accessed 8 November 2019).

28 Judith Halberstam, *The Queer Art of Failure* (Durham, NC: Duke University Press, 2011), p. 88.

29 Bonnie Ruberg, 'Playing to Lose: The Queer Art of Failing at Video Games', in Jennifer Malkowski and TreaAndrea M. Russworm (eds.), *Gaming Representation: Race, Gender, and Sexuality in Video Games* (Bloomington, IN: Indiana University Press, 2017), pp. 197–211, at p. 204.

30 *Ibid.*, p. 203.

31 Salen and Zimmerman, *Rules of Play*, p. xi.

17

ADAM ROBERTS

Coda
The Imaginaries of *Nineteen Eighty-Four*

Nineteen Eighty-Four (1949) has become part of our collective mental furniture. Its phrases structure our journalism. Its ideas inform our critiques of the present and the politics it shapes. Its future has become our past, yet its account of that future determines how we talk about the present as it continually threatens to transform into something menacing, unpredictable, and strange. That transformation, however, maps something interesting, something we might almost call perverse, about the way these imaginaries of the novel figure in contemporary culture. Dystopian vision has become a weird postmodern utopian energy, although one that looks, to many observers, like dystopia in a suntan and mirror-shades.

I'll start with two specific examples, both from latter-day TV culture. On the one hand there is the long-running BBC gameshow *Room 101*, which began on BBC radio in 1992 and was successful enough to merit transfer to BBC TV in 1994, where it ran until 2018 (versions of the show have also been broadcast on Australian, Dutch, and Israeli TV). In this show a celebrity host – usually a comedian – invites a group of celebrity guests to talk, in a whimsical, comical manner, about things they find irksome: objects, organizations, habits people have, anything that irritates or annoys them. At the end of each round the host decides who has made the best case, and then 'banishes' their pet-hate into the show's 'Room 101', thereby, according to the conceit of the show, consigning it to oblivion forever. The relationship between this 'Room 101' and Orwell's original torture facility is peculiar. Orwell's room contains that which an individual *fears* most greatly, not that which s/he most strongly dislikes – in fact, the show might more accurately have appropriated a different Orwellian phrase and called itself 'Memory Hole'. But to say so is, in one sense, to miss the point. A better way of reading the success of *Room 101* is to understand that it is the logic of contemporary popular culture to 'read' the drab existential uniformity of ordinary

citizenship as 'celebrity comedians', and more pungently still to 'read' debili-
tating somatic terror as *dislike*.

My second example has had considerably more cultural impact: the *Big
Brother* gameshow franchise. Conceived originally by Dutch TV producer
John de Mol Jr., and first broadcast in the Netherlands in 1999, this show has
been and continues to be syndicated internationally across more than fifty
countries, proving a major ratings hit in many of them. The format involves
a specially constructed house, fitted with a great many surveillance cameras
and microphones. A group of ordinary people (or, in later 'celebrity' iterations of the show, of famous people) live in the house for several months,
completely isolated from the outside world. They interact in the various ways
people interact – more or less banally, in the main – and from time to time are
given tasks to accomplish, gaining nicer food and drink if they win, and
having to make do with less varied fare and no alcohol if they fail. Mostly
contestants sit around chatting, bickering, pairing off romantically, or split-
ting up, with every interaction recorded and edited together into a nightly
highlight TV bulletin. Each week the general public are invited to vote for
their favourite contestant, and the contestant with the fewest votes is
expelled from the house, a process which continues weekly until only one
contestant is left. He or she is then awarded their cash prize and, more
importantly, their Warholian fifteen minutes of fame. Worldwide there
have been hundreds upon hundreds of series of this show, and its cultural
penetration is such that for many people the phrase 'big brother' now evokes
the TV franchise rather than the novel.

With *Big Brother* the intuitive inversion of Orwell's original vision is even
more revealing than is the case in *Room 101*. It provides, indeed, a glimpse
into the new social unconscious of an entire society. In *Nineteen Eighty-
Four*, 'telescreens' in every house are intrusive tools of an autocratic and
oppressive state apparatus; Winston Smith and Julia must find a place they
believe to be unsurveilled – the room above Charrington's shop – in order to
be able to conduct their affair. For Orwell, love and sex are properly private
interactions, mediations between specific individuals, and his understanding
of the logic of tyranny is of an ideological commitment precisely to the
annihilation of individuality and privacy. But in the TV format, people
flock eagerly to sacrifice their privacy: at the height of the show's success in
the United Kingdom, 2000–2010, tens of thousands of people applied to be
one of the small group that went into the 'Big Brother house'. Remote from
Winston and Julia's private tristes, the sexual shenanigans of the contestants,
will-they-won't-they dramatic tensions up to and including coitus, constitute
a large part of the show's appeal. This speaks not only to the lubricious

interests of the show's audience but also to assumptions about how we increasingly conceptualize our own love and sex *as* public performances.

Big Brother represents an example of what Jane Arthurs calls 'programming for the citizen consumer'. Arthurs points out that, by charging people for their phone-in voting as well as selling advertising slots, UK broadcaster Channel 4 significantly increased its revenue, thereby 'offering among other things a solution to the financing of multi-channel television'. At the height of the show's success, '*Big Brother* and its spin-off *Celebrity Big Brother*' delivered the channel's 'highest ratings for several months each year, helped by the tabloid and celebrity magazines that circulate the scandalous events precipitated by the 24-hour surveillance on which this genre depends'. Scandalous, there, should probably be in scare-quotes: the show depends upon providing for its viewers a safe performance space in which mock-scandal can titillate viewers, the externalization of gossip and lubricious interest in contestants' sex-lives. But Arthurs is quite correct when she identifies the show as predicated upon the surveillance of a closed community as a discursive space in which *collective* cultural and social questions are aired, via TV, print, and social media. She notes:

> *Celebrity Big Brother* (2007) became the centre of an international media and political furore when one participant, Bollywood star Shilpa Shetty, was the subject of alleged 'racist bullying' [by fellow contestant Jade Goody, and others]. It provoked calls for Channel 4's licence to be revoked for inciting racial hatred, while her eventual win of the [show] was used by the Government as evidence of the nation's credibility as a tolerant multicultural society.[1]

To a degree not true of other hit TV shows of its era, *Big Brother* reverted its contextual cultural idiom back upon its audience, both creating and reflecting a version of modern society in which *being watched* was constitutive of social identity, in which the policing – the shaming of Goody – and the personal validation were externalized performances. *Room 101* implies that the worst thing in the world is being forgotten, being ignored; *Big Brother* manifests that we yearn to be surveilled, because the alternative is to be ignored, which is a condition of modernity the very thought of which none can bear.

Google ngram suggests something interesting about the cultural penetration of the term 'Orwellian' (Figure 17.1). The rise in usage from 1950 through to 1970 manifestly tracks a steady increase in the novel's reputation and influence, and we can speculate that the second upslope, from 1980 to approximately 1987–88, reflects the calendrical uptick provoked by the advent of the actual year 1984 (and the release of the film adaptation directed by Michael Radford), although it may also mark a resurgence in concerns

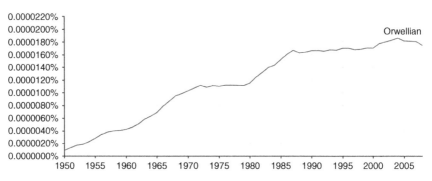

Figure 17.1 Google ngram for 'Orwellian'

about new technologies of surveillance and the political authoritarianism of the Reagan-Thatcher years. That said, it is odd that 'Orwellian' plateaus in usage through the 1970s and again through the 1990s and into the 2000s, at just the time when new technologies of surveillance were rolled out on a hitherto unprecedented scale.

More recent debates about 'fake news', post-truth politics, and surveillance often invoke Orwell's novel, although generally they do little more than draw straight parallels between Airstrip One and twenty-first-century political life. After Donald Trump's election sales of *Nineteen Eighty-Four* spiked. In the week Trump's spokesperson Kellyanne Conway spoke of the administration's 'alternate facts', Jean Seaton took to *The Guardian* newspaper to assert that 'the post-truth era certainly shares aspects of the dystopian world of Orwell's *Nineteen Eighty-Four*', and D. J. Taylor agreed: 'it's useless to pretend that this isn't all sharply reminiscent of the world of *Nineteen Eighty-Four*'.[2]

Such claims look, on their face, difficult to defend. Roger Paden makes the common-sense point that 'we tend to misuse the term "Orwellian" when we apply it to the various new techniques of observation, computerized record keeping, and behavioral control. Orwell's society actually uses these techniques less than ours. Of course, there is the telescreen, but this device seems to be used more for its intimidating effect than for "surveillance," in Foucault's sense.' He goes on:

> There seems to be little in the way of data gathering or record keeping. There is no mention of any universal testing, nor of physical examinations, nor of closely controlled administration. There is little surveillance. Computer data banks are not Orwellian. They are instruments of normalizing discipline. They are part of our society, not Orwell's.[3]

Paden's point is that 'in *Nineteen Eighty-Four* Orwell envisions a world in which torture and disappearances are used as the major methods of discipline'.[4] It is, of course, true that both these practices are widespread in many jurisdictions around the world; but it is also true that they are not the primary means by which the Western democracies maintain their power. Yet it is those latter strategies – surveillance, comprehensive bureaucracy, and behavioural control through mass media – that are the ones most likely to be described as 'Orwellian' in contemporary cultural discourse and discussion. The *Guerra Sucia* or 'Dirty War' conducted by the military dictatorship of Argentina against its own citizens between 1976 and 1983 was, in this strict sense, specifically Orwellian, relying as it did so heavily on torture and disappearances – although it is never described in these terms. The political logic of contemporary Europe and North America, various aspects of which *are* often described as Orwellian, is not. Paden's mention of Foucault, as a thinker whose ideas actually describe (more or less) the circumstances more commonly pegged as Orwellian, is *apropos*.

I think two circumstances explain the specific ways in which Orwell's nomenclature has come to be associated with such, one might think, un-Orwellian ideas as theories of simulation, culturalization, and the hyperreal. One has to do with the chronological coincidence that theorizing surveillance came into widespread vogue in the academy during the 1980s, at the same time of the second upslope of the ngram graph above. The broader interest tracks increasing penetration by, and sophistication of, actual technologies of surveillance that happened to occur historically round about the date Orwell had, howsoever arbitrarily, chosen as the title of his novel. The second is that Orwell committed himself to a plain style, and worked with the communicative logic of a journalist, where recent French avant-garde theorists and philosophers didn't and haven't.

Armand Mattelart's *La globalisation de la surveillance* (2007) traces 'surveillance' as a term back to Bentham's 1791 definition: 'a new mode of obtaining power of mind over mind, in a quantity hitherto without example', before leapfrogging straight past Orwell to the 1970s – 'the genesis of the surveillance society was brought to light by Michel Foucault in 1975 in his book *Surveiller et punir*', arguing that 'from the panoptic vision centred on surveillance as taming the body Foucault shifts to another paradigm, "bio-politics" and its project for a "security society"', a project which 'coincided with that of liberalism'.[5] The invocation of Foucault is a staple intellectual move for many interested in discussing the spread of panopticism. It is striking that Foucault himself never discussed Orwell, or Orwell's most famous novel. For all their differences of emphasis, there are clear intellectual congruences between the Frenchman and the Englishman, after all.

269

It might be that 'Orwellian' has a currency as a shorthand term for Power's surveillance and the eradication of the individual that 'Foucauldian' lacks, because the novelistic specificity of *Nineteen Eighty-Four* renders Orwell's versions of these ideas more graspable and memorable. But it's just as likely that Orwell figures as more representative of the 'Anglo' side of that notorious split in post-war philosophy that separates 'thought' between an Anglo-Saxon pragmatic, positivist camp and a 'Continental' camp, with the latter making more hyperbolic and freewheeling postmodernistic claims. When Jean Baudrillard claims that objective reality has been superseded by a logic of pure simulation, with signs no longer referring 'to a territory, a referential being or substance' but standing as 'a generation by models of a real without origin or reality: a hyperreal', he is accused by some of exaggerating his analysis to the point where it becomes hysterical and meaningless – at the height of Baudrillard's influence, Richard Poirier deprecated the 'always hyperbolic and apocalyptic' tone in which he analysed the undeniable contemporary reality of 'the electronic proliferation of signs'.[6] Maybe Orwell occupies our imaginary on these matters because of his famous advocacy for, and practice of, plain style – his repudiation of stylistic excess or fine writing. The Anglo-American side often manifests a suspicion of Continental exuberance in the articulation of important matters, although this position is itself tangled up with more-or-less malign questions of class and history – Craig Raine is surely right that Orwell's own adoption of plain writing 'hardened into an intellectual mannerism of patrician plain-speaking'.[7] But the continuing presence of Orwell, and the waning of the reputation of thinkers like Baudrillard and Foucault, suggests that Orwell's *simplesse*, faux or otherwise, the very plainness of his neologisms ('thought-crime', 'memory hole', and so on), fits better the globalized Americana of our current social-mediaverse than those more baroque Continental intricacies.

With Baudrillard this Foucauldian collective panopticism is focused not on some objective social 'facts' but rather on its own panopticism, a circumstance of systemic socio-cultural narcissism that is also (as the phrase goes) 'meta' – i.e. self-reflexive. For Baudrillard the logic of society is that of a Disney parade of pure simulacra, untethered from reality. This, again, might seem a long way from Orwell's vision. After all, the issue in *Nineteen Eighty-Four* is not that meaning floats free from signification, or that the world of Airstrip One has been 'de-realized' as per Baudrillard's *Simulacra and Simulation* (1981). On the contrary Orwell's world is only too painfully *realized*, a boot stamping on a human face forever, the physical and psychological degradations of Airstrip One life all carefully itemized. It is not that anything can mean anything in Orwell's fictional world, not that meaning has uncoupled signifiers from signified. It is, rather, that all signifiers are reduced to one signifier – the Party – and all signifieds are abolished. Nothing is real except the Party; nobody exists except Big Brother. During his long interrogation by O'Brien, Winston, not yet awoken to this reality, struggles to understand:

'Does Big Brother exist?'
'Of course he exists. The Party exists. Big Brother is the embodiment of the Party.'
'Does he exist in the same way as I exist?'
'You do not exist', said O'Brien.   (*NEF*, pp. 271–2)

What remains is suffering, the indelible mark of the party's power: not a 'thing', not 'significant' in any of the semiological or common-sense meanings of that word, but unignorable and the most potent leverage-point for power. There is no need in Orwell's novel for the elaborate technologies of twenty-first-century surveillance because there is only one thing to see in Airstrip One. The true logic of surveillance in the novel is not merely that the citizenry are observed, but rather that they *themselves can see* the one thing that guarantees their degradation. The TV show *Room 101* is like this only insofar as terror annihilates memory as it does all rational thought. Winston is taken to Room 101 in order *that he observe*. In a sense, Room 101 is the central space in the Benthamite panopticon of this novel. It's just that only one thing is visible from this surveillance space: that which terrifies you. The elaborate cage-mask device that is nearly fitted to Winston's face is constructed such that opening a gate in the copula allows the rat inside the cage to access the face inside the mask. But it is, much more importantly, designed so that the person wearing the mask *must observe the rat*. It is not having his face attacked that breaks Winston; it is his forced surveillance of the externalization of the only thing that now exists in the universe under Party rule: terror. In that respect, the ubiquity of TV culture, of which *Room 101* is an example, is profoundly Orwellian: not that TV is watching *us*, but that we are watching *it*.

The truly Orwellian perspective on the phenomena Baudrillard discusses would talk not of hyperreality so much as of monoreality. By this I mean a flattening of affective possibility and a narrowing of all social interaction and all culture into a world at once collective – just as TV, cinema, online culture, and social media barely mask their monocrop singularity with the simulation of variety – and oligarchical, with power in the hands of a very small group. Not only do we refer blithely to 'the 1%', we constantly replicate hierarchies of worth in our online worlds, by which that notoriously empty social category 'celebrity' becomes the ground of social value. We are, in other words, exactly where 'Emmanuel Goldstein' predicted we would be: both obsessed with pecking orders that concentrate power oligarchically ('celebrity', social media 'likes', and upvotes) and all defined by the same commodified global technologies of social media – it's the theory and practice of oligarchical collectivism brought to life. By some metrics, the world of 2019 has never been more democratic.[8] Social media like Twitter have enabled unprecedented intercommunication and expression. But nonetheless, the more hopeful prophecies that attended the invention of the World Wide Web in the 1990s have not been borne out. Online culture is primarily characterized by anxiety, its addictive nature, and a toxic culture of consequence-free criticism and bullying, flame wars, aggression, public shaming ('call-out culture'), mendacity, and propaganda. Even its most enthusiastic users (and I am one such) refer to Twitter as 'this hellsite'. Perhaps the wisest advice here would take Sophoclean form: the best thing is never to have been on Twitter at all, second best is to leave it soon. And yet it continues to grow in popularity.

We are confronting, in other words, a situation more profoundly Orwellian than is usually indicated by the use of that word. It is not that we are constantly being surveilled (although manifestly we are) so much as it is that *we yearn for constant surveillance*. It is not that we endure this state of affairs despite the suffering it causes us; it is that the suffering it causes us is the metric by which we measure its fundamental validity. Goldstein's book is famously dismissive of the dangers democracy poses to tyranny. 'What opinions the masses hold, or do not hold, is looked on as a matter of indifference. They can be granted intellectual liberty because they have no intellect' (*NEF*, p. 219). It's hard to think of a more on-point analysis of the online socio-political world post-Trump, post-Brexit. Indeed, Trump's rise to power is illustrative. We all know that when he says 'fake news!' he doesn't mean news that is erroneous or mendacious; he means news that puts him in a bad light, or that doesn't fit whichever narrative he is pleased to advance in that moment. Nonetheless, the fact that we all – opponents and supporters alike – know this *doesn't stop his strategy from working*. 'Fake news' is Trump's memory hole because his many supporters so urgently want to avoid the cognitive dissonance of confronting inconvenient facts that they make it real. The Republican Party (GOP) used to oppose huge national budget deficit so fiercely they were ready to shut down national government over the issue; now the GOP runs up the deficit to unprecedented levels, and there seems to be no political purchase whatsoever in anybody pointing out the inconsistency – it's the modern political version of We Have Always Been At War With Eastasia.

I don't mean to become myself, hyperbolic. The standard of living of twenty-first-century Westerners, broadly speaking, is vastly higher than the standard of living of the inhabitants of Orwell's Airstrip One. O'Brien takes it as axiomatic that suffering must be physical – must involve material deprivation – if it is going to work. But the practicalities of twenty-first-century living suggests a more nuanced iteration of his core belief: namely, that material comfort provides a more effective ground for psychological suffering than material discomfort. An individual suffering from cold or hunger will focus on the need to get warm or find food. Their distress is real, but one-dimensional. A second individual, this one clothed, sheltered, and fed, has a much greater range of possible movement where *mental* distress is concerned.

What, then, are social media? What is the internet? A global arena in which billions voluntarily expose themselves to surveillance by strangers, including very powerful governmental and commercial organizations – a global panopticon in which each user both observes and is observed. There is no question that these new technologies are being used for social control on a massive scale – and *control* could hardly be more central to Orwell's dystopian vision. Josh Lauer traces the way the business of assessing individuals' credit-worthiness has metastasized into a project for controlling the population as a whole, detailing 'the rise of consumer credit surveillance' and 'its ongoing effort to control the behaviour of American citizens and to quantify their value in a growing array of contexts'; to make citizens '"good" – morally responsible, obedient, predictable and profitable'.[9] Rachel O'Dwyer gives some concrete examples of what living in the new Surveillocene now entails:

> The maths behind the assessment of our worth is becoming harder to untangle and dispute at the very time it is playing an increasing part in shaping our future. Facebook is experimenting with a 'trustworthiness score' for its more than two billion users. And the Chinese government is developing a 'social credit' system that will assign a score to each of its 1.4 billion citizens based on an aggregation of economic and social factors. While it remains unclear what kinds of 'social' behaviour will be rewarded or penalised (one journalist wondered whether women would be penalised for remaining single or not having children), the government has made it clear that poor scores will affect people's access to public transport, employment and basic social services. The pilots are up and running, and penalties are already being applied. Figures released recently by the National Public Credit Information Centre show that by the end of 2018, the courts had banned 17.5 million 'discredited' citizens from buying plane tickets, and a further 5.5 million from travelling by train.[10]

It is an alarming prospect, which explains why so many contemporary commentators adopt a grave tone when writing about it. That seriousness is also part of the twenty-first-century imaginary of the 'Orwellian', I suppose. The denuded material existence of Orwell's Airstrip Oners stands as objective correlative for the pessimism of the novel's political vision. Orwell himself, living a materially attenuated life down and out in London and Paris, writing *Nineteen Eighty-Four* in the extraordinarily remote and spartan environment of his hut on north Jura, whilst expiring painfully of tuberculosis, a Keatsian or Kafkaesque physiological process of literal attenuation: it all contributes to a semiology of Orwell as embodying a kind of austerity. Of course, to read accounts of Orwell's actual life is to realize how far he was, in person, from being anything like the sort of socialist monk he is sometimes taken as being. More to the point, it misrepresents the novel to take it as anything as po-faced as that.

Anthony Burgess's sequel to *Nineteen Eighty-Four, 1985* (1978), opens with a lengthy introduction in which he makes two broad claims: one, that *Nineteen Eighty-Four* is a comic novel, although few people recognize it as such; and, two, that the world of the novel, with its decaying social fabric, shortages, and rationing, the smell of boiled cabbage in corridors and so on, is very precisely the world of Britain immediately after 1945 (Burgess includes a quantity of personal reminiscence to bolster this latter point). Orwell's specificity cuts two ways. One reverts back onto the more absurd elements of British life: Burgess talks about the Butlin's Holiday Camp quality of the social regimentation in the novel; the BBC-ish flavour of the Ministry of Truth, and so on. Phenomena like holiday camps, he insists astutely, prove 'that the British proletariat [is] not really averse to discipline. The working man opposed to army life not civilian freedom so much as the infusion of geniality into regimentation' (Burgess, *1985*, p. 14). Geniality seems a strange quality to discern in *Nineteen Eighty-Four*; yet Burgess is surely putting his finger on something important about the novel's imaginaries here – for it is precisely geniality that defines *Room 101* and *Big Brother* as TV phenomena; and it is a regimented kind of jollity, often brittle and snarky, that characterizes the social media to which we have surrendered our collective being.

One aspect of Orwell's novel has always bothered me: the great care and attention the senior party official O'Brien lavishes upon the torture-brainwashing of Winston Smith. It certainly works, dramatically; and it is elements from this portion of the book (the rat, Room 101, O'Brien's 'if you want a picture of the future, imagine a boot stamping on a human face – forever') that are its most famous and widely known moments. Nonetheless, it's surely, shall we say, *unlikely* that a senior officer in the Thought Police would have the time or leisure to devote to one insignificant figure. Were Winston some notorious or important celebrity, the turning of whom could be put to propaganda usage, it might make sense to invest all this time and personal attention in him. But Winston is an Outer-Party-member nobody, a mere cog in the machine, and any ruthless totalitarian power worth its salt would either send him to a camp to be re-educated by rote with thousands of others or more likely would simply shoot him. The latter seems to me the more plausible eventuality.

Of course I'm being obtuse in noting this. The book is a fable, and Winston's passage through the hands of O'Brien stands in for a larger process by which people are broken and re-made (we could compare Koestler's *Darkness at Noon* (1940), a direct influence upon Orwell, in which the two torturers seem to have endless time to work on the lone figure of Rubashov). We could also speculate that O'Brien is enjoying himself: his big speech inhabits a distinctly sexualized BDSM idiom of delight in staged humiliation even as he boasts: 'We shall abolish the orgasm' (*NEF*, p. 280). Social realism is not the idiom here, but psychological realism absolutely is. Our craving for surveillance is the deeply Orwellian truth of the novel's climax: we *want* O'Brien to give us his undivided attention, even though that means torture and tyranny. Patrick Reilly notes:

> Winston begins as our spokesman, upholding the same pieties that we revere. When he rejects these pieties, his recantation poses a problem. We are not to join him in craven capitulation to Big Brother, but neither, at the risk of being Pharisees, can we dismiss him as a weakling who has fallen miserably below our own high standard. To imply that Big Brother's good fortune was not to have us for opponents smacks of presumption. The book asks us to identify with Winston and say honestly how we would fare in his place. Orwell's mortifying intention within the text is to extort the humiliating confession that we would do no better.[11]

I think we can take this further. That the truly mortifying figuration in this text is the one that the imaginaries of its afterlife have brought to the surface: not just that we would do no better in this situation than Winston Smith, but that our unconscious desire is to *be* in his place.

If the imaginaries of *Nineteen Eighty-Four* tend towards oppression, they are also, pretty much without exception, iterations of a particular kind of digital-culture *jouissance*. The novel is playful, and the ideas it has coined into general consciousness have been comprehensively played with. Nor is play a marginal consideration. On the contrary: if these imaginaries are parlaying grimness and political pessimism, they are doing so ludically. Contemporary culture has found a dark but genuine *jouissance* in inhabiting Orwell's vision.

That inhabitation can be literal. Take, for example, *Orwell: Keeping an Eye on You* (already discussed by Soraya Murray in Chapter 16, above): a popular video game developed by Osmotic Studios in which the player assumes the role of a state operative and monitors surveillance sources to find national security threats. *Orwell: Keeping an Eye on You* was released in five instalments between October–November 2016, each episode titled with a phrase from the novel ('The Clocks Were Striking Thirteen', 'A Place Where There Is No Darkness', 'Unperson', 'Memory Hole', and 'Under the Spreading Chestnut Tree'). The player surveils a 3D video representation of a contemporary country called Nation, spying on the various characters' personal data and day-to-day activities. 'Inspired by the rise of fake news, the social media echo chamber and the death of "truth",' say the game developers, rather ominously clapping that last word in scare-quotes, '*Orwell* places the player in the shoes of a government official in a top-secret department of the Orwell program':

> A political crisis has arisen across borders, threatening to plunge The Nation and Parges into violent civil unrest. Given the power to both uncover and fabricate 'the truth', the player must decide for themselves how far they will go in the service of their country and whether the truth is sacred or ignorance is strength.[12]

The game was one of 2016's surprise hits; a sequel game, *Orwell: Ignorance is Strength*, was released in 2018, and more are planned. Nor should it surprise us that the imaginary of *Nineteen Eighty-Four* should migrate into this online medium of popular entertainment. This game proved popular for the same reason video games in general are popular: people enjoy playing it. The imaginaries of *Nineteen Eighty-Four* have proved much more ludic than the novel's dourly ideological-satiric critical reputation has prepared us for. People watched *Room 101* because it made them laugh. People watched *Big Brother* to see themselves reflected back, all inane chatter, flirtation, sex, and play. This is a show that explicitly, in its very title, interpellates the viewer – you, me – into the position of the panoptic tyrant, giving us and only us the power (provided we are prepared to pay premium-rate phone-line charges) to unperson or spare the people we are watching. People watch *Big Brother* because they love it.

In his 'Lear, Tolstoy and the Fool' essay (1947), Orwell argues that Shakespeare's *King Lear* 'contains a great deal of veiled social criticism [...] but it is all uttered either by the Fool, by Edgar when he is pretending to be mad, or by Lear during his bouts of madness. In his sane moments Lear hardly ever makes an intelligent remark' (CW, 19, p. 64). The madness in Lear is not a tragic collapse of meaning but a necessary distillation of meaning in a mad-already world, a sort of alignment of consciousness with insane reality. *Mutatis mutandis*, we might argue that the tyrannical dystopia of *Nineteen Eighty-Four* – at least as it has been received into subsequent popular culture –

is not a critique so much as it is a focusing of popular desire *for* absolute surveillance, for the surrender of individuality to the hive-mind, for the opportunity to escape individual mortality in the faux-Absolute of the celebrity-oligarchy of the online collective. We love it, and we are not so naïve as to believe love is an innocent matter of hearts and flowers.

It is not often-enough recognized that, however unconventional its form, Orwell's novel is a love story. The course of true love runs its untrue meandering path, but it does eventually find its consummation. We are entitled to take the story's last words – 'But it was all right, everything was all right, the struggle was finished. He had won the victory over himself. He loved Big Brother' (*NEF*, p. 311) – as ironic, provided we remember that *ironic* does not mean the same thing as *mendacious*. People don't love Trump for rational reasons, but people do love (or, that related valence, hate) Trump. The opposite of love is not hate, but indifference; and these are not matters of indifference to us. We win the battle against ourselves. We love *Nineteen Eighty-Four*.

Notes

1 Jane Arthurs, 'Contemporary British Television', in Michael Higgins, Clarissa Smith, and John Storey (eds.), *The Cambridge Companion to Modern British Culture* (Cambridge: Cambridge University Press, 2010), pp. 171–88, at pp. 182–3.

2 Jean Seaton, Tim Crook, and D. J. Taylor, 'Welcome to Dystopia – George Orwell Experts on Donald Trump', *The Guardian* (25 January 2017) [www.theguardian .com/commentisfree/2017/jan/25/george-orwell-donald-trump-kellyanne-conway-1984] (accessed 29 November 2019).

3 Roger Paden, 'Surveillance and Torture: Foucault and Orwell on the Methods of Discipline', *Social Theory and Practice*, 10.3 (Fall 1984), pp. 261–71, at p. 270.

4 *Ibid.*, p. 261.

5 Armand Mattelart, *The Globalization of Surveillance: the Origin of the Securitarian Order*, trans. Susan Taponier and James Cohen (Cambridge: Polity, 2010), pp. 7–8.

6 'While all this has become prophetic gospel to its adherents, it is only a hypothesis, like any other. The degree of assent you give it may depend on how little or how much the process is complicated by bringing into it the possibilities of human resistance and discrimination with respect to signs' (Richard Poirier, 'America Deserta', *London Review of Books*, 11.4 (16 February 1989), pp. 3–6, at p. 4). The Baudrillard quotation is from *Simulacra and Simulation*, trans. Sheila Faria Glaser (Ann Arbor, MI: University of Michigan Press 1994), p. 166.

7 Craig Raine, *In Defence of T. S. Eliot* (London: Picador, 2000), p. 248.

8 According to 'Freedom in the World', there were 69 properly functioning electoral democracies in 1990, accounting for 41 per cent of the global population; by 2016 this number had risen to 125, accounting for 64 per cent. See https://freedomhouse .org (accessed 30 October 2019).

9 Josh Lauer, *Creditworthy: A History of Consumer Surveillance and Financial Identity in America* (New York: Columbia University Press, 2017), p. 7.

10 Rachel O'Dwyer, 'Stained in Red', *London Review of Books*, 41.7 (4 April 2019), pp. 36–7, at p. 37.

11 Patrick Reilly, '*1984*: The Insufficient Self', in Graham Holderness, Bryan Loughrey, and Nahem Yousaf (eds.), *New Casebooks: George Orwell* (London: Macmillan, 1998), pp. 116–38, at p. 122.

12 Developers' blurb 2016 [https://store.steampowered.com/app/491950/Orwell_Keeping_an_Eye_On_You/?curator_clanid=34986443] (accessed 30 October 2019).

Bal, Sant Singh, *George Orwell: The Ethical Imagination* (Delhi: Heinemann, 1981).

Bounds, Philip, *Orwell and Marxism: The Political and Cultural Thinking of George Orwell* (London: I. B. Tauris, 2009).

Bowker, Gordon, *George Orwell* (London: Little, Brown, 2003).

Brennan, Michael, *George Orwell and Religion* (London: Bloomsbury, 2017).

Carr, Craig L., *Orwell, Politics, and Power* (New York: Bloomsbury, 2012).

Claeys, Gregory (ed.), *The Cambridge Companion to Utopian Literature* (Cambridge: Cambridge University Press, 2010).

Clarke, Ben, *Orwell in Context: Communities, Myths, Values* (Basingstoke: Palgrave Macmillan, 2007).

Colls, Robert, *George Orwell: English Rebel* (Oxford: Oxford University Press, 2013).

Cushman, Thomas and John Rodden (eds.), *George Orwell: Into the Twenty-First Century* (London: Routledge, 2004).

Davison, Peter, *George Orwell: A Literary Life* (Basingstoke: Macmillan Press, 1996).

Di Nucci, Ezio and Stefan Storrie (eds.), *'1984' and Philosophy: Is Resistance Futile?* (Chicago: Open Court, 2018).

Dwan, David, *Liberty, Equality and Humbug: Orwell's Political Ideals* (Oxford: Oxford University Press, 2018).

Fenwick, Gillian, *George Orwell: A Bibliography* (Winchester: St Paul's Bibliographies, 1998).

Fowler, Roger, *The Language of George Orwell* (Basingstoke: Macmillan, 1995).

Fyvel, T. R., *George Orwell: A Personal Memoir* (1982; London: Hutchinson, 1983).

Gleason, Abbott, Jack Goldsmith, and Martha C. Nussbaum (eds.), *On 'Nineteen Eighty-Four': Orwell and Our Future* (Princeton: Princeton University Press, 2005).

Gomis, Annette and Susana Onega (eds.), *George Orwell: A Centenary Celebration* (Heidelberg: Universitätsverlag Winter, 2005).

Gottlieb, Erika, *The Orwell Conundrum: A Cry of Despair or Faith in the 'Spirit of Man'?* (Montreal: McGill-Queen University Press, 1990).

Hammond, J. R., *A George Orwell Chronology* (Basingstoke: Palgrave, 2000).

Hitchens, Christopher, *Why Orwell Matters* (2002; New York: Basic Books, 2003).

Hunter, Lynette, *George Orwell: The Search for a Voice* (Milton Keynes: Open University Press, 1984).

Ingle, Stephen, *George Orwell: A Political Life* (Manchester: Manchester University Press, 1993).

The Social and Political Thought of George Orwell: A Reassessment (London: Routledge, 2006).

Keeble, Richard Lance (ed.), *Orwell Today* (Bury St Edmunds: Abramis, 2012).

George Orwell: Now! (New York: Peter Lang, 2015).

Lazaro, Alberto (ed.), *The Road from George Orwell: His Achievement and Legacy* (Bern: Peter Lang, 2001).

Lynskey, Dorian, *The Ministry of Truth: A Biography of George Orwell's '1984'* (London: Picador, 2019).

Marks, Peter, *George Orwell the Essayist: Literature, Politics, and the Periodical Culture* (London: Continuum, 2011).

Meyers, Jeffrey (ed.), *George Orwell: The Critical Heritage* (1975; London: Taylor & Francis, 2002).

Orwell: Life and Art (Baltimore: University of Illinois Press, 2010).

Newsinger, John, *Hope Lies in the Proles: Orwell and the Left* (London: Pluto Press, 2018).

Rees, Richard, *George Orwell: Fugitive from the Camp of Victory* (London: Secker & Warburg, 1961).

Reilly, Patrick, *'Nineteen Eighty-Four': Past, Present, and Future* (Boston: Twayne Publishers, 1989).

Rodden, John, *Every Intellectual's Big Brother: George Orwell's Literary Siblings* (Austin: University of Texas Press, 2006).

(ed.), *The Cambridge Companion to George Orwell* (Cambridge: Cambridge University Press, 2007).

The Unexamined Orwell (Austin: University of Texas Press, 2011).

Rodden, John and John Rossi, *The Cambridge Introduction to George Orwell* (Cambridge: Cambridge University Press, 2012).

Ryan, David, *Orwell on Screen: Adaptations, Documentaries, and Docudramas on Film and Television* (Jefferson: McFarland, 2018).

Saunders, Loraine, *The Unsung Artistry of George Orwell: The Novels from 'Burmese Days' to 'Nineteen Eighty-Four'* (Aldershot: Ashgate, 2008).

Shelden, Michael, *Orwell: The Authorised Biography* (New York: HarperCollins, 1991).

Slater, Ian, *Orwell: The Road to Airstrip One* (1985; Montreal: McGill-Queen's University Press, 2003).

Spurling, Hilary, *The Girl from the Fiction Department: A Portrait of Sonia Orwell* (London: Hamish Hamilton, 2002).

Stansky, Peter (ed.), *On 'Nineteen Eighty-Four'* (Stanford: Stanford Alumni Association, 1983).

Steinhoff, William R., *George Orwell and the Origins of '1984'* (Michigan: University of Michigan Press, 1975).

Stewart, Anthony, *George Orwell, Doubleness, and the Value of Decency* (New York: Routledge, 2003).

Sutherland, John, *Orwell's Nose: A Pathological Biography* (London: Reaktion, 2017).

Taylor, D. J., *Orwell: The Life* (London: Chatto & Windus, 2003).

On 'Nineteen Eighty-Four': A Biography (New York: Abrams Press, 2019).

West, W. J., *The Larger Evils: 'Nineteen Eighty-Four' – The Truth Behind the Satire* (Edinburgh: Canongate Press, 1992).

Woloch, Alex, *Or Orwell: Writing and Democratic Socialism* (Cambridge: Harvard University Press, 2016).

INDEX

French Revolution, 90
Freud, Anna, 8
Freud, Sigmund, 91
Frye, Northrop, 200
Fukuyama, Francis, 234

Galsworthy, John, 4
Garden of Eden, 84
Gardner, John, 6
General Election of 1945, 160
General Strike of 1926, 156
geopolitics, 3, 37–49, 142
glass, 86, 102, 106, 113, 171, 178,
	213, 224
Gleason, Abbott, 203
glitter, 102, 113, 169, 172, 178–9
Goldstein, Emmanuel (character), 12, 145,
	172, 177, 190, 271
	*The Theory and Practice of Oligarchical
	Collectivism* (Goldstein's book), 17, 27,
	28–30, 31, 42, 45, 54, 55, 57, 83, 84, 90,
	99, 102, 104, 105, 106, 113, 119, 145,
	146, 172, 178, 188, 205, 236, 239,
	240, 272
Gollancz, Victor, 111, 157
Gottlieb, Erika, 55, 56, 61
Gray, Maggie, 238
grease, 173
Great Expectations (Charles Dickens), 25

Halberstam, Jack, 261
Hamilton, Charles, 239
Harrigan, Pat, 250
Hate Week, 55, 91, 146, 190
The Hawthorns (school), 23
Hegel, G. W. F., 186
Heidegger, Martin, 66
Hesiod, 84
Hillegas, Mark, 114
Hilton, James, 206
Hitchens, Christopher, 2, 207
Hitler, Adolf, 37, 39, 93, 97, 99, 111, 118,
	143, 144, 187, 191
	Mein Kampf, 187
Holocaust, 191
Holt, Jenny, 34
Howe, Irving, 83
humanism, 3, 64–76
Hume, David, 186
The Hunger Games (Suzanne Collins),
	126
Hutcheon, Linda, 200, 206, 232
Huxley, Aldous, 26, 90, 102

Brave New World, 9, 26, 62, 87–8, 99, 101,
	104, 124, 127
Huxley, Julian, 66, 73

The Ice People (Maggie Gee), 130, 134
imaginaries, 265–77
In the Second Year (Storm Jameson), 98
insects, 12, 15, 71
Inside (video game), 247, 258–9
The Invisibles (Grant Morrison), 232,
	241–2, 243
It Can't Happen Here (Sinclair Lewis), 88

Jarman, Derek, 226
Jefferies, Richard, 97
Jenkins, Henry, 250
Jerome, Jerome K., 85
John, Elton, 219
Johnson, Boris, 3, 200
Jones, Aaronson, and Rutherford
	(characters), 176, 214
	photograph, 8, 58, 186
A Journal of the Flood Year (David Ely), 131
Joyce, James, 95, 171
	Finnegans Wake, 104
	A Portrait of the Artist as a Young Man, 117
Julia (character)
	boldness, 7
	bored by Goldstein's book, 29, 45, 84, 106
	promiscuity, 44, 178
	skill at mapping, 44
	as Thought Police agent, 7, 13, 150
Juvenal, 82, 92

Kakutani, Michiko, 141, 148
Kant, Immanuel, 66, 68, 69, 72, 73, 187
Kerr, Douglas, 14, 172
Keynes, John Maynard, 112
Kim Jong-un, 3
Kipling, Rudyard, 39
	'McAndrew's Hymn', 213
Koestler, Arthur, 64, 88
	Darkness at Noon, 9, 87, 88, 103, 275
Kołakowski, Leszek, 5
Kristeva, Julia, 174, 176
Kundera, Milan, 222
Kurdi, Aylan, 148, 150

The Last Man in Europe (original title), 47,
	65, 106
The Lathe of Heaven (Ursula K. Le Guin), 124
Lawrence, D. H., 115, 123
	'Psychology and the Unconscious', 26

The League of Extraordinary Gentlemen: Black Dossier (Alan Moore, with Kevin O'Neill), 232, 237, 239–40
Lenin, Vladimir, 86
Lennon, John, 219
Lennox, Annie, 221
Levenson, Michael, 134
literary context, 9, 95–107
literary dystopias, 82–6
literary inheritors, 10, 123–36
Little Brother (Cory Doctorow), 127–8, 129
London Blitz, 2, 223
London, Jack, 9, 100
  The Iron Heel, 1, 9, 88, 89, 99
Lorenzo, David J., 54
Lux Radio Theatre, 199, 201
Lynskey, Dorian, 4, 110

Maazel, Lorin, 223
Manguso, Sarah, 51
Manichaeism, 99, 181, 182, 190
Manovich, Lev, 250
maps, 16, 37, 38–40, 44, 46, 48, 251
Marrus, Michael R., 147
Marx, Karl, 67, 101, 155
masks, 117, 144, 174, 177, 179, 185, 260, 271
Mattelart, Armand, 269
McCartney, Paul, 219
memory holes, 58, 177, 265, 270, 272
Menand, Louis, 2
Merleau-Ponty, Maurice, 66, 67
mess, 102, 170, 171–2, 173
metaphor, 10, 11, 126, 161, 167, 204, 206, 224, 239
Metropolis (1927 film), 259
Meyers, Jeffrey, 200
Miller, Henry, 95–7
  Tropic of Cancer, 96
Miłosz, Czesław, 5
Ministry of Love, 7, 58, 113, 168, 175, 179, 181, 213, 248
  place where there is no darkness, 8, 73, 119, 225
Ministry of Peace, 248
Ministry of Plenty, 248
Ministry of Truth, 8, 14, 52, 54, 162, 169, 171, 173, 177, 179, 248, 274
modernism, 13, 95, 96, 106, 215
More, Thomas, 9, 92
  Utopia, 84
Morris, William, 9, 99, 102, 104
  News from Nowhere, 85, 97
Mosley, Oswald, 118
Mr Charrington (character), 8, 14, 17, 54, 173, 199, 207, 214, 216, 225, 240
  room above his shop, 7, 13, 15, 43, 44, 45, 175, 185, 266
Mr Men books, 200
Muggeridge, Malcolm, 100
Muldowney, Dominic, 213
Murdoch, Iris, 194
Murphy, Mary (actress), 199
Murray, Gilbert, 66, 74
Murray, Janet, 250
musical adaptations, 16, 213–26
Mussolini, Benito, 118

Nakamura, Asami, 232
Napoleon Bonaparte, 38, 117
nationalism, 10, 74, 113, 142, 143–5, 146, 148, 153, 256, 258
Nazism, 2, 39, 75, 99, 187, 192, 238
neoliberalism, 127, 129, 148, 219, 220
Never Let Me Go (Kazuo Ishiguro), 131
Newspeak, 47, 52, 54, 55, 92, 104, 130, 132, 190, 208, 223, 232, 240, 250, 251, 252
  the novel's appendix, 6, 55, 61, 83, 84, 90, 104, 105, 134, 135, 190, 249
Nicolson, Harold, 9
Nietzsche, Friedrich, 188–9, 191
nihilism, 68, 69
Nineteen Eighty-Four (2013 radio adaptation), 205
Niven, David, 203, 205, 207
Nohr, Rolf H., 250
Norris, Christopher, 68, 73
nursery rhymes, 213
Nussbaum, Martha C., 14, 72, 149, 150, 151, 152, 190, 203

O'Brien (character)
  agent of evil, 182, 189, 193
  authorship of Goldstein's book, 26, 55, 145
  four fingers as five, 33, 242
  as functionary, 119
  his apartment, 18, 179
  image of boot on face, 56, 81, 121, 172, 206, 274
  intelligence, 26, 32, 69
  laws of gravity, 74, 186
  omniscience, 185
  physical appearance, 14
  pity for Winston, 72
  as priest of power, 174

Cambridge Companions to ...

AUTHORS

TOPICS

Frankenstein edited by Andrew Smith

The French Enlightenment edited by Daniel Brewer

French Literature edited by John D. Lyons

The French Novel: from 1800 to the Present edited by Timothy Unwin

Gay and Lesbian Writing edited by Hugh Stevens

German Romanticism edited by Nicholas Saul

Gothic Fiction edited by Jerrold E. Hogle

The Graphic Novel edited by Stephen Tabachnick

The Greek and Roman Novel edited by Tim Whitmarsh

Greek and Roman Theatre edited by Marianne McDonald and J. Michael Walton

Greek Comedy edited by Martin Revermann

Greek Lyric edited by Felix Budelmann

Greek Mythology edited by Roger D. Woodard

Greek Tragedy edited by P. E. Easterling

The Harlem Renaissance edited by George Hutchinson

The History of the Book edited by Leslie Howsam

Human Rights and Literature edited by Crystal Parikh

The Irish Novel edited by John Wilson Foster

Irish Poets edited by Gerald Dawe

The Italian Novel edited by Peter Bondanella and Andrea Ciccarelli

The Italian Renaissance edited by Michael Wyatt

Jewish American Literature edited by Hana Wirth-Nesher and Michael P. Kramer

The Latin American Novel edited by Efraín Kristal

Latin American Poetry edited by Stephen Hart

Latina/o American Literature edited by John Morán González

Latin Love Elegy edited by Thea S. Thorsen

Literature and Disability edited by Clare Barker and Stuart Murray

Literature and Food edited by J. Michelle Coghlan

Literature and the Posthuman edited by Bruce Clarke and Manuela Rossini

Literature and Religion edited by Susan M. Felch

Literature and Science edited by Steven Meyer

The Literature of the American Renaissance edited by Christopher N. Phillips

The Literature of Berlin edited by Andrew J. Webber

The Literature of the Crusades, Volume 1, edited by Anthony Bale

The Literature of the First World War edited by Vincent Sherry

The Literature of London edited by Lawrence Manley

The Literature of Los Angeles edited by Kevin R. McNamara

The Literature of New York edited by Cyrus Patell and Bryan Waterman

The Literature of Paris edited by Anna-Louise Milne

The Literature of World War II edited by Marina MacKay

Literature on Screen edited by Deborah Cartmell and Imelda Whelehan

Lyrical Ballads edited by Sally Bushell

Medieval British Manuscripts edited by Orietta Da Rold and Elaine Treharne

Medieval English Culture edited by Andrew Galloway

Medieval English Law and Literature edited by Candace Barrington and Sebastian Sobecki

Medieval English Literature edited by Larry Scanlon

Medieval English Mysticism edited by Samuel Fanous and Vincent Gillespie

Medieval English Theatre edited by Richard Beadle and Alan J. Fletcher (second edition)

Medieval French Literature edited by Simon Gaunt and Sarah Kay

Medieval Romance edited by Roberta L. Krueger

Medieval Women's Writing edited by Carolyn Dinshaw and David Wallace

Modern American Culture edited by Christopher Bigsby

Modern British Women Playwrights edited by Elaine Aston and Janelle Reinelt

Modern French Culture edited by Nicholas Hewitt

Modern German Culture edited by Eva Kolinsky and Wilfried van der Will

The Modern German Novel edited by Graham Bartram

The Modern Gothic edited by Jerrold E. Hogle

Modern Irish Culture edited by Joe Cleary and Claire Connolly

Modern Italian Culture edited by Zygmunt G. Baranski and Rebecca J. West

Modern Latin American Culture edited by John King